READER'S DIGEST

# 30-MINUTE
# COOKBOOK

READER'S DIGEST

# 30-MINUTE
# COOKBOOK

Published by The Reader's Digest Association, Inc.
Pleasantville, New York/Montreal

**EDITORS**
Brenda Houghton, Philomena Rutherford

**ART EDITOR**
Louise Bruce

**DESIGNERS**
Kate Harris, Cécile Germain

**ASSISTANT EDITORS**
Alison Bravington, Claire Clifton, Jenni Muir, Linda Tsiricos

**EDITORIAL ASSISTANT**
Alison Candlin

**PROOFREADERS**
Roy Butcher, Barry Gage, Gilles Humbert

———•———

**CONTRIBUTORS**

**CONSULTANT**
Pat Alburey

**WRITERS**
Pat Alburey, Val Barrett, Claire Clifton, Christine France, Carole Handslip, Sybil Kapoor,
Patricia Lousada, Jenni Muir, Mary Skinner, Colin Spencer, Rosemary Stark, Berit Vinegrad

**RECIPE TESTERS**
Helen Alsop, Terry Farris

**PHOTOGRAPHERS**
Martin Brigdale, Gus Filgate, James Murphy, Peter Myers, Jon Stewart

**HOME ECONOMISTS**
Louise Pickford, Janet Smith, Linda Tubby, Berit Vinegrad

**STYLISTS**
Antonia Gaunt, Penny Markham, Helen Trent

**ILLUSTRATORS**
Diane Broadley, Stan North

———•———

In Canada: For information on this and other Reader's Digest products or to request a catalogue, please
call our 24-hour Customer Service hotline at 1-800-465-0780.
You can also visit us on the World Wide Web at http://www.readersdigest.ca
In the United States: Call 1-800-846-2100, or visit http://www.readersdigest.com

Printed in Canada

ISBN 0-7621-0460-0

———•———

**PHOTOGRAPHS:** GOAT'S CHEESE AND ARUGULA SALAD (*page 2*);
PEA AND ASPARAGUS SOUP (*page 3*); CHICKEN BREASTS WITH APPLES AND CIDER (*right*);
PASTA WITH HEARTY SAUCE (*page 6*); FRESH TROUT WITH WALNUT DRESSING (*page 7*).

# - CONTENTS -

# GREAT FOOD IN MINUTES

The skill of creative cookery is not only reserved for those who have plenty of time to spend in the kitchen. All of the recipes collected here can be prepared and cooked within half an hour, with an emphasis on fresh, healthy ingredients and a little help from a well-stocked pantry.

Fast-cooked food not only leaves you with more time to spend on other things, it also carries a health bonus, as the most valuable nutritional components of food are best conserved by reducing the amount of time they are exposed to heat.

Best of all, these dishes taste especially delicious, because when good quality ingredients are cooked for the minimum amount of time, they retain all their fresh, intense flavors.

## THREE STEPS TO SUCCESS

**HEAT** When you don't want to waste any time in the kitchen, the first important ingredient is heat: before you even wash your hands, turn on the oven or the grill to start heating it up, or put the kettle on and leave it to boil.

Domestic ovens vary a great deal in how long they take to come to the required temperature. In general, 10–15 minutes have been allowed for preheating the oven. (Convection ovens, which are hotter than standard ones, may not need to be preheated: check your manufacturer's handbook.) If you know that your oven is slow to heat up, preset it to the recipe's required temperature as long in advance as you need to, before you start to assemble the ingredients.

Grills must also be properly preheated before use. For fast, even cooking, it is best to have the grill on high in order to avoid any cool patches, and to keep an eye on the food. If any tender items such as fish steaks seem in danger of burning, drop the grill rack a slot farther away from the heat source, or take the food off the rack and sit it on the base of the grill pan.

**ORGANIZATION** After heat, the next secret of successful fast cooking is good organization. Make sure that you have all the ingredients you need close at hand—a dish can easily be ruined if you have to spend time hunting for the sesame oil while the contents of your wok are just seconds away from burning.

Before you begin to prepare a recipe, read it through to familiarize yourself with the method, so you won't have to waste time stopping to read each step. Then take a few minutes to assemble the ingredients, dishes, and tools so that everything you need is within easy reach. This is especially important when the recipe demands items that you don't use every day. The hand blender, lemon zester, and nutmeg grater are invaluable aids, but not if they are in the back of the cupboard.

Clear an adequate working space with plenty of elbow room. Remove utensils from your working area after use—clutter will slow you down.

**SIZE** The third weapon in the hands of the busy cook is size: the smaller the ingredients are, the quicker they will cook. Chopping, dicing, slicing, and grating food into fast-cooking morsels saves time—and this preparation is included in the timing of each recipe.

## BASIC INGREDIENTS

**SALT** The amount of salt to add in these recipes has been left to personal taste. But doctors advise that it is healthier to reduce salt consumption, so try to add as little as possible when you cook, and consider whether you could leave it out altogether if the recipe includes other salty items such as bacon, capers, olives, smoked foods, or soy sauce.

**PEPPER** Freshly ground whole black peppercorns taste much better than ready-ground black pepper, or white pepper, and they last much longer. When black pepper is included in a recipe, it should always be freshly ground.

**HERBS** When there is no time to develop the flavor of food through slow cooking, fresh herbs can add a welcome boost of flavor, and have been specified in most recipes. If you cannot find a particular fresh herb, you can substitute a dried one. The drying process concentrates the flavor so in general use 1–1½ teaspoons of dried herb to replace 1 tablespoon of fresh.

## USING THE RECIPES

Ingredients are given in both Imperial and metric measures, but are not precise equivalents. For this reason, use either all-Imperial or all-metric measures. All spoon measures are for a level spoon. The 15 ml cook's measuring spoon generally equals 1 level tablespoon and the 5 ml spoon equals 1 level teaspoon. Most of the recipes serve four people, but they can be halved easily for two.

## THE NUTRITIONAL BALANCE

Fast food can also be healthy food—these recipes are designed to offer a good nutritional balance. To help you plan a healthy diet, each recipe includes an analysis showing how many calories and how much carbohydrate (including sugar, natural or added), protein, and fat (including saturated fat) there are in one average serving.

Vitamins and minerals are also essential to a healthy diet. Most, such as vitamin A, are single substances, but vitamin B is a group of vitamins, which includes folate and nicotinic acid. Where the analysis shows the dish is a good source of a vitamin or mineral, one serving contains at least 30 percent of the amount the government recommends we should consume every day. These quantities are known as the Recommended Daily Allowances (RDAs) in the United States and as Recommended Nutrient Intakes (RNIs) in Canada.

*HEALTHY EATING Use fresh ingredients and oils that are high in monounsaturated fatty acids for the best nutritional value and fresh herbs and natural seasonings to enhance their flavors.*

# FAST TECHNIQUES

*There are many time-saving methods that can speed up the cooking process. And the smoother and more methodical your preparation, the quicker the finished dish will come together. Follow these tried-and-tested techniques to achieve fast results without any last-minute hassles.*

## OFF TO A QUICK START

When you are peeling, trimming, topping and tailing, slicing or chopping ingredients, it is best to form an assembly line. Stand a colander nearby for rinsing the items, and place kitchen paper or a spare basin by the chopping board to hold anything you are discarding.

If several chopped ingredients are to be added during cooking, put them into bowls or saucers and line them up in the order in which they will be used, or put very small amounts on one large plate. Then place them close to the cooker so you can reach them easily.

Have the salt and pepper to hand. If a number of flavoring ingredients are to be added at the same time, assemble them all on one saucer so that everything can be added in an instant.

*CUTTING* It is often quicker to cut up ingredients using a pair of kitchen scissors rather than a knife, for example, to snip the fat off bacon and ham, to chop herbs or cut up anchovy fillets, sun-dried tomatoes, stoned olives, or green onions. You can often snip the item directly into the pan.

It is easier to use your hands to tear up salad leaves than to use a knife. Tearing also causes less damage to the tender leaves, retaining more vitamins and minerals. Clean hands are also the fastest tool for flaking cooked fish, tearing up cooked chicken, and crumbling cheese.

*BY HAND Fingers are often the fastest tool for tearing up tender items such as salad leaves, for flaking fish or crumbling cheese.*

*COATING WITH FLOUR* To dust pieces of meat or fish quickly, put them into a plastic bag with flour and seasoning and shake it, or toss them with the flour in a mixing bowl. To dust slices of meat, sift flour over them with a small sieve or tea strainer.

*PEELING* You may not need to waste time peeling vegetables—many taste better and retain more goodness when cooked in their skins. The thick skins of older vegetables should be removed, but young, thin-skinned vegetables such as eggplants, zucchinis, new potatoes, or parsnips will need no more than a scrub. And baked eggplants, boiled potatoes, and roasted peppers can be peeled quickly after cooking.

The exception is carrots, as the advice now is to peel even young carrots because of the risk of chemical residues. You can save time by choosing organic carrots, as these only need a quick scrub.

If you are removing the flesh from an avocado to be mashed or blended, don't bother peeling it: just cut the avocado in half, remove the stone and scoop out the flesh using a large spoon.

*NO NEED TO PEEL If an avocado is going to be mashed or blended, just scoop out the flesh with a spoon.*

To peel garlic, press down on the clove with the flat blade of a large knife and the peel will split and slip off easily.

*SLIP OFF Pressing a knife down on a clove of garlic is the quickest way to remove the skin.*

It's quicker to use a garlic crusher than to chop and purée garlic with a knife. And for stir-fries, slice cloves thinly in seconds using the little slicer on the side of your hand grater. Onions are quicker to peel if you cut them in half first, trim off the top and bottom, and then peel off the skin.

SKINNING  To remove the skins easily from fruit and vegetables such as peaches, small onions, and tomatoes, pour over enough boiling water to cover them, then leave to stand for a minute or two. The skin will peel off cleanly.

To skin peppers quickly, spear them with a long fork and hold in a gas flame, turning gently, until blackened. Then peel off the skin. With a paring knife, cut them in half and roast under the grill.

To skin a fish fillet, place it skin side down on a chopping board. Insert a knife at the tail end with the blade held at an angle between the skin and the flesh, resting on the board. Pull the skin with one hand and use a gentle sawing action with the blade, folding the flesh over and out of the way as it comes clear.

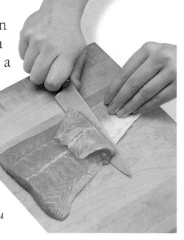

*SKINNING The skin of a fish fillet peels away quickly if you cut it free with a sharp knife.*

## FASTER COOKING

BOILING  Root vegetables will cook much faster if they are arranged in a shallow layer in a large saucepan rather than a deep layer in a small one. Add just enough water to cover them and use a pan with a tight-fitting lid to hold in the steam.

If a recipe calls for you to add stock to a dish and you are using already-prepared stock, put it in a saucepan to start warming up straightaway so that it will come to the boil faster when it is eventually needed.

FRYING AND GRILLING  If you slice meat or fish, make the slices the same size and thickness so they cook at the same rate, or cut the flesh into strips that will cook quickly. Pat burgers and patties with your hands until they are thinner and flatter than usual, so that the heat penetrates easily and they cook faster.

*THIN AND FAST For faster cooking, pat burgers between your hands to make them thin.*

---

### MADE IN MINUTES!

#### PASTA SOUP

**Make an elegant soup by simmering a handful of pasta soup shapes in some good stock—previously prepared, frozen stock would be very suitable. Garnish it with a few slices of thinly sliced lemon, some chopped coriander or parsley, and a few sliced mushrooms or snipped sun-dried tomatoes.**

#### BUTTER-GLAZED FRUIT

**For a frying pan dessert to serve 4 people, melt 2 tablespoons (25 g) of unsalted butter and 2 tablespoons (25 g) of sugar in a nonstick frying pan, then add 1 lb (450 g) of mixed, sliced fresh fruit and 1½ tablespoons of fruit liqueur. Cook over a moderate heat, basting with the sauce, until the fruits are warmed through.**

When stir-frying, the trick is to get the pan as hot as possible using a high heat, then add the fat or oil, and only add the ingredients when the fat is sizzling so that they cook very quickly. Be sure to move the food around constantly so that it does not have time to stick.

STEAMING  Cooking food in vapor rather than water or fat reduces the loss of vitamins and if you have two or three steamer baskets, you can pile them up and cook a variety of vegetables at once.

# TIME-SAVING EQUIPMENT

*You can speed up your preparation and cooking considerably by choosing the right equipment. Here is a guide to the most suitable tools for fast cooking, and how to put them to the best use.*

### POTS AND PANS

Use pots and pans that are the right size for the ingredients. It is a waste of time to boil up a large saucepan of water to cook a small quantity of vegetables, or to heat up a large frying pan for a small piece of meat or fish.

There are some exceptions: always use a large saucepan when you are cooking pasta: it will cook quicker with plenty of water to swim in. And it is better to use a large frying pan with plenty of space when you are browning meat, as in a small pan the pieces of meat will be too close together, and will steam rather than fry.

It is also important not to overcrowd the pan when stir-frying. The ingredients in a stir-fry cook most rapidly when they touch the surface of the hot pan, so choose a large wok, which gives you plenty of room. It will take a little longer to heat up, but the cooking time will be shorter.

Frying over a high heat often means that you need to shake the pan vigorously to keep the food moving around: a pan with a single, heat-proof handle is ideal for this job. And a two-handled iron

frying pan or shallow flameproof casserole that will fit underneath the grill or go into the oven is another time-saver because you don't have to transfer the food from pan to oven dish when you are making casserole dishes.

A ridged, cast-iron griddle plate will cook fish, steaks, and chops very quickly and works even faster if you preheat it under the grill and then place the food between the griddle and the grill, cooking from both sides. Griddles with fold-down handles are easiest to store.

A wok can double-up as a large saucepan and can be used for steaming, as well as for stir-frying, so make sure you buy one with a lid.

Not all pots and pans are equal when it comes to heat conduction. Heat makes food stick to the surface of a pan, so to avoid this, nonstick surfaces are designed to be relatively poor heat conductors, and are not the best choice if you want to cook

quickly. Copper pans lined with aluminum, or copper-based stainless-steel pans, are ideal heat conductors for fast cooking.

Cast-iron saucepans with a strong enamel coating also conduct heat well, though they are heavy to use. Stainless-steel saucepans are much lighter, virtually indestructible, and they perform very well. Always scour the underside of pans thoroughly when you wash them to prevent any buildup of grease, which would impede the even distribution of heat.

A pasta pan that comes with a separate strainer basket, which you just lift out, makes draining pasta quick and easy, and there is less danger of fragile stuffed pastas breaking up, as they can if they are tipped into a colander.

And whatever you are cooking, be sure to put the pan on the right size burner, so that the heat is evenly distributed.

For oven-baking when time is limited, metal ramekins and custard cups are better than porcelain, earthenware, or glass, because they conduct heat better and reduce the cooking time.

## GADGETS AND TOOLS

*BRUSHES* Invest in a small stiff brush for cleaning vegetables, and don't use it for anything else. Natural fiber or plastic bristles are both equally efficient, but natural bristles must be left to dry out completely after use to prevent them rotting.

A pastry brush is the quickest way to baste food under the grill with oil or a marinade—choose natural bristles, as plastic bristles will melt if they touch a hot surface. A pastry brush is also useful for cleaning rind out of the tiny holes in a grater.

*CHERRY-STONER* Using a single cherry-stoner is quicker than removing stones by hand; it also removes olive pits. But a double cherry-stoner is tricky to use and can be time-consuming.

*CHOPPING BOARD* Choose a large chopping board, which sits firmly in place. It will make chopping easier, and nothing will fall over the edges.

*ESSENTIALS Choosing the right equipment makes quick cooking easier. A griddle lets you grill food fast, a pasta saucepan enables you to drain pasta in an instant, and a wok makes stir-frying simple. Stainless-steel tools are easy to use—and quick to clean.*

*COOKBOOK HOLDER* Invest in a specially designed cookbook holder: you'll find it easier to keep the recipe book open in front of you.

*GRATER* A stainless-steel grater makes fast work of small items. If you need only one or two carrots, it is quicker to grate them by hand than in a food processor. Making pastry can also be quicker if you grate hard butter into the flour before rubbing in.

*JAR OPENER* A tool with large rings at the end that will grip firmly stuck jar and bottle tops and open them easily saves time and temper.

*KNIFE SHARPENER* Blunt knives slow you down. Use a knife sharpener and take a few seconds to hone the blades of knives and kitchen scissors to a fine, razor-sharp edge every time you use them. It will make short work of cutting and slicing.

*LEMON SQUEEZER* A cone-shaped hand squeezer will let you squeeze juice straight into the salad bowl or saucepan.

*POTATO MASHER* A potato masher is an essential, as electrical tools turn potatoes (and potato-based soups) into a gluey mass.

*SALAD SPINNER* A simple plastic spinner is the most effective way to dry salad leaves. Put the washed leaves into the basket and rotate it to spin the water into the bowl.

*STRAINER* Wire mesh strainers strain off all the liquid better than a colander.

*VEGETABLE PEELER* A swivel-headed potato peeler makes a smooth job of peeling other vegetables and firm fruits, or cutting vegetables such as zucchinis into ribbon shapes. It will destring celery, trim the edges off fruit, and shave chocolate and strips of Parmesan cheese. Learn to use it in long strokes away from you.

*ZESTER* A good-quality zester makes swift work of removing the rind from citrus fruit. It has tiny holes at the end of the blade that shave off thin strips of rind without lifting the pith beneath.

## ELECTRICAL EQUIPMENT

*BLENDERS* You can purée a soup or sauce in a blender in a fraction of the time it takes to push it through a sieve by hand, and the resulting mixture will be much smoother.

*COFFEE GRINDER* If you use a lot of spices, it is a good idea to invest in an extra coffee grinder for pulverizing them into powder in seconds—a much faster and easier process than crushing them with a rolling pin or grinding them with a pestle and mortar. You can also use a coffee grinder to make small quantities of breadcrumbs.

*ELECTRIC MIXER* It takes only seconds to whip cream or meringue mixtures using a handheld electric mixer, when it takes time and effort using a hand rotary beater or wire whisk.

*FOOD PROCESSORS* The chopping, grating, and shredding blades of a food processor can make the business of preparing large amounts of raw food a matter of seconds rather than minutes. They are especially useful for chopping a succession of ingredients, for instance when you are making a vegetable soup or a salsa.

Processors make soft white breadcrumbs in seconds: cut the crusts off a few slices of thick white bread and process into crumbs. For dried

### MADE IN MINUTES!

#### INSTANT SORBET

Use the food processor for an instant sorbet: tip a small basket of soft fruit, such as raspberries, into the food processor with 1–2 tablespoons of icing sugar, process until smooth, then freeze.

brown breadcrumbs, dry some slices in a low oven at 300°F (150°C) for about an hour until they become crisp and a pale brown color, then process them. They will keep in an airtight container in the refrigerator for up to a month.

A processor can also make flavored butters in seconds—if the recipe only calls for a small amount, you can make double the quantity and freeze half to save time another day.

If you only want to chop one item, it is often quicker to do so by hand, but new food processors often have an additional small bowl and cutting blade, useful for chopping herbs and other small items and for making your own mayonnaise. Keep extra processor discs and blades handy so you do not waste valuable time searching for them.

*HANDHELD FOOD MIXER* This purées soup faster than a food processor or blender as you can use it in the saucepan. The result is not quite as smooth as using a blender, but many cooks prefer the slightly thicker texture.

Handheld mixers are also useful for making milkshakes and sauces, and for taking the lumps out of sauces that have gone wrong. And they can be used to mash cooked pumpkin: it will smooth it quickly and remove any stringy pieces—they wind themselves round the blades so they can be easily removed.

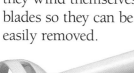

## OVENS

*CONVENTIONAL OVENS* When you are using a conventional gas or electric oven, it is worth remembering that the heat produced inside the oven will be uneven—on average, one setting higher at the top than at the bottom. Always follow instructions for preheating, to make sure that the oven is up to temperature in time for cooking.

*CONVECTION OVENS* A convection oven saves time as it preheats quicker than a conventional oven. Because of built-in fans, convection ovens cook faster at lower temperatures, as their efficient, even heat circulation makes them hotter than conventional ovens. This should be taken into account when setting the temperature.

### MICROWAVE SHORTCUTS
*(based on a 650-watt oven)*

**Soften butter from the fridge**
by warming on High for 20 seconds.

**Warm lemons**
for a few seconds on High and they
will yield more juice.

**Make crispy bacon**
by laying 3–4 bacon slices on a microwave rack over
a piece of folded kitchen paper; cook on High for
2 minutes, turn and cook 1–2 minutes more.

**Melt chocolate**
by breaking small pieces into a bowl and leaving it
uncovered. It's best to melt all chocolate on Medium or
Low and to stir and check every 10 seconds or so during
the cooking time, as chocolate will hold its shape even
when it has melted. Keep checking, and expect to
stir the last few bits of chocolate in.
To melt chocolate for a quick decoration, place it
in one corner of a microwave roasting bag and melt it in
the microwave oven. Then snip off the tip of the corner
and drizzle a pattern over a dessert or cake.

**Make fat-free poppadoms**
by cooking them, one at a time, on High for
40–60 seconds, and watch them puff up.

**Toast nuts**
such as cashew nuts; 1 oz (30 g) of nuts, cooked on
High for 5 minutes, will turn a golden, toasted color.

*MICROWAVE OVEN* Though a microwave oven does nothing that cannot be done with other more basic equipment, it speeds up preparation and cooking dramatically. Many foods cook in about a quarter of the time they take in a conventional oven. Those ovens with the clearest instructions and the fewest buttons are the most practical.

The foods that do best in a microwave are those cooked with moist heat: vegetables cooked in a few tablespoons of water, food in sauces, poached fish. And long, thin pieces of food cook faster than short thick pieces of the same weight.

But unlike with a conventional stove top, if you double the quantity of the ingredients you cook in the microwave, the cooking time is nearly doubled too. And a microwave will not brown most food, nor produce a crisp crust.

# THE SMART SHOPPER

*Every good meal starts with smart shopping, and this is particularly important for the busy cook. Take care in choosing your ingredients—some types of food take less time to prepare and cook than others. Consider, too, whether it is worth the expense of buying ready-prepared ingredients when they are available—this can save a lot of time.*

## FRESH MEAT, FISH, VEGETABLES, AND FRUIT

Start by going to the best suppliers that you can find—a reputable butcher and fish supplier, or a good supermarket that you know has a quick turnover of fresh produce.

For speedy meals, avoid joints and tough cuts of meat that need long slow cooking; use only tender pieces, cut into chops, steaks, or thin slices.

Fish is a natural fast food. Ask the clerk to prepare it for you, or buy ready-cut fillets and steaks. If the recipe calls for skinned fish, look for ready-skinned fillets.

Young vegetables require less preparation and shorter cooking time than tougher, older ones. Baby green beans, for example,

don't have any tough strings, so you don't waste time removing them. New potatoes have very thin skin, and can be washed rather than peeled.

Most citrus fruits are waxed, which prevents dehydration during transit and improves their appearance. If you want to use the rind, you must first scrub the fruit in hot water to remove the wax. Save time by choosing unwaxed fruit that does not have to be scrubbed first.

Although it is generally wise to avoid processed foods, some prewashed and ready-cut items are worth the extra money because of the time they save. Bags of ready-washed mixed salad leaves save preparation, and are not so expensive compared with the cost of putting together a similar mixture of leaves yourself. Ready-peeled, sliced pineapple or ready-made fresh fruit salad makes a delicious dessert—try draining off the syrup and using the fruit to fill a pancake dusted with icing sugar.

Buying a packet of mixed mushrooms will save the time it takes to weigh out two or more separate varieties. If some of the mushrooms have been left whole to give the pack visual appeal, be careful to cut them up into smaller pieces for faster cooking when you are preparing to use them.

Except for parmesan, which always tastes better if it is grated at the last minute, packets of ready-grated cheese, which can be melted over the top of a pizza or soup, also save time and effort.

*NATURALLY FRESH*
*Buy the freshest ingredients you can find for quicker cooking times and meals full of flavor.*

## THE WELL-STOCKED PANTRY

A busy cook needs to keep the pantry stocked with a generous selection of flavoring ingredients and staples. Group ingredients that you tend to use together, such as Indian spices, side by side so you can find all of them at a glance.

*CANS* of anchovies, beans, olives, tomatoes, and tuna fish are important pantry items as they can be combined into quick sauces for pasta, eggs, pizza toppings, and hearty soups.

Canned beans, such as white cannellini beans or red kidney beans, pale green flageolet and lima beans, borlotti or black-eyed peas and creamy chickpeas, can be rinsed and tossed with a handful of chopped parsley, some finely sliced onion and a garlicky dressing for a filling main-dish salad, perhaps with some added canned tuna, or anchovy fillets, rinsed and chopped.

A can of drained tuna can be processed with half a dozen stoned black olives, 1 teaspoon of capers, 3–4 tablespoons of olive oil and 1 teaspoon of brandy into a pâté to serve with toast.

Canned tomatoes are especially versatile, and often have more taste in winter than imported fresh varieties. Sun-dried tomatoes can be stirred into stews, risottos, or scrambled eggs, added to pasta sauces and sprinkled over pizzas.

*DRIED FRUIT AND NUTS* With little preparation, dried fruit and nuts give a lift to many savory dishes and salads, particularly those made with grated raw vegetables such as carrot, cabbage, and celery. Dried apricots, raisins, or sultanas, soaked in a spirit such as brandy, Cointreau, fruit brandy (eau-de-vie), or rum for a few minutes, also make a great instant topping for ice cream.

*OILS* Besides a bland vegetable oil for frying and a good olive oil for cooking and making salad dressings, a nut oil—walnut, almond, or hazel—is useful as it can provide a quick final touch drizzled over plainly cooked vegetables, or give instant flavor to salad dressings. Flavored oils such as chili or garlic olive oil can be drizzled over warm vegetables to add a final spicy note. Oils are best used up quickly, so buy small bottles.

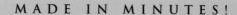

### CANNED BEAN MASH

Short of an accompaniment? Canned Bean Mash tastes great with sausages, pork chops, or cold meat. For 2 people, fry 2 crushed cloves of garlic and ½ a teaspoon of chili flakes gently in 3 tablespoons of olive oil, without letting the garlic color. Stir in some chopped rosemary, sage, or thyme leaves and a large can of flageolet beans, including the liquid. Boil gently for 10 minutes until the liquid is thick and opaque, then mash roughly and season to taste with black pepper.

### PEAR RICE PUDDING

In need of a quick dessert? For 4 people, spoon four small containers of canned rice pudding into dishes and pour on hot chocolate sauce made by melting 2¾ oz (75 g) of dark chocolate gently in 3–4 tablespoons of heavy whipping cream. Cover with slices of peeled, fresh pear and top with curls of chocolate shaved straight from the bar with a potato peeler.

*PASTA* Dried pasta is a great pantry favorite, but fresh pasta is three times faster to cook. Fresh pasta can also be frozen, and will only take a minute or two longer to cook straight from the freezer. In general, to serve four people you will need to cook 1 lb (450 g) of fresh pasta, or 12 oz (335 g) if it is dried.

Small pasta shapes are very useful items to have in the pantry: they can be used to thicken soups, as they cook much faster than rice used for the same purpose, and they are more filling. Vermicelli and fine Oriental egg noodles can also be used to thicken soup: crush the dry noodles between your hands to break them up into tiny pieces, then stir the pieces into the soup 5 minutes before you serve it.

*RICE* Presteamed white rice cooks considerably faster than plain white or brown rice. Cans of ready-cooked rice can be turned into a tasty accompaniment to a stir-fry in just a minute or two. If your family is tired of rice and you are looking for a fast substitute, try using Oriental rice noodles instead: they cook very quickly and go equally well with most Oriental dishes. Another good alternative is to serve nan bread with curry instead of rice—it heats up in the oven in a few seconds.

*SAUCES AND PURÉES* Keep a bottle or two of your favorite sauces such as Worcestershire, hot Tabasco and soy sauce in the pantry, and some good mayonnaise in the refrigerator. Don't skimp on these: if you save time by buying your mayonnaise ready-made, make sure you choose one with a good flavor.

A few small bottles of concentrated fruit purée, which can be found in most health-food shops and in some supermarkets, are also a good idea for your pantry. They are very versatile and taste delicious, and can add a quick, colorful finishing touch to a wide variety of desserts.

*SPICES* Whole spices keep better than ground ones, but they take time to prepare. Buy small quantities of the ground spices you use most often and replace them as soon as they seem musty.

*STOCK CUBES* Though they are convenient, many stock cubes are aggressively salty: try using only half a cube to the given amount of water for a more delicate flavor. Or use vegetable bouillon powder, sold in health-food shops, instead.

*VINEGAR* Use vinegar made with red or white wine, or flavored with fruit or herbs, to give immediate interest to salad dressings. Balsamic vinegar, which is caramel colored and slightly sweet, can be used not only to liven up salad dressings but also for deglazing the pan after frying meat or poultry.

## FREEZER STANDBYS

*BREAD* In the freezer, keep a loaf of good, crusty half-cooked bread, or rolls, which can go straight into the oven without defrosting. Either will add a hearty note to a soup or salad snack and can be baked while you are making them.

*ICE CREAM* A good-quality ice cream can form the basis of many delicious desserts; for some great ideas, see pages 288–289.

*PASTRY* A frozen unbaked pastry shell can be used to make a quick tart, such as Crab and Pea Tart (page 118). Puff and filo pastry and ready-made pizza bases also save time spent in preparation.

*SHRIMP* Cooked, peeled shrimp can be the basis of a quick starter or a colorful stir-fry.

*STOCK* Keep some high-quality stock in your freezer, ready to use. You can make your own stock and store it in reusable yogurt cartons or ice-cream containers, or you can buy a carton of good, ready-made stock.

*VEGETABLES* Frozen broad beans, peas, spinach, and sweet corn can be cooked straight from the freezer, and can be used to add both flavor and color to many different dishes.

# INGREDIENTS FROM AROUND THE WORLD

Many of the dishes in this book are inspired by the cuisines of India, the Middle East, the Far East, South-east Asia, and Mexico, where powerfully flavored local ingredients lend intense flavors to a wide variety of fast-cooked foods.

A long list of exotic ingredients can appear daunting if you are new to this type of cooking, and acquiring them may seem extravagant. But with a little experimentation, you will find that some new ingredients quickly become firm favorites and are used over and over again. On the other hand, if you try something and dislike it, get rid of it! You are cooking to please your own tastebuds, so you can add and discard flavorings to suit yourself.

## INDIA

**CURRY PASTE** is much easier to use than curry powder, which can taste slightly raw and is best kept for giving a lift to Western dishes—as a flavoring for mayonnaise, for example. A wide variety of curry pastes are now available, and have been blended by experts to give an authentic flavor. If you like Indian food, keep one mild and one hotter curry paste in the pantry. When you are choosing a brand, remember that spice mixtures manufactured in India are often hotter than those made in North America.

**SPICES** are essential ingredients in Indian cooking. Popular spices that can give an authentic Indian flavor to a variety of dishes are black mustard or cumin seeds, dry roasted until they begin to pop, then stirred through a vegetable dish or a grated vegetable salad (if you are using raw carrot, add some lemon or lime juice). Favorite Indian spices are cardamom, coriander seeds, and cinnamon, which are usually added whole to the dish while cooking, and left in when the meal is served. Cardamoms and coriander seeds should be crushed very lightly before use to gently release their aroma.

### MADE IN MINUTES!

#### INDIAN SAUCE

This will liven up a variety of legumes or vegetables. Fry 1 crushed clove of garlic, some grated ginger, 2 teaspoons of cumin seeds and 1 roughly chopped onion until colored. Then add a 14 oz (400 g) can of chopped tomatoes and cook, stirring, for 15 minutes until thickened. Pour over the legumes or vegetables just before serving.

All ground spices go stale quickly and it is best to buy them little and often.

**SAFFRON** can be used to tint rice a rich golden color. Steep whole saffron stamens in a little hot liquid to draw out their flavor; powdered saffron can be added directly to the dish.

**TURMERIC** is a less extravagant way to flavor and color rice. Ground turmeric produces a darker yellow color than saffron. It can also be cooked with leaf vegetables such as spinach.

**ACCOMPANIMENTS** are a very important part of Indian meals: you can add the finishing touches straight from the shelf. A handful of raisins, sultanas, or chopped dried mango slices can be added to rice or vegetable dishes. Mango and other chutneys, and lime pickle, can add an intense, spicy flavor. And ready-made poppadoms, or nan or some other Indian bread, quickly warmed through, make an authentic accompaniment.

## MADE IN MINUTES!

### CUCUMBER RAITA

A cooling sauce to serve with curries can be quickly made in a food processor. Roughly grate a cucumber then drain it in a sieve for a minute or two to release some of its water. Put it into a food processor, add a small tub of natural yogurt, salt, and fresh mint, if you have any, or a pinch of ground cumin, process to the consistency of double cream and serve.

## CHINA

**BEAN SAUCES** are useful both as a dip and for cooking. Black beans, butter beans, and yellow beans are often used to make cooking sauces. Hoisin sauce is made of fermented soybeans, and makes a particularly good dipping sauce—it is best known as the sauce served with Peking Duck. All Chinese sauces are very salty, and they should be used sparingly.

**DRIED MUSHROOMS** such as tree-ear and shiitake add flavor to many Chinese dishes, and these, and many other varieties, are now available in large supermarkets and Oriental stores. Rinse them thoroughly before use to remove most of the grit, then soak in warm water for as long as possible. Save the water used to soak them, as it can be strained through muslin—or through a sieve lined with kitchen paper—to remove any remaining grit, and added to the dish along with the sliced mushrooms.

**GINGER** is one of the key trio of Chinese flavorings along with garlic and green onions. If you find it difficult to obtain fresh ginger, you can buy a ready-minced version in a jar: 1 teaspoon of minced ginger is equivalent to 1 inch of fresh root ginger.

**SOY SAUCE** is the most basic flavor of the Far East. It is very salty—in the Orient it is used instead of table salt. To make sure you get the best flavor, look for the words "naturally brewed" on the label, which are most easily found on bottles of Japanese soy sauce.

**TOASTED SESAME OIL** is a powerful flavoring used in very small amounts. It is not an oil to use for frying because it burns easily. Instead, it is usually added toward the end of cooking, or sprinkled on just before the dish is served.

## JAPAN

**MIRIN** is a slightly sweet version of sake, or rice wine. It is a favorite flavoring agent, and can be found in Oriental stores. If you cannot find a supply, sweet sherry can be used as a substitute.

**RICE VINEGAR** has a very delicate flavor, and it can add interest to a dressing for green salads or cold vegetables.

**WASABI** is sometimes called Japanese horseradish; it has a clear, strong bite and goes superbly with grilled fish. It comes as ready-mixed paste in tubes, or as powder for mixing with water, like mustard powder.

## SOUTH-EAST ASIA

**COCONUT MILK** is made from coconut flesh, and in South-east Asia it is often the only liquid used for cooking vegetable stews, curries, and puddings, giving them a rich flavor and texture. It can be bought either in dehydrated blocks, which have to be reconstituted with hot water, or as a ready-made liquid in cans. Coconut cream is also sold in cans. The liquid forms are much quicker to use than the blocks.

**LEMONGRASS** is a favorite flavoring in Thai cookery, adding a subtle citrus flavor and aroma to soups and curries. The tough upper part of the stem should be discarded, and the lower half sliced into rounds. Dried lemongrass must be soaked in hot water until tender before use. Ground lemongrass is also available, and cuts out the time spent in preparation: 1 teaspoon is the equivalent of 1 stalk.

**TAMARIND** is used as a souring flavor in some South-east Asian and Indian dishes. It is dried in sticky blocks, which need to be soaked, or comes as a concentrate; the concentrate is quicker to use because it can be spooned directly into dishes.

**THAI FISH SAUCE** called *nam pla* or *nuoc mam*, is used as a flavoring in cooked dishes or diluted with water to use as a dip. Choose a brand with a clear, sherry-like color and check that the label lists "fish" as the main ingredient.

## THE MIDDLE EAST

**BULGUR WHEAT AND COUSCOUS** are as popular as rice in the Middle East and North Africa, and much faster to prepare as they simply need to be reconstituted in hot water.

To give rice dishes a Middle Eastern flavor, add cardamom pods, slightly cracked, an inch or two of cinnamon stick and two or three whole cloves while cooking. You can remove and discard whole spices before serving, if you wish.

**HARISSA** is a fiery chili paste that is flavored with coriander, cumin, garlic, and mint, and is sold in tubes or cans. It is traditionally served with couscous. To store leftover canned harissa, transfer into a container, cover and keep in the refrigerator.

**ORANGE FLOWER WATER AND ROSE WATER** evoke the Middle East more intensely than any other flavoring. Sweetly perfumed, they are added to cream, or to nut and date fillings for sweet dishes, or added discreetly to vegetables such

---

### MADE IN MINUTES!

#### INSTANT HUMMUS

If you have some canned chickpeas and tahini in your pantry you can make instant hummus. Put a can of drained chickpeas in a processor or blender with 2 tablespoons of tahini, 1 or 2 cloves of garlic, the juice of a lemon, and a generous pinch of salt. Thin to the consistency of thick cream with a little water while processing it. Serve with pita bread, bread sticks or sliced raw vegetables.

as spinach and carrots. They are available from Middle Eastern and Indian shops and in some large supermarkets. Avoid flower "essence," which has a synthetic flavor.

**TAHINI** is a nutty-flavored, oily paste made from sesame seeds; it can be diluted with lemon juice, milk, or water and seasoned to make a quick sauce or salad dressing.

## MEXICO

**CHILIES** can be bought fresh, canned, or bottled, and are readily available. They are used extensively to give flavor to Mexican dishes, along with fresh coriander and fresh lime juice. To save the time it takes to prepare fresh chilies, buy them flaked or crushed, or use some Tabasco, chili sauce, or cayenne pepper instead, to taste.

**SALSAS** can be found in many large supermarkets, canned, bottled, or fresh, along with a good selection of accompaniments such as corn chips, taco shells, and tortillas.

# FAST FINISHING TOUCHES

*T*hink about color, texture, and presentation when you are serving food. It need take only seconds to transform the simplest dish so that it appeals to the eye as well as the taste buds.

## PRESENTATION

Soup can be garnished with chopped herbs or a sprinkling of the main ingredient, such as a few slivers of mushroom. Alternatively, spooning a little whipping cream into each soup bowl and swirling it in with a teaspoon adds a finishing touch.

Color is as important to a sauce as flavor, and should provide a striking contrast to the main ingredient. Quickly snipped sun-dried tomatoes or finely chopped black olives can give an instant visual lift to many pale sauces. A little crumbled blue cheese or a handful of chopped walnuts can look pretty scattered over fresh dark green salad leaves. You can also vary your method of presentation—sauces often look better if they are poured carefully onto the plate first and the meat or fish laid on top of them.

Choose accompanying vegetables to contrast or complement the colors of the main course—try combining crisp green broccoli with bright scarlet, tomato-based dishes; vivid orange carrots with rich green spinach dishes; and jewel-bright peppers with grain or meat dishes.

While you are cooking, reserve a few whole ingredients that have visual appeal. Save a few whole shrimps to garnish seafood, for instance, a few sprigs of fresh herbs to place beside grilled meat or fish, and a whole strawberry or a little sliced fresh fruit to decorate desserts.

A fine dusting of icing sugar or cocoa sifted gently through a tea strainer is an elegant way to decorate a dessert. Because so little sugar is used, it will not oversweeten the dish, but icing sugar does melt quickly, so make sure you add it just before serving. Fresh fruit, such as sliced mango with a squeeze of lime, looks appetizing frosted lightly with icing sugar and dotted with some raspberries or thinly sliced strawberries, and a few leaves of fresh mint.

## GARNISHES

**Cookies, nuts, and citrus rind**
all make an attractive topping for ice cream. Use crushed almond praline, peanut brittle, macaroons or any almond cookies, raisins soaked in hot rum, toasted nuts or the thinly cut rind of an orange, lemon or lime. Curls of dark chocolate shaved off with a vegetable peeler are also very effective.

**Breadcrumbs**
can be quickly fried in very little oil or butter until golden, and used to top a vegetable or pasta dish, adding both flavor and color. They are easily made in a food processor (see pages 14–15).

**Croutons**
can be made in minutes to add a crunch to soups or salads. Cut slightly stale bread into small cubes and fry them with a little olive oil and a few slivers of garlic for extra flavor.

**Nuts and seeds**
such as flaked almonds, pine nuts, or sesame seeds, dry fried or toasted for a few seconds until they turn golden, add a pretty speckle and rich flavor to many dishes, and they also provide a good helping of protein in vegetarian recipes.

**Onions**
can be sliced and quickly deep fried to add intense flavor as a garnish over the top of rice or egg dishes. And bacon, fried until it is crisp and dry, can be crumbled over salads, grain dishes, and creamy soups.

**Orange and lemon rind,**
finely grated or taken off with a zester, can add a splash of fast color to grills and fried meat, and looks pretty on creamy desserts. If you like, blanch the shreds, or put them in a sieve and pour boiling water over them, to make them less bitter.

**Watercress**
makes a bright, peppery garnish, and is more unusual than a sprig of parsley. A handful of watercress can take the place of a separate side salad, and tastes especially good with grilled meat as it blends with the juices on the plate but retains its crispness.

## LAST-MINUTE SALADS

If you suddenly feel a dish needs a side salad but do not have any salad leaves to hand, green vegetables such as beans, zucchinis, or peas make a tasty substitute. Cook the chosen vegetable briefly so that it remains crunchy, refresh it under cold running water, and serve with mayonnaise or salad dressing and a sprinkling of fresh herbs.

Alternatively, make a salad from raw root vegetables such as carrots, turnips, and white or red cabbage, grated and tossed with a strongly flavored dressing, some caraway or mustard seeds and a pinch of curry powder or mixed spice.

If you have only a few salad leaves and you need to stretch them further, shred them finely and add other pantry items such as chopped hard-boiled eggs, crumbled cheese, and a handful of toasted flaked almonds, or some walnuts quickly fried with a tiny pinch of cayenne pepper.

Any three canned beans—kidney beans, white or green flageolet, fava beans or cannellini—will make a salad, tossed in a blue cheese or vinaigrette dressing with fresh herbs, crushed garlic, and a little coarse mustard, blended to a creamy texture.

### MADE IN MINUTES!

#### FRUIT SALAD

You can make an attractive fruit salad without making sugar syrup. Pour a thin film of bottled concentrated fruit juice onto individual plates—pink juice is the prettiest color—and arrange the sliced fruit on top. Sprinkle with icing sugar and decorate with fresh mint.

*QUICK TRANSFORMATIONS A little creative flair can turn versatile vegetables, legumes, and nuts into stunning salads using herbs, spices, and dressings and some imaginative techniques.*

# MAKING USE OF LEFTOVERS

A bowl of leftovers in the fridge can provide the basis for many wonderfully quick dishes. But be sure to chill and refrigerate leftover food as quickly as possible, and use it within two days. Cooked rice, in particular, must be cooled quickly, kept refrigerated, then reheated quickly and eaten immediately.

### MEAT AND FISH

Leftover meat, game, and poultry can be turned into crunchy croquettes, and fish into fish cakes. For extra color and flavor, top these with a fried egg or ketchup, or make a quick tomato sauce by simmering canned tomatoes with some chopped chives and parsley for a few minutes until it has thickened. For a more formal dish, accompany the croquettes with sautéed mushrooms and cherry tomatoes or grilled red tomatoes.

Slivers of leftover meat, game, or poultry can be quickly and crisply fried and tossed with salads of vegetable, rice, pasta, or mixed leaves to turn them into main-course dishes.

And you can make a delicious pâté by finely chopping or processing leftover cooked meat with a spoonful of mayonnaise and a couple of dill pickles or gherkins, and seasoning it well with salt and black pepper. Use the pâté to fill a sandwich, or serve it on top of a few mixed leaves as a starter.

### PASTA

Leftover pasta can be used to make a chunky rustic soup. Use small shapes whole and roughly chop spaghetti or fettuccine, or cut it up with a knife and fork into 2 in. (5 cm) lengths. Sauté a small sliced onion and a clove of garlic, then add the pasta, a can of broad, borlotti, kidney, or lima beans, or chickpeas, or a can of tomatoes, and enough stock, water, or wine to cover. Cook very gently until the vegetables are tender, then serve with grated Parmesan, if you have any.

### POTATOES

Leftover potatoes are particularly versatile, and their gentle, appetizing flavor makes them a very good accompaniment to a great variety of other foods. Potatoes can give substance to salads and add texture to soups, and they can be combined with other ingredients, reshaped and reheated to accompany many different meals.

Surplus mashed potatoes can be shaped into croquettes or potato cakes, coated in flour, and fried. Adding a well-beaten egg will help to hold the mixture together. If you have another leftover vegetable to hand, mash that into the potato first to make a colorful patty, or mix in canned salmon to make instant fish cakes.

Leftover new potatoes can make a delicious potato salad: toss them in a little olive oil while they are still warm enough to absorb the flavor, cool them, then put them in the refrigerator. To complete the salad, add extra flavor by dressing the potatoes with a herb mayonnaise.

Or turn cooked new potatoes into a fast and tasty accompaniment to hot or cold meat by frying them in olive oil or butter and sprinkling them with a little grated Parmesan, to melt and turn crunchy as they cook.

Leftover boiled potatoes can be turned into hash browns, to make a tasty breakfast with eggs and bacon (see recipe opposite).

### RICE

Extra cooked rice is always useful: it will make a substantial stuffing for peppers or tomatoes, or can be combined with crunchy cooked vegetables and salad dressing to make a rice salad.

Leftover risotto rice can be combined with egg and cheese to make delicious Italian rice balls (see recipe opposite). Rice balls can be served on their own with fresh tomato sauce as a starter or snack, or with a salad or vegetable for a simple lunch or supper. They are also pleasantly filling as an accompaniment to grilled sausages and ham, or to smoked, grilled, or fried fish.

Cooked rice can also be used for a fast stir-fry using whatever fresh vegetables you have to hand, such as baby corn cobs, carrots, cherry tomatoes, zucchinis, mushrooms, peppers or green onions, finely sliced or grated (see recipe opposite).

## MADE IN MINUTES!

### MEAT CROQUETTES

For 4 people, mince 14 oz (400 g) of cooked meat and combine it with the same weight of mashed potato and some chopped green onions, chives, or parsley. Shape it into patties, brush with egg, toss gently in dried breadcrumbs and fry until very crisp.

### ITALIAN RICE BALLS

For 2 people, mix 8 oz (230 g) of cooked risotto rice with a beaten egg, a little grated Parmesan, salt, and pepper. Shape the rice mixture into balls, roll them in flour and dried breadcrumbs, and fry them in a little olive oil until they turn a rich golden brown color.

### HASH BROWNS

For 4 people, fry a thinly sliced onion in a little oil in a nonstick pan until soft and golden. Slice or dice 1 lb (450 g) of cooked potatoes, add them to the onion and fry until they are brown and crunchy. Season well, add some chopped chives or parsley if available, and serve.

### FIVE-MINUTE STIR-FRY

For 2 people as an accompaniment, fry a little chopped garlic and ginger until slightly colored. Add 5½ oz (155 g) of mixed sliced vegetables and stir-fry until cooked but crunchy. Add 7 oz (200 g) of cooked rice, stir and heat through. Season with soy sauce and sesame oil.

## VEGETABLES

Vegetables that have been cooked in a sauce, such as cauliflower cheese, can be turned into a pasta bake. Put the leftovers into a buttered ovenproof dish, stir in some cooked pasta shapes, top with dried breadcrumbs and grated cheese and bake.

Almost any leftover vegetable can be turned into a delicious cold salad with the addition of some chopped red or green onion, capers, olives, or croutons, and some mayonnaise or vinaigrette dressing. To turn a leftover vegetable into a hearty main-course salad, try mixing it with some more substantial ingredients, such as drained canned beans, tuna fish, and canned artichoke hearts, or fry a few slices of bacon until they are very crisp, drain them well on kitchen paper, and crumble them into pieces; add them to the vegetables then mix in a little salad dressing.

*Tomato and Red Lentil Soup*

# SOUPS

Chilled soups for hot days, filling broths and chowders for hungry appetites, served on their own or with crusty bread, a good soup can start a meal, or make one.

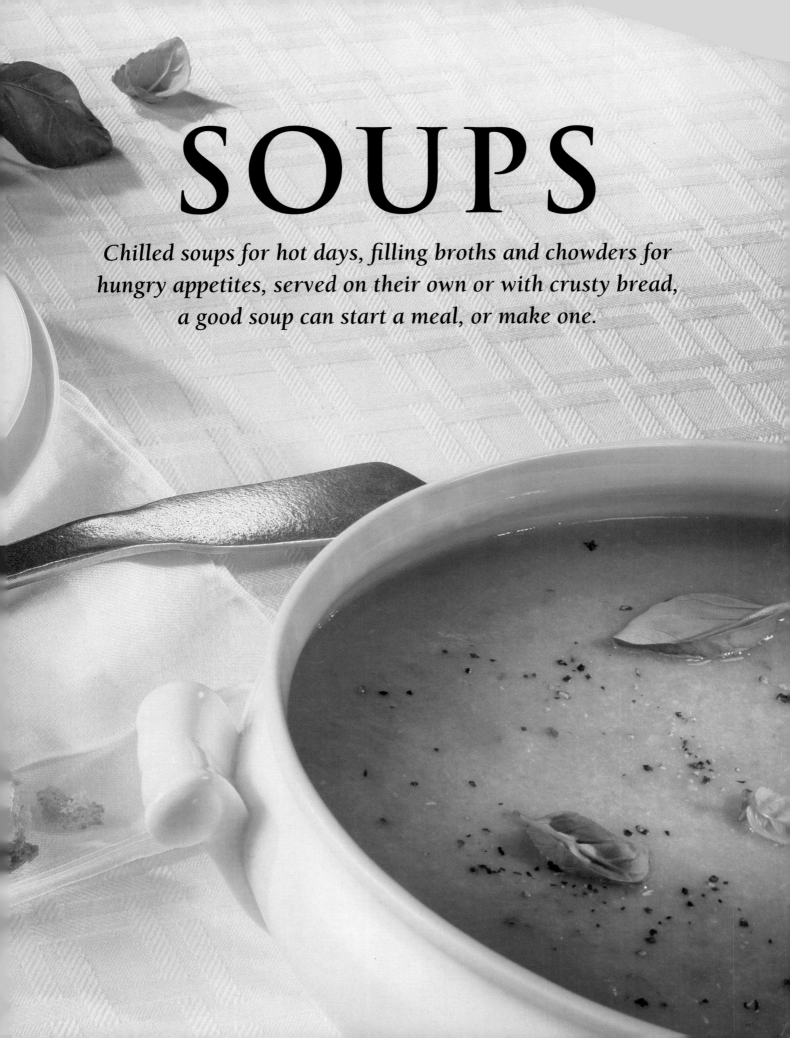

# COOL CUCUMBER SOUP

OK— NICe

*This is a great soup to make on a steamy summer's day since it requires no cooking at all. Just assemble the ingredients, mix them together, and the soup is ready to eat and enjoy.*

TIME: 15 MINUTES  SERVES: 4

| 1 large cucumber |
| 4 bushy sprigs of mint |
| 1⅔ cups (500 g) natural yogurt |
| ⅔ cup light cream |
| 2 tablespoons white wine vinegar |
| Salt and black pepper |
| *To garnish:* 4 small sprigs mint |
| *To serve:* ice cubes, optional |

**1** Chill four soup bowls in the refrigerator. Trim, rinse, and dry the cucumber, then grate it coarsely, with its skin, into a large bowl.

**2** Rinse and dry the bushy mint. Strip the leaves from the stalks and shred enough to give 4 tablespoons, or bundle the leaves together and cut them diagonally into fine strips with kitchen scissors. Add the mint to the cucumber.

**3** Stir the yogurt, cream, and vinegar into the bowl. Season well with salt and pepper and stir again.

**4** Divide the soup among the four chilled soup bowls. Add one or two ice cubes to each one if you like to chill it quickly. Garnish with the small sprigs of mint and serve.

**VARIATION**
You can use sour cream instead of light cream if you prefer a sharper taste, and use tarragon vinegar instead of wine vinegar for a herbier overtone. For a pretty contrast of taste and color, add a few peeled fresh shrimp to each soup bowl before serving.

**NUTRIENTS PER SERVING:** *calories 235, carbohydrate 6.5 g (including sugar 6 g), protein 10 g, fat 19 g (saturated fat 11 g), good source of vitamins A, B group, E, and folate and selenium.*

# GAZPACHO

*This crunchy, floating salad, one of many versions of the celebrated Spanish soup, is incomparable on a hot day.*

TIME: 30 MINUTES  SERVES: 4–6

| | |
|---|---|
| 1 thick slice dry-textured bread | 4 large cloves garlic |
| 6 tablespoons extra virgin olive oil | 1 large cucumber |
| 4 tablespoons red wine vinegar | 1 each red, yellow, and green peppers |
| Salt and black pepper | 1 fresh or dried red chili or 1 fresh green chili |
| 1 tablespoon paprika, or hot or sweet Spanish paprika | 6 large basil and/or mint leaves |
| 1 can (19 oz / 540 ml) chopped tomatoes in natural juice | 1¼ cups ice-cold water |
| 1 red onion | 12 ice cubes (if required) |

*To garnish:* 1 clove garlic, a little olive oil, and 3 slices of bread for croutons, optional

**1**  Discard the crusts from the bread, then put it into a food processor, and make it into crumbs.

**2**  Put the oil into a large serving bowl and whisk in the vinegar and salt to make a creamy emulsion. Add the paprika and breadcrumbs and stir until thoroughly combined and sloppy.

**3**  Stir the tomatoes and their juice into the mixture, then set it aside.

**4**  Peel the onion, garlic, and cucumber. Rinse, halve, and deseed the peppers and the chili, then cut them into squares.

**5**  In a food processor, coarsely chop the onion and garlic together and add them to the breadcrumb mixture. One by one, coarsely chop the cucumber, peppers, and chili, and add them to the soup.

**6**  Rinse, dry, and tear the basil or mint leaves into small pieces and add them. Stir well, taste, and season generously with salt and pepper. The flavor should be sharp and refreshing, with plenty of bite.

**7**  Stir in enough ice-cold water to give the mixture a souplike consistency, but do not make it too thin: the texture should be quite dense. Leave to chill, or stir in the ice cubes and serve immediately.

**8**  To make croutons, put the garlic into a frying pan with a little oil, over a moderate heat. Cut the bread into cubes and fry, turning often until browned. Discard the garlic; serve the croutons with soup.

VARIATION

Put some vodka into the freezer before making the gazpacho, then add 1–2 tablespoons to each bowl just before serving.

NUTRIENTS PER SERVING, WHEN SERVING 4:
*calories 261, carbohydrate 21g (including sugar 13g), protein 6g, fat 18g (saturated fat 3g), good source of vitamins A, B group, C, E, and folate.*

---

COOK'S SUGGESTION

*A food processor will make fast work of chopping the vegetables. You can chop them by hand, but it will take much longer.*

# CREAMY AVOCADO AND COCONUT SOUP

*Tropical flavors of chili, coconut, and coriander characterize this cold puréed soup, which takes its silky texture and velvety taste from luscious, ripe avocados and smooth, creamy Greek yogurt.*

TIME: 15 MINUTES   SERVES: 4

½ **vegetable stock cube**

4 **green onions**

1 **large clove garlic**

1 **fresh green chili**

A **small bunch coriander**

2 **medium avocados**

1 cup (300 g) natural Greek yogurt

⅔ **cup coconut milk**

1 **tablespoon olive oil**

A **pinch of sugar**

½ **lemon**

**Salt and black pepper**

1   Dissolve the stock cube in a small amount of boiling water in a measuring cup, then make up to 1¼ cups with chilled water.

2   Rinse, trim, and chop the green onions. Peel and crush the garlic. Rinse, deseed, and chop the chili, and set them all aside.

3   Rinse and dry the coriander. Set aside a few leaves for a garnish and roughly chop the remainder.

4   Halve and stone the avocados and scoop the flesh into a blender or food processor. Add the stock, green onions, garlic, chili, chopped coriander, yogurt, coconut milk, olive oil, sugar, and 1 tablespoon of juice from the lemon, and process until velvety and smooth.

5   Season to taste and chill for as long as possible. Garnish with the coriander leaves and black pepper.

*SERVING SUGGESTION*

Place a couple of ice cubes in the soup bowls before serving.

*NUTRIENTS PER SERVING: calories 322, carbohydrate 6 g (including sugar 5 g), protein 7 g, fat 30 g (saturated fat 9 g), good source of vitamins B group, C, and E.*

# RED PEPPER AND ORANGE VELVET SOUP

*A soup to delight the senses, this derives its stunning color from red peppers, and its heady aroma and fruity flavor from orange flower water and freshly squeezed orange juice.*

TIME: 30 MINUTES  SERVES: 4

| |
|---|
| 2 tablespoons olive oil |
| 2 lb (1 kg) red peppers |
| Salt |
| 3 oranges |
| 1 tablespoon orange flower water |
| *To garnish:* orange zest, chopped parsley or croutons, optional |

**1** Heat the oil in a large saucepan over moderate heat. Rinse, dry, deseed, and quarter the peppers lengthways. Slice them fairly coarsely in a food processor and add to the oil. Alternatively, slice them by hand, adding the first pepper to the pan while you slice the next, stirring with each addition and keeping the pan covered while you slice. Add a little salt to taste.

**2** Wash any wax from the oranges, then grate the rind from one into the pan. Cover and increase the heat to high until steam starts to escape from under the lid. Lower the heat and simmer, covered, for 15–18 minutes, shaking the pan occasionally, allowing the peppers to cook in their own juice.

**3** Meanwhile, squeeze the juice from the oranges into a measuring cup; you will need ¾ cup. Stir the orange flower water into the orange juice.

**4** When the peppers are soft, process or blend them to a smooth purée. It does not matter if some of the peppers have caramelized— this just adds to the flavor. Add the orange mixture and process or blend again.

**5** Reheat and garnish with orange zest, herbs, and croutons, if using.

**VARIATION**

In winter use blood oranges for a dramatic ruby color. You could serve the soup cold in summer.

*NUTRIENTS PER SERVING: calories 130, carbohydrate 17g (including sugar 16g), protein 2g, fat 6g (saturated fat 1g), good source of vitamins A, B group, C, and E.*

---

### COOK'S SUGGESTION

*Orange flower water is available in some supermarkets, delicatessens, and Indian and Middle-Eastern specialty stores. Check that it can be used for cooking—the beauty product orange flower water is not suitable.*

---

# MUSHROOM SOUP

*The earthy flavor of the large, dark mushrooms in this soup is given a lift by garlic, parsley, and mace.*
*It has a deep, smoky color and a rich taste that needs no cream to enhance it.*

TIME: 30 MINUTES  SERVES: 4–6

| |
| --- |
| 5 cups vegetable stock |
| 3 slices (140 g) country-style bread |
| ½ small onion or 1 shallot |
| 1½ lb (680 g) large, flat mushrooms |
| 3 sprigs of parsley |
| 2 tablespoons olive oil |
| ½ small clove garlic |
| A pinch of ground or freshly grated nutmeg |
| Salt and black pepper |

1  Put the stock on to boil. Soak the bread in a little cold water.
2  Peel and chop the onion or shallot. Clean and roughly chop the mushrooms. Rinse, dry, and chop the parsley.
3  Heat the oil in a large pan. Fry the onion or shallot over a moderate heat until lightly browned. Peel the garlic and crush it into the pan. Add the mushrooms and cook until they release their liquid; add the parsley.
4  Squeeze as much water as possible from the bread, then stir it into the mushrooms. Add the stock and nutmeg. Return the stock to the boil, half cover the pan and simmer for 15–20 minutes.
5  Purée or blend the soup until it is creamy but still slightly grainy, then reheat, season with salt and pepper and serve.

*NUTRIENTS PER SERVING, WHEN SERVING 4: calories 170, carbohydrate 21 g (including sugar 2 g), protein 7 g, fat 9 g (saturated fat 1 g), good source of vitamins B group, E, and folate and selenium.*

# GREEN BEAN SOUP

*A trio of beans—green, lima, and flageolet, fresh, frozen, and canned—come together to add their*
*individual flavors to this delicate, pale green soup, flavored with chives.*

**TIME: 30 MINUTES  SERVES: 4–6**

| |
|---|
| 2 tablespoons olive oil |
| 4 cups vegetable stock |
| 1 medium onion |
| 1 large clove garlic |
| 8 oz (230 g) thin green beans |
| 12 oz (335 g) frozen lima beans |
| 15 oz (425 g) canned flageolet beans |
| Salt and black pepper |
| *To garnish:* a small bunch of chives |

**1**  Heat the olive oil gently in a large saucepan and put the stock on to heat. Peel the onion, chop it, and add it to the oil. Peel the garlic, crush it into the onion, and stir.

**2**  Rinse, top, and tail the green beans, chop into 1 in. (2.5 cm) pieces and add them and the lima beans to the pan. Raise the heat and cook for a few minutes.

**3**  Add the stock to the pan and boil for 5 minutes, then lower the heat and simmer for 10 minutes.

**4**  Remove the saucepan from the heat and stir in the canned flageolet beans with their liquid. Stir well.

**5**  Process or blend half the soup to a purée, then return it to the pan. Season to taste, then reheat. Rinse the chives and any chive flowers, snip them over the soup and serve.

**VARIATION**
Coriander, mint, or parsley can be used as a garnish instead of chives.

*NUTRIENTS PER SERVING, WHEN SERVING 4: calories 233, carbohydrate 29 g (including sugar 4 g), protein 13 g, fat 8 g (saturated fat 1 g), good source of vitamins B group, C, E, and folate.*

# CABBAGE, POTATO, AND SAUSAGE SOUP

*This version of a Portuguese soup, caldo verde, features the traditional potato and shredded cabbage, boosted with the delicious flavors of garlic, dill, smoky chorizo sausage, and olive oil.*

TIME: 25 MINUTES  SERVES: 4

| |
| --- |
| 3 medium-size (500 g) floury potatoes |
| 2 cloves garlic |
| 2 cups green or curly cabbage |
| 1 teaspoon dried dill weed |
| 3 oz (85 g) chorizo sausage |
| Salt and black pepper |
| 4 tablespoons extra virgin olive oil |
| *To serve:* crusty bread or toast |

1  Peel and thinly slice the potatoes and put into a large saucepan. Cover with 4 cups of cold water and bring to the boil. Peel and slice the garlic and add to pan.

2  When the water reaches boiling point, skim off the white froth and lower the heat, then partially cover the pan and gently boil the potatoes for 7–10 minutes.

3  Meanwhile, trim the cabbage, removing any coarse stalks, then rinse and shred the leaves into strips, about ½ in. (1 cm) wide.

4  When the potatoes are nearly cooked, remove the pan from the heat and mash them in the water to break them up as much as possible.

5  Add the cabbage and dried dill, bring back to the boil then reduce the heat and cook for a further 4–7 minutes (depending on the variety of cabbage).

6  While the potatoes and cabbage are cooking, cut the chorizo sausage into wafer thin slices.

7  Take the pan off the heat and mash the potatoes again to reduce them to more of a purée and to help break down the cooked cabbage into the soup, though it should still retain its color and shape.

8  Season the soup generously with salt and black pepper, then ladle it into the soup plates.

9  Garnish with slices of sausage. Trickle olive oil in a zigzag pattern over each serving and grind on more black pepper. Serve with crusty bread or toast.

*NUTRIENTS PER SERVING: calories 469, carbohydrate 68g (including sugar 5g), protein 14g, fat 16g (saturated fat 4g), good source of vitamins B group, C, E, and folate.*

# SPICY CARROT SOUP o, K

*Carrots and ginger bring out the best in each other, and here they are boosted with fresh green chili and Eastern spices in a thick vegetable soup to make a real winter warmer.*

TIME: 30 MINUTES  SERVES: 4–6

| 4 cups vegetable stock or water |
| 1 small–medium potato |
| 1 medium onion |
| 1 lb (450 g) carrots |
| 2 large cloves garlic |
| Salt and black pepper |
| 1 fresh green chili |
| 2 in. (5 cm) piece root ginger |
| 1 lemon or lime |
| 2 tablespoons olive oil |
| 1 teaspoon garam masala, Chinese five-spice powder, or mixed spice |
| 1 teaspoon toasted sesame oil |
| *To garnish:* fresh coriander leaves, lemon or lime zest, or croutons |

1  Bring the stock or water to the boil in a large saucepan. Peel the potato, onion, and carrots and cut them into small chunks. Peel and quarter the garlic cloves.

2  When the stock is boiling, stir in the vegetables, garlic, and some salt. Bring it back to the boil, reduce the heat, partially cover, and boil gently for 15–20 minutes.

3  Meanwhile, rinse, deseed, and chop the chili, peel and chop the ginger, and squeeze the juice from the lemon or lime.

4  Heat the olive oil in a small pan and fry the chili and ginger for about 1 minute, but do not let them burn. Stir in the garam masala, five-spice powder or mixed spice and the juice; cook for 1 minute.

5  Add the sesame oil and stir over the heat until the mixture thickens to form a sauce. Remove the pan from the heat and set aside.

6  When the vegetables are tender, stir in the ginger sauce, then process or blend the mixture into a smooth purée. Return the purée to the pan, season with black pepper to taste, then reheat and serve with the garnish of your choice.

*NUTRIENTS PER SERVING, WHEN SERVING 4: calories 149, carbohydrate 19g (including sugar 9g), protein 3g, fat 9g (saturated fat 1g), good source of vitamins A, B group, C, and E.*

# PEA AND ASPARAGUS SOUP

*This pretty spring soup makes the most of fresh asparagus. A garnish of crispy bacon pieces and crunchy croutons adds savor, while a swirl of whipped cream provides a smooth touch.*

TIME: 30 MINUTES   SERVES: 4

| |
|---|
| 2½ cups chicken or vegetable stock |
| 8–9 green onions |
| 1 lb (450 g) frozen peas |
| 12 small (150 g) asparagus spears |
| Salt and black pepper |
| 3 slices rindless streaky bacon |
| 1–2 tablespoons vegetable oil |
| 2 slices day-old white bread |
| 3 tablespoons whipped cream |

**1** Put the stock on to heat, then rinse the green onions, trim and chop them roughly, add them to the stock with the frozen peas, and bring to the boil.

**2** Rinse the asparagus spears, remove the tips, and set them aside. Roughly chop the stems and add them to the saucepan with a pinch of salt. Reduce the heat, cover, and simmer for 10–15 minutes, or until the asparagus is tender.

**3** Meanwhile, snip the bacon slices directly into a frying pan and fry until crisp and golden. Transfer to a plate and set aside.

**4** If there is not enough bacon fat left in the pan for frying, add 1–2 tablespoons of oil and heat. Cut the bread into small dice and fry for 2–3 minutes over a high heat, turning frequently, until golden, then drain on kitchen paper.

**5** When the peas and asparagus are done, blend or process the soup to a purée.

**6** Add the reserved asparagus tips to the pea soup and simmer for 5 minutes, or until tender.

**7** Pour the soup into warmed serving bowls. Swirl a little whipped cream into each and sprinkle with the crispy bacon pieces, croutons, and some freshly ground black pepper to serve.

*NUTRIENTS PER SERVING: calories 330, carbohydrate 24 g (including sugar 5 g), protein 13 g, fat 21 g (saturated fat 9 g), good source of vitamins B group, C, E, and folate.*

# TOMATO AND RED LENTIL SOUP

*An unusual green-and-white garnish of cream cheese speckled with fresh basil adds a festive touch to this intensely flavored, richly colored soup of tomatoes, garlic, and lentils.*

TIME: 30 MINUTES  SERVES: 4

| |
| --- |
| 2½ cups chicken or vegetable stock |
| 2 tablespoons olive oil |
| 3 shallots |
| 2–3 cloves garlic |
| A few sprigs of fresh basil |
| ½ cup (100 g) split red lentils |
| 1 can (19 oz / 540 ml) canned chopped tomatoes |
| 1 packet (4½ oz / 125 g) cream cheese |
| Salt and black pepper |

1  Put the stock on to heat. Heat the oil in a large saucepan. Peel and chop the shallots and garlic and fry gently for 5 minutes, or until soft.
2  Rinse and dry the basil, reserve a few leaves for a garnish, then shred enough to give 1 tablespoon.
3  Rinse and drain the lentils, and add them to the pan with the stock and the tomatoes. Bring to the boil, cover and simmer for about 15 minutes, adding half the shredded basil after 10 minutes.

4  Beat the cream cheese in a small bowl until softened. Stir in the remaining shredded basil.
5  Blend or process the soup to a purée and season to taste with salt and pepper. Serve with spoonfuls of the cream cheese mixture; garnish with basil leaves.

*NUTRIENTS PER SERVING: calories 280, carbohydrate 20 g (including sugar 4 g), protein 10 g, fat 18 g (saturated fat 8 g), good source of vitamins B group, C, and E.*

# AROMATIC PARSNIP SOUP

*This fragrant, warming winter soup has a yogurt creaminess and subtle spicing, with a sweet undertone of apple.*

**TIME: 30 MINUTES  SERVES: 4–6**

| |
|---|
| 3½ cups vegetable stock |
| 1 large cooking apple |
| 1 lb (450 g) parsnips |
| 1 medium onion |
| 1 tablespoon sunflower oil |
| 1 clove garlic |
| 2 teaspoons ground coriander |
| 1 teaspoon ground cumin |
| 1 teaspoon turmeric |
| Salt |
| 1½ cups milk |

***To garnish:* a few sprigs of coriander; 4–6 tablespoons natural yogurt**

**1**  Warm the stock over a low heat. Peel the apple and the parsnips. Quarter and core the apple, then chop the apple and parsnips into chunks, and set aside.

**2**  Peel and chop the onion. Heat the oil in a large saucepan, add the onion, and leave it to soften.

**3**  Peel and roughly chop the garlic, add it to the pan, then add the three spices and cook for 1 minute.

**4**  Pour the warmed stock into the pan and add the apple, parsnips, and salt. Bring to the boil, then reduce the heat, cover, and simmer for 15 minutes.

**5**  Meanwhile, rinse and dry the coriander and strip off the leaves.

**6**  Remove the pan from the heat and stir in the milk. Process or blend the soup to a smooth purée, then reheat.

**7**  Ladle the soup into bowls, garnish it with the coriander, and serve. Prepare a dish of yogurt to hand around separately for people to help themselves.

*NUTRIENTS PER SERVING, WHEN SERVING 4: calories 211, carbohydrate 30g (including sugar 21g), protein 9g, fat 8g (saturated fat 2g), good source of vitamins B group, C, E, and folate and calcium.*

### COOK'S SUGGESTION

*If you are using a food processor or blender that will not take boiling liquids, cooling the soup by adding cold milk means that you can purée it immediately.*

# ZUCCHINI AND WATERCRESS SOUP

*The mellow smoothness of the zucchinis in this intensely green vegetable soup provides a subtle counterbalance to the underlying sharp, peppery flavor of the watercress leaves.*

TIME: 30 MINUTES  SERVES: 4

2 medium onions

2 tablespoons (1 oz) unsalted butter

3 cups chicken
or vegetable stock

2 lb (900 g) firm zucchinis

A large bunch of watercress

1 lemon

Salt and black pepper

**1** Peel and chop the onions. Heat the unsalted butter in a large saucepan and fry the onions over a gentle heat until they are transparent. Add the stock, cover, and bring to the boil.

**2** Rinse the zucchinis, slice them thinly, and add them to the boiling stock. Reduce the heat, cover, and simmer for 15 minutes.

**3** Rinse the watercress, discard the coarse stems, and reserve four sprigs for a garnish. Chop the remainder.

**4** When the zucchinis are tender, stir in the watercress, then remove the pan from the heat and leave to stand, covered, for 5 minutes. Meanwhile, squeeze the juice from the lemon and set aside.

**5** Blend the soup to a purée, add seasoning and lemon juice to taste. Reheat and garnish with watercress.

*NUTRIENTS PER SERVING: calories 119, carbohydrate 9 g (including sugar 7 g), protein 6 g, fat 6 g (saturated fat 4 g), good source of vitamins A, B group, C, E, and folate, and iron and zinc.*

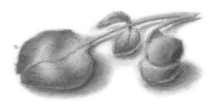

39

# CORN CHOWDER

*Substantial and warming, this soup was inspired by a traditional recipe from New England that makes good use of the local corn, while cream and potatoes add to its rich texture.*

TIME: 30 MINUTES  SERVES: 4

| |
|---|
| 1 can (12 oz / 340 ml) corn kernels |
| 5 slices pancetta, or bacon |
| 1 tablespoon sunflower oil |
| 1 large onion |
| 3 medium potatoes |
| 1¼ cups light cream |
| 1¼ cups milk |
| Salt and black pepper |
| *To garnish:* fresh parsley |

**1**  Put a kettle of water on to boil. Drain the corn kernels and purée into a chunky paste, reserving a few whole kernels for a garnish. Chop the pancetta or bacon into small strips.

**2**  Heat the oil in a pan, fry the pancetta or bacon until crisp and brown, then set aside on a plate.

**3**  While the pancetta or bacon is cooking, peel and slice the onion. Scrub the potatoes, if necessary, and cut them into ¼ in. (5 mm) cubes.

**4**  Add the onion to the fat remaining in the pan; cook over a high heat, stirring, until softened. Stir in the corn, potatoes, and 2½ cups of boiling water. Cover and simmer for 15 minutes.

**5**  Meanwhile, rinse, dry, and finely chop the parsley and set it aside. Heat the cream and milk gently in a small saucepan, but do not boil.

**6**  When the potatoes are cooked, but still retain their shape, stir in the cream and milk, and heat gently to just below boiling point. Stir in the pancetta or bacon and add salt and pepper to taste. Garnish with the chopped parsley and corn kernels and serve.

NUTRIENTS PER SERVING: *calories 545, carbohydrate 67 g (including sugar 22 g), protein 16 g, fat 26 g (saturated fat 10 g), good source of vitamins A, B group, C, E, and folate and zinc.*

### COOK'S SUGGESTION

*Pancetta, an Italian delicatessen meat, is made from pork belly, soaked in an herb and spice-flavored brine and then air-dried for several months. Unlike bacon (often used as a substitute), it can be eaten without cooking and has a sweet flavor and soft texture.*

# MINESTRONE

*You can vary the ingredients in this robust, classic soup to suit your own tastes by using any fresh, seasonal vegetables, some small pasta shapes, and a choice of canned beans.*

TIME: 30 MINUTES  SERVES: 4

| |
|---|
| 1 small leek |
| 3 tablespoons olive oil |
| 1 clove garlic |
| 2 medium sticks celery |
| 2 medium zucchinis |
| A sprig of parsley |
| 1 can (19 oz / 540 ml) cannellini beans |
| 1 can (19 oz / 540 ml) chopped tomatoes |
| 1 bay leaf |
| ⅔ cup (150 ml) dry white wine |
| ¼ cup (25 g) soup-pasta shapes |
| 1 lemon |
| 1 tablespoon (40 g) Parmesan cheese |
| 1 cup (125 g) savoy or other green cabbage |
| Salt and black pepper |
| *To serve:* loaf of crusty bread; 4 tablespoons pesto sauce, optional |

**1**   Put a kettle of water on to boil. Trim, halve, and slice the leek, rinse well, then drain in a colander.

**2**   Heat the oil in a large saucepan and fry the leek for 1 minute. Peel the garlic and crush it into the pan.

**3**   Rinse and finely slice the celery and stir it into the pan. Rinse and trim the zucchinis. Cut them in half lengthways and then into half-moon slices. Add them to the pan and cook for another 3 minutes.

**4**   Rinse the parsley and drain and rinse the beans, then add them both to the pan with the tomatoes, bay leaf, white wine, pasta and 2½ cups of boiling water. Wash any wax from the lemon, then finely pare off a strip of rind and add it to the pan. Cover, bring back to the boil, then reduce the heat and simmer for 7 minutes.

**5**   Meanwhile, add half the Parmesan cheese into the soup, then finely shred, rinse, and add the cabbage. Season to taste, then simmer for another 5 minutes.

**6**   Remove the bay leaf, transfer the minestrone into four bowls, and shake the rest of the cheese over the top of each bowl. Serve the soup with crusty bread and a small, separate bowl of pesto sauce.

*NUTRIENTS PER SERVING: calories 485, carbohydrate 65 g (including sugar 8 g), protein 21 g, fat 15 g (saturated fat 3 g), good source of vitamins A, B group, C, E, and folate, and calcium and selenium.*

### COOK'S SUGGESTION

*Instead of adding the grated cheese at the end, you can speed things up and cut costs by adding a piece of Parmesan rind to the soup along with the canned tomatoes to give a cheesy flavor. Remove the rind just before serving.*

# SMOKED HADDOCK, BEAN, AND LEEK SOUP

*Modest ingredients add up to a richly flavored family soup. Creamy butter beans, with a little onion and leek to sharpen them, have their flavor lifted by the salty, smoky taste of the fish.*

TIME: 30 MINUTES   SERVES: 4–6

| |
|---|
| 2½ cups fish, chicken, or vegetable stock |
| 1 medium onion |
| 5 medium (800 g) leeks |
| 2 tablespoons extra virgin olive oil |
| 1 can (19 oz/540 ml) flageolet beans |
| 1 lb (450 g) undyed smoked haddock |
| A small handful of parsley |
| Black pepper |
| *To garnish:* 4–6 tablespoons whipping cream, optional |

**1** Put the stock on to heat in a saucepan. Peel and finely chop the onion. Trim the leeks, cut them into thin slices, and rinse them well.
**2** Heat the oil in a medium-sized saucepan and cook the onion and leeks gently for 5 minutes, stirring occasionally. Add the stock, bring to the boil, reduce the heat, cover, and simmer for 5 minutes.
**3** Add the butter beans and their liquid to the pan and mash roughly. Return to the boil, reduce the heat, cover, and let them simmer.
**4** Skin the haddock (see page 11) and dice the flesh, removing any bones. Add to the soup and simmer until the flesh becomes opaque.
**5** Rinse, dry, and chop the parsley. Season the soup to taste with the black pepper (the smoked fish should be salty enough without adding extra). Sprinkle the chopped parsley over the soup and serve. If you like, swirl a spoonful of whipping cream into each bowl.

*NUTRIENTS PER SERVING, WHEN SERVING 4:* calories 361, carbohydrate 34 g (including sugar 7 g), protein 38 g, fat 8 g (saturated fat 1 g), good source of vitamins B group, C, E, and folate.

---

# CHUKY FISH SOUP

*Chunks of firm fish stay attractively whole in this beautifully simple soup. Herbs, tomatoes, and wine add extra flavor and a warm, inviting color, while a modest addition of cream gives it richness.*

TIME: 30 MINUTES   SERVES: 4–6

| |
|---|
| 2½ cups fish stock |
| 1 medium onion |
| 1 medium bulb fennel |
| 2 tablespoons sunflower oil |
| ⅔ cup (150 ml) dry white wine or vermouth |
| 1 can (19 oz/540 ml) chopped tomatoes |
| 1 bay leaf |
| 1 teaspoon sugar |
| Salt and black pepper |
| 1 lb (450 g) firm-fleshed fish (see box, right) |
| A few sprigs of parsley |
| 1 tablespoon cornstarch |
| 2 tablespoons milk |
| 3 tablespoons whipping cream |

**1** Put the stock on to heat. Peel and finely chop the onion and trim, rinse, and finely chop the fennel, reserving the fronds for a garnish.
**2** Heat the oil in a large, heavy saucepan, then cook the onion and fennel over a moderate heat for 5 minutes, or until softened.
**3** Pour off any surplus oil from the saucepan, then add the stock, the wine or vermouth, tomatoes, bay leaf, and sugar and season to taste. Bring to the boil, cover, and simmer for 10 minutes.
**4** Meanwhile, skin the fish, remove any bones, cut the flesh into 1 in. (2.5 cm) cubes and add it to the pan. Rinse the parsley, reserve a few leaves for a garnish, chop the rest, and add to the soup. Cover and simmer gently for 5 minutes.
**5** Blend the cornstarch and milk in a bowl. When the fish is cooked, remove the bay leaf, stir the cornstarch into the soup, and simmer until it thickens slightly.
**6** Stir in the whipping cream and let it heat gently for a minute or two. Serve the soup garnished with the reserved fennel and parsley.

*NUTRIENTS PER SERVING, when serving 4:* calories 312, carbohydrate 12 g (including sugar 8 g), protein 22 g, fat 17 g (saturated fat 8 g), good source of vitamins A, B group, C, and E.

---

### COOK'S SUGGESTION
*You can use any firm-fleshed fish, such as halibut, salmon, or swordfish to make this dish. Alternatively, you can use equal quantities of shrimps and scallops, with the scallops sliced widthwise into two discs (see page 128).*

**TWO HEARTY FISH SOUPS:** *(top right)* SMOKED HADDOCK, BEAN, AND LEEK SOUP; *(bottom left)* CHUNKY FISH SOUP.

# ORIENTAL CHICKEN BROTH

*Shiitake mushrooms, lettuce, cayenne pepper, and fresh coriander flavor this Eastern soup, which is based on chicken stock and made substantial with vermicelli and threads of beaten egg.*

TIME: 15 MINUTES  SERVES: 4

| |
|---|
| **5 cups chicken stock** |
| **¼ teaspoon cayenne pepper** |
| **3½ oz (100 g) shiitake mushrooms** |
| **1 small head of lettuce** |
| **1 large egg** |
| **A small bunch of coriander** |
| **1½ oz (45 g) vermicelli** |

**1** Bring the stock and cayenne pepper to the boil in a large saucepan.
**2** Meanwhile, clean, trim, and thinly slice the mushrooms. If necessary, remove and discard the outer leaves from the lettuce, then rinse it and shred it finely. Whisk the egg lightly and set it aside. Rinse, dry, and chop enough coriander to give 1 tablespoon.
**3** When the stock reaches boiling point, add the mushrooms, lower the heat, and simmer for 2 minutes. Crush the vermicelli lightly, add it, and simmer for 3 minutes until it is just barely cooked. Add the lettuce, then raise the heat and bring the broth to a rolling boil.

**4** Take the pan off the heat and slowly add the egg, stirring gently. It will cook very quickly to form threads. Stir in the coriander straightaway and serve immediately.
**VARIATION**
Oyster mushrooms can be used instead of shiitake, and watercress can be substituted for the lettuce.

*NUTRIENTS PER SERVING: calories 80, carbohydrate 8g (including sugar 0.5g), protein 6g, fat 2g (saturated fat 1g), good source of vitamins B group and E.*

# FRENCH VEGETABLE SOUP

*This elegant combination of fresh spring vegetables, cooked together then added to a rich tomato-flavored broth, makes a hearty soup that will serve as a main course for lunch or supper.*

TIME: 30 MINUTES  SERVES: 4

| |
|---|
| 2 tablespoons (25 g) butter |
| 2 cloves garlic |
| 2 shallots |
| 1 can (28 oz / 796 ml) chopped tomatoes |
| 1¾ cups chicken or vegetable stock |
| 1 teaspoon dried sweet basil |
| Salt and black pepper |
| ½ lb (230 g) baby new potatoes |
| 12 baby or 4 small carrots |
| 6 large radishes |
| 3½ oz (100 g) snow, or sugar, peas |
| 12 asparagus tips |
| ½ cup (125 ml) light cream |
| 8 large basil leaves |
| *To garnish:* Parmesan cheese or mature Cheddar, optional |

1  Put a kettle of water on to boil. Heat the butter very slowly in a large saucepan. Peel and chop the garlic and shallots, add them to the butter and fry gently for 3 minutes, stirring occasionally.

2  Add the tomatoes and their liquid, stock, dried basil, and some salt and pepper to the pan. Cover and simmer for 15 minutes.

3  Meanwhile, scrub and quarter the potatoes, put them into a second saucepan, and cover well with the boiling water from the kettle. Bring back to the boil, then reduce the heat and boil gently.

4  Trim, scrub, and halve the baby carrots or, if you are using larger ones, peel them and cut into 1 in. (2.5 cm) chunks. When the potatoes have been cooking for 5 minutes, add the carrots.

5  Trim and rinse the radishes, then dice them and add them to the carrots and potatoes. Rinse the asparagus tips and rinse, trim, and halve the snow, or sugar, peas and add them.

6  Cook the vegetables for a total of 10–12 minutes or until they are just tender. Meanwhile, grate the cheese, if using, and set aside.

7  Drain the vegetables and add to the tomato stock. Stir in the cream. Rinse, tear, and add the basil leaves.

8  Season to taste with salt and pepper. Serve the soup immediately, passing the grated cheese separately to sprinkle over the top, if using.

**VARIATION**
Add some cooked chicken for a delicious chicken and vegetable stew.

*NUTRIENTS PER SERVING: calories 224, carbohydrate 22 g (including sugar 14 g), protein 8 g, fat 12 g (saturated fat 7g), good source of vitamins A, B group, C, E, and folate.*

POTATO PANCAKES WITH SMOKED SALMON

# APPETIZERS & SNACKS

*Smoked salmon, mangoes, goat's cheese, bruschetta—some of the tempting ingredients that make up enticing light dishes to launch a great meal, or provide a delectable snack.*

# CHICKEN LIVERS WITH JUNIPER BERRIES

*Aromatic juniper berries, juicy grapes, fresh thyme, and a dash of dry sherry give earthy, pan-fried chicken livers a rich, sophisticated flavor to serve as a dramatic appetizer or a pasta sauce.*

TIME: 20 MINUTES  SERVES: 4

| |
|---|
| **1 lb (450 g) fresh chicken livers** |
| **1 shallot** |
| **1 clove garlic** |
| **10 juniper berries** |
| **A large bunch of fresh thyme** |
| **1 tablespoon olive oil** |
| **Salt and black pepper** |
| **2 tablespoons dry sherry** |
| **6 oz (170 g) small, seedless, green and ruby grapes** |
| **2 large, thick slices white country-style bread** |
| ***To garnish:* a small bunch of flat-leaved parsley** |

**1** Rinse the chicken livers under cold running water, trim off any sinews with scissors, then cut the flesh into bite-sized pieces. Pat dry with kitchen paper.

**2** Peel and finely chop the shallot, peel and crush the garlic, and lightly crush the juniper berries with a pestle and mortar or the end of a rolling pin. Set them all aside.

**3** Rinse and dry the thyme and parsley. Strip enough leaves from the thyme to give 2 tablespoons. Chop the parsley and set it aside for a garnish.

**4** Heat the olive oil in a large, heavy frying pan and when it is very hot, add the chicken livers and toss quickly to seal the surfaces. Cook over a high heat, stirring, for 2 minutes.

**5** Add the shallot, garlic, juniper berries, thyme, and plenty of black pepper to the pan, then lower the heat and continue cooking for a further 3–4 minutes, stirring to prevent burning.

**6** Add the sherry and grapes to the pan and add salt to taste. Cook the chicken livers for another minute, then turn off the heat, cover, and keep warm.

**7** Toast the bread and cut each slice into four triangles. Spoon the chicken livers onto individual serving plates, sprinkle with the chopped parsley and serve accompanied by the toast.

**VARIATION**
You can add ¾ cup of light whipping cream, buttermilk, or Greek yogurt, to the chicken livers and serve them as a sauce for pasta.

*NUTRIENTS PER SERVING: calories 242, carbohydrate 20 g (including sugar 8 g), protein 25 g, fat 6 g (saturated fat 1 g), good source of vitamins A, B group, C, and folate, and iron and zinc.*

# TROPICAL SALAD WITH LIME DRESSING

*Two favorite tropical fruits—rich, creamy-smooth avocado and sweet-flavored papaya—are combined with peppery watercress and a fresh lime dressing to make a light and stylish appetizer.*

**TIME: 20 MINUTES  SERVES: 4**

*For the salad:*

| |
|---|
| **A bunch of watercress** |
| **2 ripe but firm avocados** |
| **2 ripe but firm papayas** |

*For the dressing:*

| |
|---|
| **1 lime** |
| **Salt and black pepper** |
| **¼ teaspoon sugar** |
| **4 tablespoons extra virgin olive oil** |
| **4 tablespoons sunflower oil** |

**1**  First make the dressing. Wash any wax from the lime and remove the rind with a zester, or grate it finely. Squeeze out 2 tablespoons of lime juice and put it with the rind in a mixing bowl. Add salt, black pepper, and the sugar, then whisk in the oils. Taste and add more lime juice, if necessary, then stand the dressing aside.

**2**  Rinse and dry the watercress and trim off the coarse stalks.

**3**  Halve and stone the avocados, then peel and slice them widthwise. Halve the papayas, then remove the seeds, and peel and slice the flesh lengthwise.

**4**  Arrange the watercress, avocados, and papayas on individual serving plates. Pour the dressing over and serve immediately.

### VARIATION

Mangoes can be substituted for the papayas and the watercress replaced with baby spinach leaves.

*NUTRIENTS PER SERVING: calories 472, carbohydrate 20g (including sugar 19g), protein 4g, fat 42g (saturated fat 7g), good source of vitamins A, B group, and C.*

# PARMA HAM WITH PEAR AND PARMESAN

*Served on a bed of mixed salad leaves, this unusual combination makes a lovely appetizer or very light lunch. Use a good, fruity extra virgin olive oil as its particular flavor really makes the dish sing.*

TIME: 12 MINUTES  SERVES: 4

1 lime or lemon

4 small dessert pears

Salt and black pepper

4 oz (110 g) mixed salad leaves

12 thin slices Parma ham, about ½ lb (230 g) in total

2½ oz (70 g) piece Parmesan cheese

4 tablespoons extra virgin olive oil

1  Squeeze the lime or lemon and pour the juice into a mixing bowl. Rinse, dry, quarter, and core the pears. Cut each piece lengthwise into three or four slices, add them to the juice, season lightly with black pepper, and toss them gently.

2  Trim the salad leaves, then rinse and dry them if necessary. Tear any large leaves into pieces, then pile them loosely on four plates. Arrange the slices of marinated pear on top of the salad leaves, then weave the slices of Parma ham around the pears. Add salt to taste.

3  Using a potato peeler, shave wafer-thin curls of Parmesan cheese directly over the salad (see box, right). Drizzle the extra virgin olive oil over the salad and serve at once.

*NUTRIENTS PER SERVING: calories 405, carbohydrate 11g (including sugar 11g), protein 20g, fat 31g (saturated fat 11g), good source of vitamins B group and E, and calcium.*

### EASY DOES IT!

*To give you a good grip when shaving thin strips of Parmesan, buy a larger piece of cheese than you will actually use for this particular dish.*

---

# GOAT'S CHEESE SOUFFLÉS

*Light and dainty, these soufflés are made with strong-flavored cheese and coated in toasted nuts. They look and taste impressive, but are simple to make, rise well, and can be served hot or cold.*

TIME: 30 MINUTES  SERVES: 4

½ cup (50 g) ground hazelnuts, almonds, or walnuts

2 tablespoons (25 g) butter at room temperature

1 tablespoon (15 g) plain flour

5 tablespoons milk

Salt and black pepper

3½ oz (100 g) firm goat's cheese

1 large egg yolk

3 large egg whites

1  Preheat the oven to 375°F (190°C). Put a kettle of water on to boil. Spread out the ground nuts in a dry frying pan and toast them gently, stirring, until they are golden brown.

2  Use half the butter to grease the insides of four ¾ cup (200 ml) ramekins all over. Divide the toasted nuts equally among them and shake them until the sides and bottoms are evenly coated.

3  Melt the remaining butter in a saucepan, stir in the flour and cook, stirring, for about 30 seconds. Take the pan off the heat and gradually stir in the milk. Then bring the sauce to the boil, stirring, until it thickens. Season to taste.

4  Cut the goat's cheese into small squares, add just over half to the sauce, and stir well. When the cheese has just melted, take the pan off the heat and stir in the egg yolk.

5  Whisk the egg whites until they are stiff. Using a large metal spoon, fold a third into the cheese sauce to lighten it, then carefully fold in the remainder.

6  Divide the remaining cheese among the four ramekins and spoon the soufflé mixture on top. Stand the ramekins in a large roasting pan and pour in boiling water to halfway up their sides. Bake in the top half of the oven for 10 minutes, or until the soufflés have risen and

are lightly set and golden brown. Serve hot, straight from the oven.

**VARIATION**

The soufflés can be made ahead and served cold on a bed of salad leaves. Let them cool in their dishes, then chill them. To serve, run a knife round the sides then turn them out.

*NUTRIENTS PER SERVING: calories 285, carbohydrate 5g (including sugar 2g), protein 13g, fat 24g (saturated fat 10g), good source of vitamins B group and E.*

### COOK'S SUGGESTION

*Use thin, ovenproof, china ramekins for the soufflés if you can, rather than thicker ceramic ones, as china allows the heat to penetrate faster.*

**CHEESE WITH VARIATIONS:** (*top*) PARMA HAM WITH PEAR AND PARMESAN; (*bottom*) GOAT'S CHEESE SOUFFLÉS.

# WARM CHEESE AND TOMATO DIP

*Great to serve at barbecues or when you are sipping tequilas, this warm dip is based on a runny cheese and cream sauce that gets its chunky texture from tasty pieces of onion, tomato, and jalapeño pepper.*

**TIME: 25 MINUTES  SERVES: 4**

| |
|---|
| **1 large onion** |
| **2 teaspoons olive oil** |
| **5 medium tomatoes** |
| **2 jalapeño peppers or 1 tablespoon chopped jalapeño peppers in brine** |
| **½ lb (230 g) sharp Cheddar cheese** |
| **½ cup (100 ml) whipping cream** |
| **Salt and black pepper** |
| **Tabasco sauce** |
| ***To garnish:* 2 sprigs of coriander** |
| ***To serve:* corn chips, soft tortillas, or pita breads** |

**1**  Preheat the oven to moderate. Put a kettle of water on to boil.

**2**  Peel and chop the onion and fry it in the oil in a small saucepan over a low heat for 10–15 minutes, stirring occasionally, until softened.

**3**  Peel the tomatoes and cut them into quarters. Remove and discard the seeds, slice the flesh finely and set aside.

**4**  Rinse, dry, halve, deseed, and finely chop the jalapeño peppers, if necessary, and set aside. Grate the cheese and set it aside.

**5**  Put the corn chips, tortillas, or pita breads into the oven to heat.

**6**  Add the cream to the softened onions in the pan and raise the heat. Just before the cream reaches simmering point, add the cheese and stir until it melts.

**7**  Add the tomatoes and jalapeños to the pan and stir gently. Season carefully to taste with salt, pepper, and Tabasco sauce.

**8**  Rinse, dry, and strip the coriander leaves from the stems. Pour the dip into a warm serving bowl, garnish with the coriander, and serve with corn chips or with fingers of soft tortilla or pita bread.

*NUTRIENTS PER SERVING: calories 670, carbohydrate 31 g (including sugar 7 g), protein 17 g, fat 53 g (saturated fat 22 g), good source of vitamins A, B group, C, and E, and calcium.*

# AVOCADO, SHRIMPS, AND TOMATO SALAD

*Avocado and shrimps are famously good together. Here they are joined by tomatoes, and a creamy dressing of lime, yogurt, and coriander gives the combination an elegant new style and exciting taste.*

TIME: 15 MINUTES   SERVES: 4

| 1 large avocado |
| --- |
| ½ lemon |
| 2 medium tomatoes |
| 6 oz (170 g) peeled, cooked shrimps |

*For the dressing:*

| ½ lime |
| --- |
| A small bunch of coriander |
| ½ cup (125 g) natural yogurt |
| 1 teaspoon sugar |
| Salt and black pepper |

**1**  To make the dressing, wash any wax from the lime, grate the rind into a small bowl, setting a little aside for a garnish, then squeeze the juice into the bowl. Rinse and dry the coriander. Reserving a few sprigs for a garnish, finely chop enough to give 1 tablespoon. Add it to the lime juice, then stir in the yogurt, sugar, salt, and black pepper. Beat well then set aside.

**2**  Halve and stone the avocado (see box, right), peel and slice the flesh and arrange it on plates. Squeeze some lemon juice onto the slices to stop them browning.

**3**  Slice the tomatoes and arrange them and the shrimps among the avocado. Spoon over the dressing and garnish with the reserved lime rind and sprigs of coriander.

*NUTRIENTS PER SERVING: calories 223, carbohydrate 7 g (including sugar 6 g), protein 13 g, fat 16 g (saturated fat 4 g), good source of vitamins B group, C, and E.*

### EASY DOES IT!

*To halve the avocado, cut it lengthwise around then twist to separate the halves. Carefully stick the blade of a heavy kitchen knife into the stone. Twist to loosen the stone, then lift it out.*

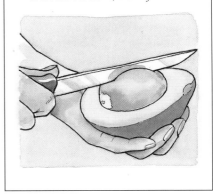

# SARDINES IN A PEPPERCORN CRUST

*Fresh sardines are always bursting with flavor, and here they are given a crunchy coating of lemon juice, olive oil, dill, garlic, and mixed peppercorns, then grilled with aromatic rosemary.*

TIME: 25 MINUTES  SERVES: 4

8 large, fresh sardines, about
1 lb (450 g) in total

1 teaspoon mixed peppercorns

A small bunch of fresh dill

1 clove garlic

2 lemons

Salt

3 tablespoons olive oil

8 small sprigs of fresh rosemary

4 crisp lettuce leaves

8 sprigs of watercress

1  Preheat the grill to the highest setting. Cut along the belly of each sardine with kitchen scissors, then pull out the insides. Rinse the fish inside and out, gently rubbing off the scales with your fingers. Dry the sardines on kitchen paper.

2  Crush the peppercorns with a pestle and mortar, or rolling pin, and put them into a small bowl.
3  Rinse, dry, and chop the dill, peel and crush the garlic, and add them to the peppercorns. Wash any wax from one lemon and finely grate the rind into the bowl. Add some salt and the olive oil and mix.
4  Rinse the rosemary. Put a sprig inside each fish, then spoon over some of the dill mixture. Turn and coat the other side, reserving any leftover mixture. Leave the sardines to marinate for 5–10 minutes.
5  Meanwhile, rinse, dry, and finely shred the lettuce leaves, rinse and dry the watercress, and arrange on plates. Cut four wedges from the other lemon, remove any pips, and put one wedge on each plate.

6  Thread each sardine lengthwise onto a metal skewer, then grill them for 2–3 minutes on each side.
7  Slide the sardines off the skewers and put two on each plate on top of the salad. Spoon the reserved dill mixture over them and the salad leaves and serve.

NUTRIENTS PER SERVING: *calories 265, carbohydrate 1 g (including sugar 0.3 g), protein 24 g, fat 19 g (saturated fat 4 g), good source of vitamins B group and E.*

### COOK'S SUGGESTION

*If you have the time, you can spread the peppercorn paste over the sardines an hour or two in advance and leave them to marinate in the refrigerator.*

# SCALLOPS GRILLED WITH PROSCIUTTO

*The subtle saltiness of Italian dried ham combines perfectly with these marinated scallops with their brilliant orange corals to make handsome brochettes that can be served on their skewers.*

TIME: 30 MINUTES  SERVES: 4

12 fresh king scallops with their
corals, about ¾ lb (335 g) in total

16 thin slices Parma ham, about
⅓ lb (150 g) in total

Black pepper

*For the marinade:*
2 large cloves garlic

A few sprigs each of fresh basil,
coriander, and parsley

½ lemon

3 tablespoons virgin olive oil

1  Rinse and dry the scallops, separate the corals from the white meat and put both into a bowl.
2  To make the marinade, peel the garlic cloves and crush them into the bowl. Rinse and dry the herbs, reserve a few sprigs of basil for a garnish, then chop the rest and add

them to the scallops. Squeeze the lemon juice into the bowl, add the olive oil, stir, and leave to marinate at room temperature for 15 minutes. Preheat the grill to high.
3  When the scallops are ready, gather a slice of ham into a ruffle, thread it onto a metal skewer, then thread on a scallop and a piece of coral. Repeat three times, finishing with ham. Prepare three more skewers the same way.
4  Lay the skewers across the grill pan, baste them with some of the marinade, and grill for 5 minutes, turning and basting them again halfway through. They are ready when the ham is crisp and the scallops are just cooked.
5  Serve on skewers, or remove and pile onto serving plates. Spoon on the pan juices, then top with black pepper and sprigs of basil.

VARIATION
Try using raw jumbo shrimps or cubes of firm white fish instead of the scallops. Any sliced air-dried ham could be used as an alternative to Parma.

NUTRIENTS PER SERVING: *calories 315, carbohydrate 4 g (including sugar 0.1 g), protein 30 g, fat 20 g (saturated fat 6 g), good source of vitamin E.*

### COOK'S SUGGESTION

*Always use fresh scallops. Frozen scallops are too watery and this will dilute the marinade, and make it difficult to grill the scallops properly.*

**GREAT SEAFOOD GRILLS:** (*top*) SARDINES IN A PEPPERCORN CRUST; (*bottom*) SCALLOPS GRILLED WITH PROSCIUTTO.

# SMOKED TROUT WITH PEAR AND ARUGULA

*Strips of smoked trout and crisp, white slivers of pear are set against the brilliant leaves of radicchio and arugula in this very decorative salad, which is served dressed with a creamy horseradish sauce.*

**TIME: 15 MINUTES  SERVES: 4**

| |
|---|
| 4 fillets of smoked trout |
| 2 dessert pears (see box, below) |
| 1 small head radicchio (red chicory) |
| 2 oz (55 g) arugula leaves |
| Salt and black pepper |
| *To serve:* walnut or brown bread |

*For the dressing:*

| |
|---|
| ½ lemon |
| 2 tablespoons extra virgin olive oil |

*For the sauce:*

| |
|---|
| 3 tablespoons light cream |
| 2 teaspoons creamed horseradish sauce |

**1**  Skin the trout fillets and slice them across into strips. Rinse, dry, halve, and core the pears. Cut them into narrow slices.

**2**  Rinse and dry the radicchio and arugula. Tear the radicchio into a bowl, add the arugula, and season.

**3**  To make the dressing, squeeze 2 teaspoons of juice from the lemon into a bowl, add the oil, and whisk together. Pour over the salad leaves, add the trout and the pears, and toss gently. Divide among four plates.

**4**  To make the sauce, mix the cream with the creamed horseradish and stir to give a pouring consistency. Spoon over the trout and salad and serve with thinly sliced bread.

*NUTRIENTS PER SERVING: calories 528, carbohydrate 31 g (including sugar 11 g), protein 39 g, fat 28 g (saturated fat 9 g), good source of vitamin E.*

---

### COOK'S SUGGESTION

*Bartlett and Bosc pears are two of the sweetest and juiciest varieties and will keep their color if they are served as soon as they are sliced. If you need to keep them for any length of time before serving, brush them with lemon juice.*

# QUAIL ON A MUSHROOM NEST

*Tiny quails, nestling on mushroom caps and topped with a favorite Italian garnish of parsley, lemon, and garlic, make a sophisticated starter, yet leave you plenty of free time to prepare the main course.*

TIME: 30 MINUTES   SERVES: 4

| |
| --- |
| 2 tablespoons olive oil |
| 2 tablespoons (25 g) butter |
| 4 oven-ready quails |
| 8 sprigs of fresh thyme |
| 4 bay leaves |
| 4 large, flat open mushrooms |
| Salt and black pepper |

*For the gremolata:*

| |
| --- |
| A small bunch of parsley |
| 1 lemon |
| 1 clove garlic |

**1**  Preheat the oven to 450°F (230°C) and heat the olive oil and butter in a shallow ovenproof dish in the top half of the oven while you prepare the quails.

**2**  Pluck any feathers from the quails, rinse, and pat dry. Rinse the thyme and put two sprigs and a bay leaf into each cavity. Clean the mushrooms and remove the stalks.

**3**  Lay the mushrooms, skin sides down, in the ovenproof dish, and place a quail on the center of each. Baste the quails and around the edges of the mushrooms with the oil and butter and season well with salt and pepper.

**4**  Roast the quails for 15–20 minutes, or until their juices run clear when the flesh is pierced with a skewer. Baste them again halfway through cooking.

**5**  Meanwhile, make the gremolata. Rinse, dry, and chop enough parsley to give 2 tablespoons. Wash any wax from the lemon, then grate half the rind. Peel and crush the garlic. Mix together in a small bowl.

**6**  A few minutes before the quails have finished cooking, sprinkle some gremolata over each and return to the oven.

*NUTRIENTS PER SERVING: calories 335, carbohydrate 1 g (including sugar 0.2 g), protein 31 g, fat 23 g (saturated fat 4 g), good source of vitamins B group and E.*

COOK'S SUGGESTION

*The Italian flavoring called gremolata can be used as a garnish and to boost the flavor of many simple dishes including pasta and vegetables.*

# SWIFT FRUITY APPETIZERS

*A fruit component in an appetizer adds a tingle to the flavor—think of that uplifting splash of orange juice in a tomato soup or a grated carrot salad. And there's another bonus: ripe, vibrant fruit needs no cooking, so you can add almost instant glamour to the appetizer menu.*

### STRAWBERRY, CUCUMBER, AND AVOCADO SALAD

*A colorful, dramatic summer presentation that can be served alone as an appetizer, or offered as the centerpiece of a sumptuous buffet to complement tender smoked chicken or succulent poached salmon.*

Lay alternating bands or concentric circles of sliced avocado, strawberries, and cucumber on a serving dish (remember to turn the avocado slices in lemon juice if the dish is not to be eaten immediately). Then dress the salad with a vinaigrette dressing made of two parts hazelnut oil to three parts olive oil and one part of raspberry or wine vinegar.

FIRST COURSE FRUIT
*For these simple presentations choose ripe fruits in flawless condition that will taste as good as they look.*

### SMOKED MACKEREL WITH GRAPEFRUIT SALSA

*The sweet-sharp freshness of lush pink grapefruit offsets the smooth saltiness of the fish in this combination of strong, smoky flavors.*

Take one fillet of smoked mackerel per person, skin it (see page 11) and cut it diagonally into strips. For four people, peel and segment a large pink grapefruit over a bowl, making sure you catch the juices. Dice the flesh of a large, ripe avocado and add it to the bowl. Snip a few fresh chives over the salsa, season generously with black pepper and stir together. Mix in the smoked mackerel and garnish with chives.

### FIGS WITH PARMA HAM

*A new twist on the classic combination of Parma ham and melon.*

Serve two ripe figs per person, halved to display their delicious flesh and arranged in a cluster beside the folds of thinly sliced, delicately folded Parma ham. The black pepper, which is traditionally grated over the melon in the classic version, can also be served with this dish. You can make it an optional extra by passing the pepper grinder around separately.

### WATERMELON AND FETA CHEESE

*The kind of colorful, fruity appetizer that is a joy to eat outdoors in the warmth of high-summer, surrounded by the aroma of tempting hot food sizzling on a barbecue.*

Mix large, bite-sized chunks of peeled watermelon, sprinkled with black pepper, with smaller pieces of crumbled Greek feta cheese. Garnish with arugula or watercress

leaves. It is the striking contrasts of flavor and texture that make this salad so exciting.

### CITRUS SALAD

*A refreshing orange and grapefruit salad is garnished with black olives and red onion rings to make a perfect appetizer to a rich meal.*

For four people, cut off the rinds and white pith from three oranges and one pink grapefruit. Separate them into segments over a bowl, cutting between the membranes, or slice them thinly across on a plate to catch the juices. Peel a red onion and slice it across thinly into rings. Pull the rings apart to separate them. Measure the orange juice and stir in an equal amount of fruity olive oil and a pinch of salt and sharpen to taste with lemon juice to make the dressing. Arrange the fruit slices on four plates, garnish with black olives and the onion rings, and pour the dressing over.

### LOCKET'S SAVORY

*A dish that takes its name from a fashionable London restaurant of the 1970s where this delicious open sandwich was served as a savory alternative to pudding. For today's tastes, it works well as an appetizer.*

Toast one thick slice of granary bread per person and cover each with a generous pile of roughly chopped watercress. Then layer overlapping peeled slices of juicy dessert pears on top of the chopped watercress and grind black pepper over the top. Cover the open sandwich with a thick layer of Stilton or any blue cheese and place under the grill until the cheese just reaches melting point. Garnish with lettuce and tomato halves.

THREE REFRESHING FIRST COURSES: (*top right*) LOCKET'S SAVORY; (*left*) SMOKED MACKEREL WITH GRAPEFRUIT SALSA; (*bottom right*) WATERMELON AND FETA CHEESE.

# GRILLED OYSTERS

*Pacific oysters are easily opened, then topped with a simple mixture of butter, garlic, breadcrumbs, and parsley before being lightly grilled on a bed of coarse salt until browned and crunchy.*

TIME: 30 MINUTES  SERVES: 4

| 12 Pacific oysters |
| 4 tablespoons (50 g) softened butter |
| 2 cloves garlic |
| 3 tablespoons toasted brown breadcrumbs (see page 14) |
| A small bunch of parsley |
| Salt and black pepper |
| *To support the oysters:* bag of coarse salt |

**1** Place the oysters, flat shells up, in a large saucepan. Add enough cold water to cover the bottom and steam, covered, over a moderate heat for 2 minutes, until they open.

**2** Remove from the heat and leave to cool. Preheat the grill to high.

**3** Mash the butter in a small bowl; peel the garlic cloves and crush them in, then mix in the breadcrumbs. Rinse, dry, and finely chop enough parsley to give 2–3 tablespoons and add it to the butter with a little salt and plenty of pepper.

**4** Half fill a grill pan with coarse salt. Open the oysters, taking care not to lose any juices. Cut the oyster from each shell and place it in the deeper one, discarding the other. Set the oysters firmly in the salt so they do not wobble, and top with some breadcrumb mixture.

**5** Grill for 1–2 minutes, or until the topping bubbles and is lightly browned. Serve immediately.

NUTRIENTS PER SERVING: *calories 141, carbohydrate 7g (including sugar 0.3g), protein 4g, fat 11g (saturated fat 7g), good source of vitamins B group and E, and zinc.*

### COOK'S SUGGESTION

*Pacific oysters, a transplant from Japan, taste better cooked than raw. They are filling, but if you expect hungry diners, allow four each rather than three.*

# SHRIMPS WITH CHILI AND MANGOES

*Luscious ripe mango and crunchy green onions, spiced with hot chili and fresh ginger, give a sweet and sour Oriental flavor to the large, stir-fried shrimps featured in this exuberant dish.*

TIME: 30 MINUTES  SERVES: 4

| 20 peeled, raw jumbo shrimps, about ½ lb (230 g) in total |
| 3–4 green onions |
| 1 in. (2.5 cm) piece fresh root ginger |
| 1 clove garlic |
| 1 small, hot, fresh red chili |
| 2 mangoes |
| 2 teaspoons tomato purée |
| 1 tablespoon soy sauce |
| 2 tablespoons medium sherry |
| ½ teaspoon toasted sesame oil |
| 4–6 red oak-leaf or other looseleaf lettuce leaves |
| 2 tablespoons peanut oil |
| Salt and black pepper |

1  Make a deep cut along the back of each shrimp. Remove the dark intestinal vein, then set them aside.

2  Rinse, dry, and trim the green onions and slice them diagonally; peel and grate the ginger; peel and crush the garlic; rinse, halve, deseed, and slice the chili. Put them all into a bowl and set aside.

3  Peel the mangoes, then remove the flesh from the stones and cut it into ¼ in. (5 mm) thick slices.

4  Mix the tomato purée, soy sauce, sherry, and sesame oil in a small bowl.

5  Rinse and dry the lettuce leaves and arrange them on individual serving plates. Set aside.

6  Heat the peanut oil in a wok or large frying pan. Add the green onion mixture and stir-fry for 1 minute. Add the shrimps and continue stir-frying until they are just beginning to turn pink. Add the mango slices and stir-fry until the shrimps turn completely pink and unfold, and the mango is heated through.

7  Add the soy sauce mixture and bring it to the boil. Season to taste, then spoon over the salad and serve.

*NUTRIENTS PER SERVING: calories 198, carbohydrate 21 g (including sugar 20 g), protein 13 g, fat 7 g (saturated fat 1 g), good source of vitamins A, B group, C, and E.*

# MELTED CAMEMBERT WITH CRANBERRIES

*Slices of crusty Italian bread topped with creamy French cheese and smothered with fresh herbs are
lightly grilled and served with a cool green salad and a refreshingly sharp cranberry sauce.*

TIME: 25 MINUTES  SERVES: 4

| |
|---|
| ½ packet (175 g) fresh or frozen cranberries |
| ¼ cup (40 g) soft, light brown sugar |
| 1 small orange |
| 2–3 large sprigs of parsley |
| A small bunch of chives |
| A small sprig of fresh thyme |
| 1 small clove garlic |
| 2 tablespoons olive oil |
| Black pepper |
| 1 loaf of ciabatta or crusty bread |
| 1 round ripe but firm Camembert |
| Watercress and looseleaf lettuce leaves |

**1** Preheat the grill to the highest setting. Remove the stalks from the cranberries, if necessary, then rinse the berries and put them into a small saucepan with the sugar and a tablespoon of water.

**2** Wash any wax from the orange, grate the rind into the saucepan, cover and cook the berries over a moderate heat for 8–10 minutes, or until they are soft and the juice has thickened slightly. Remove from the heat and keep warm.

**3** Meanwhile, rinse and dry the parsley, chives, and thyme. Chop the parsley and chives, strip the leaves from the thyme, then put all the herbs onto a large plate. Peel the garlic and crush it over the herbs, then mix in the olive oil and black pepper to taste.

**4** Cut four thick slices from the loaf. Lightly coat both sides with some of the herb and garlic mixture and place on the grill rack.

**5** Cut the Camembert vertically into 10 thin slices then discard the slice of rind from each end. Coat the 8 remaining slices with the rest of the herb mixture.

**6** Lightly toast the bread on one side, then turn them over and top each with two slices of Camembert. Grill until the cheese begins to run down the sides of the bread.

**7** Meanwhile, rinse and dry the salad leaves and arrange them on individual serving plates.

**8** Place one cheesy slice of toast on each plate, spoon over the cranberry sauce and serve.

**VARIATION**
You can substitute bottled cranberry sauce for the fresh version, or the cranberries can be cooked in advance and warmed through before serving.

NUTRIENTS PER SERVING: *calories 225, carbohydrate 18 g (including sugar 13 g), protein 11 g, fat 15 g (saturated fat 7 g), good source of vitamins B group and E.*

---

**COOK'S SUGGESTION**

*Wet the blade of the knife before you begin to slice the Camembert—it will make cutting easier and the slices of cheese will not stick to the knife.*

---

# GOAT'S CHEESE AND ARUGULA

*This warm salad of roasted goat's cheese served on a bed of salty bacon and peppery leaves has a dressing flavored with garlic and wholegrain mustard and is guaranteed to sharpen the appetite.*

### TIME: 20 MINUTES  SERVES: 4

½ lb (230 g) smoked back bacon

1 tablespoon vegetable oil

2 small, round, soft goat's cheeses, about ¼ lb (110 g) each

3 oz (85 g) arugula or watercress

*For the dressing:*

1 clove garlic

1 teaspoon wholegrain mustard

2 teaspoons white wine vinegar

2 tablespoons extra virgin olive oil

Salt and black pepper

**1** Preheat the oven to 475°F (240°C). Derind and dice the bacon. Heat the oil and fry the bacon until crisp then drain it on kitchen paper.

**2** To make the dressing, peel the garlic, crush it into a small bowl, then whisk in the mustard, vinegar, and extra virgin olive oil. Season to taste with salt and pepper.

**3** Line a baking sheet with baking paper. Cut the goat's cheeses in half horizontally and lay the rounds on the paper. Bake for 5 minutes or until they begin to melt and turn a toasty brown on top.

**4** Meanwhile, trim, rinse, and dry the arugula or watercress and put it into a mixing bowl with the bacon. Pour the dressing over and toss lightly, then arrange in circles on individual plates.

**5** Remove the cheese from the oven, place one round in the center of each salad and serve immediately.

**VARIATION**
For a vegetarian version, use toasted pine kernels or almonds instead of the bacon.

*NUTRIENTS PER SERVING: calories 333, carbohydrate 2 g (including sugar 1 g), protein 17 g, fat 29 g (saturated fat 11 g), good source of vitamins A, B group, C, and E.*

# ONION AND SHALLOT PASTRIES WITH SALAD

*Red onions and shallots are particularly well suited to rapid baking as they will not lose any of their flavor or crispness.*

**TIME: 30 MINUTES  SERVES: 4**

| |
|---|
| 2 small red onions |
| 4 large shallots |
| ½ lb (230 g) ready-made puff pastry |
| 1 medium egg |
| 12 sprigs of fresh thyme |
| 4 tablespoons olive oil |
| Salt and black pepper |

*For the salad:*

| |
|---|
| ½ cup (85 g) baby spinach leaves |
| 3 oz (85 g) watercress |
| 1 oz (30 g) walnut pieces |
| 1¼ oz (35 g) Roquefort cheese |
| 3 tablespoons whipping cream |
| 1 tablespoon walnut oil |
| 1 teaspoon sherry vinegar |

### EASY DOES IT!

*Using a stout wooden spoon makes it an easy job to mash the Roquefort cheese and cream together when you are preparing the salad dressing.*

**1**  Preheat the oven to 425°F (220°C). Peel the red onions and thinly slice them, then peel and quarter the shallots. Set them both aside.

**2**  Lightly flour a work surface, then cut the pastry in half and roll out each piece to a rectangle of about 12 × 6 in. (30 × 15 cm). Cut two large rounds from each, using a 5–6 in. (13–15 cm) diameter saucer as a template, and place the rounds on a large baking sheet.

**3**  Beat the egg lightly and brush it over the pastry rounds, taking care not to let it trickle over the edges.

**4**  Pile a quarter of the onions and shallots in the center of each round, leaving a border of ¾ in. (2 cm) all around. Rinse and dry the thyme and tuck three sprigs on top of each pile.

**5**  Brush the onions and shallots lightly with the olive oil and season them to taste with salt and black pepper. Put the pastries into the oven and bake them for 20 minutes, or until they are puffed up and golden brown.

**6**  Meanwhile, prepare the salad. Rinse, dry, and trim the spinach leaves and watercress and put both into a salad bowl. Roughly chop the walnut pieces and add them to the salad leaves.

**7**  Put the Roquefort cheese into a small bowl. Pour in the whipping cream and mash the two together (see box, above). Then beat in the walnut oil and sherry vinegar and season to taste with black pepper (the Roquefort will add enough salty flavor). Pour the dressing over the salad and toss gently.

**8**  When the pastries are cooked, serve them on individual plates, accompanied by the dressed salad.

**VARIATION**

If you prefer a milder flavor, you can replace the Roquefort with either Gorgonzola or a Danish blue cheese.

*NUTRIENTS PER SERVING: calories 571, carbohydrate 28 g (including sugar 4 g), protein 11 g, fat 47 g (saturated fat 10 g), good source of vitamins A, B group, C, E, and folate and calcium.*

# INDIAN SCRAMBLED EGGS

*These unusual scrambled eggs are flavored with herbs and spices from the East and topped with a crisp garnish of fried onion.*

TIME: 25 MINUTES  SERVES: 2

| |
|---|
| Oil for deep-frying |
| 1 medium–large onion |
| 3 tablespoons (50 g) butter |
| 1 in. (2.5 cm) piece fresh root ginger |
| 1–2 green chilies |
| A small bunch of coriander |
| 4 large eggs |
| 1 teaspoon turmeric |
| Salt and black pepper |

*To serve:* ready-made poppadoms or nan bread; mango chutney

**1**  Heat 2 in. (5 cm) of oil in a small saucepan. Peel the onion and halve it lengthwise. Finely slice one half; deep-fry it over a low–medium heat until it is crisp and brown but not burned. Drain on kitchen paper.

**2**  Melt the butter in another small saucepan. Finely chop the other half of the onion and fry it gently over a low heat for 6–7 minutes until softened, stirring frequently.

**3**  Meanwhile, peel and grate the ginger and rinse, halve, deseed, and finely slice the chilies. Stir them into the onion and cook for another minute, then remove from the heat.

**4**  Heat the nan bread in the oven, if using. Rinse and chop enough coriander to give 2 tablespoons and set it aside.

**5**  Break the eggs into a bowl, then add the turmeric, some salt, and a generous amount of pepper, and beat lightly. Stir the eggs into the onion mixture and cook over a very low heat, stirring, until thick and slightly chunky but not dry.

**6**  Stir in the coriander and serve the scrambled eggs sprinkled with the fried onions and accompanied by poppadoms, or nan bread, and some mango chutney.

*NUTRIENTS PER SERVING: calories 666, carbohydrate 15g (including sugar 4g), protein 23g, fat 58g (saturated fat 20g), good source of vitamins A, B group, E, and folate, and iron and zinc.*

# POTATO PANCAKES WITH SMOKED SALMON

*The humble potato is transformed into a sophisticated appetizer when it is sharpened with onion, made into crisp pancakes, and topped with sour cream and dainty strips of smoked salmon.*

TIME: 30 MINUTES  SERVES: 4–6
(MAKES 12 PANCAKES)

| |
|---|
| 1 lb (450 g) floury potatoes, such as Idaho |
| 1 medium onion |
| 1 large egg |
| 2 tablespoons whole-wheat flour |
| Salt and black pepper |
| Sunflower oil for frying |
| 7 oz (200 g) smoked salmon |
| ⅔ cup (150 ml) thick, sour cream |
| *To garnish:* sprigs of fresh dill or flat-leaved parsley |

**1**  Preheat the oven to low. Peel and grate the potatoes and finely chop the onions; put them both in a sieve. Press with a spoon to squeeze out as much starchy liquid as possible.

**2**  Transfer to a bowl, add the egg, flour, salt, and pepper and mix well.
**3**  Pour the oil into a frying pan to a depth of about ⅜ in. (8 mm) and heat it until it shows a haze.
**4**  Put a tablespoon of the potato mixture into the oil, flattening it to a small pancake about 2 in. (5 cm) in diameter. Keep adding more tablespoons of the mixture to the pan, cooking four to six at a time. Fry them for about 1 minute or until they are golden on the bottom, then turn them over and cook the other side until they are crisp and golden but still soft in the center.
**5**  Remove the pancakes from the pan, drain them on kitchen paper, and keep them warm in the oven while you cook the remainder.

**6**  Cut the salmon into small strips. Rinse and dry the dill or parsley. Serve each pancake topped with a spoonful of sour cream and a few strips of salmon, and garnished with the dill or parsley.

*NUTRIENTS PER SERVING, WHEN SERVING 4: calories 342, carbohydrate 28 g (including sugar 4 g), protein 20 g, fat 18 g (saturated fat 6 g), good source of vitamins B group, C, E, and folate and selenium.*

---

#### COOK'S SUGGESTION

*Ask your fish store for smoked salmon trimmings. They do not need to be chopped up, taste as good as sliced smoked salmon, and are considerably cheaper.*

# SPEEDY EGGS BENEDICT

*A simple blend of mayonnaise, whipping cream, horseradish, and herbs makes a quick but equally luxurious alternative to the classic hollandaise sauce of authentic eggs Benedict.*

TIME: 25 MINUTES  SERVES: 4

A few sprigs each of basil, chives, parsley, and thyme

½ cup (125 ml) whipping cream

½ cup (125 ml) mayonnaise

1 teaspoon horseradish sauce

2 English muffins

4 thick slices ham carved off the bone (see box, opposite)

4 large eggs

Salt and black pepper

**1** Preheat the grill to high. Rinse, dry, and chop the herbs, setting the parsley aside for a garnish.
**2** Combine the rest in a saucepan with the cream, mayonnaise, and horseradish. Heat gently, but do not allow to boil. Remove from the heat, cover, and keep warm.
**3** Halve the muffins and toast them on both sides under the grill. Turn off the heat, put a slice of ham on each muffin, and leave under the grill to warm through.

**4** Cook the eggs in an egg poacher, or bring some water and a dash of vinegar to simmering point in a frying pan. Break each egg into a cup, carefully slide it into the water and poach for 2–3 minutes, or until the white is set, then drain on kitchen paper.
**5** Put a half muffin with ham on each plate and place a poached egg on top. Spoon over the sauce, add salt and pepper to taste, and garnish with the chopped parsley.

**VARIATION**

For a slightly richer taste, you can fry the ham gently in a little olive oil to heat it through.

*NUTRIENTS PER SERVING: calories 638, carbohydrate 21 g (including sugar 2 g), protein 23 g, fat 52 g (saturated fat 17 g), good source of vitamins A, B group, and E and selenium.*

# CHEESE AND SHERRY PÂTÉ

*Fresh herbs and sweet sherry flavor two strong cheeses in a creamy paste that can serve as an appetizer or cheese course.*

**TIME: 10 MINUTES  SERVES: 4**

| |
|---|
| 2¾ oz (75 g) hard goat's or sheep's cheese |
| 2¾ oz (75 g) blue cheese such as Roquefort or Gorgonzola |
| A small bunch of chives |
| 6 fresh sage leaves |
| 1 clove garlic |
| 3–4 tablespoons sweet sherry |
| *To serve:* water biscuits, bread sticks, or oatcakes |

**1** Remove any rind from the cheeses. Trim, rinse, and dry the chives and sage and peel the garlic. Then put them all into a food processor or blender and process them to a thick paste.

**2** Add the sherry gradually, blend until smooth, then spoon into a dish to serve. If not using immediately, cover with plastic wrap and store in a cool place, but do not refrigerate.

**3** Serve with water biscuits, bread sticks, or oatcakes.

**VARIATION**

Vary the cheeses and herbs to taste, or use brandy instead of sherry.

*NUTRIENTS PER SERVING: calories 171, carbohydrate 2 g (including sugar 1 g), protein 9 g, fat 13 g (saturated fat 8 g), good source of vitamin E.*

# EGGPLANT PÂTÉ

*Warm eggplant pâté packed with herbs and spices makes a fine
smoky-flavored dish to start a meal or serve as a snack.*

**TIME: 30 MINUTES   SERVES: 4**

| |
|---|
| 2 tablespoons olive oil |
| 1 medium onion |
| 1 large, firm eggplant |
| 10 sun-dried tomatoes |
| 6 small gherkins |
| 3 cloves garlic |
| A few sprigs of fresh thyme |
| A few sprigs of fresh parsley |
| 1 teaspoon wholegrain mustard |
| 1 teaspoon balsamic vinegar |
| 2 teaspoons capers |
| 1 loaf of French bread |
| Salt and black pepper |

**1**   Heat the oil gently in a frying
pan. Peel the onion, chop it finely,
and fry for 5 minutes, or until soft.
**2**   Rinse the eggplant and cut it
into ½ in. (1 cm) cubes. Add
them to the onion and stir over a
moderate heat for 8–10 minutes,
or until they have softened.
**3**   Drain and chop the sun-dried
tomatoes and the gherkins and add
them to the eggplants. Peel the
garlic cloves and crush them in.
**4**   Rinse and dry the thyme and
parsley. Strip off the leaves and chop
finely. Reserve some parsley for a
garnish and add the rest of the
herbs to the pan, with the mustard,
vinegar, and capers. Simmer,
stirring frequently, for 5 minutes.
**5**   Meanwhile, cut and toast the
French bread, or dry fry it on a
striped griddle.
**6**   Season the eggplant mixture,
then blend it in a food processor or
mash it to a paste by hand.
**7**   Spoon the pâté onto individual
plates, sprinkle with the reserved
parsley, and serve with the toast.

**NUTRIENTS PER SERVING:** *calories 357,
carbohydrate 55 g (including sugar 8 g),
protein 10 g, fat 12 g (saturated fat 1 g),
good source of vitamins B group, C, and E
and selenium.*

---

### COOK'S SUGGESTION

*As this pâté tastes equally good
either hot or cold, it can be made in
advance and served chilled, or
reheated just before serving.*

# GRILLED VEGETABLE BRUSCHETTA

*Grilling brings out all the sweet flavors of an assortment of Mediterranean vegetables, which are then piled on top of crusty bread that has been rubbed with garlic and tomato to give it extra zest.*

TIME: 30 MINUTES  SERVES: 4

| 1 medium red pepper |
| --- |
| 1 medium yellow pepper |
| 2 small zucchinis |
| 1 medium head fennel |
| 1 red onion |
| 5 tablespoons olive oil |
| 2 cloves garlic |
| 1 small tomato |
| 1 loaf of ciabatta bread, or 1 baguette |
| Salt and black pepper |
| 6 large basil leaves |

**1**  Preheat the grill to high. Rinse and dry the peppers, zucchinis, and fennel. Cut the peppers lengthwise into eight, then remove their stems and any seeds. Trim the zucchinis and slice them diagonally. Trim the fennel, then cut it lengthwise into thin slices. Peel the onion and slice it into rings.

**2**  Cover the grill rack with a single layer of vegetables, laying the peppers skin-sides down. Brush with olive oil and grill, on one side only, until they are lightly browned but still slightly firm. If necessary, cook them in batches and keep the first batch warm in the oven.

**3**  Meanwhile, peel and halve the cloves of garlic and rinse, dry, and halve the tomato. Cut the loaf down and then across into quarters and toast on both sides.

**4**  Rub the top of each slice with the cut garlic and tomato, then pile the grilled vegetables on top. Trickle over the remaining oil and season the bruschetta to taste. Rinse, dry, and tear the basil leaves and scatter them over the top.

*NUTRIENTS PER SERVING: calories 224, carbohydrate 26g (including sugar 10g), protein 11g, fat 16g (saturated fat 2g), good source of vitamins A, B group, C, E and folate.*

# GREAT SANDWICH FILLINGS

*With the wonderful array of tasty breads offered in most supermarkets, you can transform the humble sandwich into a mouthwatering creation. All it takes is a little imagination.*

We all have our favorite sandwich fillings: tender ham with lettuce and mustard; roast beef and horse-radish; egg and watercress or the classic BLT of bacon, lettuce, and tomato. But with a little imagination you can ring the changes.

Instead of butter or margarine, try spreading the bread with mayonnaise or a little pesto, a smear of powerful tapenade or sun-dried tomato paste, or some new and delicious chutney.

Here are six imaginative fillings that combine unusual ingredients to turn a snack into a treat.

### HUMMUS AND NATURAL DATES
Toast a pita bread lightly on each side, then slit it open. Spread hummus on both sides of the interior and push in four or five split and stoned natural dates and some chopped fresh coriander leaves to make a vegan sandwich.

### PEANUT BUTTER WITH CRANBERRIES
Spread two slices of granary bread thickly with crunchy peanut butter. Top one slice lightly with cranberry sauce, bought or homemade, then add a generous topping of shredded iceberg lettuce mixed with chopped celery. Season to taste with salt and pepper and place the second slice of bread on top.

### BRIE WITH GRAPES
Cut a baguette into two or three pieces and cut each one open lengthwise, stopping just short of cutting all the way through. Thinly slice some well-ripened Brie and pack it into the unbuttered lengths of the baguette, squashing the cheese down slightly. Grind some black pepper over the cheese. Halve some seedless grapes, either ruby or green, or a mixture of both and lay them on top. Fold the tops of the baguettes over the filling and decorate each serving plate with a small cluster of grapes.

### SMOKED SALMON WITH CUCUMBER AND CREAM CHEESE
Split a bread roll or bagel in half and toast it for a minute on each side. Spread one half with plain cream cheese, arrange slices of smoked salmon in folds on top and cover the salmon with wafer-thin slices of cucumber and a sprinkling of chopped dill. Grind on some black pepper and sandwich in place with the remaining half.

### TURKEY, AVOCADO, AND PESTO
Split four large croissants in half and spread the cut surfaces evenly with a little pesto. Thinly slice an avocado and arrange the slices over one half of each croissant. Top with some wafer-thin slices of turkey, scrunching them up slightly, and arrange a few strips of drained sun-dried tomatoes over the turkey. Sprinkle lightly with salt and black pepper, press the two halves of each croissant together and serve.

### MASHED RASPBERRY AND BANANA
Finally, for a great sweet filling, toast slices of brioche or raisin bread and fill them with banana mashed with a few raspberries (these can be fresh or thawed from frozen).

FRUITY SANDWICH FILLINGS: (*left*) BRIE WITH GRAPES; (*center*) PEANUT BUTTER WITH CRANBERRIES; (*right*) HUMMUS AND NATURAL DATES; (*bottom left*) TURKEY, AVOCADO, AND PESTO.

# PUNJABI POTATO PATTIES

*In India, these aromatic and scrumptiously spicy potato patties, known as aloo tiki, are eaten hot or cold as a teatime snack with mint chutney, tomato ketchup, or sweet tamarind relish.*

TIME: 30 MINUTES  MAKES: 8 PATTIES

| |
|---|
| 1 lb (450 g) potatoes |
| Salt |
| 1 medium onion |
| ¼ teaspoon chili powder |
| 1 teaspoon garam masala |
| ½ lemon |
| A handful of fresh coriander |
| 3 tablespoons vegetable oil |
| 1 tablespoon (15 g) butter |

**1**  Peel and cube the potatoes, put them into a pan and cover with cold salted water. Cover, bring to the boil, and boil gently for 10 minutes, until the potatoes are tender but not disintegrating.

**2**  Peel and roughly grate the onion onto a double thickness of kitchen paper. Squeeze out any juice then put it into a bowl. Add the chili, garam masala, and a pinch of salt.

**3**  Squeeze 2 teaspoons of lemon juice into the onion. Rinse and dry the coriander. Reserve a few sprigs for a garnish, chop the remaining leaves, and add to the bowl.

**4**  Drain the potatoes, add them to the onions, and mash roughly together. Shape into eight patties, each about 2 in. (5 cm) wide.

**5**  Heat the oil and butter in a large frying pan until sizzling, then fry the patties for 2–3 minutes on each side until crisp and golden.

**6**  Drain the patties on kitchen paper and serve them hot, garnished with the reserved coriander, and with chutney or ketchup if desired, or set aside to eat cold later.

*NUTRIENTS PER SERVING, 2 PATTIES: calories 194, carbohydrate 21 g (including sugar 3 g), protein 3 g, fat 12 g (saturated fat 3 g), good source of vitamins B group and C.*

---

#### COOK'S SUGGESTION

*The patties can also be made from leftover potatoes and can be mixed and shaped in advance, then kept chilled in the refrigerator until needed.*

---

# PESTO AND GOAT'S CHEESE CROUTONS

*Grilled croutons spread with spicy red pesto and topped with melted goat's cheese are teamed with an unusual tomato salad that marries fresh tomatoes with the intense flavor of the sun-dried variety.*

TIME: 15 MINUTES  SERVES: 4

| 6–8 small tomatoes |
| --- |
| 12 sun-dried tomatoes in oil |
| 3 tablespoons extra virgin olive oil |
| 1 tablespoon balsamic vinegar |
| Salt and black pepper |
| 1 loaf of French bread |
| 4–5 tablespoons red pesto, or 2 tablespoons wholegrain mustard |
| 6 oz (170 g) soft goat's cheese |

**1** Preheat the grill to high. Cut the fresh tomatoes into thin slices and arrange them on four plates. Drain and thinly slice the sun-dried tomatoes and scatter them over the fresh ones.

**2** Drizzle the oil and vinegar over the tomatoes and season to taste.

**3** To make the croutons, cut 12 diagonal slices, each about 1 in. (2.5 cm) thick, from the French bread. Spread each slice with some red pesto or mustard, put a spoonful of goat's cheese on top, and season with black pepper.

**4** Put the croutons under the hot grill for 1–2 minutes, or until the cheese has melted slightly.

**5** Place three grilled croutons on each plate with the tomato salad and serve.

*NUTRIENTS PER SERVING: calories 567, carbohydrate 27g (including sugar 6g), protein 17g, fat 44g (saturated fat 11g), good source of vitamins A, B group, C, and E.*

---

### COOK'S SUGGESTION

*The cheese croutons can be assembled ahead of time, kept in the refrigerator, and grilled just before serving.*

# THREE EASY APPETIZERS

## AVOCADO AND WATERCRESS CREAM

*A blend of creamy avocado and hot watercress, this pretty purée can be eaten with a spoon or served as a dip.*

**TIME: 18 MINUTES SERVES: 4**

| |
|---|
| A bunch of watercress |
| A few sprigs of parsley |
| A few green onions |
| 1 clove garlic |
| 1 lemon |
| A few basil leaves |
| 4 tablespoons olive oil |
| 2 large avocados |
| Salt and black pepper |
| 1 tablespoon green peppercorns in brine |

**1** Discard the stalks from the watercress, then rinse and dry the leaves. Rinse and dry the parsley and strip the leaves from the stems.
**2** Rinse the onions, chop the green tops, leaving the whites for another dish, and put them into a blender or food processor with the parsley and watercress.
**3** Peel the garlic and crush it into the parsley and watercress. Wash any wax from the lemon, grate the rind, squeeze out the juice, and add both to the blender or processor. Rinse and dry the basil leaves, then chop a few and set them aside for a garnish. Add the remaining leaves to the mixture with the olive oil.
**4** Halve and stone the avocados. Leaving the shells intact, spoon the flesh into the blender or processor and season. Process until smooth.
**5** Spoon the purée into the shells, sprinkle it with the peppercorns and reserved basil, and serve.
*VARIATION*
Garnish the plate with looseleaf lettuce and serve with Melba toast.

*NUTRIENTS PER SERVING: calories 321, carbohydrate 2 g (including sugar 1 g), protein 3 g, fat 33 g (saturated fat 6 g), good source of vitamins B group, C, and E.*

## FRESH HERB DIP WITH CHICKPEA CRÊPES

*A feast of summery herbs is packed into this lemon-flavored dip, served with tasty little pancakes.*

**TIME: 30 MINUTES SERVES: 4**

| *For the herb dip:* |
|---|
| A few sprigs each of basil, chives, dill, and/or parsley |
| ¾ cup (200 ml) whipping cream |
| ½ lemon |
| 1 small clove garlic |
| Salt and black pepper |

| *For the crêpes:* |
|---|
| ½ cup (115 g) gram (chickpea) flour |
| ½ cup (115 g) plain flour |
| 2 tablespoons olive oil |
| 1⅔ cups lukewarm water |

**1** To make the herb dip, rinse, dry, and finely chop enough herbs to give 4 tablespoons. Put the herbs into a small bowl with the cream and 1 tablespoon of lemon juice. Peel the garlic and crush it into the dip, mix well and add salt and pepper to taste.
**2** To make the crêpes, put the gram and plain flour into a bowl. Add the oil and water gradually, whisking until the batter is smooth. Transfer to a measuring jug.
**3** Heat a 6 in. (15 cm) nonstick frying pan over a high heat, then pour in just under ¼ cup (50 ml) of the batter, tilting the pan so it covers the base evenly. Fry the crêpe for 30 seconds or until it is golden, then flip it over and cook the other side for about 15 seconds.
**4** Turn the crêpe onto a plate and roll it up. Keep it warm while you cook and roll the rest of the crêpes, then cut them in half and serve them with the dip.

*NUTRIENTS PER SERVING: calories 429, carbohydrate 38 g (including sugar 3 g), protein 10 g, fat 27 g (saturated fat 14 g), good source of vitamins B group and E.*

## SALMON PÂTÉ

*Cream cheese is given a kick by hot chili sauce for an almost instant salmon pâté. Great as a starter, it could also fill a glamorous sandwich.*

**TIME: 30 MINUTES SERVES: 4**

| |
|---|
| A small bunch of chives |
| A small bunch of fresh dill |
| A small bunch of fresh parsley |
| 1 can (14½ oz / 418 g) canned salmon |
| 1 packet (4½ oz / 125 g) cream cheese |
| 1 lemon |
| 1 teaspoon Tabasco sauce |
| Salt and black pepper |
| *To serve:* brown bread, toast, Melba toast, or water biscuits |

**1** Rinse, dry, chop, and mix the chives, dill, and parsley.
**2** Drain the salmon and remove any bones and skin. Put it into a bowl and mix in the cream cheese.
**3** Squeeze the lemon and add the juice to the salmon mixture a little at a time, until it is sharp enough to suit your taste. Stir in the Tabasco sauce and the chopped herbs, and blend the mixture until it forms a smooth purée using a hand blender, a potato masher, or a wooden spoon, which will give a slightly coarser texture.
**4** Season to taste with salt, pepper, and more lemon juice, then spoon into a serving bowl or individual ramekins and chill for 15 minutes.
**5** Serve the pâté with bread, toast, or water biscuits as desired.

*NUTRIENTS PER SERVING: calories 362, carbohydrate 16 g (including sugar 2 g), protein 22 g, fat 24 g (saturated fat 12 g), good source of vitamins A, B group, and E and selenium.*

**THREE CREAMY APPETIZERS:**
(*top left*) AVOCADO AND WATERCRESS CREAM; (*center*) SALMON PÂTÉ; (*bottom*) FRESH HERB DIP WITH CHICKPEA CRÊPES.

# HOT CORN CAKES WITH SALAD

*Crispy corn pancakes spiced with Tabasco sauce and served hot are accompanied by a salad of cool lettuce, sweet pepper, and rich avocado, with a sour-cream dressing on the side.*

**TIME: 30 MINUTES  SERVES: 4**

½ lb (230 g) canned or frozen corn

½ cup milk

Salt and black pepper

A few drops of Tabasco sauce

1 medium iceberg lettuce

2 avocados

1 yellow pepper

4 tablespoons olive oil

1 tablespoon wine vinegar

¾ cup (100 g) self-raising flour

2 large eggs

2–3 tablespoons vegetable oil

*For the dressing:*

3 green onions

4–5 sprigs of dill

⅔ cup sour cream

Salt and black pepper

**1**  Drain canned corn, set aside and mix the milk, salt, pepper, and Tabasco in a bowl. Put frozen corn into a pan with the milk, salt, pepper, and Tabasco and shake over a low heat for 1 minute. Then turn off the heat and leave to thaw.

**2**  To make the dressing, rinse, trim, and finely slice the green onions, rinse and chop the dill, reserving 1 sprig for a garnish, mix them into the sour cream and season to taste.

**3**  Rinse and dry the lettuce leaves and put them into a salad bowl. Peel and slice the avocados, rinse, deseed, and slice the pepper, and add both to the bowl. Mix the olive oil and vinegar together, season, and toss gently into the salad.

**4**  Put the flour into a bowl, make a well in the center and break in the eggs. Add the seasoned milk, or strain in the milk from the defrosted corn, beat until smooth, then stir in the corn.

**5**  Take two frying pans and heat 1–1½ tablespoons of vegetable oil in each. Drop six tablespoons of batter into each pan. Fry gently for 4–5 minutes until golden underneath and set at the edges. Turn and fry another 1–2 minutes.

**6**  Divide the salad among four plates. Drain the corn cakes and arrange three with each salad. Garnish with fronds of dill and serve the dressing separately.

*NUTRIENTS PER SERVING: calories 667, carbohydrate 40 g (including sugar 12 g), protein 13 g, fat 52 g (saturated fat 13 g), good source of vitamins A, B group, C, and E, and folate and calcium.*

# APPLE AND CHEESE GRILLS

*Cut thick slices from a large loaf of good whole-wheat bread for this fruity version of cheese on toast where a sweet layer of dessert apple lies hidden beneath the golden topping.*

TIME: 15 MINUTES  MAKES: 4

---

**2 small red dessert apples**

**4 thick slices whole-wheat bread cut from a large loaf**

**5 oz (140 g) Cheddar, Cheshire, or Emmental cheese**

**Butter for spreading**

**8 sage leaves**

**Black pepper**

**1**  Preheat the grill to the highest setting. Rinse the apples, then quarter, core, and slice them finely.

**2**  Toast the bread on one side under the grill. Meanwhile, finely slice or grate the cheese.

**3**  Turn the bread over and spread the untoasted side with butter. Arrange the apple slices on top and cover with cheese. Grill for 4–5 minutes, until the cheese melts and the apples heat through.

**4**  Meanwhile, rinse, dry, and finely chop the sage leaves. When the grilled dishes are ready, sprinkle them with the chopped sage and black pepper and serve immediately.

*NUTRIENTS PER SERVING: calories 357, carbohydrate 26 g (including sugar 5 g), protein 14 g, fat 23 g (saturated fat 14 g), good source of vitamins A, B group, and E, and calcium and selenium.*

---

### COOK'S SUGGESTION

*The grilled items will taste different depending on the cheese you use. Cheddar and Emmental melt well and give a strong, nutty flavor. Cheshire has a light, salty taste that goes very well with apple.*

# BAKED EGGS WITH CRAB

*Baked and served in dainty ramekins, these eggs on a layer of crab meat flavored with brandy make a rich but simple snack.*

**TIME: 25 MINUTES  SERVES: 4**

| |
|---|
| Butter for greasing |
| 6 oz (170 g) canned crab meat |
| 4 teaspoons brandy |
| 4 large eggs |
| Salt and black pepper |
| 4 tablespoons light cream |
| Cayenne pepper |
| *To garnish*: a few sprigs of chervil or parsley |
| *To serve*: bread for toast, butter for spreading |

**1** Preheat the oven to 375°F, (190°C). Lightly grease four ramekins with the butter.

**2** Put a quarter of the crab meat into the bottom of each of the dishes and sprinkle a teaspoon of brandy over each.

**3** Break an egg carefully into each dish. Season with salt and pepper, then spoon a tablespoon of cream around the yolk of each egg. Dust lightly with cayenne pepper.

**4** Put the dishes onto a baking sheet and bake for 10–15 minutes, or until the egg whites are set but the yolks are still soft.

**5** Meanwhile, rinse, dry, and chop the chervil or parsley, and make and butter the toast.

**6** Serve the eggs hot, in their dishes, sprinkled with the chervil or parsley, accompanied by the toast.

**VARIATION**
Strips of smoked salmon and a dash of sherry can be used instead of the crab and brandy, or you could use 2 chopped anchovy fillets with a very little chopped thyme and a sprinkling of brandy.

*NUTRIENTS PER SERVING: calories 293, carbohydrate 25 g (including sugar 2 g), protein 19 g, fat 13 g (saturated fat 5 g), good source of vitamins A, B group, and E, and selenium and zinc.*

---

### COOK'S SUGGESTION

*Canned crab is inexpensive yet high in quality as it tends to include only the white meat. A dash of brandy is an excellent flavor enhancer for crab or any creamy seafood dishes.*

# PITA PIZZAS

*When there's no time to make pizza dough, try these zesty little alternatives made of pita bread topped with chili and tomato sauce, three different cheeses, and a mixture of tasty vegetables.*

TIME: 27 MINUTES  SERVES: 2

| |
|---|
| **Oil for greasing** |
| **2 whole-wheat pita breads** |
| **3 tablespoons tomato ketchup** |
| **½ teaspoon Tabasco sauce** |
| **2 oz (55 g) each of Mozzarella, mature Cheddar, and Pont-l'Évêque or Chaumes cheese** |
| **1 medium red onion** |
| **2 medium tomatoes** |
| **½ large red or green pepper** |
| **1 clove garlic** |
| **1 tablespoon olive oil** |
| **4 black olives** |

*To garnish:* **a few sprigs each of fresh marjoram and basil, 2 teaspoons (25 g) Parmesan cheese**

**1** Preheat the oven to 375°F (190°C). Lightly oil a baking sheet.

Open the pitas out and split in half with a sharp knife.

**2** Mix the tomato ketchup with the Tabasco sauce. Spread some on each pita half and arrange on the baking sheet.

**3** Grate the Mozzarella and the Cheddar cheese together and sprinkle over the pitas.

**4** Slice or dice the Pont-l'Évêque or Chaumes cheese and spread evenly over the grated cheese.

**5** Peel the onion and slice into thin wedges. Rinse and dry the tomatoes and the pepper. Slice the tomato into rounds. Deseed and finely chop the pepper. Arrange the onion and tomatoes on top of the cheese and scatter with the chopped pepper.

**6** Peel and crush the garlic, mix it with the olive oil, and drizzle it over

the pizzas. Place an olive in the center of each and bake on the top shelf of the oven for 10 minutes.

**7** Meanwhile, rinse and dry the herbs, strip off the leaves, and put them into a bowl. Add the Parmesan and mix.

**8** Remove the pitas from the oven, sprinkle with the herbs and Parmesan mixture, and serve hot.

*VARIATION*

Instead of whole-wheat pitas, which make soft pizza bases, use white pitas, which have a crunchier texture when baked.

*NUTRIENTS PER SERVING: calories 628, carbohydrate 53 g (including sugar 16 g), protein 27 g, fat 36 g (saturated fat 13 g), good source of vitamins A, B group, C, E, and folate, and calcium and zinc.*

MELON, AVOCADO, AND SHRIMP SALAD

# SALADS

The refreshing taste of summer leaves and herbs, the aroma of oils and spices, a wealth of special ingredients—here are salads from the simple to the substantial for every meal.

# SALMON AND ASPARAGUS SALAD

*A velvety mango, yogurt, and mustard dressing with a subtle hint of aniseed gives the freshly cooked salmon in this salad a luxurious, tropical taste that is just right for a summer dinner party.*

TIME: 25 MINUTES   SERVES: 4

| 4 salmon fillets, about 1½ lb (680 g) |
| 1 tablespoon olive or sunflower oil |
| ½ lb (230 g) asparagus spears |
| 1 large stick celery |
| ⅔ lb (300 g) mixed salad leaves |

*For the dressing:*

| 2 large mangoes |
| 4 chives |
| 1 small container (125 g) natural yogurt |
| 1 teaspoon wholegrain mustard |
| 1 tablespoon Pernod |
| Black pepper |

**1**  Put a kettle of water on to boil. Skin the salmon, remove any bones, and cut it into large cubes. Heat the oil in a frying pan and stir-fry the salmon for 2–3 minutes until just cooked through and lightly browned. Drain on kitchen paper.

**2**  Rinse and trim the asparagus spears, cut them into 1½ in. (4 cm) pieces, cover with the boiling water, and blanch for 2 minutes. Rinse under cold water and drain.

**3**  To make the dressing, peel the mangoes and cut into cubes: you need about 1 lb (450 g). Place in a food processor or bowl. Rinse and dry the chives and snip them into the mango. Add the yogurt, mustard, and Pernod and purée. Add black pepper to taste.

**4**  Rinse and finely slice the celery. Put it into a bowl with the salmon and asparagus. Pour the dressing over the top, holding a little back in case there is more than you need. Toss gently, taking care not to break up the salmon.

**5**  Trim, rinse, and dry the salad leaves, then arrange them on four serving plates and top with the salmon salad.

*VARIATION*

You can use white vermouth as a substitute for the aniseed flavor of the Pernod.

*NUTRIENTS PER SERVING: calories 576, carbohydrate 33 g (including sugar 32 g), protein 48 g, fat 28 g (saturated fat 5 g), good source of vitamins A, B group, C, E, and folate, and selenium and zinc.*

### COOK'S SUGGESTION

*The dressing can be made and the fish fried in advance and both stored in the refrigerator, leaving the salad to be assembled at the last minute.*

# WILD RICE AND FENNEL SALAD

*Grapes, an orange, and a handful of raisins add sweetness to a salad redolent with the earthy flavors of wild rice, chopped hazelnuts, and a nut oil, herb, and white wine vinegar dressing.*

TIME: 30 MINUTES  SERVES: 4–6

| |
|---|
| 6 oz (170 g) easy-cook **wild rice and long grain mixture** |
| Salt |
| 2 medium cucumbers |
| 1 large fennel bulb |
| 6 green onions |
| 4 oz (110 g) seedless red grapes |
| 2 oz (55 g) skinned hazelnuts |
| 2 tablespoons (25 g) raisins |
| 1 orange |

*For the dressing:*

| |
|---|
| 3 sprigs of chervil |
| 2 sprigs each of tarragon and parsley |
| 6 tablespoons hazelnut or walnut oil |
| 1 tablespoon white wine vinegar |
| Salt and black pepper |
| *To garnish:* 4–6 sprigs tarragon |

**1** Bring 2 cups of water to the boil, add the rice and a little salt, cover and simmer for 18–20 minutes, or until the rice is cooked and all the water absorbed.

**2** Meanwhile, rinse and dry the cucumber, fennel, green onions, and grapes. Finely cube the cucumber; trim and thinly slice the fennel and green onions, and halve the grapes. Put them all into a salad bowl. Chop the hazelnuts and add them, with the raisins.

**3** Wash any wax from the orange and grate the rind into the salad.

**4** To make the herb dressing, squeeze 3 tablespoons of juice from the orange and pour it into a small bowl. Rinse, dry, and finely chop the herbs and add them to the juice with the oil and vinegar. Whisk together then season to taste.

**5** Drain the cooked rice and rinse it briefly under a cold tap. Drain well, mix it into the salad vegetables, and pour the dressing over. Garnish with sprigs of tarragon.

NUTRIENTS PER SERVING, WHEN SERVING **4**: *calories 459, carbohydrate 50 g (including sugar 12 g), protein 7 g, fat 26 g (saturated fat 2 g), good source of vitamins B group, C, and E.*

### COOK'S SUGGESTION

*This salad can be made in advance and left to stand for 30 minutes before serving. It makes an excellent accompaniment to game or chicken.*

# THAI-STYLE BEEF SALAD

*Rare lean beef and a variety of crunchy fresh vegetables are combined with the fragrant Eastern flavorings of lemongrass, lime, and pungent herbs in this main-course salad.*

TIME: 30 MINUTES  SERVES: 4

| |
|---|
| 12 oz (335 g) crisp lettuce leaves |
| 1 medium cucumber |
| 2 medium carrots |
| ¼ lb (110 g) fresh bean sprouts |
| 1 clove garlic |
| 1 stalk lemongrass |
| 1 lb (450 g) lean beef steak |
| A small bunch of fresh coriander |
| A small bunch of basil |
| 2 teaspoons vegetable oil |
| 2 limes |
| 2 tablespoons olive oil |
| 1 tablespoon sweet chili sauce |

**1** Rinse, dry, and shred the lettuce. Rinse, dry, and cube the cucumber. Peel and coarsely grate the carrots. Rinse and drain the bean sprouts. Arrange them on a large serving dish or on individual plates.

**2** Peel and crush the garlic. Remove the outer leaves from the lemongrass and chop enough of the inner stalk to give 1 teaspoon. Thinly slice the beef and set aside. Rinse, dry, and finely chop the herbs and set them aside.

**3** Heat the vegetable oil in a large frying pan and gently cook the garlic and lemongrass for about 30 seconds, until just golden brown.

**4** Add the beef to the pan and fry over a high heat for 1–2 minutes, stirring continuously to keep the slices separate. Then remove the meat from the pan and place it on top of the salad vegetables.

**5** Squeeze 2 tablespoons of juice from the limes and add it to the pan with the herbs, olive oil, and chili sauce. Cook, stirring, for 1 minute, then pour the dressing over the beef and salad and serve.

*NUTRIENTS PER SERVING: calories 272, carbohydrate 7g (including sugar 6g), protein 29g, fat 14g (saturated fat 4g), good source of vitamins A, B group, C, E, and folate.*

# GREEK SALAD

*This pretty variation on the classic Mediterranean salad mixes sweet cherry tomatoes with salty feta cheese and olives.*

TIME: 15 MINUTES  SERVES: 4–6

| |
|---|
| 20 cherry tomatoes |
| 1 cucumber |
| 13 oz (375 g) feta cheese |
| 4 tablespoons extra virgin olive oil |
| ½ lemon |
| 12 good black olives |
| Black pepper |

**1** Rinse and dry the cherry tomatoes, then cut them in half and place them in a serving bowl. Rinse, dry, and halve the cucumber, then cut each half into ½ in. (1 cm) slices and add them to the tomatoes.

**2** Drain the cheese and crumble it into the bowl. Sprinkle in the oil and 1 tablespoon of juice from the half lemon. Add the black olives and pepper to taste (the cheese is salty already). Toss well and serve.

*NUTRIENTS PER SERVING, WHEN SERVING 4: calories 365, carbohydrate 5g (including sugar 5g), protein 16g, fat 31g (saturated fat 15g), good source of vitamins A, B group, C, and E, and calcium.*

87

# THAI SALAD WITH COCONUT DRESSING

*Creamy coconut milk, smooth peanut butter, and fiery chili sauce are combined with lime to make
a dressing for this Oriental-style salad of fresh, crunchy vegetables and Chinese cabbage.*

TIME: 25 MINUTES   SERVES: 4

½ lb (230 g) Chinese cabbage

3 medium sticks celery

2 medium carrots

7 oz (200 g) baby corn

4 green onions

*For the dressing:*

2 limes

5 tablespoons coconut milk

3 tablespoons smooth
peanut butter

½ teaspoon chili sauce

1 teaspoon Thai fish sauce
or light soy sauce, optional

Salt and black pepper

**1** Rinse and dry the Chinese cabbage, tear the leaves into pieces, and put them into a salad bowl.
**2** Rinse, dry, and trim the celery; peel the carrots. Cut them into thin matchsticks and add to the bowl.
**3** Rinse and dry the corn and green onions, slice them diagonally, and add them to the salad.
**4** To make the coconut dressing, squeeze 3 tablespoons of juice from the limes and pour it into a screw-top jar. Add the coconut milk, peanut butter, chili sauce, fish or soy sauce, if using, and season. Close the lid and shake the jar. Taste and adjust the seasoning.

**5** Pour the dressing over the salad vegetables, toss them well together, and serve immediately.

NUTRIENTS PER SERVING: *calories 165, carbohydrate 15 g (including sugar 6 g), protein 6 g, fat 9 g (saturated fat 2 g), good source of vitamins A, B group, C, E, and folate.*

---

### COOK'S SUGGESTION

*Chinese cabbage looks like pale, elongated lettuce. The whole vegetable can be eaten, apart from any tattered outer leaves.*

---

# MOZZARELLA WITH TOMATO DRESSING

*A simple salad of mild mozzarella cheese and mixed lettuce leaves is given a rich tomato and fresh herb dressing, which can also be used as a sauce for pasta or as a pizza topping.*

TIME: 15 MINUTES  SERVES: 4

¼ lb (110 g) mixed salad leaves

1 lb (450 g) fresh
mozzarella cheese

*For the dressing:*
5½ oz (155 g) sun-dried
tomatoes in oil

A small bunch of basil

A small bunch of parsley

A small bunch of marjoram
or oregano

1 tablespoon balsamic vinegar

1 tablespoon capers

1 clove garlic, optional

Black pepper

**1**  To make the dressing, take the sun-dried tomatoes from the jar and put them into a food processor or blender. Pour ⅔ cup (150 ml) of oil from the jar into a measuring jug. If there is not enough, top it up with some olive or vegetable oil. Rinse and dry the fresh herbs.
**2**  Add the herbs, vinegar, and capers to the processor. Peel the garlic, if using, and add it, with the oil, then process to a thick purée. Or, process the ingredients in a bowl with a handheld mixer.
**3**  Season the dressing to taste with pepper. It should not need any salt because the capers are salty.

**4**  Trim, rinse, and dry the mixed salad leaves and arrange them on four serving plates.
**5**  Drain and slice the mozzarella and arrange it on top of the salad leaves. Spoon the dressing over the top and serve.

*VARIATION*
Tiny balls of mozzarella make an attractive alternative to the sliced cheese.

*NUTRIENTS PER SERVING: calories 520, carbohydrate 7g (including sugar 1g), protein 33g, fat 40g (saturated fat 17g), good source of vitamins A, B group, and E, and calcium.*

# Warm Duck Breast Salad with Red Wine and Apple

*Crunchy apple and lettuce make a delicious base for fried duck breast, sliced and served warm with a red wine dressing.*

TIME: 30 MINUTES   SERVES: 4

| |
|---|
| 4 boneless duck breasts, about 6 oz (170 g) each |
| Salt and black pepper |
| 2 lettuce hearts |
| 1 small bunch radicchio (red chicory) |
| 1 small bunch watercress |
| 1 small red onion |
| 1 red dessert apple |
| 1 tablespoon olive oil |
| 2–3 tablespoons red wine |

*For the dressing:*

| |
|---|
| A handful of fresh mint or parsley |
| 1 clove garlic |
| Salt and black pepper |
| 1 teaspoon sugar |
| 2 teaspoons Dijon or wholegrain mustard |
| 2 tablespoons red wine |
| 3 tablespoons olive oil |

**1**   Remove the skin and sinew from each duck breast. If the breasts are uneven in size, cut the larger ones in half horizontally. Season the meat generously with salt and black pepper and set aside.

**2**   For the dressing, wash, dry, and chop the mint or parsley and put it into a salad bowl. Peel the garlic and crush it in. Season with salt and black pepper, add the sugar, mustard, red wine, and olive oil and whisk to a creamy paste.

**3**   Trim, rinse, and dry the lettuce and radicchio. Tear into small pieces and add them to the salad dressing. Trim, wash, and dry the watercress. Halve, peel, and thinly slice the red onion. Rinse, dry, quarter, core, and slice the apple. Add them to the salad bowl in turn. Toss gently.

**4**   Heat the olive oil in a frying pan, add the duck breasts and fry them over a moderate heat for 4–5 minutes on each side until they are golden brown but still slightly pink in the center. If you prefer them well done, fry the breasts for a few minutes longer.

**5**   Remove the duck breasts to a board and leave them to stand for 2–3 minutes. Meanwhile, pour off the excess fat from the frying pan, raise the heat, add the red wine and bring it to the boil, stirring and scraping the residue from the bottom of the pan.

**6**   Slice the duck breasts thinly on the diagonal and add them to the salad. Pour the pan juices over the salad, then toss it well and serve.

**VARIATION**
Chicken breasts may be substituted for the duck, using white wine with the juices instead of red. Chicken needs more cooking time than duck, so allow a little longer.

*NUTRIENTS PER SERVING: calories 397, carbohydrate 8 g (including sugar 7.5 g), protein 36 g, fat 23 g (saturated fat 5 g), good source of vitamins B group, C, E, and folate, and iron and zinc.*

# CREAMY MIXED BEAN SALAD

*This hearty salad mixes a variety of fresh and canned vegetables into a nutritious dish packed with strong flavors. Fresh basil infuses a creamy yogurt and mustard dressing.*

TIME: 25 MINUTES  SERVES: 4

| |
|---|
| ½ lb (230 g) green beans |
| 1 can (19 oz / 540 ml) kidney beans |
| 1 can (19 oz / 540 ml) cannellini beans |
| 1 can (19 oz / 540 ml) lentils |
| 6 oz (170 ml) artichoke hearts in oil |
| 15 small (150 g) button mushrooms |
| 5–6 green onions |
| 1 soft, round lettuce |

*For the dressing:*

| |
|---|
| ½ cup (225 g) natural yogurt |
| ½ lemon |
| 1–2 teaspoons Dijon mustard |
| A large handful of fresh basil |
| Salt and black pepper |

**1**  Bring a saucepan of water to the boil. Rinse, top, tail, and halve the green beans. Cook them for 5–6 minutes or until just tender. Rinse under cold water then drain.

**2**  Rinse the kidney and cannellini beans and lentils, drain and spread them on a tea towel to dry.

**3**  Drain the artichoke hearts on kitchen paper and cut them into quarters. Clean and slice the mushrooms; trim, rinse, and slice the green onions.

**4**  To make the dressing, put the yogurt into a large bowl, squeeze in the lemon juice, add mustard to taste, and stir well.

**5**  Rinse and dry the basil, reserve a few sprigs for a garnish, tear the rest and add them to the dressing. Season to taste.

**6**  Rinse and dry the lettuce leaves and arrange them on a serving dish.

Mix the vegetables into the yogurt and mustard dressing. Spoon on top of the leaves and garnish with the reserved basil.

*VARIATION*

Diced cheese, strips of cooked ham, chicken or turkey, or peeled shrimps can be added to this creamy salad.

*NUTRIENTS PER SERVING: calories 598, carbohydrate 64 g (including sugar 9 g), protein 32 g, fat 24 g (saturated fat 5 g), good source of vitamins B group, C, and folate.*

# CANTALOUPE, AVOCADO, AND SHRIMP SALAD

*Ripe and richly scented cantaloupe and avocado combined with pale pink shrimps and garnished with aromatic coriander leaves make a pretty summer salad that is filling, but not too rich.*

TIME: 20 MINUTES   SERVES: 6

| |
|---|
| A few sprigs of coriander |
| 1 cantaloupe |
| 2 avocados |
| 2 oz (55 g) mixed salad leaves |
| ½ lb (230 g) cooked, peeled shrimps |

*For the dressing:*

| |
|---|
| 1 small shallot |
| ½ cup (125 ml) whipping cream |
| 2 tablespoons extra virgin olive oil |
| 1 tablespoon cider vinegar |
| A pinch of sugar |
| Salt and black pepper |

**1** To make the dressing, halve, peel, and finely chop the shallot. Put it into a bowl and add the cream, olive oil, vinegar, and sugar. Stir well, season with salt and pepper, and set aside.

**2** Rinse and dry the coriander, strip off the leaves and set them aside for a garnish.

**3** Cut the cantaloupe into quarters and discard the seeds. Remove the skin and cut the flesh lengthwise into narrow slices.

**4** Halve and stone the avocados, then peel them and cut the flesh lengthwise into slices the same thickness as the cantaloupe.

**5** Trim, rinse, and dry the salad leaves and divide them among six plates. Arrange the slices of cantaloupe and avocado prettily among them. Scatter the shrimps on top and drizzle the dressing over using a spoon. Garnish with the reserved coriander leaves and serve.

*NUTRIENTS PER SERVING: calories 324, carbohydrate 7g (including sugar 6g), protein 16g, fat 26g (saturated fat 9g), good source of vitamins B group, C, and E.*

# ENDIVE, PEAR, AND ROQUEFORT SALAD

*This simple but elegant salad, a mixture of orchard fruit, blue cheese, fresh nuts, and bitter leaves,
is at its best in the autumn when the new season's crop of walnuts is available.*

TIME: 15 MINUTES   SERVES: 4–6

**6 whole fresh walnuts
or 12 shelled walnut halves**

**3 endives**

**2 Bartlett, Bosc, or Orient pears**

**3 oz (85 g) Roquefort cheese**

*To garnish:* **a small bunch of chervil
or 4 sprigs of tarragon, optional**

*For the dressing:*

**1 tablespoon wine vinegar**

**Salt**

**2 tablespoons virgin olive oil**

**3 tablespoons walnut oil**

**1** If using fresh walnuts, crack
the shells and remove the kernels
(see box, right). Roughly chop the
kernels or halves and set aside.

**2** Rinse, dry, and separate the
endive leaves, and arrange them on
individual plates. Rinse, dry,
quarter, and core the pears. Cut
each quarter into three slices and
lay them over the endive.

**3** Crumble the cheese and scatter
it, and the walnuts, over the pears.
Rinse and dry the herb, if using,
strip off the leaves and set aside.

**4** To make the dressing, put the
vinegar into a bowl, add salt and
both oils and whisk, then pour a
little over each salad. Scatter with
the chervil or tarragon, if using.

*NUTRIENTS PER SERVING, WHEN SERVING 4:
calories 306, carbohydrate 9 g (including
sugar 7 g), protein 6 g, fat 28 g (saturated
fat 7 g), good source of vitamin B group.*

### EASY DOES IT!

*Fresh walnuts, available
in the autumn, have an incomparable
flavor and should feel heavy in the
hand. To prepare them, crack the
shells, remove the kernels, and rub
off the thin, dark inner skin.*

# SALAD NIÇOISE

*A popular summer lunch dish or late-night supper, this classic Provençal salad of eggs and fish has many variations, so it can be made up from the pantry and enjoyed at any time of the year.*

TIME: 25 MINUTES  SERVES: 4

| |
|---|
| 4 medium eggs |
| 14 oz (400 g) canned tuna |
| 1 medium red onion |
| 1 can (2 oz / 60 g) anchovy fillets |
| 3 tablespoons (50 g) capers |
| 4 oz (110 g) stoned black olives |
| 3 lettuce hearts |
| 6 oz (170 g) cherry tomatoes |

*For the croutons:*

| |
|---|
| 2 thick slices whole-wheat bread |
| 1 clove garlic |
| 2 tablespoons olive oil |

*For the dressing:*

| |
|---|
| ½ teaspoon sugar |
| 1 tablespoon white wine vinegar |
| Salt |
| 1 clove garlic |
| 1–2 teaspoons Dijon mustard |
| 3 tablespoons extra virgin olive oil |

**1** Put the eggs into a pan and cover them with water. Bring them to the boil, then reduce the heat and simmer for 4 minutes. Take the pan off the heat, cover, and leave the eggs to stand.

**2** To make the croutons, cut the bread into ½ in. (1 cm) cubes. Peel the garlic, crush it into a frying pan, add the oil, and fry over a moderate heat. Add the croutons and fry until crisp and golden, stirring frequently, then drain and leave to cool.

**3** To make the dressing, put the sugar and vinegar into a large salad bowl with salt to taste. Peel the garlic and crush it into the bowl, then add the mustard and olive oil and mix to a thick paste.

**4** Drain the tuna and flake it into the dressing. Peel the onion, slice it very thinly, and add it to the bowl, with the anchovies and their oil, the capers and olives. Toss gently.

**5** Separate, rinse, and dry the lettuce, slicing the hearts into small pieces, and add them to the tuna mixture. Rinse, dry, and halve the cherry tomatoes and scatter them in the bowl.

**6** Shell the eggs and slice them into quarters, lengthwise. Toss the salad, making sure every leaf is coated with dressing, then add the egg quarters. Serve the croutons in a separate dish.

**VARIATION**
You can also add artichoke hearts, sliced red peppers, or cooled steamed green beans to the salad when you add the tomatoes.

NUTRIENTS PER SERVING: *calories 525, carbohydrate 17 g (including sugar 6 g), protein 33 g, fat 37 g (saturated fat 6 g), good source of vitamins A, B group, C, E, and folate, and selenium and zinc.*

### COOK'S SUGGESTION

*Anchovies are very salty, so add only a little salt to this salad. If you are using sea salt, remember that it is not as strong as table salt.*

# FAVA BEAN, SHRIMP, AND FETA SALAD

*A pretty salad of fava beans, speckled with fresh mint and scattered with juicy shrimps, gets an added punch from cubes of salty feta cheese and a strong, refreshing, lemon and garlic dressing.*

TIME: 20 MINUTES  SERVES: 4

| |
| --- |
| 1 can (19 oz / 540 ml) frozen fava beans |
| 2–3 sprigs of fresh mint |
| ½ lb (230 g) feta cheese |
| ½ lb (230 g) peeled, cooked shrimps |

*For the dressing:*

| |
| --- |
| 1 large lemon |
| 6 tablespoons extra virgin olive oil |
| 1 clove garlic |
| Salt and black pepper |

1  Put a kettle of water on to boil. Put the beans into a saucepan with a sprig of mint. Cover with boiling water and simmer for 6 minutes. Drain and rinse the beans, then drain them again.

2  Drain and dice the cheese. Put it into a salad bowl; add the shrimps.

3  To make the dressing, squeeze half the lemon, mix 2 tablespoons of the juice with the olive oil, then peel the garlic and crush it into the dressing. Rinse, dry, and finely chop the remaining mint, whisk it into the dressing, then add salt and pepper to taste.

4  Add the drained beans to the cheese and shrimps and stir in the dressing. Serve with wedges cut from the rest of the lemon.

*NUTRIENTS PER SERVING: calories 428, carbohydrate 16 g (including sugar 2 g), protein 29 g, fat 28 g (saturated fat 9 g), good source of vitamins B group, C, and E, and calcium and zinc.*

# BEAN SPROUT, FETA, AND HAZELNUT SALAD

*A nutritious mix of crunchy salad vegetables, salty white cheese, fresh citrus fruit, and roasted hazelnuts with a tangy orange and nut oil dressing makes a great salad for the winter months.*

TIME: 20 MINUTES  SERVES: 4

2 in. (5 cm) piece of cucumber

2 sticks celery

¾ lb (335 g) fresh bean sprouts, or a mixture of bean and alfalfa sprouts

3½ oz (100 g) hazelnut kernels, ready-skinned

1 orange

5 oz (140 g) feta cheese

*To garnish:* 1 bunch watercress

*For the dressing:*

1 orange

2 tablespoons hazelnut, or walnut, oil

Salt and black pepper

1 teaspoon wholegrain mustard

**1** Preheat the oven to 400°F (200°C) and bring a saucepan of water to the boil.

**2** Rinse and dry the cucumber and celery, chop them into small pieces, and place in a salad bowl.

**3** Place the bean sprouts in the boiling water for 1 minute to blanch, then drain and rinse. Alfalfa sprouts do not need blanching.

**4** Press the hazelnuts in half with a rolling pin. Toast on a tray in the oven for 3–4 minutes until golden.

**5** Cut the peel and pith from the orange and, holding it over the celery to catch any juice, cut the segments from the connecting tissue and let them fall into the bowl.

**6** To make the dressing, squeeze the juice from the orange into a small bowl or jug and whisk in the nut oil, seasoning, and mustard.

**7** Drain the cheese and crumble it into the salad bowl, then add the sprouts and hazelnuts. Rinse and dry the watercress. Pour the dressing onto the salad, toss gently, and garnish with watercress.

*NUTRIENTS PER SERVING: calories 352, carbohydrate 9 g (including sugar 7 g), protein 13 g, fat 30 g (saturated fat 7 g), good source of vitamins B group, C, E, and folate and calcium.*

# SPECIAL SALADS FOR SIDE DISHES

### SNOW PEAS AND PICKLED GINGER SALAD

*The sharp taste of pickled ginger blended into natural yogurt turns a simple vegetable salad into a great accompaniment for plain roasts or grills of beef, chicken, or fish.*

TIME: 15 MINUTES  SERVES: 4

| ¾ lb (335 g) snow peas |
| Salt |
| A small bunch of chives |

*For the dressing:*

| 1¾ oz (50 g) pickled (sushi) ginger (see box, below) |
| 3 tablespoons natural yogurt |
| Black pepper |

1  Put a pan of water on to boil. Top, tail, and rinse the snow peas. Add them to the pan with a little salt, bring back to the boil, and cook for 1 or 2 minutes, until tender but still crisp. Drain and set aside.
2  To make the dressing, put the pickled ginger and its liquid into a salad bowl and separate the pieces. Add the yogurt and black pepper to taste and mix until creamy.
3  Add the snow peas to the bowl and toss well. Rinse and dry the chives and snip them over the salad.

VARIATION
You can substitute a tablespoon of pickled green peppercorns, rinsed but left whole, for the ginger.

*NUTRIENTS PER SERVING: calories 60, carbohydrate 7g (including sugar 6g), protein 5g, fat 1g (saturated fat 0.6g), good source of vitamins B group, C, and E.*

---

COOK'S SUGGESTION

*Finely sliced pickled ginger, sometimes called sushi ginger, is served with Japanese dishes, and may be found in the ethnic section of larger supermarkets, in Oriental stores, and in health-food stores.*

---

### CARROT AND GINGER SALAD

*A simple salad with a surprising citrus dressing, sharpened with ginger and sweetened with honey, this makes an excellent accompaniment to grilled fish.*

TIME: 30 MINUTES  SERVES: 4

| ½ cup (125 g) sultanas |
| ¾ lb (335 g) young carrots |
| Salt |
| ½ teaspoon honey or sugar |
| 1¾ oz (50 g) chopped peanuts, pecans, or walnuts |

*For the dressing:*

| 2 in. (5 cm) piece fresh root ginger |
| 1 lemon |
| 1 orange |
| ½ cup (225 ml) sour cream or natural yogurt |

1  Put a little water into a kettle and put it on to boil. Put the sultanas into a small bowl, then cover them with the boiling water and set them aside.
2  To make the citrus dressing, peel and finely grate the ginger into a small mixing bowl.
3  Wash any wax off the lemon and orange, then finely grate half the rind from each into the bowl. Squeeze the juice from half of each of them and add it to the ginger in the mixing bowl. Stir in the sour cream or yogurt and set the dressing aside.
4  Peel the carrots and grate them into a serving bowl, then drain the sultanas and add them.
5  Stir the dressing into the carrot and sultana mixture, then season with salt and add honey or sugar to taste. Finally, stir in the chopped nuts and serve.

*NUTRIENTS PER SERVING: calories 315, carbohydrate 35g (including sugar 33g), protein 7g, fat 18g (saturated fat 8g), good source of vitamins A, B group, and E.*

---

### LETTUCE, CUCUMBER, AND RED ONION SALAD

*Looseleaf lettuce, escarole, and radicchio (red chicory) make a bittersweet salad that is particularly good served with a hearty stew or a rich main course.*

TIME: 10 MINUTES  SERVES: 4

| 1 head looseleaf lettuce |
| 1 head escarole |
| 1 head radicchio |
| 2 medium cucumbers |
| 1 small red onion |
| 1¾ oz (50 g) walnut halves |

*For the dressing:*

| 1 clove garlic |
| 3 tablespoons walnut oil |
| 1 tablespoon white wine vinegar |
| Salt and black pepper |

1  Separate, rinse, and dry the leaves of the lettuce, escarole, and radicchio—you will save time if you use a salad spinner. Put all the leaves into a large salad bowl and mix them together.
2  Rinse, dry, peel, and finely slice the cucumber, and peel and finely slice the onion. Put them into the salad bowl, then add the walnuts.
3  To make the dressing, peel the garlic and crush it into a small bowl, then pour the walnut oil into the bowl with the wine vinegar, add salt and black pepper to taste, and whisk them well together.
4  Just before serving, trickle the walnut dressing over the salad and toss gently.

*NUTRIENTS PER SERVING: calories 187, carbohydrate 5g (including sugar 4g), protein 4g, fat 17g (saturated fat 2g), good source of vitamin B group.*

**VERSATILE SIDE SALADS:** (*top*) LETTUCE, CUCUMBER, AND RED ONION; (*center*) SNOW PEAS AND PICKLED GINGER; (*bottom*) CARROT AND GINGER.

# CAESAR SALAD

*Anchovies add extra flavor to this Caesar salad, a strongly flavored combination of hearty lettuce, Parmesan cheese, and crunchy croutons, bathed in a velvety dressing of olive oil, egg, and lemon juice.*

TIME: 25 MINUTES  SERVES: 4

| |
|---|
| 2 heads romaine (cos) lettuce |
| 5 thick slices white bread |
| 2 tablespoons peanut oil |
| 8 tablespoons olive oil |
| 2 cloves garlic |
| 1 large egg |
| 8 anchovy fillets |
| 1 lemon |
| Salt and black pepper |
| 3 oz (85 g) Parmesan cheese |

1  Discard the outer lettuce leaves, rinse and dry the rest, and put them into a salad bowl.

2  Put a small saucepan of water on to boil for the egg.
3  To make the croutons, remove and discard the crusts from the bread, and cut the slices into ½ in. (1 cm) cubes. Heat the peanut oil with 2 tablespoons of the olive oil in a frying pan. Peel the garlic, crush it into the pan, add the bread and fry, stirring, until the croutons are crisp. Drain on kitchen paper.
4  When the water boils, add the egg and boil it for 1 minute, then remove it from the water and set aside. Roughly chop the anchovy fillets and set aside.

5  To make the salad dressing, squeeze 2 tablespoons of juice from the lemon, mix in the remaining olive oil and some salt and black pepper, then whisk in the egg.
6  Pour the salad dressing over the lettuce, toss, then add the anchovies and croutons and toss again.
7  Cut thin strips of Parmesan, place them on top and serve.

*NUTRIENTS PER SERVING: calories 523, carbohydrate 27 g (including sugar 3 g), protein 18 g, fat 39 g (saturated fat 9 g), good source of vitamins B group, E, and folate, and calcium and selenium.*

# CUCUMBER, RADISH, AND MELON SALAD

*A wonderful combination of fruit, vegetables, and crunchy almonds mixed with a honey and walnut oil dressing, this salad makes an ideal accompaniment to cold or smoked meats and poultry.*

TIME: 20 MINUTES  SERVES: 4

| |
| --- |
| 1 lb (450 g) piece of watermelon or honeydew melon |
| 1 small cucumber |
| Salt |
| Olive oil for frying |
| 2 tablespoons (25 g) flaked almonds |
| 3½ oz (100 g) fresh bean sprouts |
| 8–10 medium radishes |
| 4 green onions |
| A small bunch of watercress |

*For the dressing:*

| |
| --- |
| 1½ teaspoons clear honey |
| 3 tablespoons walnut oil |
| 1 tablespoon cider vinegar |
| Black pepper |

**1**  Deseed and cube the melon; rinse, dry, and cube the cucumber. Put both into a colander, add a little salt and toss them together. Place a saucer on top and leave to drain.
**2**  Heat a little oil in a frying pan and fry the almonds until golden, then drain on kitchen paper.
**3**  Rinse the bean sprouts and drain them well, then rinse, dry, and trim the radishes and green onions. Quarter the radishes, slice the onions, and mix all three together in a salad bowl.
**4**  Whisk the dressing ingredients together and pour over the salad.
**5**  Trim the watercress, rinse and dry it, and arrange it in a shallow serving dish. Add the melon and cucumber to the salad bowl, toss the salad gently, then spoon it onto the watercress. Scatter the almonds over the top to serve.

*NUTRIENTS PER SERVING: calories 231, carbohydrate 15 g (including sugar 14 g), protein 4 g, fat 18 g (saturated fat 2 g), good source of vitamins B group, C, and E.*

101

# CAJUN POTATO SALAD

*Green pepper, celery, and onion are called the "holy trinity" of Cajun cooking and form the basis of many dishes, including this substantial salad that is ideal for picnics and barbecues.*

TIME: 30 MINUTES  SERVES: 4

| 3 medium (1 lb/450 g) potatoes |
| --- |
| Salt and black pepper |
| 1 small green pepper |
| 2 sticks celery |
| 1 small red onion |

*For the dressing:*

| ⅔ cup (150 ml) mayonnaise |
| --- |
| 2 teaspoons Dijon mustard |
| A few dashes of Tabasco sauce |

**1** Put a kettle of water on to boil. Scrape the potatoes and put them into a pan with boiling water and some salt. Return to the boil and simmer for 15–20 minutes or until the potatoes are tender.

**2** Rinse, dry, halve, and deseed the pepper, slice it into strips, and put it into a salad bowl. Rinse, dry, and finely slice the celery; reserve the leaves for a garnish and add the rest to the pepper. Peel the onion, halve it lengthwise, and slice it lengthwise again into crescents. Add it to the bowl.

**3** To make the dressing, mix the mayonnaise and mustard in a small bowl and add Tabasco to taste.

**4** Drain the potatoes, cool under running water, drain again, and add to the salad. Add the dressing, grind pepper over the salad, and mix. Garnish with celery leaves.

**VARIATION**

Add chopped hard-boiled eggs to the salad to turn it into a meal.

*NUTRIENTS PER SERVING: calories 346, carbohydrate 19 g (including sugar 4 g), protein 3 g, fat 29 g (saturated fat 4 g), good source of vitamins B group, C, and E.*

### COOK'S SUGGESTION

*Small, firm-fleshed potato varieties are the best type to use when you are making potato salads.*

# SPINACH AND BABY CORN SALAD

*Succulent morsels of rich avocado in oil and vinegar are strewn throughout this pretty combination of dark, tender spinach and arugula tossed with tiny cobs of crunchy corn.*

TIME: 15 MINUTES  SERVES: 4

8 cobs (100 g) baby corn
Salt
3 oz (85 g) arugula
1 packet (250 g) baby spinach leaves

*For the dressing:*
1 avocado
1 clove garlic
3 tablespoons extra virgin olive oil
1 tablespoon white wine vinegar
1 teaspoon sugar
1 teaspoon Tabasco sauce

**1** Bring a small saucepan of water to the boil. Cut the baby corn across in half and add them to the boiling water with some salt. Simmer for 1 minute then drain.

**2** Rinse the arugula and spinach leaves and leave them to drain.

**3** Meanwhile, make the dressing. Cut the avocado in half, remove the stone, and use a spoon to scoop the flesh into a large salad bowl.

**4** Peel the garlic and crush it into the bowl, then add the oil, vinegar, sugar, and Tabasco sauce. Season to taste with salt, then stir the dressing

together: some of the avocado will merge into the oil, but the diners should find some small chunks in the salad.

**5** Add the well-drained corn, arugula, and spinach leaves to the dressing, toss well and serve.

**VARIATION**
If arugula is unavailable, peppery watercress makes a good substitute.

*NUTRIENTS PER SERVING: calories 174, carbohydrate 8 g (including sugar 3 g), protein 3 g, fat 15 g (saturated fat 3 g), good source of vitamins A, B group, C, E, and folate.*

GRILLED SOLE WITH BUTTERY ZUCCHINIS

# FISH & SHELLFISH

*From grilled sole to monkfish ragout, from homely cod steaks to scallops with Thai flavorings, here are tempting, no-fuss recipes for a whole shoal of different fishes.*

# Fresh Trout with Walnut Dressing

*Plain grilled trout is dramatically transformed with the help of herbs and nuts, spiced vinegar, and a pinch of paprika.*

TIME: 25 MINUTES   SERVES: 4

| |
|---|
| 2 teaspoons vegetable oil |
| 4 trout fillets, about 6 oz (170 g) each |
| ¼ teaspoon paprika |
| 10 walnut halves |
| 4½ oz (125 g) arugula, watercress, or mixed salad leaves |

*For the dressing:*

| |
|---|
| 1 shallot or 2 green onions |
| A few sprigs of fresh dill, or celery leaves |
| 2 tablespoons spiced rice vinegar, or sherry vinegar |
| 6 tablespoons walnut oil |
| Salt and black pepper |

**1**  Preheat the grill to the highest setting. To make the dressing, peel and finely chop the shallot, or rinse, trim, and finely chop the green onions, and place them in a small bowl. Rinse, dry, and chop the dill or celery leaves and add them to the bowl with the vinegar, walnut oil, salt and pepper. Mix well and set aside.

**2**  Grease the grill pan with half the vegetable oil and lay the trout fillets on top, skin sides down. Season them with salt and paprika. Grill the fish for 5–8 minutes, on one side only, until the flesh is opaque in the center and delicately brown at the edges.

**3**  While the fillets are cooking, heat the remaining vegetable oil in a small frying pan and gently fry the walnuts, shaking and stirring constantly so that they color but do not burn. Drain them on kitchen paper, then chop them roughly.

**4**  Rinse and dry the salad leaves and arrange on four plates. Lay a fillet of trout on each. Stir the dressing, spoon it over the fish, and scatter the walnuts on top.

*SERVING SUGGESTION*
Tiny new potatoes go well with the clear flavors of this dish. Put them on to boil before you start cooking the trout.

*NUTRIENTS PER SERVING: calories 451, carbohydrate 1g (including sugar 0.5g), protein 37g, fat 33g (saturated fat 4g), good source of vitamins B₁ and C.*

# BALTIMORE SEAFOOD CAKES

*These rich crab and shrimp cakes are spiced with mustard, Worcestershire sauce, and a little cayenne pepper, then coated in breadcrumbs and fried until the outside is a crunchy golden brown.*

TIME: 30 MINUTES  SERVES: 4

2 slices dry bread, about
4½ oz (125 g) altogether

½ cup milk

2 cans (4 oz / 120 g) fresh crab meat

½ lb (230 g) peeled, cooked shrimps

2 large eggs

2 teaspoons Dijon mustard

1 tablespoon Worcestershire sauce

½ cup (60 g) ground almonds

A large pinch of cayenne pepper

1 tablespoon thick mayonnaise

A handful of fresh parsley

*For the coating:*
⅓ cup (40 g) plain flour

1½ cups dried breadcrumbs

Sunflower oil for frying

**1**  Soak both slices of bread in the milk for 5 minutes. Flake the crab meat, put it into a bowl, chop the shrimps and add them to the crab.

**2**  Separate the eggs and set the whites aside. Add the yolks, mustard, Worcestershire sauce, almonds, cayenne, and mayonnaise to the crab. Rinse, dry, and chop enough parsley to give a tablespoon and add it to the bowl.

**3**  Squeeze the bread dry, add it to the crab, and stir until soft but not sloppy: add some breadcrumbs if the mixture is too moist.

**4**  To make the coating: put the flour onto one plate and the breadcrumbs onto another. Whisk a tablespoon of water into the egg whites. Divide the crab mixture into eight portions and shape them into cakes. Dip them into the flour, shake off the excess, then dip them into the egg whites, and coat with the breadcrumbs.

**5**  Heat ½ in. (1 cm) of oil in a large frying pan over a fairly high heat. Fry the fish cakes for 2–3 minutes

on each side until they are crisp and golden, then drain them on kitchen paper and serve two per person.

*SERVING SUGGESTION*
Serve with lemon wedges, tartar or seafood sauce, lettuce, and tomatoes, or a spicy salsa. To make a heartier meal, use the seafood cakes and salad to fill burger buns.

*NUTRIENTS PER SERVING: calories 595, carbohydrate 56 g (including sugar 6 g), protein 38 g, fat 26 g (saturated fat 4 g), good source of vitamins B group, and E, and calcium, selenium, and zinc.*

# SALMON PIZZAS WITH YOGURT AND DILL

*Salmon makes an unusual topping for pizza, and thick yogurt flavored with dill adds a creamy texture that complements the richness of the fish better than the cheese normally used for pizzas.*

TIME: 30 MINUTES  SERVES: 4

2 small skinless salmon fillets, about ¾ lb (335 g) in total

2 large tomatoes

1 small mild, white or red onion

2 thin 10 in. (25 cm) pizza bases

Salt and black pepper

8 sprigs of fresh dill

6 oz (170 g) Greek yogurt

*To serve:* 4 tablespoons mango chutney, optional

1   Preheat the oven to 425°F (220°C). Remove any bones from the salmon fillets, then dice the flesh.

2   Rinse, dry, and finely chop the tomatoes and peel and finely chop the onion. Place the pizza bases on baking trays; spread the tomatoes and onion over each. Arrange the salmon on top and add salt and pepper to taste.

3   Bake for 15–20 minutes, or until lightly browned, swapping the trays around half way through.

4   Rinse and dry the dill. Set aside a few sprigs for a garnish, finely chop the remainder, and mix it into the yogurt, with some pepper.

5   Remove the pizzas from the oven, spoon some yogurt over each, and garnish with the reserved dill.

6   Cut each salmon pizza into quarters and serve two portions per person, accompanied by mango chutney, if using.

NUTRIENTS PER SERVING: *calories 509, carbohydrate 37g (including sugar 6g), protein 25g, fat 29g (saturated fat 15g), good source of vitamins B group and E.*

---

### COOK'S SUGGESTION

*Salmon is quite a fatty fish so the pizzas do not need to be brushed with oil before they are baked, making this dish a healthy alternative to ordinary pizzas.*

---

# SPICY CRAB WITH CHILI MAYONNAISE

*Fresh crab meat mixed with milky ricotta cheese, crunchy sweet pepper, chilies, and onions
is served with a spicy dressing to make a lunch dish that is both decorative and satisfying.*

TIME: 20 MINUTES  SERVES: 4

| |
| --- |
| 1 green chili |
| 1 small green pepper |
| 1 small red onion |
| 3 green onions |
| 4 dressed crabs in their shells, to yield 1 lb (450 g) crab meat |
| 3 oz (85 g) ricotta cheese |
| Salt and black pepper |
| 1¼ cups (300 ml) French mayonnaise |
| 1 teaspoon dried chili flakes |
| 4 slices of white bread |

**1**  Preheat the grill if you will need it to make the toast.

**2**  Rinse, dry, deseed, and finely slice the green chili and the pepper. Halve, peel, and thinly slice the red onion. Rinse, dry, trim, and slice the green onions, including some of the green parts, and put them all into a mixing bowl.

**3**  Take the crab meat out of the shells and add it to the mixing bowl with the ricotta cheese, stirring until well combined. Season to taste with salt and pepper.

**4**  Stir the chili flakes into the mayonnaise and season with salt and pepper if necessary. Place in a serving bowl and set aside.

**5**  Toast the bread, cut it into quarters in triangles, and arrange them on a serving platter. Pile the crab mixture in the center and place the bowl of chili mayonnaise on one side.

**6**  Let each person help themselves to the crab mixture, spreading it on the toast and topping it with the chili-flavored mayonnaise.

*NUTRIENTS PER SERVING: calories 821, carbohydrate 22 g (including sugar 4 g), protein 33 g, fat 68 g (saturated fat 11 g), good source of vitamins B group, C, and E, and selenium and zinc.*

# COD STEAKS WITH CREAMY BROCCOLI

*Fish steaks cook easily in the oven while you make a delicious accompaniment of emerald broccoli with cream and tarragon.*

TIME: **30 MINUTES** SERVES: **4**

| 4 thick fresh cod steaks, about 6 oz (170 g) each |
| 2 tablespoons extra virgin olive oil |
| Salt and black pepper |
| 1 shallot |
| ¾ lb (335 g) broccoli florets |
| 10 sprigs of fresh tarragon |
| ¾ cup (200 ml) whipping cream |

**1** Preheat the oven to 350°F (180°C). Dry the cod steaks, then brush them with a tablespoon of oil and season well.

**2** Cut four pieces of foil, each large enough to enclose a steak. Put one steak on each piece of foil, fold the edges together to make a roomy parcel, and crimp to seal. Lay the four steaks on a baking sheet and cook for 15 minutes.

**3** Meanwhile, peel and grate the shallot. Rinse the broccoli and trim it into small florets.

**4** Heat the remaining oil in a frying pan and fry the shallot until it is translucent.

**5** Add the broccoli to the pan, stems down, with ⅔ cup of water, and bring to the boil, then cover and simmer for 4–5 minutes until the broccoli is barely tender. Remove the lid, raise the heat, and cook until only 1–2 tablespoons of water remain in the pan. Do not let the broccoli burn.

**6** Rinse and dry the tarragon. Reserve four sprigs for a garnish, then strip the leaves off the rest and add them to the broccoli. Stir in the cream, season to taste with salt and pepper, and keep warm.

**7** Remove the foil steaks from the oven, unwrap them, and transfer the fish onto four warmed plates. Spoon the broccoli over the fish, garnish with the tarragon, and serve.

**SERVING SUGGESTION**
Accompany this dish with a salad and slices of crusty bread, or try Sweet Potato Rösti (page 266).

*NUTRIENTS PER SERVING: calories 473, carbohydrate 3 g (including sugar 3 g), protein 37 g, fat 35 g (saturated fat 18 g), good source of vitamins A, B group, C, and E, and folate and selenium.*

# BAKED COD PLAKI

*Plaki is a baked dish with a thick sauce made in many forms all over Greece. This is a simpler version of the original, but still has the robust Mediterranean flavors of peppers, tomatoes, lemon, and garlic.*

TIME: 30 MINUTES  SERVES: 4 – 6

| 2 tablespoons olive oil |
| 1 medium onion |
| 1 green pepper |
| 6 Italian tomatoes |
| 1 clove garlic |
| 1½ lb (680 g) skinless cod fillet |
| 1½ lemons |
| A handful of fresh parsley |
| 3 tablespoons dry white wine |
| 3 tablespoons tomato purée |
| Salt and black pepper |

**1**  Slowly heat the olive oil in a large, flameproof casserole. Peel the onion and slice it thinly. Rinse, dry, and deseed the pepper and slice into thin strips. Rinse, dry, and slice the Italian tomatoes.

**2**  Put the vegetables into the casserole, peel the garlic, and crush it in. Cover and cook over a high heat for 6–8 minutes, shaking the casserole occasionally so that the vegetables do not stick.

**3**  Meanwhile, cut the cod fillet into 2 in. (5 cm) cubes and sprinkle them with the juice from the half lemon. Rinse, dry, and finely chop the parsley and set it aside.

**4**  Stir the wine and tomato purée into the vegetables. Wash any wax from the whole lemon, cut it into very fine slices, and arrange in a single layer on top.

**5**  Put the fish on top of the lemon slices. Season with salt and pepper and sprinkle with the parsley. Reduce the heat to moderate, cover, and simmer for 15 minutes; uncover for the last 5 minutes if the sauce seems too liquid. The fish is cooked when the flesh turns opaque and flakes easily.

**SERVING SUGGESTION**
Serve with crusty bread or steamed rice, and a green salad with feta or soft goat's cheese, and black olives.

**VARIATION**
Other types of fish can be used instead, such as haddock, halibut, or whitefish. If fresh Italian tomatoes are not available, use drained, canned Italian tomatoes.

**NUTRIENTS PER SERVING, WHEN SERVING 4:** *calories 256, carbohydrate 11 g (including sugar 10 g), protein 35 g, fat 8 g (saturated fat 1 g), good source of vitamins A, B group, C, and E.*

# COD BAKED WITH PESTO

*Given a flourish of herby pesto and baked in the oven, firm, fresh fish makes a fine family supper dish, especially when accompanied by crushed garlic potatoes enriched with butter and cream.*

TIME: 30 MINUTES  SERVES: 4

---

| 1½ lb (680 g) floury potatoes, such as Idaho |
| :---: |
| Salt and black pepper |
| 4 thick pieces of cod fillet, or cod steaks, about 6 oz (170 g) each |
| 1 tablespoon green or red pesto |
| 1 tablespoon olive oil |
| 1 clove garlic |
| 3 tablespoons (50 g) butter |
| ¼ cup (50 ml) light cream |
| *To garnish:* 4 sprigs of basil |

**1**  Preheat the oven to 400°F (200°C) and put a kettle of water on to boil.
**2**  Scrub the potatoes and cut them into ¾ in. (2 cm) cubes. Put the cubes into a saucepan, cover with boiling water, and add salt. Cover,

bring back to the boil, and boil for 10–15 minutes, until cooked.
**3**  Meanwhile, line a small roasting pan with foil. Wipe the cod with kitchen paper and lay the fillets in the pan. Spread the pesto evenly over each and season. Drizzle with olive oil and bake on the top shelf of the oven for 15–20 minutes or until the flesh flakes easily.
**4**  Drain the potatoes and return them to the pan. Peel the garlic, crush it into the potatoes, and mash. Stir in the butter and cream and reheat gently. Serve with the fish and garnish with the basil.

*SERVING SUGGESTION*
Accompany with a simply cooked vegetable such as steamed beans, char-grilled vegetables, or Italian Baked Endive (page 258).

*NUTRIENTS PER SERVING: calories 431, carbohydrate 23 g (including sugar 2 g), protein 37 g, fat 22 g (saturated fat 10 g), good source of vitamins B group, C, and E.*

---

### COOK'S SUGGESTION

*Pesto is a velvety Italian sauce that is made from fresh basil, pine kernels, garlic, olive oil, and Parmesan or Pecorino cheese, pounded together with a pestle and mortar. Red pesto also includes sun-dried tomatoes.*

# SWEDISH FRIED HERRING

*Tender fillets of fresh herring sandwiched together with beaten egg, chopped red onion, and dill make a simple and inexpensive dish that is nevertheless packed with flavor and goodness.*

TIME: 20 MINUTES SERVES: 4

| 4 large or 8 small herrings, filleted |
| --- |
| 1 small egg |
| Salt and black pepper |
| 1 large red onion |
| A bunch of fresh dill |
| Flour for dusting |
| Oil for frying |

**1** Wash the herring fillets and pat them dry. In a small bowl, whisk the egg with some seasoning.
**2** Peel the onion, cut two slices widthwise from the center, separate into rings, and set them aside for a garnish, then finely chop the rest. Rinse and dry the dill, and finely chop enough to give 1 tablespoon, reserving four sprigs for a garnish.
**3** Liberally dust a board with flour and lay half the herring fillets on it,

skin sides down. Brush them with the seasoned egg, then divide the chopped onion and chopped dill between the fillets, spreading them along the center of each.
**4** Brush the fleshy sides of the remaining fillets with the beaten egg and arrange them on the onion-topped fillets, flesh sides down, to sandwich the filling. Pat firmly together and dredge with flour, brushing off any surplus.
**5** Heat enough oil to just cover the base of a large frying pan. When the oil is hot, lay the herring sandwiches carefully in the pan and fry them over a moderate to high heat for 2–3 minutes, until lightly browned underneath. Turn them over carefully and cook them for another 2–3 minutes, or until the flesh is opaque and cooked through.

**6** Drain the herrings on kitchen paper then serve, garnished with the reserved onion rings and sprigs of dill. Watch out for any bones.
*SERVING SUGGESTION*
Serve with boiled red potatoes and beets, or fried apple slices.

*NUTRIENTS PER SERVING: calories 520, carbohydrate 5g (including sugar 2g), protein 45g, fat 36g (saturated fat 9g), good source of vitamins B group and E, and zinc.*

---

### COOK'S SUGGESTION

*Herring must be very fresh, so look for shining, silver fish with bright eyes and buy them the day they will be cooked. Ask your fish supplier to gut and fillet the fish for you.*

---

# FISH WITH FLAVORED BUTTERS

### SALMON WITH LIME HERB BUTTER

*This aromatic butter is infused with the South-east Asian flavors of ginger, coriander, and lime.*

TIME: 30 MINUTES  SERVES: 4

| |
|---|
| 2 in. (5 cm) piece fresh root ginger |
| 12 sprigs of fresh coriander |
| 2 limes |
| ¼ lb (110 g) butter |
| Salt and black pepper |
| Cayenne pepper |
| 2 tablespoons sunflower oil |
| 4 salmon fillets, 6 oz (170 g) each |

1  Preheat the oven to 425°F (220°C). Peel and slice the ginger and put it into a food processor. Rinse and dry the coriander, set some sprigs aside, and add the rest to the ginger. Wash the limes. Cut one into wedges for a garnish. Grate the zest of the other, squeeze the juice, and add to the mixing bowl with the butter, salt, pepper, and cayenne, then blend.
2  Shape the mixture into a sausage then wrap the sausage in foil and chill it in the freezer.
3  In the meantime, brush a baking tray with a little oil, place the salmon fillets on it and brush with the remaining oil. Sprinkle with salt and bake for 8 minutes, or until the flesh flakes easily.
4  Take the butter from the freezer and cut it into thick rounds.
5  Transfer the fish to four plates, lay a round of butter on each and garnish with the lime and coriander.
*SERVING SUGGESTION*
Serve with couscous, which you can leave to soak while you cook the salmon. Or try Glazed Onions (page 272) and Spinach and Baby Corn Salad (page 103).

*NUTRIENTS PER SERVING: calories 624, carbohydrate 2 g (including sugar 0.4 g), protein 26 g, fat 57 g (saturated fat 33 g), good source of vitamins A and E.*

### TUNA STEAKS WITH WASABI BUTTER

*East meets west in this exciting, well-flavored butter containing hot wasabi, sesame seeds, and soy sauce.*

TIME: 25 MINUTES  SERVES: 4

| |
|---|
| 1 teaspoon sesame seeds |
| ½ lemon |
| A few sprigs each of basil, chives, coriander, and parsley |
| ¼ lb (110 g) unsalted butter |
| 1 tablespoon wasabi paste |
| 1 tablespoon soy sauce |
| 3 drops Tabasco sauce |
| 4 tuna steaks, 6 oz (170 g) each |
| 1 tablespoon olive or sunflower oil |

1  Dry roast the sesame seeds in a small frying pan until lightly colored then set aside.
2  Squeeze 1 teaspoon of juice from the lemon and add it to the seeds. Rinse, dry, and finely chop the herbs, reserving a few sprigs for a garnish, then stir the chopped herbs into the sesame seeds with the butter, wasabi paste, soy sauce, and Tabasco. Beat until smooth.
3  Shape the flavored butter into a sausage, wrap it in foil, and chill in the freezer.
4  Heat a griddle or frying pan over a moderately high heat. Brush both sides of the tuna with the oil and fry for 3–4 minutes on each side.
5  Cut the butter into rounds. Place the steaks on four plates, lay a round of butter on top of each and garnish with the sprigs of herb.
*SERVING SUGGESTION*
Radishes, pickled ginger, bean sprouts, and watercress all make good garnishes for this dish. Steamed new potatoes are a good foil for the flavored butter.

*NUTRIENTS PER SERVING: calories 512, carbohydrate 1 g (including sugar 0.8 g), protein 42 g, fat 38 g (saturated fat 19 g), good source of vitamins A, B group, and E, and selenium.*

### HALIBUT WITH HORSERADISH BUTTER

*The pungent flavor of chive and horseradish butter is a zesty finishing touch for quickly pan-fried fish.*

TIME: 25 MINUTES  SERVES: 4

| |
|---|
| A small bunch of fresh chives |
| 1½ tablespoons hot horseradish sauce |
| ¼ lb (110 g) butter |
| 4 halibut steaks or fillets, 6 oz (170 g) each |
| Salt and black pepper |
| 2 teaspoons corn oil |

1  Snip about 2 tablespoons of the fresh chives into a small mixing bowl and combine them with the horseradish sauce and all but 1 tablespoon of the butter.
2  Shape the butter mixture into a sausage, then wrap the sausage in foil and chill it in the freezer.
3  Wipe the halibut pieces with kitchen paper and season them on both sides with salt and pepper. Heat the remaining butter and the oil in a pan. Cook the fish over a high heat for about 4–6 minutes, until it flakes easily. If you are using halibut fillets, they will cook faster than steaks.
4  Cut the butter into rounds, then transfer the cooked fish onto four serving plates and top each with a circle of butter.
*SERVING SUGGESTION*
Steamed spinach, or Orange and Sesame Carrots (page 256), would go well with this recipe.

*NUTRIENTS PER SERVING: calories 438, carbohydrate 1 g (including sugar 1 g), protein 38 g, fat 31 g (saturated fat 18 g), good source of vitamins A, B group, and E.*

**THREE TASTY FISHES:** (*top*) HALIBUT WITH HORSERADISH BUTTER; (*center*) TUNA STEAKS WITH WASABI BUTTER; (*bottom*) SALMON WITH LIME HERB BUTTER.

# BAKED SKATE

*Tender skate wings dotted with nuts of butter and sprinkled with shallots and vinegar are simply baked in the oven. A final flourish of capers and chopped gherkins adds extra flavor.*

TIME: 30 MINUTES  SERVES: 4

| |
| --- |
| 2 shallots |
| 3 small gherkins |
| 5 tablespoons (85 g) butter |
| 2 large skate wings, about 1 lb (450 g) each |
| 2 tablespoons balsamic or sherry vinegar |
| Salt and black pepper |
| 2 tablespoons capers |

**1**  Preheat the oven to 375°F (190°C). Peel and chop the shallots and the gherkins and set them aside separately.

**2**  Use a little of the butter to grease a shallow baking dish, which must be large enough to hold the skate wings laid flat in one layer. Rinse the skate, then cut each wing into two pieces, place them in the baking dish, and dot them with the remaining butter.

**3**  Sprinkle the fish with the chopped shallots and the balsamic or sherry vinegar and season with salt and pepper. Bake the skate, uncovered, for 20 minutes, or until the thickest part of the skate wing flakes easily when it is tested gently with a fork.

**4**  Sprinkle the pieces of fish with the capers and chopped gherkins and baste with the cooking juices just before serving.

*SERVING SUGGESTION*
Accompany with some tomato halves, roasted alongside the fish. New potatoes would provide a mild contrast to the strong flavor of the skate, and can be boiled or steamed while the fish is baking.

*NUTRIENTS PER SERVING: calories 321, carbohydrate 0.5 g (including sugar 0.5 g), protein 38 g, fat 18 g (saturated fat 12 g), good source of vitamins A, B group, and E.*

# SALMON WITH TROPICAL FRUIT SALSA

*Hearty steaks of grilled salmon are given a tropical taste when served with an exciting salsa—a finely chopped sauce mixture of exotic mango and papaya, laced with lime, ginger, and cooling mint.*

### TIME: 25 MINUTES  SERVES: 4

| |
|---|
| 4 salmon steaks, 6 oz (170 g) each |
| 1 tablespoon olive oil |

*For the salsa:*

| |
|---|
| 1 small mango |
| 1 small papaya |
| 1 in. (2.5 cm) piece fresh root ginger |
| A handful of mint leaves |
| 1 lime |
| Salt and black pepper |

**1** Preheat the grill to moderate and cover the rack with foil.

**2** To make the salsa, cut the mango in half, remove the flesh, dice it finely, and put it into a bowl. Cut the papaya in half, scoop out and discard the seeds, finely dice the flesh, and add it to the mango.

**3** Peel the ginger and grate it into the bowl. Rinse, dry, and chop the mint and add to the bowl.

**4** Wash the wax off the lime. Remove a few shreds of zest for a garnish, grate the rest, and add it to the salsa. Squeeze the juice and add half to the bowl, reserving the rest.

**5** Season the salsa with salt and plenty of pepper and mix well.

**6** Put the salmon steaks, skin sides down, onto the foil on the grill rack. Brush them with the olive oil, season, and sprinkle with the remaining lime juice. Grill for 6–8 minutes without turning. The fish is done when the flesh flakes easily.

**7** Serve the grilled salmon garnished with the lime zest and accompanied by the salsa.

*SERVING SUGGESTION*
Serve with a plain green salad and perhaps some new potatoes.

*NUTRIENTS PER SERVING: calories 424, carbohydrate 15 g (including sugar 14 g), protein 26 g, fat 29 g (saturated fat 15 g), good source of vitamins A, C, and E.*

---

### COOK'S SUGGESTION

*If you grill the salmon skin side down on a piece of ungreased foil it does not need turning, and is easy to lift away from the skin to serve.*

---

# FRESH FROM THE CAN

*A well-stocked pantry is the best defense against sudden pangs of hunger, and cooks have always reached for the can opener in emergencies. Canned fish, in particular, provides a good basis for a wide range of dishes from quick toasted snacks to sturdy main courses.*

### SARDINE AND TOMATO BRUSCHETTA

*Sardines on toast get a new twist.*
SERVES 2:

- 1 ciabatta loaf
- 1 clove garlic
- 2–3 firm, ripe tomatoes
- Salt and black pepper
- Olive oil
- 4½ oz (125 g) canned sardines
- Basil, arugula, or watercress
- Lemon juice or balsamic vinegar, optional

Toast four thick slices from the ciabatta, then rub one surface of each with the cut clove of garlic. Cut the tomatoes into chunks, pile them onto the bruschetta, season, and drizzle generously with olive oil. Drain the sardines and lay them on top. Scatter leaves of basil, arugula, or watercress around the plate. If you feel the fish is too oily, sprinkle a little lemon juice or some balsamic vinegar on the salad.

### SMOKED OYSTER AND POTATO PAN-FRY

*Canned smoked oysters need no cooking and they add a rich, unusual flavor to this one-pan meal.*
SERVES 2:

- 1 clove garlic
- 2 tablespoons olive oil
- 1 lb (450 g) potatoes
- A bunch of green onions or chives
- 3½ oz (100 g) canned smoked oysters
- 4 sun-dried tomatoes
- Salt and black pepper

Peel and thickly slice the garlic and fry it very gently for 3–4 minutes in the olive oil in a large, non-stick frying pan. Peel or scrub the potatoes and cut them into ½ in. (1 cm) cubes. Remove the garlic from the pan and discard it, add the diced potatoes in a single layer, and fry over a fairly high heat, stirring

often, until they are golden brown. Trim, rinse, and chop the green onions or chives. Drain the oysters and cut them in half, then drain and chop the sun-dried tomatoes. When the potatoes are nearly done, add the onions or chives and cook for 1 minute. Stir in the oysters and tomatoes and heat through for 2 minutes. Season and serve.

### SALMON FILO WRAPS

*Chilled filo pastry means you don't have to wait for the pastry to defrost.*
SERVES 2 AS A MAIN COURSE,
4 AS AN APPETIZER:

- 4 tablespoons (50 g) butter
- 3 tablespoons (25 g) plain flour
- ½ cup milk
- 1 can (7½ oz / 213 g) red salmon
- ½ can (12 oz / 341 ml) asparagus tips
- A sprig of fresh dill or ½ teaspoon of dried dill weed
- Salt and black pepper
- 2 sheets filo pastry

Preheat the oven to 375°F (190°C). Make a sauce by whisking together half the butter with the flour and milk in a saucepan over a moderate heat, until it comes to the boil and thickens. Let it simmer for 1 minute, then pour it into a bowl. Drain the salmon, remove any skin and bones, and flake the flesh into the sauce. Drain and add the asparagus tips. Snip or stir in the dill; season generously.

Melt the remaining butter. Lay the sheets of filo pastry on top of each other, cut out four 7 in. (18 cm) squares, and brush each with melted butter. Spoon a quarter of the salmon mixture into the center of each square and fold up the corners to make a wrap. Brush the outside with butter and place on a greased baking tray. Bake for 12–15 minutes, until golden.

### CRAB AND PEA TART

*A prebaked pastry case is quickly filled with crab in a creamy sauce to make a mouthwatering flan.*
SERVES 4:

- 2 medium eggs
- Salt and black pepper
- ½ teaspoon ground mace
- 2 cans (4 oz / 120 g) crab meat
- ½ cup (100 g) frozen peas
- 2 green onions
- ⅓ cup (100 ml) whipping cream
- 3 tablespoons cooking sherry
- 2 tablespoons grated Parmesan
- 9 in. (23 cm) prebaked pastry case

Preheat the oven to 400°F (200°C). In a bowl, beat the eggs with seasoning and mace. Stir in the crab meat and its liquor. Defrost the peas in boiling water and drain, chop the green onions, and add both to the bowl. Stir in the cream, sherry, and some Parmesan.

Use the mixture to fill the flan case and place it, in its foil container, on a heavy baking sheet. Sprinkle the rest of the Parmesan on top and bake two-thirds of the way up the oven for 20 minutes.

### NOODLES WITH ANCHOVY SAUCE

*A truly simple sauce from Sicily and Venice gets its impact from the intense flavor of anchovies.*
SERVES 4:

- ½ lb (230 g) buckwheat or plain noodles
- 2 tablespoons currants
- 1 large clove garlic
- 1 sprig fresh rosemary
- 3 tablespoons olive oil
- 1 lemon
- 2 cans (2 oz / 50 g) anchovies
- 2 tablespoons pine kernels
- Black pepper
- Fresh mint, optional

Boil a large pan of water, add the noodles, and cook them according to the directions on the package.

Put the currants to soak in a spoon-ful of boiling water from the pasta pan. Fry the garlic and rosemary in the olive oil over a moderate heat until they begin to color, then discard them. Grate the lemon rind.

Place the frying pan on top of the pan of boiling pasta as the next step needs only a very gentle heat, and stir in the canned anchovies, their oil, the pine kernels, and the drained currants and lemon rind.

Cook until the anchovies melt to form a sauce. If the mixture seems too dry, add 1–2 tablespoons of hot water from the pasta. Season with black pepper, pour it over the drained noodles, and garnish, if you like, with chopped mint.

## TUNA SALAD
*A very substantial salad that tastes especially good made in the morning to eat in the garden for lunch.*
*SERVES 4:*
> *4 eggs*
> *1 cup (225 g) frozen peas*
> *1¼ lb (560 g) canned new potatoes*
> *2 cans (6 oz / 170 g) tuna in oil*
> *2 medium carrots*
> *1 lemon*
> *Salt and black pepper*
> *1¼ cups (300 ml) mayonnaise*
> *A bunch of chives or flat-leaved parsley*

Hard-boil the eggs and put the peas into a pan of boiling water to cook for 3 minutes. Drain the potatoes, rinse, and pat dry, then slice them into a serving bowl. Drain the oil from the tuna into a measuring jug, flake the tuna onto the potatoes, and peel and grate in the carrots.

Drain the peas and rinse under a cold tap. Cool and shell the eggs, cut them into quarters, and add them and the peas to the bowl.

Squeeze the lemon juice into the tuna oil. Add salt, black pepper, and enough mayonnaise to make it up to 1½ cups (350 ml). Whisk and stir through the salad. Sprinkle with chopped chives or parsley, cover, and chill. Garnish with chives.

CANNED FISH TRANSFORMATION:
TUNA SALAD.

# Smoked Salmon with Stir-fried Vegetables

*This unusual supper dish features delicate baby vegetables and smoked salmon with a light touch of Oriental flavorings.*

**TIME: 25 MINUTES  SERVES: 4**

| |
|---|
| ½ lb (230 g) mixed salad leaves |
| 1 fresh green chili |
| 3 oz (85 g) fine green beans |
| 3 oz (85 g) baby carrots |
| 3½ oz (100 g) shallots |
| 3 oz (85 g) fine asparagus |
| 1 tablespoon olive oil |
| 1 tablespoon sesame oil |
| 1 clove garlic |
| ⅓ cup (100 ml) dry sherry |
| ¼ lb (110 g) smoked salmon trimmings, or slices |
| 1 tablespoon light soy sauce |
| ½ teaspoon sugar |
| *To garnish:* a few coriander leaves |

**1**  Rinse and dry the salad leaves and arrange on a serving plate.
**2**  Rinse, dry, deseed, and slice the chili. Rinse, dry, and top and tail the beans and carrots, halving the carrots lengthwise if they are thick.
**3**  Peel the shallots and cut them into halves or quarters. Rinse, dry, and trim the asparagus, and cut it into 1 in. (2.5 cm) lengths. Rinse and dry the coriander leaves.
**4**  Heat the olive oil and sesame oil in a large frying pan. Peel the garlic and crush it into the pan, then add the sliced chili and stir-fry over a moderate heat for 1 minute. Add the beans and carrots and continue to fry for 1–2 minutes more.
**5**  Add the shallots and asparagus and stir-fry for another minute. Then add the sherry, cover the pan, and cook for 1 minute more.
**6**  Cut the smoked salmon into strips, if necessary, add them to the pan, cover, and cook for 1 minute. Then add the soy sauce and sugar, stir well, and let the sauce heat through.
**7**  Spoon the mixture over the salad leaves and serve sprinkled with the coriander leaves.

*SERVING SUGGESTION*
A bowl of steamed new potatoes is an excellent accompaniment to this crunchy stir-fry.

*NUTRIENTS PER SERVING: calories 155, carbohydrate 5 g (including sugar 4 g), protein 10 g, fat 8 g (saturated fat 1 g), good source of vitamins A, B group, C, E, and folate.*

# MACKEREL WITH DILL MAYONNAISE

*Fresh, grilled fish fillets and lightly boiled new potatoes are enlivened by a creamy yogurt and mayonnaise dressing flavored with delicate fronds of dill and piquant capers.*

TIME: 30 MINUTES  SERVES: 4

| |
| --- |
| **A small bunch of fresh dill** |
| **1½ lb (680 g) new potatoes** |
| **Salt** |
| **1 teaspoon mixed peppercorns** |
| **Oil for greasing** |
| **4 mackerel fillets, 6 oz (170 g) each** |
| **4 tablespoons mayonnaise** |
| **4 tablespoons natural Greek yogurt** |
| **1 full tablespoon (25 g) capers** |
| ***To garnish:* 1 lemon** |

**1** Put a kettle of water on to boil. Rinse and dry the dill, remove the fine fronds from the stalks, and set both aside separately.
**2** Scrub the new potatoes and put them into a large saucepan with some salt and the dill stalks. Cover the potatoes with boiling water from the kettle, return to the boil, and cook for 15–20 minutes.
**3** Meanwhile, preheat the grill to high. Crush the peppercorns with a pestle and mortar or a rolling pin. Lightly oil the grill rack, lay the fillets on it, skin sides down, and sprinkle with the peppercorns.
**4** Grill the fillets for 5 minutes, then turn them over, reduce the heat to medium, and grill them for another 5 minutes, or until the skins are blistered. Turn over once more and grill for a further 2 minutes.
**5** While the fish is cooking, blend the mayonnaise and yogurt in a bowl. Chop the dill fronds and capers, and mix them in. Cut the lemon into wedges and set aside.
**6** When the mackerel is cooked, sprinkle the flesh sides with a little salt. Drain the potatoes and remove the dill stalks. Serve the mackerel with the potatoes, dill, mayonnaise, and lemon wedges.

*SERVING SUGGESTION*
You could accompany this dish with Leek and Carrot Stir-fry (page 256), or green salad and cherry tomatoes.

*NUTRIENTS PER SERVING: calories 883, carbohydrate 26 g (including sugar 3 g), protein 39 g, fat 70 g (saturated fat 32 g), good source of vitamins B group, C, and E.*

---

### COOK'S SUGGESTION

*You will need two large mackerel. To be sure they are absolutely fresh, buy the fish the day you need them and ask your fish supplier to fillet them for you.*

---

# GRILLED SOLE WITH BUTTERY ZUCCHINIS

*A light, delicate dish of grilled white fish and buttery shredded zucchinis is a perfect choice for an elegant summer supper.*

TIME: 30 MINUTES   SERVES: 4

1¼ lb (560 g) zucchinis

Salt and black pepper

4 soles, about 1 lb (450 g) each, dark skin and heads removed by your supplier

A small bunch of chives

A few sprigs of dill

A few sprigs of parsley

5 tablespoons (70 g) butter

Oil for greasing

1½ lemons

1   Preheat the grill to high. Rinse, dry, and trim the zucchinis, then shred them coarsely in a food processor or grate by hand. Put them into a colander with a little salt, toss gently together, and set aside to drain.

2   Rinse and dry the fish and make three diagonal cuts through the white skin on each one.

3   Rinse, dry, and chop enough chives, dill, and parsley to give a tablespoon of each, and put them into a small bowl with 3 tablespoons of the butter. Season well with pepper, mash with a fork, divide the mixture into four, and set aside.

4   Melt the remaining butter in a frying pan. Fry the zucchinis over a moderate heat for 10 minutes, until cooked but still slightly firm. Shake the pan gently from time to time to keep the shreds separate.

5   Meanwhile, lightly oil a large grill pan and place the soles in it, white skin sides up. Grill the fish for 5 minutes, then turn them over and sprinkle with the juice from the half lemon. Cook for 2–3 minutes, until the flesh flakes easily.

6   Cut the whole lemon into eight wedges and set them aside. Place a portion of herb butter on each sole and warm under the grill for a few seconds until the butter starts to melt. Serve accompanied by the zucchinis and the lemon wedges.

*SERVING SUGGESTION*
Grill some halved tomatoes with the soles and serve them with fresh granary bread, or with Roast New Potatoes with Rosemary (page 267).

*VARIATION*
Cod, haddock, or salmon steaks can be used instead of sole. Brush them with melted butter before cooking.

*NUTRIENTS PER SERVING: calories 554, carbohydrate 2 g (including sugar 2 g), protein 84 g, fat 23 g (saturated fat 10 g), good source of vitamins A, B group, C, E, and folate, iron, selenium, and zinc.*

### COOK'S SUGGESTION

*If your grill pan is not large enough for four soles, you can cook them on a large baking tray in the oven instead. Preheat the oven to 425°F (220°C). Then bake the soles, white skin sides up, for 15–20 minutes.*

# SMOKED HADDOCK WITH NOODLES

*Fine smoked haddock is served on a bed of choice baby vegetables, stir-fried with rice noodles, which is enriched with a sweet and sour Oriental sauce to make an easy and unusual dish.*

TIME: 30 MINUTES  SERVES: 4

| |
| --- |
| 4 smoked haddock fillets, 6 oz (170 g) each |
| ½ lb (230 g) rice vermicelli noodles |
| 1 green chili |
| 3 oz (85 g) baby carrots |
| 3 oz (85 g) baby green beans |
| ½ lb (230 g) fine asparagus |
| 1 tablespoon peanut or canola oil |
| 1 clove garlic |
| 1–2 tablespoons Thai fish sauce or soy sauce |
| 3 tablespoons white wine |
| 1 tablespoon clear honey |
| 1 teaspoon toasted sesame oil |

1  Put a kettle of water on to boil. Skin the fish (see page 11). Put the noodles into a bowl, cover them with boiling water, leave to stand for 5 minutes, then drain.

2  Meanwhile, rinse, dry, deseed, and chop the chili. Peel the carrots; rinse, dry, and trim the green beans and asparagus. Slice the asparagus into lengths to match the beans.

3  Heat the oil in a wok or large frying pan with a lid. Peel the garlic and crush it into the oil, then add the chili and sweat over a low heat for 2 minutes to flavor the oil.

4  Add the vegetables, increase the heat, then add the Thai fish or soy sauce, wine, and honey.

5  Lay the haddock fillets on top of the vegetables, cover and cook for 5 minutes. With a slotted spoon, remove the fish; keep it warm.

6  Add the drained noodles to the pan, toss them with the vegetables in the pan juices and stir in the sesame oil. Toss the mixture for a minute or two longer to warm the noodles through.

7  Divide the stir-fry among four serving plates and arrange the haddock fillets on top.

*NUTRIENTS PER SERVING: calories 451, carbohydrate 59 g (including sugar 7 g), protein 38 g, fat 6 g (saturated fat 1 g), good source of vitamins A, B group, E, and folate.*

# STEAMED WHOLE FISH CHINESE STYLE

*A whole fish steamed in the Chinese way with ginger, soy sauce, and sesame oil looks spectacular, yet is easy to prepare.*

TIME: 30 MINUTES  SERVES: 4

| |
|---|
| **1 whole round fish, ready-gutted, such as sea bass or snapper, weighing about 2 lb (900 g)** |
| **Salt** |
| **2 in. (5 cm) piece fresh root ginger** |
| **4 green onions** |
| **2 tablespoons soy sauce** |
| **1 tablespoon toasted sesame oil** |
| **4 cloves garlic** |
| **3 tablespoons vegetable oil** |

**1**  Clean and rinse the fish, gently rub it with salt, inside and out, and set it aside for 10 minutes.

**2**  Peel and grate the ginger, then rinse the green onions, cut them into 3 in. (7–8 cm) lengths, shred them finely, and set aside. Stir the soy sauce and sesame oil together in a small bowl.

**3**  Fill a steamer or wok with water to a level of 2–3 in. (5–8 cm) and bring it to the boil. If using a wok, place a trivet in the bottom.

**4**  Rinse the salted fish under cold water then dry it with kitchen paper. Place it on a heatproof plate, sprinkle with ginger, and lower it into the steamer basket or wok: do not let the plate touch the water. Cover, reduce the heat, and steam gently for 15–20 minutes, or until the fish is cooked.

**5**  While the fish is steaming, peel the garlic and cut it into thin slices. Heat the vegetable oil in a small frying pan and cook the garlic quickly over a high heat until it is just barely colored.

**6**  Transfer the fish to a serving dish and sprinkle it with the green onions and fried garlic slices. Pour the soy sauce and sesame oil mixture over the top and serve.

*SERVING SUGGESTION*

White rice would go well with the fish and can be cooked while it is steaming. Oriental noodles cook even faster and can be garnished with sesame seeds and some finely chopped red chili. A side dish of crisp, stir-fried vegetables would be a worthwhile addition.

*VARIATION*

Other whole fish such as haddock, mackerel, sea trout, and char can be cooked in this way. Make three or four slashes down to the bone on each side of the fish and rub salt into the cuts.

*NUTRIENTS PER SERVING, USING SEA BASS: calories 372, carbohydrate 2 g (including sugar 0.4 g), protein 50 g, fat 18 g (saturated fat 2 g), good source of vitamin $B_{12}$, and calcium and iron.*

---

### COOK'S SUGGESTION

*If you do not have a large enough wok or steamer, you can use a roasting pan with a wire rack to steam the fish. Lay the fish on its plate on the rack and cover the pan with foil, tucking it under the rim to keep the steam in.*

---

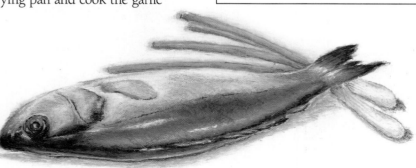

# MONKFISH RAGOUT WITH VERMOUTH

*Monkfish retains its shape, succulent texture, and flavor when cooked in a stew. The meaty white fish, a favorite in Europe, is combined in French style with garlic, tomatoes, lemon, and whipping cream.*

TIME: **30 MINUTES**  SERVES: **4**

| |
|---|
| 1 lb (450 g) trimmed monkfish |
| Salt and black pepper |
| 3 tablespoons olive oil |
| 1 small onion |
| 2 cloves garlic |
| 1 lb (450 g) tomatoes |
| ⅓ cup white vermouth, or dry Martini |
| 1 sprig tarragon |
| 1 lemon |
| 2 tablespoons whipping cream |

**1**  Boil a kettle of water for the tomatoes. Cut the monkfish into cubes and season lightly with salt and pepper. Heat the oil in a frying pan over a high heat and fry half the fish for 2 minutes, until it turns white and looks cooked on the outside. Remove, fry the second batch of fish, then remove that.

**2**  Peel and chop the onion and garlic, and fry them in the oil left in the pan until softened.

**3**  Put the tomatoes into a bowl, cover with boiling water, and leave a minute or two, then drain and peel. Finely dice the flesh and stir it into the onions.

**4**  Add the vermouth or Martini to the pan and increase the heat. Rinse, dry, and strip the tarragon leaves and add them to the pan. Wash any wax from the lemon, then grate the rind and add it to the pan. Boil rapidly for 5 minutes.

**5**  Return the monkfish to the frying pan, stir in the whipping cream, reduce the heat at once, and simmer gently for 5 minutes, or until the fish is cooked through.

***SERVING SUGGESTION***
You could serve the fish with a rice pilaf, cooked while you make the ragout, followed by a green salad.

*NUTRIENTS PER SERVING: calories 257, carbohydrate 6 g (including sugar 5 g), protein 21 g, fat 14 g (saturated fat 5 g), good source of vitamins B group, C, and E.*

# ROAST MONKFISH WITH PEA PURÉE

*A creamy, colorful pool of sweet-tasting pea purée complements the earthy flavor of Indian spices that are roasted to form a golden brown crust around firm-textured white monkfish.*

TIME: 30 MINUTES  SERVES: 2

1 monkfish tail, skinned,
weighing at least 1 lb (450 g)

1 clove garlic

½–1 fresh red chili

1 tablespoon olive oil

1 teaspoon ground cumin

1 teaspoon ground coriander

½ teaspoon sugar

½ lemon

*For the pea purée:*

½ pack (12½ oz / 350 g) frozen peas

1½ cups vegetable stock

1 clove garlic

1 tablespoon light cream

Salt and black pepper

**1**  Preheat the oven to 400°F (200°C). Trim the tail of any fins and tough outer membrane and place on a rack in a baking tray.

**2**  Peel and crush the garlic. Rinse, deseed, and finely chop the chili, and place them in a small bowl with the olive oil, cumin, coriander, and sugar. Add 1 teaspoon of juice from the lemon and stir to make a thick paste.

**3**  Spread the paste evenly over the monkfish tail, then roast it in the oven for 20 minutes or until cooked.

**4**  Meanwhile, make the pea purée. Put the peas into a pan with the stock and bring it to the boil. Peel the garlic, crush it into the peas, and simmer, uncovered, for 5 minutes, skimming off any scum.

**5**  When the peas are tender, drain the stock into a measuring jug. Blend the peas with the cream and ⅔ cup of the stock to make a textured purée. Season to taste, and keep warm.

**6**  When the fish is cooked, cut the fillets carefully from both sides of the central bone. Divide the pea purée between two plates; serve the monkfish on top.

*NUTRIENTS PER SERVING: calories 259, carbohydrate 10 g (including sugar 4 g), protein 37 g, fat 10 g (saturated fat 2 g), good source of vitamins B group, C, and E.*

# SCALLOPS WITH A HERB DRESSING

*A piquant dressing made with a heady bunch of fresh herbs, capers, and olives accompanies sweet-flavored scallops, seared over a high heat and served with long strands of pasta.*

TIME: 30 MINUTES    SERVES: 4

| |
|---|
| **1 lb (450 g) fresh scallops, with or without corals** |
| **12 oz (335 g) dried tagliatelle** |
| **3 tablespoons olive oil** |

*For the dressing:*

| |
|---|
| **A bunch of parsley** |
| **A bunch of mint** |
| **A bunch of chives** |
| **1 lemon** |
| **2 tablespoons wine or sherry vinegar** |
| **5 tablespoons extra virgin olive oil** |
| **1 tablespoon capers** |
| **6 large stoned black olives** |
| **Salt and black pepper** |

**1**  Put a large pan of water on to boil for the pasta. To make the dressing, rinse and dry the herbs. Chop the parsley and mint, snip the chives and put them in a measuring jug; you need ¾ cup.

**2**  Wash any wax from the lemon, then grate the rind and add it to the jug with the wine or sherry vinegar and the extra virgin olive oil. Roughly chop the capers and olives and add them, then season to taste with salt and black pepper, mix well, and set aside.

**3**  Check each scallop has had the small tough muscle removed, then rinse and dry. If you are using large scallops, reserve the corals, slice them (see box, right), and season.

**4**  Add the pasta to the boiling water and cook according to the package instructions.

**5**  Meanwhile, heat the olive oil in a large frying pan over a high heat and fry the scallops for 4–6 minutes until lightly browned and only just cooked through.

**6**  Remove from the heat and pour on the dressing. Drain the pasta well and serve it topped with the dressed scallops.

*NUTRIENTS PER SERVING: calories 687, carbohydrate 77g (including sugar 9g), protein 39g, fat 25g (saturated fat 4g), good source of vitamin E.*

## EASY DOES IT!

*Smaller scallops cook faster. Save cooking time if you have bought large scallops by slicing them widthwise into two or three small discs.*

# SCALLOPS WITH THAI FLAVORINGS

*Fragrant flavors of Thailand—lemongrass and kaffir lime leaves—are combined with the tropical taste of coconut milk in a stir-fry to give fresh scallops an intriguing, exotic flavor.*

TIME: 20 MINUTES  SERVES: 4

| ½ cup chicken stock |
| 2 shallots |
| 1 stalk lemongrass |
| 3 fresh or dried kaffir lime leaves |
| ¾ lb (335 g) fresh scallops |
| 6 oz (170 g) snow peas |
| 2 tablespoons peanut oil |
| 2 teaspoons Thai green curry paste |
| ⅔ cup (150 ml) coconut milk |
| A few sprigs of fresh coriander |

1  Heat the stock in a small saucepan over a moderate heat.
2  Peel the shallots and chop them finely. Remove and discard the outer section of the lemongrass, then chop the stalk finely. Chop or crumble the kaffir lime leaves.

3  Rinse the scallops and pat them dry, leaving any corals intact. If the scallops are large, cut them into discs (see box, page 128). Rinse the snow peas, top and tail them, and cut them in half crosswise.
4  Heat the oil in a heavy frying pan until it shows a faint haze. Add the shallots, lemongrass, kaffir lime leaves, scallops, and snow peas to the pan and stir-fry for 3 minutes.
5  Stir the curry paste into the stock, then add it to the pan with the coconut milk. Bring to the boil, then reduce the heat and simmer for 3 minutes.
6  Meanwhile, rinse, dry, and chop the coriander leaves. Transfer the cooked scallops to a serving dish and sprinkle the coriander on top.

**SERVING SUGGESTION**
For a Thai feast, match this dish with Thai Salad with Coconut Dressing (page 88), Thai-style Beef Salad (page 86) and rice.

*NUTRIENTS PER SERVING: calories 186, carbohydrate 7g (including sugar 4g), protein 23g, fat 8g (saturated fat 1g), good source of vitamins B group, C, and E.*

---

**COOK'S SUGGESTION**

*Kaffir lime is a South-east Asian citrus fruit whose leaves and rind both have a strong, flowery, lime-and-lemon scent. You will find fresh and/or dried leaves in larger supermarkets or Oriental grocery stores.*

---

# SEARED TUNA WITH HOT PEPPER SAUCE

*A richly flavored, peppery-hot purée of char-grilled peppers, chili, onion, and garlic makes the perfect partner for a firm, meaty fish steak that is cooked quickly over a high heat.*

TIME: 20 MINUTES  SERVES: 4

4 tuna, or swordfish, steaks,
about 6 oz (170 g) each

*For the sauce:*

| |
| --- |
| 2 medium red peppers |
| 1 medium onion |
| 2 cloves garlic |
| 1 small fresh red chili |
| 1 large slice whole-wheat bread |
| 1 lime |
| 1 tablespoon tomato purée |
| 4 tablespoons olive oil |
| Salt and black pepper |

**1** Preheat the grill to high. To make the sauce, rinse, deseed, and halve the red peppers lengthwise. Halve the onion across. Put them onto the grill, skin sides up, with the unpeeled cloves of garlic. Grill for 10 minutes or until the skins are slightly charred.

**2** While the vegetables are grilling, rinse, deseed, and chop the chili. Dice the bread. Wash any wax from the lime, then grate the rind and squeeze the juice.

**3** When the grilled peppers, onion, and garlic are cool enough to handle, peel them and put the flesh into a food processor with the chili, bread, tomato purée, and 3 tablespoons of olive oil. Add half the lime rind and juice, reserving the rest. Process the mixture to a purée, then season to taste with salt and black pepper. Transfer the sauce to a serving bowl and set aside.

**4** Brush a ridged griddle pan or a large, heavy-based frying pan with the remaining oil and place it over a very high heat. Lightly season the fish steaks and fry them for 4–6 minutes, until golden brown on the outside and cooked through, turning them over once.

**5** Sprinkle the steaks with the remaining lime rind and juice and serve with the hot pepper sauce, either spooned around the fish or served separately in a bowl.

*SERVING SUGGESTION*
The cool flavors of Spinach and Baby Corn Salad (page 103) would complement the hot sauce.

*NUTRIENTS PER SERVING: calories 409, carbohydrate 14 g (including sugar 7 g), protein 44 g, fat 20 g (saturated fat 4 g), good source of vitamins A, B group, C, and E, and selenium.*

---

# BLACKENED WHITE FISH

*Fillets of sturdy white fish are given a crunchy cornmeal crust, seasoned with a fiery mixture of spices and herbs, before being seared over a fierce heat in the Cajun style and served with lemon.*

TIME: 20 MINUTES  SERVES: 4

| |
| --- |
| 1 teaspoon black peppercorns |
| 1 teaspoon each of fennel seeds, dried oregano, and thyme |
| ½–1 teaspoon cayenne pepper |
| Salt |
| 3 cloves garlic |
| 2 tablespoons cornmeal |
| 4 fillets fish, about 6–8 oz (170–230 g) each (see box, right) |
| 3 tablespoons peanut oil |
| *To garnish: 1 lemon* |

**1** Crush the peppercorns and put them into a large bowl. Add the dried herbs, cayenne pepper, and some salt. Peel the garlic and crush it into the bowl, then add the cornmeal and stir thoroughly.

**2** Skin the fish fillets if necessary (see page 11), add them to the herb and spice mixture, and press it on firmly to coat them well.

**3** Heat the peanut oil in a large frying pan until it begins to smoke. Add the fish and fry for 1½ minutes on each side, or until the fillets are lightly browned and cooked through.

**4** Meanwhile, cut the lemon into wedges. Drain the cooked fish on kitchen paper, then transfer the fillets to a warmed serving dish and garnish with the lemon wedges.

*SERVING SUGGESTION*
Serve this spicy fish with steamed new potatoes and a green salad or, to continue the Louisiana theme, the Cajun Potato Salad (page 102).

*NUTRIENTS PER SERVING, USING BREAM: calories 258, carbohydrate 9 g (including sugar 0.1 g), protein 34 g, fat 10 g (saturated fat 2 g), good source of vitamin E.*

> ### COOK'S SUGGESTION
> *Any round white fish, such as cod, haddock, halibut, or Boston bluefish is suitable for this dish. As an alternative, you could use either monkfish or shark, but you will have to allow them a little longer to cook—they will each need about 6–8 minutes.*

**TWO HOT FISH DISHES:** (*top*) SEARED TUNA WITH HOT PEPPER SAUCE; (*bottom*) BLACKENED WHITE FISH.

# SEARED SQUID WITH MINT AND BUTTER

*Fresh squid, quickly fried, is juicy and tender. Tossed with shredded lettuce that is bathed in a warm, buttery onion and lime sauce, it makes a perfect light lunch or an elegant first course.*

TIME: 30 MINUTES  SERVES: 4

| |
|---|
| 1 lb (450 g) prepared squid (the pouch without head and tentacles) |
| 3 lettuce hearts |
| 2 shallots |
| 2 limes |
| 6 sprigs of mint |
| 5 tablespoons (85 g) butter |
| 2 cloves garlic |
| 2 tablespoons cooking oil |
| Salt and black pepper |
| *To serve:* French or Italian bread |

**1** Halve the prepared squid lengthwise. If the flat triangles are more than 4 in. (10 cm) long, cut them in half again. Score the inner surfaces in a diamond pattern with a sharp knife, then set aside.

**2** Trim the lettuces, discarding the outer leaves, slice across into fine strips, and put them into a large serving bowl.

**3** Peel and chop the shallots. Wash any wax from the limes, then grate the rind of one and squeeze out the juice. Slice the other lime and set it aside. Rinse and dry the mint and chop the leaves finely.

**4** Warm the butter in a saucepan. Peel the garlic and crush it into the pan. Add the shallots and cook them very gently for about a minute. Then stir in the lime rind and juice and pour the mixture over the strips of lettuce.

**5** Heat the oil in a large frying pan until very hot and fry the squid in batches, for 2–3 minutes each

batch, until the pieces have become opaque and tightened into curls.

**6** Transfer to the serving bowl with all the juice and residue from the pan, season to taste, and toss gently into the lettuce.

**7** Scatter the finely chopped mint over the salad and serve it garnished with the reserved slices of lime and accompanied by warm bread.

**SERVING SUGGESTION**
The squid can be paired with the sunny Mediterranean flavor of Greek Salad (page 87).

*NUTRIENTS PER SERVING: calories 536, carbohydrate 47g (including sugar 3g), protein 28g, fat 26g (saturated fat 13g), good source of vitamins A, B group, and E, and folate and selenium.*

# SHRIMPS MASALA

*This simple Indian-inspired dish of sweet-tasting shrimps has a gentle, spicy flavor, balancing the coolness of coconut cream with the heat of cumin, coriander, turmeric, and aromatic ginger.*

TIME: 20 MINUTES  SERVES: 4

| |
|---|
| 1 medium onion |
| 2 cloves garlic |
| 2 in. (5 cm) piece fresh root ginger |
| 2 tablespoons sunflower oil |
| 2 teaspoons ground coriander |
| 2 teaspoons ground cumin |
| 1 teaspoon ground turmeric |
| 1 lb (450 g) peeled, cooked tiger shrimps |
| ¾ cup (200 ml) coconut cream |
| Salt and black pepper |
| A small bunch of fresh coriander |

**1**   Peel and chop the onion and garlic and peel and finely chop the ginger. Heat the oil in a heavy frying pan, add the onion and garlic and fry them for a few minutes until they have softened. Then add the ginger and the ground coriander, cumin, and turmeric and cook for another 1–2 minutes until the spices have released their fragrance.
**2**   Add the shrimps and the coconut cream to the frying pan, taste and season with salt and black pepper. Then bring the mixture to the boil, reduce the heat, and let it simmer for 2–3 minutes.
**3**   Meanwhile, rinse and dry the coriander. Set aside a few sprigs to use as a garnish and chop the rest. Pour the shrimp mixture into a serving dish, scatter the chopped coriander over the top; do this last to keep the coriander tasting fresh. Garnish with the sprigs and serve.

*SERVING SUGGESTION*
This light dish could be served with just steamed long-grain rice or some nan bread. Or you could add Potato and Green Bean Curry (page 253) and Dahl (page 252) to make a much more substantial meal.

*NUTRIENTS PER SERVING: calories 341, carbohydrate 7g (including sugar 5g), protein 26g, fat 24g (saturated fat 16g), good source of vitamins B group and E, and selenium and zinc.*

PLUM-GLAZED PORK WITH SPICY CABBAGE

# BEEF, LAMB, & PORK

*Please the family or delight guests with nourishing, richly flavored main course dishes from classic steaks and bacon pie to spiced lamb kabobs and plum-glazed pork.*

# BEEF STROGANOFF

*Cocktail gherkins and hot green peppercorns offset the richness of sour cream, mushrooms, and slivers of fillet steak in this stroganoff to bring a new dimension to a traditional favorite.*

TIME: 30 MINUTES  SERVES: 4

| |
|---|
| 3 tablespoons olive oil |
| 1 large red onion |
| ½ lb (230 g) small chestnut mushrooms |
| 1¼ lb (560 g) beef fillet |
| 2 teaspoons fresh green peppercorns in brine |
| Salt |
| 2 tablespoons Dijon mustard |
| 1¼ cups (300 ml) sour cream |
| 8 small drained cocktail gherkins |
| A small bunch of chives |

**1** Heat a tablespoon of the oil in a large frying pan. Halve, peel, and thinly slice the onion, then fry over a moderate heat for 2–3 minutes, until slightly softened.

**2** Meanwhile, clean and halve the mushrooms and add them to the pan. Increase the heat and cook, stirring, for about 5 minutes, until they have softened and most of the liquid has evaporated.

**3** While the mushrooms are cooking, slice the beef fillet very thinly, then cut it across the grain into thin strips (piling several slices on top of one another will speed up this process).

**4** When the mushrooms are cooked, tip them and the onion into a large bowl and set aside.

**5** Add another tablespoon of oil to the pan and increase the heat to high. Add half the beef and stir-fry for 2–3 minutes, or until very lightly browned, then remove it. Heat the remaining oil and cook the rest of the beef the same way.

**6** Return the onion, mushrooms, and the first batch of beef with any juices to the frying pan. Crush the green peppercorns, add them to the pan with some salt, and heat through for 1–2 minutes.

**7** Blend the mustard and sour cream together and stir into the beef with the gherkins. Heat through gently, without boiling. Trim, rinse, and dry the chives, snip them over the top and serve.

*SERVING SUGGESTION*

Serve with rice, mashed potatoes or noodles, which can be boiled while the beef is cooking, and a green side salad.

*VARIATIONS*

The stroganoff can also be made with pork fillet, lean neck of lamb fillet, or chicken breasts. Button mushrooms can be used in place of chestnut mushrooms and, if you prefer, the gherkins can be chopped.

*NUTRIENTS PER SERVING: calories 563, carbohydrate 14 g (including sugar 11 g), protein 35 g, fat 41 g (saturated fat 16 g), good source of vitamins A, B group, E, and folate, and iron, selenium, and zinc.*

# SPICED STEAK WITH SPEEDY RATATOUILLE

*Zucchinis, eggplants, and tomatoes, gently flavored with wine and herbs, provide a melting ratatouille that perfectly complements steak rubbed with a mixture of hot spices.*

TIME: 30 MINUTES   SERVES: 4

| |
|---|
| 4 tablespoons olive oil |
| 2–3 shallots |
| 2 cloves garlic |
| 1 lb (450 g) zucchinis |
| ⅔ lb (300 g) baby, or small, eggplants |
| ½ teaspoon dried thyme |
| ½ teaspoon dried oregano |
| 4 tablespoons red wine |
| 1 can (19 oz / 540 ml) chopped tomatoes |
| 2 tablespoons tomato purée |
| Salt |
| 1 teaspoon ground coriander |
| 1 teaspoon ground cumin |
| 1 teaspoon ground paprika |
| ½ teaspoon cayenne pepper |
| 4 sirloin or rump steaks, about 6 oz (170 g) each |

**1** Heat 2 tablespoons of oil in a large saucepan. Peel and chop the shallots and garlic, add them to the pan, and cook over a moderate heat for 3–4 minutes.

**2** Meanwhile, rinse, dry, and trim the zucchinis and eggplants and cut them into ½ in. (1 cm) chunks. Stir them into the shallots with the thyme and oregano, and cook gently for 5 minutes.

**3** Add the wine, the tomatoes and their juice, tomato purée, and a little salt, then cover and simmer gently for about 15 minutes, stirring occasionally, until the vegetables have softened.

**4** While the ratatouille is cooking, put the spices into a small bowl, add a pinch of salt, and mix them together. Season each steak on both sides with the spice mixture.

**5** Heat the remaining olive oil in a heavy-based frying pan until a faint haze rises, then fry the steaks for 4–4½ minutes each side for rare steak, 5½–6 for medium-rare or 6–8½ for well done, depending on the thickness of the meat. Serve with the ratatouille.

**SERVING SUGGESTION**
For a hearty meal, add Polenta with Smoked Cheese (page 271).

*NUTRIENTS PER SERVING: calories 407, carbohydrate 9 g (including sugar 8 g), protein 46 g, fat 20 g (saturated fat 5 g), good source of vitamins A, B group, C, E, and folate, iron, and zinc.*

# STYLISH SAUCES FROM THE FRYING PAN

*When you fry meat, whether it is steak, chicken breasts, lamb, or pork chops, there is a great bonus. After you remove the meat, it leaves behind in the pan the delicious sticky juices exuded during cooking, just waiting to be made into a quick sauce by the technique known as deglazing.*

Each of the deglazing sauces that follow will make enough to serve four people. First, remove the cooked meat from the frying pan and put it in a low oven to keep warm. Then pour off all but about 1 tablespoon of fat or oil from the pan, being careful to leave all the sticky residue behind. Then make the sauce.

### SHALLOTS IN RED WINE
*The classic sauce for sirloin or blade steaks.*

Peel and slice four shallots, then peel and crush a clove of garlic. Sizzle both in the pan juices for 1–2 minutes then stir in 1 cup of red wine and 1 tablespoon of chopped parsley. Bring the wine to the boil over a medium heat, stirring and scraping the deposits from the bottom of the pan, until the liquid is reduced to about a third. Season to taste, then spoon over the steaks, and sprinkle them with more chopped parsley.

### MUSTARD AND CREAM SAUCE
*A sophisticated finish for butter-fried chicken or veal.*

Stir 1¼ cups (300 ml) of rich whipping cream into the frying pan, then mix in 2 tablespoons of Dijon or tarragon mustard (tarragon mustard is particularly good with chicken). As soon as the sauce begins to bubble, season it with salt and black pepper to taste and pour it over the meat.

To make an even faster sauce, mix the mustard, salt and black pepper with the cream while the meat is cooking, then stir the mixture into the pan juices to deglaze.

---

## FRIED STEAK

One of the most delicious fast meat dishes of all is a tender fried steak with a dark and crusty exterior surrounding still-juicy meat.

1 Brush a large heavy frying pan, ridged or flat, with oil and heat it until very hot.

2 Sprinkle the steaks with black pepper and fry them for 1–1½ minutes each side.

3 Then cook them (turning the meat over halfway through) for a further 3 minutes for rare steak, for 4½ minutes for medium steak, and for 5–7 minutes for a well-done steak. For rare steaks, keep the heat very high all the time. For medium and well-done steaks, lower it to moderate after the initial browning.

---

### SAGE AND APPLE SAUCE
*Especially good on pork chops or roast pork.*

Grate in an unpeeled cooking apple (about 8 oz / 230 g), discarding the core. Shred eight fresh sage leaves and add half of them, with 1 tablespoon of cider vinegar and 2–3 tablespoons of water. Stir over the heat until the apple is soft. Add more water if necessary, but keep the sauce chunky. Chop half a small red onion and add it to the pan with the remaining sage. Season to taste and serve.

### SPICED RED WINE AND RED CURRANT SAUCE
*An excellent dressing for lamb chops or venison steaks.*

Stir 2 teaspoons of cumin seeds, and ½ teaspoon each of paprika, ground cinnamon, and ground coriander into the pan juices with 1¼ cups of red wine. Swirl and stir, scraping up the sediment, until the wine comes to the boil then add 2–3 teaspoons of red currant jelly, mashing it to help it melt. Cook, stirring frequently, for 5 minutes until the liquid is reduced by almost half. Season and pour over the meat.

### CHUNKY TOMATO SAUCE
*Everybody's favorite sauce for sausages, it goes well with lamb or pork chops too.*

Fry a finely chopped clove of garlic in the frying pan until soft, then add 1 cup (200 g) of canned chopped tomatoes in tomato juice.

Boil the sauce fast for a couple of minutes to let it thicken, scraping up the sediment from the bottom of the pan. Season to taste, add a teaspoon of Worcestershire sauce and, if you like, a dash of Tabasco, and serve.

### BRANDY CREAM SAUCE
*A smooth, luxurious sauce for any lean red meat, but particularly beef or venison steaks.*

Stir 4 tablespoons of brandy into the pan juices and allow it to bubble gently for 1–2 minutes, stirring and scraping up the residue.

Add 1 tablespoon of chopped fresh thyme (or 1 teaspoon of dried thyme), 1 tablespoon of tomato purée, and 1 tablespoon of balsamic vinegar, and simmer for 1 minute, stirring until smooth.

Finally stir in ½ cup of heavy cream and bring it to the boil. Add salt and black pepper to taste and spoon over the meat.

FLASH IN THE PAN SAUCE:
SHALLOTS IN RED WINE.

# BEEF AND BEAN CHILI

*Nothing is quite as hearty as a bowl of tingling-hot chili con carne made with extra-lean minced beef,
cooked with sturdy kidney beans and served with tortillas in the easy Mexican style.*

TIME: 30 MINUTES   SERVES: 4

| |
|---|
| 1 small red pepper |
| 1 small, fresh red chili |
| 1 medium onion |
| 2 tablespoons sunflower oil |
| 1 lb (450 g) extra-lean minced beef |
| 1 tablespoon paprika |
| 1 tablespoon ground cumin |
| 3 cloves garlic |
| 1 can (19 oz / 540 ml) chopped tomatoes |
| 2 teaspoons tomato purée |
| 1 teaspoon dried oregano |
| ½ cup red wine, or beef stock |
| Salt |
| ½ teaspoon sugar |
| 2 green onions |
| 1 can (19 oz / 540 ml) kidney beans |
| 8 soft flour tortillas |
| 4 tablespoons sour cream |

**1**   Rinse, dry, deseed, and chop the pepper and the chili. Set the chili aside. Peel and chop the onion.

**2**   Heat the sunflower oil in a large, flameproof casserole and fry the pepper, onion, beef, paprika, and cumin over a moderate heat. Stir constantly, until the meat browns.

**3**   Peel and crush the garlic. Add it to the casserole with the chili, the canned tomatoes and their juice, tomato purée, oregano, wine or stock, salt, and sugar. Bring to the boil, reduce the heat, cover, and simmer for 15 minutes.

**4**   Rinse, dry, and chop the green onions; set them aside. Preheat the grill to high to warm the tortillas.

**5**   When the beef chili has been cooking for 15 minutes, drain and rinse the kidney beans, stir them into the casserole, and cook for a further 5 minutes. Heat the tortillas under the grill.

**6**   Transfer the chili to four serving dishes, then add a tablespoon of sour cream to each, sprinkle the green onions over the top, and serve with the tortillas.

*SERVING SUGGESTION*
A simple green salad, perhaps with some hard cheese, adds a cool, crisp freshness to this rugged chili.

*NUTRIENTS PER SERVING: calories 575, carbohydrate 53 g (including sugar 12 g), protein 39 g, fat 22 g (saturated fat 8 g), good source of vitamins A, B group, C, and E, and iron and zinc.*

### COOK'S SUGGESTION

*Tortillas are soft, thin pancakes made from corn or wheat flour, which you can roll and stuff with a spicy meat or bean sauce. Corn tortillas can also be cut into small triangles that are then deep-fried and sprinkled with salt to make corn chips.*

# MEATBALLS WITH CREOLE SAUCE

*Tender meatballs are easy to prepare for a filling family supper and come with a syrupy sauce of crisp, crunchy fresh vegetables, both spiced with cayenne pepper and hot paprika.*

TIME: 30 MINUTES  SERVES: 4

*For the meatballs:*

| |
|---|
| 1 large onion |
| 1⅓ lb (600 g) minced beef |
| 1 large egg |
| 3 tablespoons plain flour |
| ¼ teaspoon cayenne pepper |
| ¼ teaspoon hot paprika |
| Salt and black pepper |
| 2 tablespoons olive oil |

*For the sauce:*

| |
|---|
| 1 tablespoon olive oil |
| 1 medium green pepper |
| 1 medium red pepper |
| 2 cloves garlic |
| 2 sticks celery |
| 1 can (19 oz / 540 ml) chopped tomatoes |
| 1 bay leaf |
| 1 teaspoon cayenne pepper |
| 1 teaspoon hot paprika |
| 1 teaspoon molasses |

**1** To make the meatballs, peel and chop the onion. Put half into a large bowl with the beef, egg, flour, cayenne, paprika, salt, and pepper. Mix them together until thoroughly combined, then set aside.

**2** To make the Creole sauce, heat the oil in a large saucepan over a moderate heat, fry the remaining onion until softened, then rinse, deseed, and chop the peppers and stir them into the onion.

**3** Peel the garlic and crush it into the pan. Rinse and chop the celery and stir it into the pan. Cook for another 2 minutes.

**4** Add the tomatoes and their juice, the bay leaf, cayenne, paprika, molasses, and ½ cup of water and bring the mixture to the boil. Then let it simmer, uncovered, for 15 minutes or until the sauce is thick but the vegetables still retain a little crunch.

**5** While the sauce is simmering, cook the meatballs. Heat the oil slowly in a very large frying pan. With wet hands, shape the meat mixture into 16 balls, about the size of golf balls, and put them carefully into the hot oil. Fry them over a high heat for 10 minutes, until they are browned all over and just cooked on the inside.

**6** Season the Creole sauce to taste with salt and pepper and serve with the meatballs.

*SERVING SUGGESTION*
A steaming mound of mixed white and wild rices, or some Cajun Potato Salad (page 102), would be a good accompaniment.

*NUTRIENTS PER SERVING: calories 526, carbohydrate 19 g (including sugar 10 g), protein 35 g, fat 35 g (saturated fat 12 g), good source of vitamins A, B group, C, E, and folate and zinc.*

# BEEF BALTI

*Balti dishes are stir-fried curries that originated in Kashmir and are traditionally served with a bread accompaniment.*

TIME: 25 MINUTES  SERVES: 4

| | |
|---|---|
| 2 tablespoons sunflower oil | 1 red pepper |
| 1 medium onion | 3 medium tomatoes |
| 1 lb (450 g) steak | ½ lemon |
| 1 clove garlic | 1 tablespoon garam masala |
| 1½ in. (4 cm) piece fresh root ginger | 1 teaspoon ground cumin |
| 1 small, fresh red chili | Salt |
| 1 green pepper | *To garnish:* 3 tablespoons desiccated coconut, flaked or shredded |
| | *To serve:* 4 nan breads |

1  Preheat the oven to a low setting to keep the beef warm later. Heat up 1 tablespoon of oil in a large balti pan, wok, or frying pan. Peel and thinly slice the onion, and fry it over a fairly high heat for 3–4 minutes, stirring occasionally, until it is soft and lightly browned.

2  Meanwhile, trim any excess fat from the beef, then slice it into very thin strips. Peel and crush the garlic, then peel and grate the ginger, and rinse, deseed, and chop the chili. Add them all to the onion and cook over a fairly high heat for 5 minutes, stirring occasionally, until the beef is lightly colored. Remove from the heat and keep warm in the oven.

3  Rinse, deseed, and thinly slice the peppers. Add them to the pan, with the remaining oil, if necessary, and continue frying for 3 minutes, stirring occasionally, until they are softened and lightly browned.

4  Meanwhile, rinse and roughly chop the tomatoes, then squeeze the juice from the lemon and preheat the grill to a high setting.

5  Stir the garam masala and the cumin into the frying pan and cook, stirring continuously, for 1 minute. Add the tomatoes, lemon juice, and some salt and simmer, stirring, for about 3–4 minutes. If the mixture becomes dry, add a little water.

6  Sprinkle the breads with water and grill for about a minute each side. Return the beef to the pan and heat it through. Sprinkle with the coconut and serve with the bread.

NUTRIENTS PER SERVING: *calories 923, carbohydrate 90g (including sugar 16g), protein 43g, fat 46g (saturated fat 12g), good source of vitamins A, B group, C, E, and folate, and calcium, iron, selenium, and zinc.*

### COOK'S SUGGESTION

*Nan is a flat, tear-shaped bread from India that is authentically baked on the walls of a tandoor oven. To approximate this at home, sprinkle the nans with water before grilling to help them puff up and turn deliciously soft and light.*

# STEAK SKEWERED WITH TWO ONIONS

*A powerfully aromatic basting sauce made by combining Dijon mustard, Worcestershire sauce, and red wine vinegar tenderizes cubes of steak grilled on skewers with crunchy red and green onions.*

TIME: 25 MINUTES   SERVES: 4

1½ lb (680 g) sirloin or rump steak, trimmed of all fat

2 medium red onions

8 fat green onions

1 tablespoon Dijon mustard

1 teaspoon Worcestershire sauce

½ teaspoon red wine vinegar

Salt and black pepper

4 tablespoons light olive oil

*For the sauce, optional:*
6 tablespoons red wine

1   Preheat the grill to high. Cut the meat into 20 equal cubes. Peel, top, and tail the red onions, cut them in half widthwise and cut each half into four wedges. Rinse the green onions, trim to lengths of 4 in. (10 cm) and cut in half lengthwise.

2   Onto each of four metal skewers, about 16 in. (40 cm) long, thread five pieces of meat, alternating them with a combination of red and green onions.

3   Lay the skewers across the grill pan or a roasting pan, balancing their ends on the rim.

4   Mix the mustard, Worcestershire sauce, vinegar, salt, and pepper in a small bowl, then whisk in the oil.

5   Brush half the mixture over the top of the kabobs, then grill, close to the heat source, for 3–5 minutes. Turn the skewers, brush with the remaining mixture and grill for a further 3–5 minutes. If they start to burn, lower the pan a little.

6   The kabobs can be served on their own, but taste even better with a sauce. Remove the kabobs from the grill and keep them warm. Pour the wine into the roasting pan and stir over a moderate heat, scraping up any sediment from the bottom of the pan. Cook until the sauce is reduced by half, then season to taste, and serve with the kabobs.

*SERVING SUGGESTION*
Serve with mashed potatoes and a green vegetable or Orange and Sesame Carrots (page 256).

*NUTRIENTS PER SERVING: calories 375, carbohydrate 8 g (including sugar 6 g), protein 43 g, fat 20 g (saturated fat 5 g), good source of vitamins B group and E, and zinc.*

# ARABIAN-STYLE BEEF WITH FLAT BREAD

*Minced meat with pine nuts, flavored with cumin and allspice, is served with salad in this easy Eastern-style dish.*

TIME: 30 MINUTES   SERVES: 4

| |
|---|
| 1 cup (100 g) pine nuts |
| 1 tablespoon olive oil |
| 1 large onion |
| 1 lb (450 g) lean minced beef or lamb |
| 1 tablespoon ground cumin |
| 1 teaspoon ground allspice |
| 1 can (10 oz / 284 ml) chopped tomatoes |
| A bunch of coriander |
| 1 cucumber |
| ½ crisp lettuce |

*To serve:* ¾ cup (200 ml) sour cream, 8 soft flour tortillas or pita breads

**1** Preheat the oven to warm the bread. Dry-fry the pine nuts in a large frying pan, shaking the pan and stirring the nuts frequently until lightly browned. Transfer to a bowl and set aside.

**2** Add the olive oil to the pan and heat slowly. Halve, peel, and chop the onion, then fry over a moderate heat for 3 minutes, or until it has softened. Add the meat and fry it until brown, stirring to break up any lumps. Then stir in the cumin, allspice, and tomatoes and their juice and simmer for 10–15 minutes, stirring occasionally.

**3** Rinse, dry, and chop enough coriander to give 4 tablespoons and set aside. Rinse, dry, and chop the cucumber; rinse, dry, and shred the lettuce. Place them in separate serving bowls. Put the bread into the oven to warm.

**4** When the meat is cooked, stir in the coriander and pine nuts, heat

## EASY DOES IT!

*If you use pita bread instead of tortillas, make a pocket for the filling by cutting a slit in the side of the warm bread. Place a spoonful of the meat mixture inside, then stuff with shredded lettuce and chopped cucumber. Top the salad with a spoonful of sour cream and eat with the fingers.*

through for a minute or two, then transfer to a serving bowl. Put the bread into a napkin-lined serving basket to keep it hot.

**5** At the table, each diner takes a tortilla, places a spoonful of meat in the center, tops it with lettuce, cucumber, and some sour cream, then rolls it up, holds it in the fingers, and eats it. If using pita breads, make a slit in one side of each and spoon the meat and salad into the pocket (see box, above).

*NUTRIENTS PER SERVING: calories 689, carbohydrate 41 g (including sugar 10 g), protein 38 g, fat 43 g (saturated fat 13 g), good source of vitamins A, B group, C, E, and folate, and iron and zinc.*

# CALF'S LIVER WITH BALSAMIC VINEGAR

*Simple liver and onions is transformed into a memorable meal by a richly flavored sauce made with Italian balsamic vinegar, French mustard, a dash of cream, and a sprinkling of fresh sage.*

TIME: 25 MINUTES SERVES: 4

| |
|---|
| 1 large Spanish onion |
| 2 tablespoons olive oil |
| A small bunch of fresh sage |
| 4 slices calf's liver, about 4½ oz (125 g) each |
| Black pepper |

*For the sauce:*

| |
|---|
| 3 tablespoons balsamic vinegar |
| 1 tablespoon Dijon mustard |
| ½ cup (125 ml) light cream |

**1** Preheat the oven to low. Halve, peel, and thinly slice the onion.
**2** Heat half the olive oil in a large frying pan over a high heat and fry the onion, stirring, for 1 minute. Lower the heat, cover, and cook for 6 minutes, or until the onion is just tender and is beginning to brown, then transfer to a plate and keep warm.
**3** Meanwhile, rinse and dry the sage, strip off the leaves, and chop enough to give 1 tablespoon, then set aside.
**4** Season the liver with black pepper. Add the remaining oil to the frying pan and, when it is very hot, fry the liver for a minute or two on each side, until it changes color. Remove and keep warm.
**5** To make the sauce, bring the vinegar and 3 tablespoons of water to the boil in the pan, stirring and scraping up the browned residue. Reduce the heat and stir in the mustard and cream.
**6** Return the liver and onions to the pan, reheat them very gently in the sauce for 1–2 minutes, sprinkle with sage, and serve.

*SERVING SUGGESTION*
Serve with creamed potatoes. Put them on to cook before preparing the onion, and mash them while the liver is reheating.

*VARIATION*
The sauce can also be served with lamb's liver, fried chicken, or pork.

*NUTRIENTS PER SERVING: calories 271, carbohydrate 8 g (including sugar 6 g), protein 25 g, fat 15 g (saturated fat 5 g), good source of vitamins A, B group, C, E, and folate, and iron, selenium, and zinc.*

---

### COOK'S SUGGESTION

*Balsamic vinegar is carefully aged in fragrant wooden barrels—a process that slowly develops a deep and distinctive sweet-sour flavor.*

---

# VEAL PICCATA WITH SAGE AND LEMON

*A single fresh sage leaf pressed onto each tender slice of veal adds an unusual touch and a delicate fragrance to these escalopes, which are served in a refreshing lemon and butter sauce.*

TIME: 15 MINUTES  SERVES: 2

| 1 tablespoon plain flour |
| Salt and black pepper |
| 2 escalopes of veal, about 3½ oz (100 g) each |
| 6 fresh sage leaves |
| 1 tablespoon oil |
| 3 tablespoons (40 g) butter |
| ½ lemon |
| 4 tablespoons chicken stock or water |

**1** Preheat the oven to low to keep the veal warm later. Sprinkle the flour onto a board or large plate and season it well with salt and pepper. Cut each veal escalope into three equal pieces, press a sage leaf firmly onto each, then turn in the flour until well coated.

**2** Heat the oil and half the butter in a frying pan until the butter has melted. Add the veal to the pan and fry for 2 minutes on each side, then remove it and keep it warm.

**3** Squeeze the juice from the half lemon into the pan, then add the stock or water, and swirl over a medium heat until the liquid has reduced by half. Add the remaining butter and continue to swirl the mixture until all the butter has been absorbed into the sauce.

**4** Return the veal escalopes to the pan and cook for a few seconds on each side to heat them through. Serve immediately.

*SERVING SUGGESTIONS*

Serve the veal piccata with boiled new potatoes and a simply prepared green vegetable, such as frozen peas or fresh broccoli, or a side dish of Italian Baked Endive (page 258) or Zucchinis, Apples, and Persillade (page 260).

*NUTRIENTS PER SERVING: calories 324, carbohydrate 4 g (including sugar 0.2 g), protein 24 g, fat 24 g (saturated fat 12 g), good source of vitamins A, B group, and E and zinc.*

# LAMB CHOPS PROVENÇALE

*This lamb hotpot has a fine herby flavor and is quickly made on top of the stove with tender canned cannellini beans and tomatoes, and served with glorious onion and garlic-flavored mashed potatoes.*

TIME: 30 MINUTES  SERVES: 4

| |
| --- |
| 4–6 medium floury potatoes |
| Salt and black pepper |
| 2 tablespoons olive oil |
| 2 medium onions |
| 2 cloves garlic |
| 8 lamb chops, about 3½ oz (100 g) each |
| 4 sprigs fresh rosemary |
| ½ lb (230 g) Italian or cherry tomatoes |
| ¾ cup lamb or chicken stock |
| 1 can (19 oz / 540 ml) cannellini beans |
| Celery salt |
| 3–4 tablespoons milk |

1  Put a large saucepan of water on to boil. Peel and dice the potatoes and add them to the boiling water with some salt. Reduce the heat, cover the pan, and cook gently for 15–20 minutes, or until tender.

2  Meanwhile, heat the oil in a large frying pan or flameproof casserole. Halve, peel, and slice the onions and add them to the pan. Peel the garlic and crush it in. Fry over a fairly high heat until the onion has softened and is well browned, then transfer to a plate and set aside.

3  Add the chops to the pan and fry them over a moderately high heat for 2–3 minutes on each side, or until lightly browned.

4  While the chops are cooking, rinse the rosemary and strip the leaves from the stems. Rinse and roughly chop the tomatoes.

5  Return half the onions and garlic that you set aside to the lamb in the pan. Add the chopped tomatoes, stock, and rosemary, then increase the heat to high.

6  Drain the cannellini beans and add them to the pan with celery salt and black pepper to taste. Bring to the boil then simmer, uncovered, for 8–10 minutes.

7  Meanwhile, drain the potatoes, mash them with the milk, then stir in the remaining fried onion and garlic. Add a few extra chopped rosemary leaves to the potatoes if you like. Season to taste and serve with the lamb.

*NUTRIENTS PER SERVING: calories 711, carbohydrate 45 g (including sugar 7 g), protein 39 g, fat 43 g (saturated fat 18 g), good source of vitamins B group, C, E, and folate and zinc.*

# ORIENTAL LAMB MEDALLIONS

*Succulent rounds of the most tender lamb are served with an assembly of crisp, stir-fried green vegetables and baby corn, brightened with the Oriental flavors of fresh ginger and soy sauce.*

TIME: 30 MINUTES  SERVES: 4

| |
|---|
| ½ in. (1 cm) piece fresh root ginger |
| ¼ lb (110 g) broccoli florets |
| ¼ lb (110 g) leek |
| 1 bunch of watercress |
| ¼ lb (110 g) snow peas |
| ¼ lb (110 g) baby corn |
| 1 lb (450 g) lamb fillet, or 8 noisettes of lamb |
| 1–2 tablespoons olive oil |
| Salt and black pepper |
| 2 tablespoons peanut oil |
| 3 tablespoons lamb or chicken stock |
| 1–2 tablespoons light soy sauce |

**1**  Peel and chop the ginger and set it aside. Rinse the vegetables. Cut the broccoli into slices, the leek into matchstick-thin strips. Chop the watercress, top and tail the snow peas, leave the baby corn whole. Set them all aside.

**2**  If using lamb fillet, cut it into eight 1 in. (2.5 cm) thick medallions. Brush them, or the noisettes, with the olive oil and season with salt and pepper.

**3**  Warm a frying pan over a moderate heat, add the lamb, and dry fry it for 2 minutes, or until browned underneath. Turn and fry for 3–4 minutes until cooked but slightly pink in the center. Cover the pan and keep warm.

**4**  Meanwhile, heat the peanut oil in a wok or large frying pan. Add the ginger and the vegetables and stir-fry them for 3–4 minutes, until just tender.

**5**  Add the stock and soy sauce to the vegetables and season to taste, then cover and cook for 2 minutes more, stirring occasionally.

**6**  Lay two lamb medallions on each plate and spoon the vegetables over and alongside them.

SERVING SUGGESTION

As an accompaniment, try the Wild Rice and Fennel Salad (page 85).

*NUTRIENTS PER SERVING: calories 405, carbohydrate 8g (including sugar 3g), protein 30g, fat 28g (saturated fat 10g), good source of vitamins A, B group, C, and E and zinc.*

---

COOK'S SUGGESTION

*If you cannot find lamb fillet or noisettes, cut the eye of meat from eight lamb chops and use these instead.*

---

# LAMB CHOPS WITH RED CURRANTS

*Grilled lamb chops get a sophisticated crusty coating of whole cumin seeds and ground spices. Served with a sauce of red currants cooked in red wine and spices, this is a decorative and festive dish.*

TIME: 25 MINUTES  SERVES: 4

4 well-trimmed lamb chops, about
4½ oz (125 g) each

*To garnish: a bunch of watercress*

*For the sauce:*
2 teaspoons cumin seeds
1 teaspoon ground coriander
1 teaspoon ground cinnamon
1 teaspoon paprika
Black pepper
¾ cup red wine
3 tablespoons (50 g) sugar
7 oz (200 g) fresh red currants

**1** Preheat the grill to high. To make the sauce, mix all the spices with a good grinding of black pepper. Put half the mixture into a small saucepan with the wine and sugar, and set the rest aside.

**2** Rinse the red currants and reserve a few sprigs for a garnish. Run a fork down the remaining sprigs to remove the red currants; add them to the wine. Bring to the boil over a moderate heat, stirring gently, then lower the heat and simmer for 12–15 minutes, or until the liquid is slightly syrupy.

**3** Rub the reserved spice mixture into both sides of the chops and grill them for 6–8 minutes, turning once. Meanwhile, rinse, dry, and trim the watercress, discarding any coarse stems.

**4** Pour some sauce onto each plate and place a chop on top. Garnish with the watercress and red currants.

**SERVING SUGGESTION**
Serve with a green vegetable or with some mixed salad.

**VARIATION**
Fresh or frozen cranberries can be used instead of the red currants.

*NUTRIENTS PER SERVING: calories 400, carbohydrate 16 g (including sugar 15 g), protein 24 g, fat 24 g (saturated fat 11 g), good source of vitamins B group, C, and E, and iron and zinc.*

# LAMB NOISETTES WITH SPINACH

*Stir-fried spinach studded with the Middle Eastern flavors of raisins and pine nuts is a great partner to lamb noisettes, flavored with mustard, then roasted until tender.*

TIME: 30 MINUTES  SERVES: 4

| |
|---|
| 2 tablespoons olive oil |
| 2 tablespoons mustard (honey or herb-flavored) |
| 8–12 lamb noisettes, about 1¾ lb (790 g) in total |
| 2 large sprigs rosemary, optional |
| Salt and black pepper |
| ½ red onion |
| 3 cloves garlic |
| 1 medium tomato |
| 3 full tablespoons (50 g) pine nuts |
| 3 full tablespoons (40 g) raisins |
| 2 packs (450 g) young spinach |
| *To serve: crusty bread* |

**1**  Preheat the oven to 425°F (220°C). Use a little of the oil to grease a small baking tray.

**2**  Using half the mustard, spread some on top of each noisette. Rinse and dry the rosemary, if using, and snip some over the noisettes. Season with salt and pepper and set aside until the oven is hot enough.

**3**  Peel and thinly slice the onion and garlic; rinse and chop the tomato. Set them aside.

**4**  Roast the noisettes on the top tray of the oven for 10 minutes, then turn them over, spread with the remaining mustard, scatter with more rosemary, if using, and season. Roast for another 5–8 minutes, until cooked but still slightly pink. If you prefer them well done, cook a few minutes longer.

**5**  While the lamb is cooking, heat the remaining oil in a large pan. Add the onion and garlic, cover and cook over a low heat for 5 minutes, or until the onion is soft but not colored. Add the pine nuts and raisins and fry for 3 minutes.

**6**  Trim the spinach, then rinse and dry it thoroughly. Add the tomato to the pan and cook for 1 minute. Then add the spinach and a pinch of salt and stir for 3–4 minutes, until the spinach wilts and is only just cooked. If there is too much spinach to stir easily, cover the pan for a minute until the spinach wilts slightly, then uncover and stir-fry.

**7**  Divide the mixture among individual serving plates and arrange the lamb on top. Serve with crusty bread to mop up the juices.

NUTRIENTS PER SERVING: *calories 705, carbohydrate 48 g (including sugar 14 g), protein 54 g, fat 34 g (saturated fat 9 g), good source of vitamins A, B group, C, E, and folate and calcium, iron, selenium, and zinc.*

151

# LAMB'S LIVER WITH BACON AND ONION

*The wonderfully warm and mellow flavor and appetizing fragrance of fresh sage transforms
traditional liver and bacon, while onions in a creamy sauce lend a melting richness.*

TIME: 25 MINUTES  SERVES: 4

| 1 large onion |
| 8 large, fresh sage leaves |
| 2 tablespoons olive oil |
| 4 slices lamb's liver, about 3 oz (85 g) each |
| 2 tablespoons plain flour |
| Salt and black pepper |
| 1¼ cups lamb stock |
| 4 lean, rindless slices smoked back bacon |
| ⅔ cup (150 ml) sour cream |
| *To garnish:* small, fresh sage leaves, optional |

**1**  Preheat the oven to low to keep the bacon warm later. Halve, peel, and slice the onion. Rinse, dry, and shred the large sage leaves.

**2**  Heat 1 tablespoon of olive oil in a frying pan, add the onion, and fry it over a moderate heat for 4–5 minutes, until lightly browned.

**3**  Meanwhile, rinse the liver and pat it dry with kitchen paper. Put the flour onto a plate, season it well with pepper, then coat each slice of liver with the flour.

**4**  Stir the leftover flour and the shredded sage into the onions and cook, stirring, for 1 minute. Add the stock and bring to the boil, stirring. Reduce the heat; leave to simmer.

**5**  Heat the remaining olive oil in a frying pan and fry the bacon for 1–2 minutes on each side, then remove it from the pan and keep it warm in the oven. Add the liver to the pan and fry over a moderate-to-high heat for 2 minutes each side, or until lightly browned.

**6**  Return the bacon to the pan. Add the sauce and stir, scraping up any residue from the bottom. Simmer for 3–4 minutes, or until the liver is cooked but still slightly pink in the center.

**7**  Stir the cream into the pan and season to taste, but be cautious with the salt as the bacon may be salty. Simmer for 1–2 minutes to heat the cream.

**8**  Transfer to a warmed serving dish, garnish with the small sage leaves, if using, and serve.

*SERVING SUGGESTION*
Accompany with plain boiled new potatoes or mashed potatoes and sautéed zucchinis.

*NUTRIENTS PER SERVING: calories 374, carbohydrate 10 g (including sugar 5 g), protein 26 g, fat 26 g (saturated fat 10 g), good source of vitamins A, B group, C, E, and folate and iron, selenium, and zinc.*

# LAMB CUTLETS WITH FLAGEOLET BEANS

*A rustic dish of lamb cutlets fried with rosemary and accompanied by mixed beans gets a great boost of flavor from the sharp saltiness of capers simmered in a wine and cream sauce.*

TIME: 30 MINUTES  SERVES: 4

| |
|---|
| ⅔ cup (150 ml) lamb or chicken stock |
| ¼ lb (110 g) fine green beans |
| Salt and black pepper |
| 1 tablespoon olive oil |
| 5 tablespoons (70 g) butter |
| 1 lemon |
| 2 sprigs of fresh rosemary |
| 8 lamb cutlets or lean loin chops, about 3½ oz (100 g) each |
| 1 medium onion |
| 2 cans (15 oz / 425 g) flageolet beans |
| 2 cloves garlic |
| 1¼ cup (300 ml) dry white wine |
| 2 teaspoons cornstarch |
| 4 tablespoons heavy cream |
| 2 tablespoons capers, or 1 oz (30 g) caper berries |

**1**  Put a kettle of water on to boil. Preheat the oven to a low setting, then heat the stock.

**2**  Top and tail the green beans, rinse and cut them into 1 in. (2.5 cm) pieces. Put them into a saucepan with a little salt, cover with boiling water, and cook them for 5–6 minutes, until tender.

**3**  Meanwhile, put the oil and 1½ tablespoons of the butter into a frying pan and place it over a moderate heat. Wash any wax from the lemon, then grate the rind into the frying pan. Rinse and add the rosemary sprigs and increase the heat.

**4**  Season the lamb cutlets with pepper. When the butter starts to sizzle, put them into the pan, lower the heat to moderate and fry them for 4–5 minutes on each side, until golden brown and cooked but still slightly pink in the center.

**5**  Melt the remaining butter in a second frying pan. Peel and chop the onion, add it to the pan and fry over a moderate heat for 5 minutes.

**6**  Rinse the canned beans in a colander, then drain the cooked green beans into the same colander.

**7**  Peel the garlic, crush it into the onion, and cook for 30 seconds. Add all the beans, season to taste, and stir. Lower the heat and leave to heat through, stirring occasionally.

**8**  Remove the lamb cutlets and rosemary from the first frying pan. Keep them warm in the oven.

**9**  Pour off the fat from the pan, leaving the residue from the lamb behind. Add the wine and the juice from half the lemon and boil rapidly until reduced by half.

**10**  Meanwhile, blend the cornstarch with 1 tablespoon of water and stir it into the hot stock.

Stir the stock into the wine, bring to the boil, reduce to a simmer and stir in the cream. Add seasoning and the capers or caper berries and heat through. Do not allow the sauce to boil, as it will curdle.

**11**  Return the lamb cutlets and rosemary to the pan, stirring in any juices, and heat through. Serve with the mixed beans.

*NUTRIENTS PER SERVING: calories 944, carbohydrate 26 g (including sugar 4 g), protein 33 g, fat 73 g (saturated fat 39 g), good source of vitamins A, B group, and E and selenium and zinc.*

# LAMB BROCHETTES WITH PITA BREAD

*This is a delectable barbecue dish of grilled lamb coated in hot spices, served in warmed pita bread with crunchy mixed salad and topped with a cooling Greek yogurt sauce.*

TIME: 30 MINUTES  SERVES: 4

2 tablespoons olive oil
2 cloves garlic
2 teaspoons ground cumin
½ teaspoon cayenne pepper
1½ lb (680 g) lamb fillet or lean leg steak
1 lettuce heart
4 sprigs fresh mint
½ cucumber
4 tomatoes
1 red onion
Salt and black pepper
⅔ cup (200 g) natural Greek yogurt
8 small pita breads

1  Preheat the grill to high. Put the oil into a bowl, peel the garlic, and crush it in, then stir in the spices.
2  Cut the meat into 1 in. (2.5 cm) cubes, or kabobs. Toss in oil, thread onto brochettes, and set aside.
3  Rinse, dry, trim, and shred the lettuce and put it into a salad bowl. Rinse and dry the mint, cucumber, and tomatoes. Then shred the mint leaves, reserving a few whole leaves for a garnish, dice the cucumber, chop the tomatoes, peel and finely chop the onion, and add them all to the salad bowl.
4  Season the kabobs and grill for 4–6 minutes, turning once.

5  Thin the yogurt with a little water, and season to taste.
6  Remove the kabobs from the grill and set them aside. Heat the pitas until they puff up, turning them over once.
7  Slit open the pitas and fill with salad. Slide the grilled lamb on top, spoon over the yogurt sauce, garnish with the mint, and serve.

NUTRIENTS PER SERVING: *calories 899, carbohydrate 95 g (including sugar 10 g), protein 53 g, fat 37 g (saturated fat 15 g), good source of vitamins A, B group, C, E, and folate and calcium, iron, selenium, and zinc.*

# LAMB SAUSAGES WITH TOMATO SALSA

*Tender, lean lamb is blended to a smooth paste with spices and yogurt, then molded around a skewer to make tasty sausages, served with a mouthwatering fresh salsa and rice.*

TIME: 30 MINUTES  SERVES: 4

1 tablespoon (15 g) butter
1 medium onion
1½ cups (300 g) long-grain rice
Salt and black pepper
¼ in. (5 mm) fresh root ginger
1 clove garlic
1 lb (450 g) minced lamb
A small bunch of fresh coriander
1 tablespoon mango powder (amchoor), or lemon juice
1 teaspoon garam masala
1 teaspoon ground cumin
1 teaspoon chili powder
1½ tablespoons chickpea (gram) flour
3 tablespoons natural Greek yogurt
1–2 tablespoons vegetable oil

*For the salsa:*
3 tablespoons olive oil
1 tablespoon white wine vinegar
1 can (10 oz / 284 ml) chopped tomatoes
1 clove garlic
1 small fresh, green or red chili

1  Put a kettle of water on to boil. Melt the butter in a saucepan. Peel the onion, finely slice one quarter, and fry it gently for 3 minutes. Stir in the rice and fry for 1 minute.
2  Pour 3 cups of boiling water onto the rice, add salt, cover, and return to the boil. Reduce the heat and simmer for 15 minutes. Preheat the grill to high.
3  Peel and chop the ginger and garlic, roughly chop the remainder of the onion, then put them all into a food processor with the lamb.
4  Rinse and chop the coriander leaves, reserving a few for a garnish. Set two-thirds of the chopped herbs aside and add the rest to the food processor with the mango powder or lemon juice, the spices, chickpea flour, yogurt, and some salt and pepper. Blend to a paste.
5  Divide the mixture into eight equal portions and mold each into a sausage shape around a metal skewer. Brush with the oil and grill for 6–8 minutes, turning once.

6  To make the salsa, whisk the oil, vinegar, and tomatoes in a bowl. Peel, crush, and add the garlic, then rinse, dry, and finely chop the chili and add it, with the remaining chopped coriander. Season to taste.
7  Spoon the rice onto serving plates, top with the sausages, and spoon the salsa over them. Garnish with coriander.

NUTRIENTS PER SERVING: *calories 683, carbohydrate 69 g (including sugar 4 g), protein 36 g, fat 29 g (saturated fat 5 g), good source of vitamins B group, C, and E.*

## COOK'S SUGGESTION

*Gram flour, made from ground chickpeas, is available from larger supermarkets and Asian grocers, along with mango powder (amchoor).*

EASTERN PROMISE: *(top)* LAMB BROCHETTES WITH PITA BREAD; *(bottom)* LAMB SAUSAGES WITH TOMATO SALSA.

# MIGHTY BURGER

*This giant minced lamb and pork burger provides an unusual spicy pizza-style base for the family's favorite vegetable toppings—you can follow these suggestions or choose your own.*

TIME: 30 MINUTES  SERVES: 4

| |
|---|
| Oil for greasing |
| ⅔ lb (300 g) lean minced lamb |
| ⅔ lb (300 g) lean minced pork, or half pork and half lean minced beef |
| 2 teaspoons dried Italian herb mix, or mixed herbs |
| 1 small egg |
| 3 tablespoons (85 g) fresh white or brown breadcrumbs |
| Salt and black pepper |
| A few drops of Worcestershire sauce |
| 2 tablespoons olive oil |
| 1 medium onion |
| 1 large clove garlic |
| 1–2 teaspoons chili powder, optional |
| 1 small red pepper |
| 2 tomatoes |
| 3 oz (85 g) button mushrooms |
| ¼ lb (110 g) mozzarella cheese |
| ¼ lb (110 g) yellow cheddar cheese |

**1** Preheat the oven to 375°F (190°C) and lightly oil a 10 in. (25 cm) solid-base pizza sheet or a baking pan.

**2** Put the lamb and pork into a bowl. Add the herbs, then stir in the egg, breadcrumbs, salt, pepper, and a good splash of Worcestershire sauce. Mix well together.

**3** Press the mixture evenly onto the pizza sheet, or put onto the baking tray and shape into a 10 in. (25 cm) round. Cook the burger in the oven for 15–20 minutes.

**4** Meanwhile, heat the olive oil in a frying pan. Peel and chop the onion and garlic, add them to the oil, and fry for 5 minutes, or until soft. Stir in the chili powder, if using, then remove from the heat.

**5** Rinse the pepper and tomatoes and clean the mushrooms. Deseed the pepper and dice it, then slice the tomatoes and mushrooms. Cut the mozzarella into thin slices and grate the cheddar.

**6** Remove the burger from the oven and drain off any liquid, then increase the oven temperature to 425°F (220°C).

**7** Spread the onion mixture over the burger, add pepper, tomatoes, and mushrooms and sprinkle the cheese on top. Bake for 5 minutes, or until the cheese melts.

**8** Serve in wedges, with crusty bread, salad, and tomato ketchup.

**VARIATION**
Any combination of minced meats can be used, including poultry or venison. The herb seasoning can also be altered: an all-lamb mighty burger could be seasoned with rosemary and mint, a pork and beef burger flavored with sage. The toppings can include corn, olives, or any other pizza topping you like.

*NUTRIENTS PER SERVING: calories 630, carbohydrate 23 g (including sugar 6 g), protein 48 g, fat 39 g (saturated fat 15 g), good source of vitamins A, B group, C, and E, and calcium and zinc.*

# SPICY PORK BURGERS WITH GUACAMOLE

*These hot burgers, spiked with chilies, coriander, and cumin, make a fine lunch or supper dish
accompanied by a rich avocado sauce sharpened with the juice of a lemon or lime.*

TIME: 30 MINUTES  SERVES: 4

| |
|---|
| 3 tablespoons sunflower oil |
| 2 cloves garlic |
| 1 small onion |
| 2 fresh red or green chilies |
| 1 teaspoon ground coriander |
| 1 teaspoon ground cumin |
| A small bunch of fresh coriander |
| 1 lb (450 g) minced pork |
| 1 small egg |
| Salt and black pepper |
| 1 lemon or lime |
| 1 large avocado |

*To serve:* corn chips, or soft tortillas

**1**  Heat a tablespoon of sunflower oil in a small frying pan. Peel and crush 1 clove of garlic, peel and finely chop the onion, add them to the pan, and fry until soft.

**2**  Rinse and finely chop the fresh chilies, including the seeds. Set half aside for the guacamole and add the remainder to the onion. Stir in the spices and fry gently for 3 minutes more, or until the mixture is soft but not browned.

**3**  Rinse, dry, and roughly chop enough fresh coriander leaves to give 2 tablespoons and add half to the reserved chilies. Put the rest of the chopped coriander into a large bowl and add the fried onion mixture, pork, egg, salt, and pepper. Wash any wax from the lemon or lime, finely grate the rind into the bowl and stir the mixture, which should be slightly soft.

**4**  Heat the remaining oil in a large frying pan. Divide the mixture into four and pat each piece into a fairly flat burger. Fry over a moderate heat for 5–6 minutes on each side, until cooked through.

**5**  Meanwhile, make the guacamole. Squeeze the juice from half the lemon or lime and put it into a bowl with the reserved chilies. Peel the remaining garlic clove and crush it in. Halve and stone the avocado, and scoop the flesh into the bowl. Season, then mash together well.

**6**  Drain the burgers on kitchen paper and serve with the guacamole and corn chips or soft tortillas.

*VARIATION*

For a more substantial dish, fill lightly toasted rolls with the burgers, sauce, and a little salad.

*NUTRIENTS PER SERVING: calories 678, carbohydrate 33 g (including sugar 2 g), protein 32 g, fat 48 g (saturated fat 11 g), good source of vitamins B group and E, and zinc.*

---

### COOK'S SUGGESTION

*Use a food processor to speed up the guacamole. Process all the coriander, remove what you need for the burgers, then add the other guacamole ingredients and blend.*

157

# PORK FILLET WITH MUSTARD SAUCE

*Tender medallions of pork, with sweet apples and a splash of apple-flavored Calvados, are served in a mustard sauce.*

TIME: **30** MINUTES   SERVES: **4**

| |
|---|
| ¾ **cup chicken stock** |
| 1⅓ **lb (600 g) pork fillet** |
| **2 small dessert apples** |
| **4 green onions** |
| **2 tablespoons olive oil** |
| **1 level tablespoon plain flour** |
| **1 sprig of fresh thyme** |
| **3 tablespoons wholegrain mustard** |
| **Salt and black pepper** |
| **5 tablespoons heavy cream** |
| **2 tablespoons Calvados or brandy** |
| *To garnish:* **4 sprigs of thyme** |

**1**  Put the chicken stock on to warm through. Trim off any fat and tissue from the pork fillet, then cut it into ½ in. (1 cm) slices.

**2**  Rinse, quarter, core, and slice the apples, and rinse, trim, and chop the green onions. Set them aside.

**3**  Heat the oil in a large frying pan, add the pork fillet slices and fry over a high heat for 1 minute on each side or until the meat is very lightly browned.

**4**  Stir the flour into the pan and cook for 2 minutes, stirring. Then add the onions and stock and bring to the boil, still stirring.

**5**  Rinse and dry 1 sprig of thyme, then strip the leaves and add them to the pan with the apples and the mustard, salt and pepper. Continue cooking over a moderate heat for a further 4 minutes, or until the pork is cooked through.

**6**  Stir the cream into the sauce, then simmer gently for 2 minutes. Pour in the Calvados or brandy, increase the heat slightly and cook gently for a further 2 minutes, then transfer onto four individual plates to serve, and garnish each with a sprig of thyme.

*SERVING SUGGESTION*

Tender baby peas mixed with shreds of wilted lettuce, and a bowl of smooth Chestnut and Celeriac Purée (page 254), make good accompaniments to this dish.

*NUTRIENTS PER SERVING: calories 520, carbohydrate 11 g (including sugar 9 g), protein 36 g, fat 35 g (saturated fat 16 g), good source of vitamins A, B group, and E, and selenium and zinc.*

# GINGERED PORK ON WILTED WATERCRESS

*Slices of warm potato and seared pork fillet, garnished with ribbons of sesame omelette, make a
sandwich for fresh watercress that will wilt slightly and absorb the delicious Oriental sauce.*

TIME: 30 MINUTES  SERVES: 2

| |
| --- |
| A bunch of watercress |
| ½ lb (230 g) pork fillet |
| 1½ teaspoons minced ginger |
| ½ lb (230 g) potatoes |
| Salt and black pepper |
| 2 teaspoons sesame seeds |
| 1 large egg |
| 2 teaspoons sesame oil |
| 2 tablespoons vegetable oil |
| ½ teaspoon cornstarch |
| 3 tablespoons dry sherry |
| 1 tablespoon soy sauce |

**1**  Preheat the oven to a low
setting. Trim, rinse, and drain the
watercress and set aside.

**2**  Trim any fat and tissue off the
pork, then cut it into ½ in. (1 cm)
slices and place in a bowl. Stir in
the ginger and set aside.

**3**  Scrub the potatoes, cut them
into ½ in. (1 cm) thick slices and put
them into a saucepan. Cover with
cold water, add salt, and bring to
the boil. Then cover and boil gently
for 10–12 minutes, or until tender.

**4**  Meanwhile, fry the sesame seeds
in a dry frying pan, shaking them
over a moderate heat until lightly
toasted, then leave to cool.

**5**  In a small bowl, lightly beat the
egg with salt and pepper, and stir in
the sesame seeds. Heat the sesame
oil and 1 teaspoon of vegetable oil in
the frying pan. Add the egg and
swirl it over the base to make a thin
omelette. Turn it out onto a plate,
roll it up, and slice it thinly.

**6**  In a small jug or bowl, blend the
cornstarch with 2½ tablespoons of
cold water, then stir in the sherry
and soy sauce.

**7**  Heat the remaining oil in the
frying pan over a high heat and fry
the pork slices for 1–2 minutes on
each side until golden brown, then
transfer to a plate and keep warm.

**8**  Pour the cornstarch mixture into
the pan and stir over a moderate
heat until it boils and thickens.

Return the pork to the pan with any
juices and heat through.

**9**  Drain the potatoes and arrange
on two plates. Place the watercress
and pork on top and pour the sauce
over; garnish with omelette ribbons.

*NUTRIENTS PER SERVING: calories 508,
carbohydrate 19 g (including sugar 1 g),
protein 34 g, fat 31 g (saturated fat 6 g),
good source of vitamins A, B group, and C,
and selenium and zinc.*

# PLUM-GLAZED PORK WITH SPICY CABBAGE

*Plum jam, soy sauce, warm spice, and hot cayenne pepper go particularly well with pork chops, while the crisp cabbage served alongside gets its own spicy boost from chili and garlic.*

TIME: 30 MINUTES  SERVES: 4

| |
|---|
| 1½ lb (680 g) crisp green cabbage, such as savoy |
| 1 large, fresh red chili |
| 2 cloves garlic |
| 3 tablespoons good plum jam |
| 1½ tablespoons soy sauce |
| ½ teaspoon ground allspice |
| ½ teaspoon cayenne pepper |
| 4 pork loin chops, about 6 oz (170 g) each |
| 2 tablespoons cider vinegar |
| Salt and black pepper |
| 3 tablespoons olive oil |

**1** Preheat the grill to high. Halve the cabbage and discard the woody center. Coarsely chop the leaves, rinse them well, then drain them in a colander.

**2** Rinse, halve, and deseed the chili, and slice it finely. Peel and roughly chop the garlic. Set them both aside.

**3** Gently warm the plum jam and soy sauce in a small pan, season with the allspice and cayenne, then sieve, if necessary.

**4** Arrange the chops on the grill rack and cook for 5–7 minutes each side, brushing the warm plum glaze over them halfway through cooking each side.

**5** Meanwhile, mix the cider vinegar with 3 tablespoons of water and some salt and pepper.

**6** Heat the oil in a large saucepan, add the chili and garlic and fry them for 30–40 seconds. Add the cabbage and toss it in the oil. Stir in the diluted vinegar, cover, and cook for 4 minutes.

**7** Uncover the pan, raise the heat, and continue to cook the cabbage until all the liquid has evaporated. Serve the spicy cabbage with the plum-glazed chops.

*SERVING SUGGESTION*
Plain steamed rice provides a good contrast to the heat of this dish and helps to soak up the juices.

*NUTRIENTS PER SERVING: calories 568, carbohydrate 19 g (including sugar 18 g), protein 32 g, fat 41 g (saturated fat 13 g), good source of vitamins A, B group, C, E, and folate, and selenium and zinc.*

# PORK WITH EGG NOODLES

*French and Oriental flavors combine in this intriguing stir-fry of pork and vegetables, with whipping cream and pungent wholegrain mustard providing a velvety sauce that soaks into the noodles.*

TIME: 20 MINUTES    SERVES: 4

| |
| --- |
| Salt and black pepper |
| 1 lb (450 g) pork fillet |
| 8 green onions |
| ⅔ lb (300 g) celery |
| ⅔ lb (300 g) small button mushrooms |
| 1 tablespoon olive oil |
| ½ lb (230 g) egg noodles |
| 3 tablespoons wholegrain mustard |
| ¾ cup whipping cream |

**1**  Preheat the oven to a low setting to keep the pork warm later. Put a large pan of lightly salted water on to boil for the noodles.

**2**  Cut the pork into thin strips; season with pepper. Trim, rinse, and slice the onions and celery; clean and slice the mushrooms.

**3**  Heat half the olive oil in a wok or frying pan over a high heat and stir-fry the pork for 4–5 minutes, until lightly colored. Remove and keep warm.

**4**  Add the remaining oil to the wok or pan with the celery and half the green onions and stir-fry them for 5 minutes. Add the mushrooms and cook until soft.

**5**  Add the noodles to the boiling water, cook them for 3 minutes, then drain them well.

**6**  Stir the mustard and whipping cream into the vegetables and bring the mixture to the boil. Add the pork, let it heat through, then season to taste.

**7**  Serve the pork stir-fry spooned over the noodles, sprinkled with the remaining green onions.

**VARIATION**
Beef fillet or chicken can be used instead of pork.

*NUTRIENTS PER SERVING: calories 662, carbohydrate 48 g (including sugar 4 g), protein 40 g, fat 36 g (saturated fat 16 g), good source of vitamins B group and folate, and selenium and zinc.*

# SAUSAGES WITH SPICED WINE AND APPLES

*The family's favorite sausages get a delicate new flavor when they are poached in white wine and then browned in butter, and served with a sauce of apples, cinnamon, and shallots.*

TIME: 25 MINUTES  SERVES: 2

| |
|---|
| 1¼ cups dry white wine |
| ½ lb (230 g) good-quality pork or chicken sausages |
| 1 shallot or ½ small onion |
| 2 crisp dessert apples |
| 5 tablespoons (70 g) butter, at room temperature |
| ¾ cup chicken or vegetable stock |
| 2 tablespoons light brown sugar |
| ½ teaspoon ground cinnamon |

1  Bring the wine to the boil in a large frying pan and poach the sausages gently for 10 minutes.
2  Meanwhile, peel and grate the shallot or onion and peel, quarter, core, and slice the apples.

3  Gently melt a small knob of the butter in a second frying pan. Remove the sausages from the first pan, reserving the wine. Discard any loose skins and fry the sausages slowly in the butter until they have browned all over.
4  Meanwhile, add the shallot or onion to the white wine in the first pan, with the apples, stock, brown sugar, cinnamon, and the remaining butter. Then bring the mixture to the boil, reduce the heat, and simmer it until the apples become tender and the liquid is reduced to a thin syrup. Serve the sausages with the apple sauce.

SERVING SUGGESTION
This is an excellent brunch dish followed by coffee and croissants or chocolate cake. To make it into a main meal, add some mashed potatoes, green salad, and Glazed Onions (page 272) or Sautéed Brussels Sprouts (page 255).

*NUTRIENTS PER SERVING: calories 929, carbohydrate 42 g (including sugar 31 g), protein 15 g, fat 69 g (saturated fat 34 g), good source of vitamins A, B group, and E.*

---

COOK'S SUGGESTION

*Good-quality sausages are essential, but choose a mild variety, otherwise the flavor may clash with the apple sauce. Chicken, or chicken-and-turkey sausages are available from some supermarkets and specialist sausage shops.*

---

# ITALIAN SPIRALS WITH BURST TOMATOES

*Cherry tomatoes are guaranteed to be full of flavor, and here they are cooked to bursting point on a bed of oregano, chili, and garlic to complement the spicy flavor of Italian sausage.*

TIME: 30 MINUTES  SERVES: 4

| |
|---|
| 1 lb (450 g) length of thin Italian sausage (*salsiccia*), peppered or spiced |
| 2 tablespoons olive oil |
| 2 cloves garlic |
| 1 teaspoon dried oregano |
| ½ teaspoon dried chili flakes |
| 1½ lb (680 g) cherry tomatoes |
| Salt and black pepper |
| *To garnish:* fresh basil leaves |

1  Preheat the grill to high. Cut the sausage into quarters and wind up each length into a coil. Pass a thin metal skewer horizontally through each coil to hold it in place, then arrange all four on the rack of the grill pan.
2  Heat the oil in a large frying pan. Peel the garlic and crush it into the oil. Then add the oregano and the chili flakes and fry them gently for about 30 seconds, without allowing the crushed garlic to change color.
3  Spread the tomatoes in a single layer on top of the garlic and chili, cover and cook over a low heat for about 10–12 minutes, or until most of the tomatoes have burst and are half-submerged in the juices.
4  Meanwhile, grill the sausage coils for 5–6 minutes on each side, turning them about to ensure that they become evenly crusty and brown on all sides.
5  Uncover the tomatoes, raise the heat to moderate, and cook for a further 5 minutes, or until the juices have reduced and thickened. Press lightly now and then with the back of a spoon to ensure that all the tomatoes have burst.
6  Season the tomato sauce to taste with salt and pepper, then pour it onto four warmed serving plates and put a sausage coil in the center of each. Rinse and dry the basil leaves, strip them from their stems, and scatter them over the top.

SERVING SUGGESTION
Mashed potatoes or Polenta with Smoked Cheese (page 271) would both provide a creamy contrast to the chili sauce.

VARIATION
Other thin, spicy sausages can be used instead of *salsiccia*. Untwist the links and smooth the sausage meat into a solid column with your fingers, before winding it into coils.

*NUTRIENTS PER SERVING: calories 472, carbohydrate 6.5 g (including sugar 6 g), protein 30 g, fat 36 g (saturated fat 15 g), good source of vitamins B group, C, and E.*

SPICY SAUSAGE DISHES: (*top*) SAUSAGES WITH SPICED WINE AND APPLES; (*bottom*) ITALIAN SPIRALS WITH BURST TOMATOES.

# QUICK CASSEROLE

*These lean pork sausages, casseroled with flageolet and cannellini beans in a herby tomato and mustard sauce, elevate humble sausages and beans into the realms of haute cuisine.*

TIME: 30 MINUTES  SERVES: 4

| 8 large, lean pork sausages |
| 1/4 lb (110 g) rindless smoked bacon |
| 1 tablespoon corn oil |
| 1 large onion |
| 2 cloves garlic |
| 1 can (15 oz / 425 g) flageolet beans |
| 1 can (19 oz / 540 g) cannellini beans |
| 1 can (19 oz / 540 g) chopped tomatoes |
| 1–2 teaspoons dried mixed herbs |
| 1 tablespoon wholegrain mustard |
| 3 tablespoons tomato purée |
| Salt and black pepper |

**1**  Cut the sausages into 1 in. (2.5 cm) pieces with kitchen scissors, and dice the bacon. Heat the oil in a large flameproof casserole and add the sausages and bacon. Fry them over a moderate-to-high heat for 8 minutes, turning frequently, until the sausages are golden.

**2**  Meanwhile, halve, peel, and slice the onion. Peel and crush the garlic. Rinse and drain the beans; you don't have to keep them separate.

**3**  Remove the sausages and bacon from the casserole, drain on kitchen paper, and set aside. Pour away all but 2 tablespoons of fat from the casserole. Add the onion and garlic and cook over a moderate heat for 5 minutes, until softened.

**4**  Stir the tomatoes and their juice into the onion, and add the herbs, mustard and tomato purée. Rinse out the tomato can with 1/3 of a can of water and add it to the mixture. Bring to the boil, stirring, then add the drained beans.

**5**  Return the sausages and bacon to the casserole and season to taste.

Reduce the heat, cover, and cook gently for 10 minutes, or until the sausages are cooked through.

*SERVING SUGGESTION*
Serve the casserole accompanied by a green salad and mashed potatoes, or some warm, crusty bread.

*NUTRIENTS PER SERVING: calories 700, carbohydrate 41g (including sugar 10g), protein 29g, fat 47g (saturated fat 17g), good source of vitamins B group, C, and E.*

---

### COOK'S SUGGESTION

*Flageolet and cannellini beans are used here, but you can use kidney, pinto, or lima beans instead if you have them in the cupboard, or you can replace one can of beans with 1/2 lb (230 g) of frozen corn, peas, or fava beans.*

---

# HAM AND LEEK PIE

*An excellent casual supper, this variation on shepherd's pie pairs the smoky flavor of ham with the delicate sweetness of leeks in a mature Cheddar sauce, enhanced by juicy cherry tomatoes.*

TIME: 30 MINUTES  SERVES: 4

| |
|---|
| 2 lb (900 g) potatoes |
| Salt and black pepper |
| 1 lb (450 g) leeks |
| 5 tablespoons (70 g) butter |
| 1 lb (450 g) lean ham steaks |
| 3 oz (85 g) mature Cheddar cheese |
| ¼ lb (110 g) cherry tomatoes |
| 2 tablespoons plain flour |
| 1 teaspoon mixed dried herbs |
| 1¼ cups milk, plus 1–2 tablespoons |
| *To garnish:* a few sprigs of parsley |

1   Put a kettle of water on to boil. Peel and dice the potatoes and put them into a saucepan. Add salt, cover with boiling water, and cook, covered, for 8–10 minutes until the potatoes are tender.

2   Slice, rinse, and drain the leeks. Melt 1½ tablespoons of butter in a frying pan over a moderate heat and fry for 6–8 minutes, stirring frequently, until softened but not browned. Preheat the grill to high.

3   Derind and dice the ham. Melt 1 tablespoon of the remaining butter in a flameproof casserole about 10 in. (25 cm) wide and 2 in. (5 cm) deep, or in a frying pan with a flameproof handle. Fry the diced ham over a moderate heat for 5 minutes, stirring frequently.

4   Grate the cheese, cut the cherry tomatoes in half, and set aside.

5   Stir the flour and herbs into the ham and cook for 1 minute. Add the milk and stir until it comes to the boil. Add the cheese, stir until it melts, then add the leeks, season to taste, and reduce the heat to low.

6   Drain and mash the potatoes with black pepper, the remaining butter, and 1–2 tablespoons of milk. Place large spoonfuls of mash in a circle around the top of the ham and leek mixture and lay the cherry tomatoes in the center.

7   Grill the pie for 2–3 minutes, or until the top of the mash is golden.

Rinse and dry the parsley, snip it over the pie, and serve.

*SERVING SUGGESTION*
Serve with a green vegetable, such as Brussels sprouts.

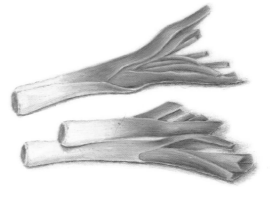

*NUTRIENTS PER SERVING: calories 576, carbohydrate 42 g (including sugar 8 g), protein 37 g, fat 30 g (saturated fat 18 g), good source of vitamins A, B group, C, E, and folate and calcium.*

# PORK CHOPS WITH GRAPEFRUIT

*This unusual combination works very well, as the slightly tangy sweetness of the pink grapefruit and spicy sweet ginger in the sauce counteracts the salty savor of the juicy pork chops.*

TIME: 20 MINUTES  SERVES: 4

1¼ cups (250 g) long-grain white rice

Salt and black pepper

2 ruby or pink grapefruits

1¾ oz (50 g) stem ginger in syrup

4 tablespoons stem-ginger syrup from the jar

4 lean pork chops, about ¼ lb (110 g) each

A bunch of watercress

1  Bring a large saucepan of water to the boil. Add the rice and some salt, then return to the boil and cook for 12–15 minutes, or until the rice is just tender.

2  Meanwhile, cut the peel and all the white pith from the grapefruits. Then, holding the fruit over a bowl to catch the juice, cut the segments of grapefruit from the connecting tissue and add them to the juice in the bowl.

3  Roughly chop the ginger and add it to the grapefruit segments with the ginger syrup.

4  Heat a large frying pan. Snip the fatty edges of the chops to prevent them from curling up. Dry fry the chops for 2–2½ minutes on each side, or until golden. Drain off any excess fat from the pan.

5  Add the ginger and grapefruit mixture to the pan. Bring it to the boil and allow it to bubble gently

for about 1 minute, then season with black pepper to taste.

**6** Meanwhile, rinse and dry the watercress and discard the stems.

**7** Drain the rice and arrange it on plates with the watercress. Top with the chops and the sauce.

*SERVING SUGGESTION*
Steam a mixture of green beans, broccoli, carrots, and snow peas and toss them in a little whipping cream or sour cream before serving.

*NUTRIENTS PER SERVING: calories 580, carbohydrate 72 g (including sugar 26 g), protein 40 g, fat 15 g (saturated fat 6 g), good source of vitamins B group, C, and E, and zinc.*

# HAM STEAKS WITH HOT SHERRY SAUCE

*Juicy ham steaks are quickly fried until brown then topped with a light sherry sauce spiced with cloves and Dijon mustard.*

TIME: 20 MINUTES  SERVES: 4

| 4 unsmoked ham steaks, about ½ in. (1 cm) thick and ½ lb (230 g) each in weight |
| --- |
| 1½ tablespoons (25 g) butter |
| 3 cloves |
| ¾ cup medium-dry sherry |
| 2 teaspoons Dijon mustard |

**1** Preheat the oven to a low setting to keep the ham warm later.

**2** Trim the fat from the steaks and pat them dry with kitchen paper. Heat the butter in a large frying pan until sizzling, add the cloves, then fry two steaks over a fairly high heat for 3 minutes each side, until browned. Transfer them to a serving dish and keep warm.

**3** Cook the other two steaks and add them to the dish.

**4** Add the sherry to the frying pan and bring it to the boil, stirring and scraping up the sediment from the bottom of the pan. Stir in the mustard, then boil the mixture for 2 minutes until the sauce has reduced and looks glossy. Discard the cloves, pour the sauce over the ham steaks, and serve.

*SERVING SUGGESTION*
Serve with rice and a vegetable such as broccoli or Celery and Apple (page 272). Or try it with Wild Rice and Fennel Salad (page 85).

*NUTRIENTS PER SERVING: calories 648, carbohydrate 4 g (including sugar 4 g), protein 40 g, fat 47 g (saturated fat 19 g) good source of vitamins B group and zinc.*

*Chicken with Mushroom Sauce*

# POULTRY & GAME

*Chicken, duck, turkey, game birds, rabbit, and venison all bring their healthy, lean meat to tempting grills, roasts, and casseroles, packed with deep, satisfying flavors.*

# CHICKEN WITH MUSHROOM SAUCE

*Tender, pan-fried breast of chicken is simmered gently in a smooth sauce of button mushrooms and green onions, laced with cream, to produce a luxurious and very satisfying dish.*

TIME: 30 MINUTES  SERVES: 4

| |
|---|
| 1 tablespoon olive oil |
| 1½ tablespoons (25 g) butter |
| 4 boneless, skinless, chicken breasts, about 6 oz (170 g) each |
| Salt and black pepper |
| 4 green onions |
| ¾ lb (335 g) button mushrooms |
| 1 tablespoon plain flour |
| ⅔ cup chicken stock |
| ⅔ cup light cream |

**1**  Preheat the oven to a low setting to keep the chicken warm later. Put the olive oil and butter into a frying pan and heat until they are sizzling hot. Meanwhile, season the chicken breasts on both sides with salt and black pepper.

**2**  Add the chicken to the pan and cook for 2–3 minutes on each side until golden, then reduce the heat to low, cover, and continue cooking for 8–10 minutes, turning once.

**3**  Meanwhile, trim, rinse, and thinly slice the green onions. Clean and thinly slice the mushrooms.

**4**  When the juices of the chicken run clear, transfer the breasts to a plate, cover, and keep warm.

**5**  Add the green onions and the button mushrooms to the pan, spread them out, and fry them over a moderate heat for 3–4 minutes, or until softened.

**6**  Stir the flour into the pan and cook for a minute, then add the stock, and bring to the boil, stirring constantly. Cook the mushroom

sauce for 2–3 minutes, then reduce the heat, add the cream, and stir in. Return the chicken breasts, and any juices, to the pan and heat through for 2–3 minutes more.

**7**  Put the cooked chicken breasts onto warmed plates, spoon over the mushroom sauce, and serve them immediately.

*SERVING SUGGESTION*
New potatoes and green beans, or a refreshing salad, such as Cucumber, Radish, and Melon Salad (page 101), would make a good accompaniment to the chicken.

*NUTRIENTS PER SERVING: calories 371, carbohydrate 4 g (including sugar 2 g), protein 41 g, fat 21 g (saturated fat 10 g), good source of vitamins A, B group, and E.*

# CHICKEN BREASTS WITH TARRAGON

*Tarragon, with its slight aniseed flavor, is one of the most delicate of all fresh herbs and is particularly well suited to this combination of simple chicken breasts with whipping cream.*

TIME: 30 MINUTES  SERVES: 4

| 4 boneless, skinless chicken breasts, about 6 oz (170 g) each |
| 2 tablespoons plain flour |
| Salt and black pepper |
| 1½ tablespoons (25 g) unsalted butter |
| 1½ tablespoons sunflower oil |
| 2 shallots |
| 4 sprigs of fresh tarragon |
| ¾ cup dry white wine |
| 1⅓ cups chicken stock |
| 4 tablespoons whipping cream |

**1** Preheat the oven to low. Trim any excess fat from the breasts and pat dry with kitchen paper. Dust with the flour and season lightly.

**2** Heat the butter and a tablespoon of the oil in a frying pan over a moderate heat and fry the breasts for about 6 minutes on each side.

**3** Peel and chop the shallots. Rinse and dry the tarragon, snip off the ends, and reserve for a garnish; strip the leaves from the remaining stems, chop, and set aside.

**4** Transfer the chicken to the oven to keep warm. Add the shallots to the pan with the rest of the oil, and fry, stirring, for 1 minute. Add the wine and half the chopped tarragon. Boil until the wine has reduced by half. Add the chicken stock and reduce by half again.

**5** Stir in the whipping cream and the remaining chopped tarragon, return the chicken to the pan, and warm it through for 1 minute on each side. Adjust the seasoning and serve, garnished with tarragon tips.

*SERVING SUGGESTION*

A selection of steamed vegetables, or Grilled Endive and Beet (page 259), would make a delicious accompaniment to this dish.

*NUTRIENTS PER SERVING: calories 405, carbohydrate 5 g (including sugar 1 g), protein 40 g, fat 21 g (saturated fat 10 g), good source of vitamin E.*

# CHICKEN STRIPS WITH GARLIC SAUCE

*Some of the great traditional flavors of France—garlic, wine vinegar, and Dijon mustard—are combined with chicken to give a full-flavored, creamy dish, served with light vermicelli noodles.*

TIME: 30 MINUTES  SERVES: 4

| |
|---|
| 1 lb (450 g) boneless, skinless chicken breasts |
| 4–6 cloves garlic |
| 2 tablespoons Dijon mustard |
| 1 tablespoon tomato purée |
| 2 tablespoons wine vinegar |
| 4 tablespoons chicken stock or water |
| 4 green onions |
| 2 tablespoons olive oil |
| ½ lb (230 g) vermicelli |
| Salt and black pepper |
| 2 teaspoons cornstarch |
| ¾ cup light cream |

**1**  Put a saucepan of water on to boil for the vermicelli. Cut the chicken breasts diagonally into long, thin strips.

**2**  Peel the garlic and crush it into a bowl. Stir in the mustard, tomato purée, vinegar, and stock or water.

**3**  Rinse and dry the green onions. Holding them together firmly, slice the green parts finely and push to one side, then slice the white parts finely and keep the two separate.

**4**  Heat 1½ tablespoons of oil in a frying pan over a high heat. Stir-fry the chicken for 1–2 minutes, until it turns white.

**5**  Stir the garlic and vinegar mixture into the pan and add the white parts of the green onions. Bring to the boil, cover, and simmer gently for 5 minutes.

**6**  Meanwhile, add the vermicelli and some salt to the pan of boiling water. Return to the boil and cook for 3 minutes, then drain well and toss in the remaining olive oil.

**7**  Blend the cornstarch with a little cream and stir it into the chicken. Add the green parts of the green onions, reserving some for a garnish, then add the remaining cream and season to taste. Stir over a moderate heat for 2–3 minutes until the sauce thickens.

**8**  Serve the chicken and sauce over the vermicelli and garnish with the reserved slices of green onion.

*SERVING SUGGESTION*
Sautéed Brussels Sprouts (page 255) are a good accompaniment as the sweetness of its diced bacon would balance the garlic and vinegar sauce.

*VARIATION*
A fresh pasta such as spaghetti can be substituted for the vermicelli.

*NUTRIENTS PER SERVING: calories 563, carbohydrate 56 g (including sugar 4 g), protein 36 g, fat 22 g (saturated fat 9 g), good source of vitamins A, B group, and E.*

---

### COOK'S SUGGESTION

*Chicken strips for this dish should be cut very thin, on the diagonal. You can save time by buying ready-cut strips, but make sure it is breast meat, which is tender and needs very little cooking.*

# SPANISH-STYLE CHICKEN

*Salty black olives, sweet red and yellow peppers, spicy chorizo sausage, and white wine bring the
flavors of the Mediterranean to joints of rich, dark chicken for an easy family casserole.*

TIME: 30 MINUTES SERVES: 4

| |
|---|
| **2 tablespoons olive oil** |
| **8 boneless, skinless chicken thighs** |
| **1 medium red onion** |
| **1 clove garlic** |
| **1 red pepper and 1 yellow pepper** |
| **1 can (19 oz / 540 ml) chopped tomatoes** |
| **⅔ cup dry white wine** |
| **1 tablespoon paprika** |
| **2¾ oz (75 g) chorizo sausage** |
| **1 tablespoon (25 g) pitted black olives** |
| **Salt and black pepper** |
| *To garnish:* **a bunch of parsley** |
| *To serve:* **crusty white bread** |

**1** Heat the oil in a large flameproof
casserole, then cut the chicken
thighs in half and fry them over a
high heat until golden.

**2** Peel and thinly slice the onion
and peel and crush the garlic. Add
them to the chicken. Rinse and slice
the peppers (see box, right) and add
them too. Fry until they are lightly
browned and slightly softened.

**3** Stir in the tomatoes, wine, and
paprika and bring to the boil. Slice
the chorizo thickly and add it, then
simmer for 15 minutes, or until the
chicken is cooked.

**4** Halve the olives, add them to
the casserole, then season to taste.
Rinse, dry, and chop the parsley.
Garnish with the parsley and serve
with some crusty bread.

*NUTRIENTS PER SERVING: calories 566,
carbohydrate 49 g (including sugar 13 g),
protein 44 g, fat 21 g (saturated fat 5 g),
good source of vitamins A, B group, C, E,
and folate and selenium.*

### EASY DOES IT!

*Cut peppers in half lengthwise
then cut away the stem, seeds, and
white membrane. Turn the halves
cut-side down and tap sharply on the
chopping board—any remaining seeds
will fall out. Slice shiny side down so
the knife does not slip on the skin.*

# GRILLED ROSEMARY CHICKEN

*Tender grilled chicken thighs imbued with the scent of rosemary, served with crushed new potatoes, are perfectly finished with a warm dressing of creamy, garlic-flavored mayonnaise.*

TIME: 30 MINUTES  SERVES: 4

| |
| --- |
| 8 sprigs of rosemary, each about 2 in. (5 cm) long |
| 8 large chicken thighs |
| 1 lb (450 g) new potatoes |
| Salt and black pepper |
| 5 tablespoons olive oil |
| 2 large cloves garlic |
| 6 tablespoons good-quality mayonnaise |

**1** Preheat the grill to high and put a kettle of water on to boil. Rinse and dry the rosemary and insert a sprig under the skin on each of the chicken thighs.

**2** Scrub the potatoes, put them into a saucepan, cover them with boiling water, and add a little salt. Bring back to the boil and cook for about 15 minutes, until tender.

**3** Meanwhile, arrange the chicken thighs, skin-sides down, on the grill rack. Brush with 1½ tablespoons of the oil, sprinkle with salt and pepper, and cook for 10 minutes, about 4 in. (10 cm) below the grill. Turn the thighs over, brush with a further 1½ tablespoons of oil, season, and cook for 10 minutes more, until the skin is golden and crisp. Turn off the grill, but leave the chicken under it to keep warm.

**4** While the chicken is cooking, put the remaining oil into a small saucepan. Peel the garlic, crush it into the oil, and shake over a moderate heat until it begins to sizzle, but do not let it color. Turn off the heat. Beat in the mayonnaise with 2 tablespoons of very hot water from the kettle, then cover it, and keep it warm.

**5** Drain the potatoes, return them to their pan, and crush them with a fork until they are roughly broken open and slightly flattened.

**6** Divide the chicken thighs and potatoes among 4 plates. Spoon over the mayonnaise, sprinkle with black pepper, and serve.

*NUTRIENTS PER SERVING: calories 552, carbohydrate 19 g (including sugar 2 g), protein 31 g, fat 40 g (saturated fat 7 g), good source of vitamins B group, C, and E.*

# RICOTTA CHICKEN WITH TOMATO SALSA

*Pesto sauce gives a wonderfully intense flavor to this dish and reveals its deep color when the chicken breast is sliced open, while a tomato, basil, and red onion salsa adds refreshing piquancy.*

TIME: 25 MINUTES  SERVES: 4

| 4 boneless, skinless chicken breasts, about 6 oz (170 g) each |
| 3½ oz (100 g) ricotta cheese |
| 5 tablespoons pesto sauce |
| 2 teaspoons olive oil |
| Black pepper |
| 2 beef tomatoes |
| 1 small red onion |
| 1 clove garlic |
| A small handful of basil leaves |
| 1 loaf Italian bread |

**1**  Preheat the grill. Cut a deep slit lengthwise down the side of each chicken breast to make a pocket.
**2**  Put the ricotta cheese into a small bowl with 1 tablespoon of pesto sauce and mix them together.

Spoon a quarter of the mixture into each breast pocket, then fold the chicken over to enclose the filling.
**3**  Place the breasts in an oiled grill pan, brush with the olive oil, and season with pepper. Cook under a fairly hot grill for 7–8 minutes each side until cooked through.
**4**  Meanwhile, rinse and finely chop the tomatoes, then peel and finely chop the onion and garlic, mix them together, and season with pepper. Rinse and tear the basil leaves and add to the salsa.
**5**  Cut four slices of bread and spread them with the remaining pesto. Place the grill rack over the chicken, lay the bread on top and grill until beginning to brown. Serve with the chicken and salsa.

**VARIATION**
If soft, mild-flavored Italian ricotta cheese is not available, use a curd or cream cheese instead, or some finely grated hard cheese, such as Gruyère or Cheddar.

**NUTRIENTS PER SERVING:** *calories 420, carbohydrate 21 g (including sugar 6 g), protein 53 g, fat 21 g (saturated fat 7 g), good source of vitamins A, B group, C, and E.*

### COOK'S SUGGESTION

*Use a food processor to speed up the chopping of the tomatoes, onion, and garlic, but take care to process each of them for just a few seconds, to leave some texture in the salsa.*

# CHICKEN BREASTS WITH PEPPER SALSA

*The fiery tang of a sweet roasted pepper and hot chili salsa, dressed in rich olive oil and fresh citrus juice, turns simple, grilled chicken breasts into a fiesta of color and taste.*

TIME: 30 MINUTES  SERVES: 4

1 red pepper and 1 yellow pepper

1 fresh green Anaheim chili,
or 1 fat green chili

5 tablespoons extra virgin olive oil

2 small cloves garlic

4 boneless chicken breasts,
about 6 oz (170 g) each

Salt and black pepper

½ lime or ½ lemon

**1** Preheat the grill to high, then rinse and dry the peppers and chili. Quarter the peppers, discarding the seeds, and put them, skin sides up, on the grill rack. Add the chili and grill for 15 minutes, or until the skins are blistered and brown, but not burned. Turn the chili over halfway through.

**2** Meanwhile, pour ½ tablespoon of oil into a large bowl and the rest into a small salad bowl. Peel the garlic and crush 1 clove into each.

**3** Add the chicken breasts to the larger bowl and turn them in the oil until they are evenly coated. Season them with pepper and put them, skin sides up, on the grill rack alongside the peppers. Grill for 7–8 minutes, until the skins are golden and blistered, then turn them over and cook them for another 7–8 minutes.

**4** When the peppers and chili are blistered, transfer them to a bowl, cover and set aside until they are cool enough to handle.

**5** While the chicken finishes cooking, squeeze the juice from the half lime or lemon into the salad bowl, with salt and pepper to taste.

**6** Peel the peppers and dice them finely. Peel, halve, deseed, and finely dice the chili. Stir both into the dressing and serve the salsa poured over the grilled chicken.

*SERVING SUGGESTION*
Add a vegetable side dish, such as Italian Baked Endive (page 258).

*VARIATION*
The salsa also goes well with grilled fish and can be made 1–2 days ahead and stored in the refrigerator.

*NUTRIENTS PER SERVING: calories 352, carbohydrate 5 g (including sugar 4 g), protein 39 g, fat 20 g (saturated fat 4 g), good source of vitamins A, B group, C, and E.*

---

### COOK'S SUGGESTION

*Anaheim chilies have a lively, mild heat and sweet aftertaste. Fat chilies are easiest to grill as they won't slip between the bars, and grilling gives them a smoky flavor.*

---

# LIME CHICKEN WITH WATER CHESTNUTS

*Scents of lime and coconut rise from this dish of spicy, stir-fried sliced chicken and crunchy water chestnuts tossed in a creamy sauce and served with almost instant rice noodles.*

TIME: 25 MINUTES   SERVES: 4

| ¼ lb (110 g) rice noodles |
| 1 lb (450 g) boneless, skinless chicken breasts |
| 1 oz (30 g) fresh root ginger |
| 1 fresh green chili |
| 2 cloves garlic |
| 3 limes |
| 1 can (7 oz / 199 ml) water chestnuts |
| 1 tablespoon peanut oil |
| ½ teaspoon sugar |
| 5 green onions |
| ½ cup (125 ml) coconut milk |
| Thai fish sauce, or soy sauce |

**1**  Put a kettle of water on to boil. Put the rice noodles into a large bowl, cover them with boiling water and leave them to stand, according to the cooking instructions given on the package.

**2**  Slice the chicken into thin strips and set it aside. Peel the ginger and finely chop it, then rinse, deseed, and dice the chili and peel and crush the garlic.

**3**  Wash any wax from the limes and finely grate the rind from two of them onto the ginger. Squeeze the juice from all three limes and set aside. Drain the water chestnuts, cut them in half, and set aside.

**4**  Pour the oil into a wok or large frying pan, add the ginger, chili, garlic, and grated rind and place over a high heat. When the oil is very hot, add the chicken and stir-fry for 2 minutes.

**5**  Add the lime juice, sugar, and water chestnuts to the chicken. Stir well, then cover, and cook over a moderate heat for 3–5 minutes, until the chicken is cooked through.

**6**  Meanwhile, trim, rinse, dry, and thinly slice the green onions.

**7**  Drain the rice noodles well, add them to the chicken with the green onions and the coconut milk, and toss together. Add fish sauce or soy sauce to taste (you won't need to add any salt) and serve immediately.

*VARIATION*
You can get an equally flavorful dish if you substitute thin slices of veal or turkey breast for the chicken.

*NUTRIENTS PER SERVING: calories 313, carbohydrate 32 g (including sugar 4 g), protein 30 g, fat 7 g (saturated fat 2 g), good source of vitamins B group and E.*

# CURRIED CHICKEN

*Tender diced chicken is flavored with gentle Indian spices, raisins, and almonds and finished with
smooth yogurt and cream, to make a mild curry that will charm the whole family.*

TIME: 30 MINUTES   SERVES: 4

| | |
|---|---|
| 1⅓ cups chicken or vegetable stock | |
| 1 medium onion | |
| 2 cloves garlic | |
| 3 tablespoons vegetable oil | |
| 3 tablespoons plain flour | |
| 2 tablespoons mild curry powder | |
| 1½ lb (680 g) boneless, skinless chicken breasts | |
| A small handful of fresh coriander | |
| 2 level tablespoons seedless raisins | |
| 3 tablespoons (25 g) flaked almonds | |
| ½ lemon | |
| 2 tablespoons natural yogurt | |
| 2 tablespoons heavy cream | |
| Salt and black pepper | |

**1** Put the stock on to boil. Peel and chop the onion and garlic and fry gently in the oil in a large frying pan for about 5 minutes, until soft.
**2** Mix the flour and curry powder in a large bowl, then cut the chicken into 1 in. (2.5 cm) cubes and toss them in the mixture until evenly coated. Add the chicken and flour mixture to the pan and fry, stirring, for 3 minutes.
**3** Rinse, dry, and chop enough coriander to give 1 tablespoon and reserve a little for a garnish. Add the rest to the chicken with the raisins and hot stock. Bring to the boil, stirring, then reduce the heat and simmer for 10 minutes.

**4** Toast the almonds in a dry frying pan. Squeeze the juice from the half lemon and set it aside.
**5** When the chicken is cooked, remove the pan from the heat and stir in the almonds, lemon juice, yogurt, cream, and salt and pepper to taste. Reheat very gently, but do not allow it to boil. Garnish with the reserved coriander.
*SERVING SUGGESTION*
Serve with rice, cooked while the chicken is simmering.

*NUTRIENTS PER SERVING: calories 508, carbohydrate 22 g (including sugar 14 g), protein 46 g, fat 26 g (saturated fat 8 g), good source of vitamins B group and E.*

# CHICKEN AND SPINACH CURRY

*This delicate chicken curry, lightly flavored with spices and spinach, is easily made in one large saucepan and served simply with hot nan bread for a relaxed but satisfying supper.*

TIME: 25 MINUTES   SERVES: 4

| |
|---|
| 3 tablespoons sunflower oil |
| 1 small onion |
| 1 clove garlic |
| 2 thin slices fresh root ginger |
| ½ teaspoon ground turmeric |
| ½ teaspoon ground cumin |
| ½ teaspoon ground coriander |
| ¼ teaspoon ground chili |
| ¼ teaspoon garam masala |
| 2 ripe tomatoes |
| 4 boneless, skinless chicken breasts, about 6 oz (170 g) each |
| Salt and black pepper |
| ⅔ cup (150 ml) heavy cream |
| 4 large nan breads |
| 1 pack (10 oz / 284 g) baby spinach |

**1**  Heat the oil in a large saucepan over a moderate heat. Peel and chop the onion and fry it in the oil. Peel and crush the garlic and stir it into the onion.

**2**  Peel and finely chop the ginger and stir it into the onion with the spices. Cook for a minute, or until the onion is slightly crisp.

**3**  Rinse the tomatoes, roughly chop them, and add them to the saucepan. Fry over a gentle heat for 7 minutes, until the tomatoes cook down to a dry pulp.

**4**  Meanwhile, remove any tough sinews from the chicken and cut it into bite-sized chunks.

**5**  Preheat the grill to high for the bread. When the tomatoes are ready, increase the heat to high, add the chicken, and stir-fry it until all the pieces have turned white. Season with salt and pepper, then pour in the cream and simmer for 6 minutes.

**6**  Put the nans under the grill to heat through. Meanwhile, rinse and dry the spinach, if necessary.

**7**  Add the spinach to the curry, press it down, and stir continuously until it wilts. Bring to the boil, then remove from the heat at once and serve, with the nans.

*NUTRIENTS PER SERVING: calories 1010, carbohydrate 85 g (including sugar 13 g), protein 55 g, fat 53 g (saturated fat 14 g), good source of vitamins A, B group, E, and folate, and calcium and selenium.*

# CHICKEN BREASTS WITH APPLES AND CIDER

*This lovely, creamy sauce for chicken breasts is made with sweet, crisp dessert apples caramelized in brown sugar and imbued with the tang of dry cider and Worcestershire sauce.*

TIME: 30 MINUTES    SERVES: 2

| |
|---|
| 1 tablespoon olive oil |
| 1 tablespoon (15 g) butter |
| 2 shallots |
| 2 crisp, red-skinned dessert apples, about 6 oz (170 g) each |
| ½ tablespoon light brown sugar |
| 2 boneless, skinless chicken breasts, about 6 oz (170 g) each |
| ⅔ cup (150 ml) dry cider |
| 1–2 teaspoons Worcestershire sauce |
| 2 tablespoons whipping cream |
| Salt and black pepper |

**1**  Put the oil and butter into a frying pan or flameproof casserole and heat gently over a low heat.

**2**  Peel and finely chop the shallots. Add them to the oil and butter in the pan or casserole, increase the heat to moderate, and fry, stirring occasionally, for 3–4 minutes, or until they are soft.

**3**  While the shallots are cooking, rinse, dry, quarter, core, and slice the dessert apples, then add them to the shallots and sprinkle them with the brown sugar. Raise the heat to fairly high and fry until the mixture starts to turn a golden caramel color.

**4**  Lift the shallots and apple slices from the frying pan or casserole with a slotted spoon and set aside.

**5**  Add a little more oil to the pan, if necessary. Add the chicken breasts and fry them over a fairly high heat for about 6 minutes, turning once, until golden.

**6**  Pour the cider over the chicken. Bring it to the boil and simmer, uncovered, for about 8–10 minutes, stirring occasionally and turning the chicken once more, until it is cooked. The chicken is ready if the juices run clear when it is pierced with the tip of a knife.

**7**  When the chicken is ready, stir in the Worcestershire sauce and whipping cream, and season to taste with salt and black pepper. Return the shallots and apple slices to the pan and warm them through for another 1–2 minutes, but do not allow the sauce to boil.

*SERVING SUGGESTION*
Serve the chicken with microwaved jacket potatoes (see box, below), or with rice or buttered noodles and a green salad or vegetables.

*VARIATION*
The sauce can be made with a dry white wine or richly flavored chicken stock instead of cider, if you prefer, but you must use dessert apples as cooking apples would lose their shape.

*NUTRIENTS PER SERVING: calories 495, carbohydrate 28 g (including sugar 28 g), protein 40 g, fat 23 g (saturated fat 11 g), good source of vitamins $B_1$, C, and E.*

---

### EASY DOES IT!

*Microwaved jacket potatoes can make a speedy accompaniment to many main course dishes. Prick the skins of two evenly sized potatoes. Place on a piece of kitchen paper in the microwave and cook on high for 6–8 minutes, turning them over halfway through. Wrap in foil and leave to stand for 3–4 minutes.*

# SPICED TURKEY BURGERS

*These healthy burgers have Oriental flavorings of chili, coriander, garlic, and lime, enhanced with
a dash of soy sauce, and are perfect for a quick, filling family lunch or supper.*

TIME: 30 MINUTES  SERVES: 4

| |
|---|
| 2 fresh mild chilies |
| 2 cloves garlic |
| A handful of fresh coriander |
| 2 limes |
| 1½ lb (680 g) raw minced turkey |
| 2 teaspoons soy sauce |
| 2 teaspoons sesame oil |
| 1 tablespoon cornstarch |
| Salt and black pepper |
| 1 tablespoon corn oil |
| ¾ lb (335 g) snowpeas |
| ½ lb (230 g) fresh bean sprouts |
| *To serve:* extra soy sauce |

**1**  Preheat the grill to medium, then rinse, deseed, and finely chop the chilies and put them into a large bowl. Peel and crush the garlic, then rinse, dry, and chop enough coriander to give 3 tablespoons, and add them both to the chilies.

**2**  Wash any wax from the limes, grate the rind from one and add it to the garlic and coriander, and reserve the other for a garnish.

**3**  Add the minced turkey, soy sauce and sesame oil, cornstarch, and seasoning. Work the ingredients together with your hands quickly, until they become well blended and stick together.

**4**  Divide the mixture into four equal portions, shape each of them into a burger, then flatten them on both sides using the blunt edge of a knife with a crisscross, chopping movement. The burgers should be about 4 in. (10 cm) wide.

**5**  Brush one side of each turkey burger with corn oil, then place them, oiled sides down, on the rack of the grill pan. Brush the tops with the remaining oil and grill them for 10–12 minutes, turning halfway through, until they are golden brown and thoroughly cooked.

**6**  Meanwhile, bring some water to the boil in a steamer, then rinse, top, and tail the snowpeas, and rinse and drain the bean sprouts.

**7**  When the water in the steamer has come to the boil, place the snowpeas in the steamer basket and sprinkle with salt. Cover and steam for 3 minutes. Then add the bean sprouts, cover again, and steam for 1–2 minutes more.

**8**  Arrange the vegetables on plates, lay the burgers on top, and garnish with the second lime, cut into wedges. Serve hot, with extra soy sauce as an accompaniment.

*NUTRIENTS PER SERVING: calories 282, carbohydrate 9g (including sugar 4g), protein 43g, fat 8g (saturated fat 2g), good source of vitamins B group, C, E, and folate, and selenium and zinc.*

### EASY DOES IT!

*To top and tail the snowpeas quickly, gather them into a bunch, tap them on the work surface to even up the ends then cut across with a pair of kitchen scissors. Turn and snip the other end.*

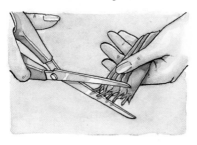

# RED-HOT TURKEY WITH CASHEWS

*Tender morsels of turkey, water chestnuts, and bean sprouts are given a fiery Eastern flavor and a rich honey and soy dressing, which balances well with the plain rice accompaniment.*

TIME: 30 MINUTES  SERVES: 4

| |
|---|
| 1½ cups (300 g) long-grain rice |
| 4 tablespoons plus 2 teaspoons peanut oil |
| Salt |
| 8–10 tiny dried red chilies |
| 1 clove garlic |
| 2 tablespoons cornstarch |
| 1 large egg white |
| 1 lb (450 g) boned turkey breast |
| 2 tablespoons runny honey |
| 6 tablespoons soy sauce |
| 2 tablespoons sake or dry sherry |
| 1 can (7 oz / 199 ml) water chestnuts |
| 8 green onions |
| 7 oz (200 g) fresh bean sprouts |
| 3 oz (85 g) roasted, salted cashew nuts |
| 2 teaspoons rice vinegar, or white wine vinegar |

1 Put a kettle of water on to boil. Put the rice into a saucepan and add 1 teaspoon of the oil, some salt and 3 cups of boiling water from the kettle. Cover, bring back to the boil, then simmer for 10–15 minutes.

2 Put the chilies in a pan of water, add 1 teaspoon of oil, bring to the boil, and simmer for 10 minutes.

3 Peel the garlic and crush it into a bowl, then stir in the cornstarch and egg white. Cut the turkey into cubes, add them to the egg-white mixture, coat well, then set aside.

4 Blend the honey, soy sauce, and sake or sherry with 4 tablespoons of water and set aside.

5 Drain, rinse, and dice the water chestnuts. Trim and rinse the green onions, cut them into chunks the size of the chestnuts, and mix them together. Drain the chilies. Rinse and drain the bean sprouts.

6 Heat 3 tablespoons of the oil in a wok or large frying pan over a high heat, until it smokes. Add the turkey and stir-fry until it begins to turn white. Add the cashews and the drained chilies and stir-fry for 30 seconds, then stir in the vinegar. Transfer the turkey to a bowl with a slotted spoon.

7 Add the remaining peanut oil to the pan, heat until it smokes, then add the diced water chestnuts and the green onions and stir-fry for 30 seconds.

8 Return the turkey mixture to the pan, with the bean sprouts. Stir for 30 seconds, then pour in the honey and soy sauce mixture and stir well to heat it through.

9 Drain the rice, and serve the turkey stir-fry on top.

*NUTRIENTS PER SERVING: calories 811, carbohydrate 82 g (including sugar 10 g), protein 43 g, fat 34 g (saturated fat 8 g), good source of vitamins B group, C, and E, and iron.*

# TURKEY ESCALOPES WITH LEMON AND PARSLEY

*Thin, tender slices of turkey served in a light sauce scented with fresh lemon make an elegant, aromatic dish.*

TIME: 20 MINUTES  SERVES: 4

| 2 lemons |
| --- |
| 8 sprigs of fresh parsley |
| 4 thin slices turkey breast, or turkey escalopes, about 4½ oz (125 g) each |
| Salt and black pepper |
| 2 tablespoons olive oil |
| 3 tablespoons (50 g) unsalted butter |
| 5 tablespoons chicken stock |

**1**  Squeeze the juice from one lemon into a bowl and set it aside. Wash any wax from the other lemon, cut it into thin slices and set aside for a garnish. Rinse and dry the parsley and set 4 sprigs aside for a garnish; finely chop the rest and set it aside.

**2**  Place the turkey slices or escalopes, one at a time, between two sheets of plastic wrap and pound them gently with a rolling pin until they are extremely thin. Season with salt and pepper.

**3**  Heat the oil and half the butter in a large frying pan over a high heat, until bubbling. Quickly fry the escalopes, two at a time if necessary, for 1½ minutes each side, until lightly browned and no longer pink in the middle. Then transfer them to a warm dish.

**4**  Pour the stock into the pan and heat, stirring and scraping up any residue from the bottom. Add half the lemon juice, the remaining butter, and the parsley. Reduce the heat to a simmer, add the escalopes, overlapping them if necessary, and any juices, and heat them through for 30 seconds on each side. Season to taste, and add more lemon juice if you like, then serve garnished with the lemon slices and parsley.

*SERVING SUGGESTION*

A mixed-leaf salad and crusty bread would be simple accompaniments. Alternatively, try a vegetable dish, such as Leek and Carrot Stir-fry (page 256) or Roast New Potatoes with Rosemary (page 267).

*NUTRIENTS PER SERVING: calories 281, carbohydrate 0.5 g (including sugar 0.5 g), protein 31 g, fat 17 g (saturated fat 8 g), good source of vitamins A, B group, and E.*

# TURKEY SALTIMBOCCA BROCHETTES

*This variation on the classic veal saltimbocca uses slices of turkey breast rolled with ham, fresh sage, and red pesto—beautifully moist and full of flavor—and served on rice strewn with cherry tomatoes.*

### TIME: 25 MINUTES   SERVES: 4

| |
|---|
| 1¼ cups (225 g) long-grain rice |
| Salt and black pepper |
| 1 lb (450 g) sliced turkey breast |
| 2 tablespoons red pesto sauce |
| 4 slices Parma ham, about 2 oz (55 g) in total |
| 12 large fresh sage leaves |
| Oil for greasing |
| 8 cherry tomatoes |
| 2 lemons |

**1**   Preheat the grill to high and put a kettle of water on to boil.
**2**   Put the rice into a pan and add salt and 2½ cups of boiling water. Stir to separate the grains, cover and simmer for 10 minutes. Remove from the heat and leave to stand, covered, for 5 minutes.
**3**   Meanwhile, rinse and dry the sage leaves. Place the turkey slices between two sheets of plastic wrap and pound them with a rolling pin until about ½ in. (1 cm) thick. Spread the pesto over one side of each turkey slice, cover with a slice of ham, and lay a sage leaf on top, then season with pepper.
**4**   Roll up each piece of turkey and ham from the long side. With a very sharp knife, cut the rolls into pieces about 1 in. (2.5 cm) long.
**5**   Holding each piece firmly to prevent it unrolling, divide the rolls among 4 skewers, carefully inserting the skewers sideways.
**6**   Lightly oil a baking tray, lay the brochettes on it and grill them for 5–6 minutes on each side, or until the rolls are golden and the turkey juices are no longer pink.
**7**   Rinse and halve the cherry tomatoes and add them to the rice. Wash any wax from the lemons.

Finely grate the rind of one lemon over the rice and mix thoroughly. Cut the other lemon into wedges and set them aside.
**8**   Spoon the rice onto warmed plates, place the skewers on top, and pour over any pan juices. Serve garnished with the lemon wedges.
*SERVING SUGGESTION*
A simple green salad is all you need to serve with this delicious dish.

*NUTRIENTS PER SERVING: calories 437, carbohydrate 46 g (including sugar 1 g), protein 40 g, fat 10 g (saturated fat 3 g), good source of vitamins B group and E.*

# DUCK BREASTS WITH GINGER SAUCE

*A wonderful sauce made with four different kinds of ginger makes a splendid accompaniment to duck, served on a bed of lightly stir-fried leeks and finished with fruity raspberry vinegar.*

TIME: 30 MINUTES  SERVES: 4

| | |
|---|---|
| 4 boneless duck breasts, about ½ lb (230 g) each | 3 tablespoons raspberry vinegar |
| | 2 tablespoons stem ginger syrup |
| 1 tablespoon (20 g) fresh root ginger | ¾ cup (200 ml) green ginger wine |
| 1 piece preserved stem ginger | 1 cup chicken stock |
| 2 medium leeks | 1 tablespoon (15 g) butter |
| | Salt and black pepper |

**1**  Preheat the oven to a low setting to keep the duck warm later. Dry fry the duck breasts, skin sides down, over a moderate heat for about 8 minutes, turn and cook for a further 6 minutes.

**2**  While the duck is cooking, peel the fresh ginger and cut it into thin strips. Chop the stem ginger and set both aside.

**3**  Trim the leeks, cut them in half lengthwise, rinse them well, then cut them into matchstick-sized strips and set them aside.

**4**  Transfer the cooked duck to the oven to keep warm. Drain off all but about a tablespoon of the duck fat. Add the vinegar and bring it to the boil, scraping up the brown residue, then add the fresh and stem ginger, ginger syrup, ginger wine, and stock. Bring back to the boil, reduce the heat and simmer for 8–10 minutes, until the liquid has reduced by half.

**5**  Meanwhile, melt the butter in a small frying pan, add the leeks, season with salt and pepper, and stir-fry gently for 3–4 minutes until just tender.

**6**  Return the duck breasts to the ginger sauce, reheat for 2 minutes, then add salt and pepper to taste.

**7**  Arrange the leeks on a serving dish, lay the duck breasts on top, and spoon over the ginger sauce.

*SERVING SUGGESTION*
Sweet Potato Rösti (page 266) or potato pancakes complement the spicy flavor of the duck breasts.

*VARIATION*
If you would prefer a thicker sauce, dissolve 1 teaspoon of arrowroot in 3 tablespoons of cold water, then pour it into the sauce and simmer for 2 minutes before you return the duck to the pan.

*NUTRIENTS PER SERVING: calories 914, carbohydrate 15 g (including sugar 14 g), protein 27 g, fat 78 g (saturated fat 23 g), good source of vitamins B group, and zinc.*

# DUCK BREASTS WITH BLACKBERRY SAUCE

*This simple but extravagantly flavored dish of tender duck breasts coated in exotic spices is served in a fruity wine sauce, and is perfect for a dinner party or a special celebration.*

TIME: 25 MINUTES   SERVES: 4

---

4 boneless duck breasts with skin, about 6 oz (170 g) each

¼ teaspoon Chinese five-spice powder

Salt and black pepper

5 tablespoons crème de mûres

5 tablespoons red wine

½ small cinnamon stick

1 star anise, optional

1 small orange

10 oz (280 g) fresh blackberries

2 level teaspoons arrowroot

---

**1** Remove any sinews from the duck and lightly score the fat into a diamond pattern. Mix the five-spice powder with some salt and pepper and rub it over the breasts.

**2** Put the crème de mûres, wine, cinnamon, and star anise, if using, into a small pan. Wash any wax from the orange, grate the rind into the pan, then bring to the boil.

**3** Meanwhile, cook the duck, skin sides down, in a dry frying pan over a moderate heat for 4–5 minutes, until the skins have turned a golden brown and enough fat has been released to cook the other sides. Turn and cook 5–6 minutes more for medium-rare, longer for well-done. Spoon off excess fat.

**4** While the duck is cooking, rinse the blackberries and add them to the wine. Squeeze the orange. Add half the juice to the wine, return to the boil, reduce the heat, and simmer gently for 5 minutes. Blend the rest of the juice with the arrowroot.

**5** Strain the blackberries into a bowl and set them aside. Return the liquid to the pan and stir in the blended arrowroot. Bring back to the boil, stirring, until it thickens, then add the blackberries and heat through. Slice the duck breasts and serve with the blackberry sauce.

*SERVING SUGGESTION*
Cut up boiled new potatoes and mix them with whipping cream.

*VARIATION*
Crème de cassis (black currant liqueur) makes a very good alternative to crème de mûres (blackberry liqueur). Both liqueurs are sold in most liquor stores.

*NUTRIENTS PER SERVING: calories 772, carbohydrate 13 g (including sugar 11 g), protein 24 g, fat 65 g (saturated fat 19 g), good source of vitamins B group, C, and E, and zinc.*

# DUCK KABOBS WITH HONEY AND ORANGE

*A classic combination, Duck à l'Orange is given a Chinese touch in these sophisticated kabobs, infused with the flavors of orange juice, honey, and soy sauce and served with scented rice.*

TIME: 20 MINUTES  SERVES: 2

| ¾ cup (150 g) white long-grain or basmati rice |
| Salt |
| 1 bay leaf or cinnamon stick |
| 1 large green pepper |
| 2 unskinned, boneless duck breasts, about ¾ lb (335 g) altogether |
| 1 orange |
| 4 tablespoons thick honey |
| 2 teaspoons soy sauce |

**1** Put a kettle of water on to boil, and preheat the grill to high.

**2** Put the rice, a pinch of salt, and the bay leaf or cinnamon stick in a large saucepan and add boiling water to reach 1 in. (2.5 cm) above the surface of the rice. Bring the water back to the boil, cover, and simmer gently for 15 minutes or until the rice is tender.

**3** Meanwhile, rinse, dry, and deseed the green pepper. Cut the pepper and the unskinned duck breasts into equal-sized cubes and thread them alternately onto two metal skewers.

**4** To make the basting sauce, wash any wax from the orange, finely grate the rind—or use a zester to remove it—and put it into a small pan. Squeeze 2 tablespoons of juice from the orange and add it to the pan, with the honey and soy sauce.

**5** Place the kabobs on the rack of the grill pan and baste them with the sauce. Grill for 4–5 minutes, then turn them over, baste with more sauce and any pan juices, and grill for a further 4–5 minutes.

They are ready when the duck is cooked, the skin is crispy at the edges, and the peppers have softened and browned a little.

**6** Warm the remaining sauce. Drain the rice, removing the bay leaf or cinnamon stick, and serve it with the kabobs. Pour the juices from the grill pan into the sauce, heat through, and transfer to a jug to accompany the kabobs.

*SERVING SUGGESTION*
A simple stir-fry of bean sprouts, snowpeas, and thinly sliced carrots and zucchinis would be the best accompaniment.

*NUTRIENTS PER SERVING: calories 1110, carbohydrate 101 g (including sugar 40 g), protein 30 g, fat 66 g (saturated fat 19 g), good source of vitamins B group and C, and zinc.*

# MUSTARD-CRUSTED RABBIT

*Mild mustard, lemon, and thick yogurt make a crisp coating for tasty pieces of grilled rabbit.*
*Mouthwatering, golden potatoes fried in rich fat are the only accompaniment they need.*

TIME: 30 MINUTES  SERVES: 2

| |
|---|
| 4 medium potatoes |
| Salt and black pepper |
| 2 boneless rabbit joints, about 5 oz (140 g) each |
| 1 tablespoon vegetable oil |
| 2 teaspoons Dijon or tarragon mustard |
| 3 tablespoons natural Greek yogurt |
| ½ lemon |
| 4 tablespoons (50 g) duck, goose, or pork fat, or 2 tablespoons olive oil and 1½ tablespoons (25 g) butter |
| *To garnish:* 2 sprigs of tarragon |
| *To serve:* ½ lemon |

**1**  Preheat the grill to high and put a kettle of water on to boil.

**2**  Scrub the potatoes and put them into a pan with some salt. Cover with boiling water, bring back to the boil and cook for 8 minutes, then drain them and leave to cool.

**3**  Meanwhile, arrange the grill so the meat will be about 4 in. (10 cm) from the heat, and lay the rabbit joints on the grill rack.

**4**  Mix the vegetable oil with the mustard, yogurt, 1 teaspoon of lemon juice, and seasoning. Brush half the mixture over the rabbit joints, grill them for 6–7 minutes, then turn them over, brush with the remaining mixture, and grill for a further 6–7 minutes.

**5**  Meanwhile, cut the cooled potatoes into 1¼ in. (3 cm) cubes. Heat the fat or the olive oil and butter in a frying pan and fry them for 10–12 minutes over a moderate heat, shaking the pan and turning them frequently until they are golden. Drain on kitchen paper and sprinkle with salt.

**6**  Rinse and dry the tarragon and cut the lemon half into wedges.

**7**  Transfer the cooked rabbit onto two serving plates and garnish each joint with a sprig of tarragon. Serve them with the fried potatoes and wedges of lemon.

NUTRIENTS PER SERVING: *calories 724, carbohydrate 49 g (including sugar 6 g), protein 41 g, fat 42 g (saturated fat 16 g), good source of vitamins A, B group, C, E, and folate, and selenium and zinc.*

# PHEASANT BREASTS WITH PANCETTA AND YELLOW PEPPERS

*Breast of pheasant, an exotic dinner party dish, is enveloped in a protective wrap of Italian smoked pork and bay leaves and roasted with eye-catching yellow peppers.*

TIME: 30 MINUTES   SERVES: 4

| |
| --- |
| **Black pepper** |
| **4 pheasant breast fillets, about 4 oz (110 g) each** |
| **4 slices pancetta, about ½ oz (15 g) each (see box, page 40)** |
| **4 bay leaves** |
| **2 large yellow peppers** |
| **1–2 tablespoons olive oil** |

**1**   Preheat the oven to 450°F (230°C). Grind black pepper over the pheasant breasts and wrap a slice of pancetta around each of them, tucking a bay leaf between the breast and the ham.
**2**   Rinse, dry, quarter, and deseed the peppers, remove the white pith, then brush them all over with a little of the olive oil.
**3**   Spread the remaining oil over a roasting pan. Then arrange the wrapped-up breasts in the pan with the peppers, skin sides up, and bake them on the top rack of the oven for 20 minutes. The dish is ready when the breasts are cooked, the pancetta is crisp, and the peppers are scorched.

*SERVING SUGGESTION*
Serve the pheasant with golden roast potatoes (see box, above right) and watercress or a green salad, and follow with fresh bread and a soft or blue cheese. Roast celeriac, kohlrabi, or other root vegetables would also go well with this dish.

---

### COOK'S SUGGESTION

*If you would like to serve golden roast potatoes, the traditional accompaniment to roast game, the best potatoes to use are a good baking variety such as Idaho. Scrub 4 potatoes, slice them into rounds ⅛ in. (3 mm) thick and place on a greased baking tray. Sprinkle with a mixture of melted butter and oil, scatter with salt, and cook with the pheasant for 25 minutes, or until golden brown.*

---

*VARIATION*
Boned breast fillets of pheasant are available from traditional butchers and some supermarkets in winter and late fall. However, you can also have excellent results if you substitute breast fillets from guinea fowl or free-range chicken for the pheasant.

*NUTRIENTS PER SERVING: calories 253, carbohydrate 5g (including sugar 5g), protein 33g, fat 11g (saturated fat 1g), good source of vitamins B group, C, and E.*

# PHEASANT BREASTS WITH WINE SAUCE

*Tender pheasant breasts are given a protective coating of herbs and flash-fried to keep them moist,
then served with a delicate white wine and orange sauce and a sprinkling of parsley.*

TIME: 30 MINUTES  SERVES: 4

| |
|---|
| ¾ cup game, veal, or chicken stock |
| A small bunch of parsley |
| 2 tablespoons olive oil |
| 2 teaspoons dried mixed Italian herbs |
| Salt and black pepper |
| 1¾ lb (790 g) boneless pheasant breasts |
| 1 large orange |
| 3 tablespoons (50 g) butter |
| 2 tablespoons brandy |
| ½ cup dry white wine |
| 1½ tablespoons plain flour |
| 1 teaspoon sugar |
| 3 tablespoons whipping cream |

1  Preheat the oven to a low setting to keep the pheasant warm later, then put the stock on to heat. Rinse and dry the parsley and set 4 sprigs aside to use for a garnish, then chop enough of the remaining parsley to give 3 tablespoons and put it into a mixing bowl.

2  Add the oil to the bowl with the dried herbs, salt, and a generous grinding of black pepper.

3  Skin the pheasant breasts and cut each one horizontally into two thin slices. Add them to the bowl and turn them gently until evenly coated with the herb mixture.

4  Wash any wax from the orange and finely grate the rind, or remove it with a zester, and set it aside.

Squeeze the juice from the orange and set it aside.

5  Melt half the butter in a large frying pan until sizzling hot, setting the rest aside to soften, then add the sliced pheasant and fry over a fairly high heat for 1 minute on each side, or until lightly browned. Do not overcook it as it will become dry.

6  Add the orange rind and brandy and cook for 1–2 minutes until the brandy has almost evaporated. Then transfer the meat to a plate, cover, and keep warm in the oven.

7  Pour the orange juice and wine into the pan and boil until the liquid reduces by half. Meanwhile, blend the remaining butter with the flour to make a smooth paste.

8  Add the hot stock to the pan and bring it to the boil, then gradually whisk in knobs of the butter-and-flour paste. Reduce the heat, stir in the sugar, and let the sauce simmer, uncovered, for 3 minutes. Then add the whipping cream and heat through for 1 minute.

9  Transfer the pheasant slices to individual plates, pour over the sauce, and garnish the dish with the remaining parsley.

SERVING SUGGESTION
The best accompaniment for this rich dish is some green fettuccine, which will cook while you make the sauce.

*NUTRIENTS PER SERVING: calories 559,
carbohydrate 8 g (including sugar 3 g),
protein 53 g, fat 32 g (saturated fat 16 g),
good source of vitamins A and E.*

# ROAST PARTRIDGES IN MARMALADE SAUCE

*Roast partridges with their subtle, delicate flavor are partnered here with a deliciously unusual, fruity sauce made from a blend of sweet, thick-cut orange marmalade and white wine.*

TIME: 30 MINUTES  SERVES: 4

| 4 young, oven-ready partridges at room temperature |
| 2½ tablespoons (40 g) butter |
| 3 tablespoons olive oil |
| Salt and black pepper |
| 4–6 bay leaves, optional |
| 1 lemon |
| ½ cup dry white wine |
| 3 tablespoons thick-cut orange marmalade |

**1** Preheat the oven to 450°F (230°C). Cut each of the partridges in half using poultry shears or a sharp knife and place, cut sides down, in a roasting pan.
**2** Heat the butter and oil in a small pan until sizzling hot, then pour over the partridge. Season well with salt and pepper and tuck in the bay leaves, if using. Roast on the top rack for 15 minutes until golden brown and just cooked through.
**3** Meanwhile, wash any wax off the lemon, then grate the rind, and squeeze the juice into a small pan. Add the wine and marmalade and stir over a moderate heat until the marmalade melts and the mixture becomes smooth, then lower the heat and keep warm.
**4** Transfer the cooked partridges to a heated serving dish, discarding the bay leaves. Add the marmalade sauce to the juices in the roasting pan and bring to the boil, stirring in any sediment. Pour it into a jug to accompany the partridges.

***SERVING SUGGESTION***
Try Chestnut and Celeriac Purée (page 254) as an elegant side dish. Or for something more substantial, serve the roast partridges with a delicious Wild Rice and Fennel Salad (page 85).

***NUTRIENTS PER SERVING:*** *calories 910, carbohydrate 13 g (including sugar 13 g), protein 121 g, fat 40 g (saturated fat 13 g), good source of vitamins B group and iron.*

---

### COOK'S SUGGESTION

*For this recipe, you must use tender young partridges, which are at their best in early to mid fall. Tougher, older birds will not roast in the time available.*

---

# CRANBERRY-GLAZED VENISON STEAKS

*Venison steaks are given a fruity coating of port-flavored sauce and sprinkled with crushed allspice and juniper berries before being grilled and served with a delicious root vegetable purée.*

TIME: 30 MINUTES  SERVES: 4

| |
|---|
| 1 lb (450 g) large carrots |
| 1 lb (450 g) turnip |
| Salt and black pepper |
| 4 venison steaks, about 4 oz (110 g) each |
| 3 tablespoons cranberry sauce |
| 1 tablespoon port or red wine |
| 1 tablespoon olive oil |
| 1 teaspoon allspice berries |
| 10 juniper berries |
| 3 tablespoons (50 g) butter |
| *To garnish:* a handful of fresh parsley, preferably flat-leaved |

**1** Put a kettle of water on to boil. Peel the carrots and turnips and cut into small chunks. Put them into a saucepan, cover with boiling water, and add some salt. Bring back to the boil, then cover and simmer for 12 minutes or until tender.

**2** Meanwhile, preheat the grill to high. Rinse and dry the parsley, keep 4 sprigs whole, chop the rest, and set aside for a garnish.

**3** Place the venison steaks on the rack of the grill pan, then mix the cranberry sauce, port or wine, and the oil and brush half the mixture over the steaks, reserving the rest.

**4** Coarsely crush the allspice and juniper berries with a pestle and mortar, or put them in a plastic bag and crush them with a rolling pin. Sprinkle half over the steaks, then season with pepper.

**5** Grill the steaks on a high setting for 7–8 minutes, sprinkling them with salt after 5 minutes. Turn the steaks, spread them with the rest of the cranberry mixture and sprinkle with the remaining spices and more black pepper. Grill for 5 minutes, then sprinkle with salt.

**6** Drain the vegetables and return them to the pan over a low heat. Shake to dry off excess water, then mash with the butter and season with pepper. Scatter the parsley over the purée and serve with the steaks.

*NUTRIENTS PER SERVING: calories 324, carbohydrate 19 g (including sugar 18 g), protein 27 g, fat 15 g (saturated fat 8 g), good source of vitamins A, B group, C, and E, and iron and zinc.*

# VENISON SAUSAGES WITH STILTON MASH

*An old favorite with a distinctive new flavor: game sausages and a designer mash of celeriac, potatoes, and blue cheese—just the thing, with a bottle of hearty red wine, for a warming supper.*

TIME: 30 MINUTES   SERVES: 4

| |
|---|
| 1½ lb (680 g) floury potatoes, such as Idaho |
| 14 oz (400 g) celeriac |
| Salt and black pepper |
| 2 tablespoons olive oil |
| 8 fat venison sausages, about 2¾ oz (75 g) each |
| 3 tablespoons milk |
| 3 tablespoons (50 g) butter |
| 3 tablespoons (50 g) Stilton cheese |
| A pinch of ground mace |
| *To serve:* mustards, chutneys and pickles |

**1**  Put a kettle of water on to boil; preheat the oven to a low setting. Peel the potatoes and the celeriac, cut them into small chunks and put them into separate saucepans. Cover both with boiling water, add salt, and cook gently for 15 minutes, or until soft.

**2**  Meanwhile, heat the oil over a moderate heat and fry the sausages for 10 minutes, turning frequently to brown them well all over, then transfer to the oven to keep warm.

**3**  Drain the celeriac and purée it with the milk in a blender, or by

hand. Drain the potatoes, add the butter, and mash them by hand. Combine the celeriac and potato purées, then crumble in the Stilton cheese, season with salt, pepper, and mace, and mash again.

**4**  Pile the purée onto a warm dish and arrange the sausages around or on top. Serve with a selection of mustards, chutneys, and pickles.

*NUTRIENTS PER SERVING: calories 531, carbohydrate 41 g (including sugar 4 g), protein 29 g, fat 60 g (saturated fat 27 g), good source of vitamins A, B group, C, E, and folate.*

# VENISON TERIYAKI WITH SWEET POTATO

*Serve steak and french fries with a difference! Lean, ginger-coated venison steaks are simmered in a dark, sweet-and-sour rice wine sauce and accompanied by chunky sweet potato fries.*

TIME: 30 MINUTES  SERVES: 4

| 2 in. (5 cm) piece fresh root ginger |
| 1 teaspoon sea salt |
| 4 well-trimmed venison steaks, each about 4 oz (110 g) |
| 5 sweet potatoes |
| Cooking oil for deep frying |
| 2½ tablespoons sake |
| 2½ tablespoons sweet sherry |
| 2 tablespoons dark soy sauce |

1 Preheat the oven to a low setting to keep the venison warm later. Peel and grate the ginger and mix it with the salt. Smear the mixture over one side of each venison steak and leave to marinate for 10 minutes.

2 Meanwhile, thinly peel the sweet potatoes and cut them lengthwise into long, fat french fries.

3 Pour cooking oil into a deep-fat fryer or large wok to a depth of about 3 in. (8 cm) and heat it to a temperature of 340°F (170°C), or until the oil is hot enough to brown a small cube of bread in about 45 seconds. Sweet potatoes need to be fried over a gentler heat than you would use for ordinary potato fries. Add the sweet potato fries and deep-fry for 12 minutes.

4 While the fries are cooking, smear a frying pan with a little cooking oil and heat until a faint haze rises from the pan. Add the venison steaks and fry for 2 minutes on each side, then lift them out of the pan and transfer to the oven to keep warm.

5 Pour the sake, sherry, and soy sauce into the pan and stir over the heat until the liquid bubbles,

scraping up the pan juices. Return the steaks to the pan and cook for 3 minutes on each side.

6 Drain the french fries. Arrange the venison on warmed plates, pour the sauce over or alongside the steak, and serve with the fries.

NUTRIENTS PER SERVING: *calories 497, carbohydrate 33 g (including sugar 2 g), protein 28 g, fat 27 g (saturated fat 4 g), good source of vitamins B group, and iron and zinc.*

# PEPPERED VENISON STEAKS

*Lean venison steaks with a peppery coating are served with a rich and sumptuous flambéed sauce of brandy, red wine, and heavy cream, spiked with aromatic juniper berries for extra flavor.*

TIME: 20 MINUTES    SERVES: 4

| 1 tablespoon black peppercorns |
| 1½ tablespoons (25 g) plain flour |
| Salt |
| 2 tablespoons olive oil |
| 4 venison steaks, about 5½ oz (155 g) each |
| 6 juniper berries |
| 3 tablespoons brandy |
| ⅔ cup red wine, or port |
| ⅔ cup (150 ml) heavy cream |

**1** Preheat the oven to a low setting. Crush the peppercorns coarsely with a pestle and mortar, or put them into a plastic bag and crush them with a rolling pin. Tip them onto a plate, add the flour and a little salt, and mix.

**2** Heat the olive oil in a frying pan. Lightly coat the venison steaks with the seasoned flour, pressing the peppercorns firmly into the flesh. As soon as the oil is hot, fry the steaks briskly over a high heat for 2½–4 minutes on each side, depending on whether you like them rare or well-done.

**3** Meanwhile, crush the juniper berries using the same method that you used for the peppercorns, and measure out the brandy.

**4** When the steaks are done, reduce the heat, pour in the brandy, and set it alight carefully, standing well back. When the flames die down, remove the steaks from the pan, put them onto a plate, cover and keep warm in the oven.

**5** Pour the red wine or port into the pan, add the juniper berries, and bring to the boil, stirring and scraping up the brown residue from the bottom. Continue boiling until reduced by half.

**6** Reduce the heat, then stir in the cream and cook for 2 minutes. Pour the sauce over the steaks and serve.

*SERVING SUGGESTION*
Serve with new potatoes sprinkled with sea salt, and runner beans.

*NUTRIENTS PER SERVING: calories 477, carbohydrate 10 g (including sugar 6 g), protein 35 g, fat 26 g (saturated fat 13 g), good source of vitamins A, B₂, and E, and iron and zinc.*

---

### COOK'S SUGGESTION

*Most venison sold in supermarkets is farmed, and is more tender than wild venison. You can cook farmed venison steaks just like lean beef steaks.*

FETTUCCINE WITH BROCCOLI

# PASTA & GRAINS

*Simple bases of pasta, rice, cracked wheat, and couscous are transformed in minutes with colors, flavors, and textures from all over the world into a feast of memorable dishes.*

# PAPPARDELLE WITH CHICKEN LIVERS AND PORT

*The powerful flavors of chicken livers, sage, and port are combined in this rich, dark sauce served on ribbon noodles.*

**TIME: 25 MINUTES  SERVES: 4 AS AN APPETIZER, 2 AS A MAIN COURSE**

| |
|---|
| 3 tablespoons olive oil |
| 1 small onion |
| 2 cloves garlic |
| 2 large sprigs of parsley |
| 1 sage leaf |
| 1 lb (450 g) fresh chicken livers |
| 8 oz (230 g) fresh pappardelle or tagliatelle, or 6 oz (170 g) dried |
| Salt and black pepper |
| 1 tablespoon vegetable oil |
| 5 tablespoons port |
| 2 tablespoons (25 g) butter |

**1** Bring a large saucepan of water to the boil and preheat the oven to a low setting. Heat the olive oil in a frying pan over a low heat. Peel and chop the onion and add it to the oil. Peel the garlic and crush it into the pan, then leave to fry gently.

**2** Rinse, dry, and chop the herbs and add them to the frying pan.

**3** Cut away any discolored areas and tough sinews from the chicken livers, then slice them into large pieces and set them aside.

**4** Add the pasta, some salt, and the vegetable oil to the boiling water, return it to the boil, and cook fresh pasta for about 3 minutes, dried for 10–12 minutes, or until al dente. Drain and keep warm.

**5** Meanwhile, raise the heat under the onion, add the chicken livers and stir-fry them until they are nicely browned. Then pour in the port and boil vigorously until the liquid has reduced by half.

**6** Stir in the butter and season with salt and black pepper. Add the chicken livers to the pasta, toss gently together, and serve.

*SERVING SUGGESTION*

For a main-course meal, serve the dish with a large green salad.

*VARIATION*

Duck livers can be used instead of chicken livers, and sherry instead of the port.

*NUTRIENTS PER SERVING, WHEN SERVING 4: calories 434, carbohydrate 31 g (including sugar 4 g), protein 28 g, fat 21 g (saturated fat 6 g), good source of vitamins A, B group, C, E, and folate, and iron and zinc.*

# FETTUCCINE WITH BROCCOLI

*A buttery Dijon mustard sauce, flavored with basil and parsley, makes an unusual spicy dressing for ribbon noodles of fresh egg pasta, crunchy green florets of fresh broccoli, and juicy cherry tomatoes.*

TIME: 20 MINUTES  SERVES: 4

| |
|---|
| 10 fresh basil leaves |
| 3 sprigs of parsley |
| 2 green onions |
| 2 small cloves garlic |
| 2 tablespoons Dijon mustard |
| ¼ lb (110 g) softened butter |
| 2 large heads broccoli, to give 1 lb (450 g) florets |
| 1 tablespoon olive oil |
| Salt and black pepper |
| 1 lb (450 g) fresh fettuccine, or tagliatelle |
| *To garnish:* 10 cherry tomatoes |

**1** Put a large saucepan of water on to boil for the pasta. Rinse and dry the basil and parsley and chop them finely. Trim and rinse the green onions; finely slice the green tops and set aside, then slice the white bulbs. Peel and crush the garlic.

**2** Blend the mustard and butter in a bowl then stir in the sliced onion bulbs, garlic, and herbs, crushing them against the bottom of the bowl to release their flavors. Set aside.

**3** Rinse and trim the broccoli into florets. Add the oil, salt, pasta, and broccoli to the boiling water, return to the boil, and cook for 4 minutes, or until the pasta is al dente.

**4** Meanwhile, rinse and halve the cherry tomatoes.

**5** Thoroughly drain the pasta and broccoli. Quickly melt the flavored butter in the pasta pan. Return the pasta and broccoli to the pan and toss them gently in the butter over a moderate heat until the pasta is well coated, but do not allow it to fry.

**6** Transfer the pasta onto a serving platter, season, and garnish with the green onion tops and tomatoes.

*NUTRIENTS PER SERVING: calories 450, carbohydrate 32 g (including sugar 5 g), protein 12 g, fat 31 g (saturated fat 18 g), good source of vitamins A, B group, C, E, and folate.*

201

# FARFALLE WITH PESTO AND BACON

*This nourishing mixture of pasta shapes, potatoes, and peas is flavored with smoked bacon, fried
onion, and pesto and given a creamy flourish with a choice of sour cream or Greek yogurt.*

TIME: 30 MINUTES  SERVES: 4

| |
|---|
| 1 lb (450 g) boiling potatoes |
| 10 oz (280 g) smoked back bacon |
| 1 medium onion |
| ½ lb (230 g) dried farfalle (bow ties), or other small pasta shapes |
| Salt and black pepper |
| 6 oz (170 g) frozen peas |
| 1½ tablespoons olive oil |
| 3 oz (85 g) pesto |
| 1¼ cups (300 ml) sour cream, or 10 oz (280 g) natural Greek yogurt |
| *To garnish:* fresh basil leaves |
| *To serve:* 1 full tablespoon (40 g) Parmesan cheese |

1  Bring a large saucepan of water
to the boil for the pasta, and a
medium one for the potatoes.
2  Peel the potatoes and cut them
into ½ in. (1 cm) cubes. Discard the
rind and excess fat from the bacon,
then cut it into ½ in. (1 cm) cubes.
Peel and chop the onion.
3  Add the pasta and some salt to
the large pan and cook, uncovered,
for 6–10 minutes, then add the peas
and cook for 4 minutes, or until the
pasta is al dente.
4  Add salt to the medium pan and
cook the potatoes, partially covered,
over a moderate heat for 7 minutes
or until tender. Drain and keep hot.
5  Meanwhile, heat half the olive oil
in a frying pan and fry the bacon
over a high heat, stirring frequently,
for 2–3 minutes, until it is cooked.
Transfer to a plate and set aside.
6  Heat the remaining oil in the
same pan, add the onion, and cook
gently for 5 minutes, until soft but
not brown. Return the bacon to the
pan and stir in the pesto and sour
cream or yogurt. Season well with
pepper, cover, and keep warm.
7  Rinse and dry the basil leaves.
Drain the pasta and peas and return
them to their pan. Add the potatoes
and gently stir in the bacon and

pesto mixture. Serve garnished with
the basil leaves and sprinkled with
freshly grated Parmesan.

*NUTRIENTS PER SERVING: calories 855,
carbohydrate 75 g (including sugar 14 g),
protein 33 g, fat 48 g (saturated fat 21 g),
good source of vitamins A, B group, C, E,
and folate, and calcium and zinc.*

### COOK'S SUGGESTION

*Look for dry-cured bacon
slices with no added water: they taste far
better than conventionally cured slices
and have the added advantage
of leaving no residue of water in the
pan after they have been fried.*

# PASTA WITH HEARTY SAUCE

*Children will love this simple family meal of chunky pasta shapes, peas, tomatoes, and pork sausage meat that is a fast, filling, and inexpensive alternative to spaghetti bolognese.*

**TIME: 25 MINUTES  SERVES: 4**

| |
|---|
| 1 medium onion |
| 1 clove garlic |
| 1 tablespoon olive oil |
| 1 lb (450 g) lean, traditional pork sausages |
| 3 tablespoons brandy, white wine, or chicken stock |
| 1 can (19 oz / 540 ml) chopped tomatoes |
| Salt and black pepper |
| 1 lb (450 g) fresh penne or 12 oz (335 g) dried |
| 5 oz (140 g) frozen peas |
| *To garnish:* a small bunch of chives |
| *To serve:* Parmesan cheese |

**1** Bring a large saucepan of water to the boil for the pasta. Peel and coarsely chop the onion and peel and crush the garlic. Fry them in the oil over a moderate heat for about 4 minutes, until the onion is soft, stirring occasionally.

**2** Coarsely chop the sausages, or remove their skins and break them up with a fork. Add the sausages to the pan and stir over a high heat for 7 minutes, or until browned.

**3** Add the brandy, wine, or stock, and the tomatoes, and season to taste. Bring to the boil, reduce the heat and simmer for 10 minutes, stirring occasionally.

**4** When the water comes to the boil, add the fresh pasta, peas, and some salt, bring back to the boil and cook for 4–5 minutes, or until the pasta is al dente. If using dried pasta, cook for 6–7 minutes before adding the peas.

**5** Meanwhile, trim, rinse, and snip or chop the chives.

**6** Drain the pasta and peas and toss them in the tomato sauce. Taste and adjust the seasoning, garnish with the chives, and serve with freshly grated Parmesan.

**NUTRIENTS PER SERVING:** *calories 662, carbohydrate 80 g (including sugar 7 g), protein 36 g, fat 22 g (saturated fat 8 g), good source of vitamins B group, C, and E, and calcium and zinc.*

---

### COOK'S SUGGESTION

*The choice of sausage is crucial to the success of this dish. Use a really meaty, coarse-cut variety of sausage, or a very high quality sausage meat.*

# SPAGHETTI ALLA VONGOLE

*Canned clams, briefly cooked in a simple tomato and white wine sauce, make a light and refreshing alternative to the heavier meat and cheese sauces for spaghetti.*

**TIME: 30 MINUTES  SERVES: 4–6**

| |
|---|
| 2 tablespoons olive oil |
| 1 large clove garlic |
| 1 can (19 oz / 540 ml) chopped tomatoes |
| 2 cans or jars (5 oz / 142 g) small clams (vongole) |
| 4 tablespoons dry white wine |
| 12 oz (335 g) dried spaghetti |
| Salt and black pepper |
| *To garnish:* fresh parsley, optional |

**1** Bring a large saucepan of water to the boil for the pasta. Meanwhile, heat the olive oil in a saucepan. Peel the garlic and crush it into the oil, allow it to sizzle briefly, then add the canned tomatoes and their juice.

**2** Drain the clams, reserving the liquid. Set the clams aside. Add half the liquid to the tomatoes with the wine; cook over a moderate heat, stirring occasionally, for 20 minutes, or until the mixture is reduced to a thick sauce.

**3** When the saucepan of water comes to the boil, add the spaghetti, some salt, and the remaining liquid from the clams, if you wish. Return to the boil and cook the spaghetti, uncovered, for 10–12 minutes, until it is al dente.

**4** While the pasta is cooking, rinse, dry, and chop enough parsley, if using, to give 2 tablespoons.

**5** Stir the clams into the thickened tomato sauce and heat them through gently, without allowing the sauce to boil. Season to taste with salt and black pepper.

**6** Drain the spaghetti, transfer it to a serving bowl or individual plates, and spoon the clam sauce on top. Sprinkle with parsley, if using. It is not usual to serve grated cheese with fish sauces for pasta.

**VARIATION**
If you prefer, canned tuna or peeled shrimps could be added to the sauce instead of clams.

*NUTRIENTS PER SERVING, WHEN SERVING 4: calories 415, carbohydrate 70 g (including sugar 6 g), protein 18 g, fat 8 g (saturated fat 1 g), good source of vitamins B group, C, and E, and iron.*

# FUSILLI WITH HAM AND GORGONZOLA

*A scattering of crunchy poppy seeds tops a powerful smoked ham and blue cheese sauce that is softened with button mushrooms and freshly grated nutmeg and swirled over pretty pasta spirals.*

**TIME: 25 MINUTES  SERVES: 4**

| |
|---|
| 6 oz (170 g) thickly sliced smoked ham (or meat left over from a baked ham) |
| ½ lb (230 g) button mushrooms |
| ¾ cup (200 ml) heavy cream |
| ¼ teaspoon freshly grated nutmeg (see box, below) |
| Salt and black pepper |
| 1 lb (450 g) fresh fusilli (twists) or other small shapes |
| 2 oz (55 g) Gorgonzola cheese |
| A few sprigs of flat-leaved parsley |
| 1½ teaspoons poppy seeds |

### EASY DOES IT!

*Grating a fresh nutmeg straight into your dishes gives them far more flavor than using the ready-ground variety.*

**1** Bring a large saucepan of water to the boil. Trim off and discard any excess fat and rind from the ham, then cut it into cubes.

**2** Clean and slice the mushrooms. Put them into a heavy saucepan with the cream, nutmeg, and some black pepper. Bring to the boil, reduce the heat to moderate, and cook, stirring frequently, until the cream starts to thicken.

**3** Add the pasta and some salt to the saucepan of boiling water, then bring back to the boil, and cook gently, uncovered, for 3–5 minutes, until al dente.

**4** Meanwhile, crumble the cheese into small pieces and rinse, dry, and chop the parsley.

**5** When the cream has thickened enough to coat the back of a spoon, remove the pan from the heat, add the cheese, and stir until it melts.

**6** Add the ham to the sauce, then return the pan to the heat and warm it through gently. Stir in the parsley and keep warm.

**7** Drain the pasta, transfer it to a serving bowl, and sprinkle with the poppy seeds. Pour over the sauce, toss gently, and serve.

*NUTRIENTS PER SERVING: calories 653, carbohydrate 56 g (including sugar 3 g), protein 25 g, fat 39 g (saturated fat 22 g), good source of vitamins A, B group, and E.*

**TWO EASY PASTA DISHES:** *(top)* SPAGHETTI ALLA VONGOLE; *(bottom)* FUSILLI WITH HAM AND GORGONZOLA.

# "STRAW AND HAY" WITH SMOKED SALMON

*Italians call this combination of yellow and green pasta "straw and hay" because of its colors.*
*It looks especially pretty served with richly flavored smoked salmon in a wine sauce.*

TIME: 25 MINUTES  SERVES: 6 AS AN
APPETIZER, 4 AS A MAIN COURSE

---

**1 small onion**

---

**6 tablespoons white wine,
or white vermouth**

---

**13 oz (375 g) fresh "straw and hay,"
or other narrow yellow and green
pasta such as linguine
or fettuccine, or 10 oz (280 g)
dried yellow and green pasta**

---

**Salt and pepper**

---

**12 oz (335 g) smoked salmon, or
smoked salmon trimmings**

---

**4 large sprigs of fresh dill**

---

**1 full tablespoon (25 g) capers**

---

**1**  Bring a large pan of water to the
boil for the pasta. Peel and finely
chop the onion and set it aside.
**2**  Bring the wine or vermouth to
the boil in a frying pan and allow it
to boil for 1–2 minutes until the

liquid has reduced by half. Stir in
the chopped onion and cook it until
it has softened, then reduce the
heat to very low.
**3**  Add the pasta and some salt to
the pan of boiling water and stir it
with a fork. Return to the boil, then
reduce the heat a little and cook
fresh pasta for 4–5 minutes, dried
for 10–12 minutes, until al dente.
**4**  While the pasta is cooking, cut
the smoked salmon or smoked
salmon trimmings into small strips.
Add them to the onion and wine
mixture in the frying pan and heat
them through gently.
**5**  Rinse, dry, and roughly chop
the dill and the capers. Stir them
into the onion and salmon mixture
in the frying pan.
**6**  As soon as the pasta is cooked,
drain it well and transfer it into a
large serving bowl.

**7**  Season the salmon mixture with
black pepper to taste (it won't need
any salt because the capers are very
salty), then spoon it over the pasta.
Stir gently and serve.
*VARIATIONS*
If you cannot find fresh dill, try
mint or flat-leaved parsley instead,
while diced green olives or gherkins
would make an agreeable substitute
for the capers.
*SERVING SUGGESTION*
Serve the pasta as an appetizer, or
turn it into a substantial main
course by adding a mixed green
salad or some thinly sliced tomatoes
with fennel, black olives, and a
lemon and olive oil dressing.

*NUTRIENTS PER SERVING, WHEN SERVING 6:
calories 249, carbohydrate 31g (including
sugar 1g), protein 21g, fat 4g (saturated
fat 0.8g), good source of vitamins B group.*

# TAGLIATELLE WITH BREADCRUMBS

*Pine kernels and freshly toasted breadcrumbs provide a tasty crunch in this extraordinarily simple combination of long ribbons of pasta with garlic and plenty of fresh herbs.*

TIME: 30 MINUTES  SERVES: 4

| 4 slices of crusty white bread |
| A bunch of flat-leaved parsley |
| A few sprigs of oregano |
| A few chives |
| ½ cup (125 ml) extra virgin olive oil |
| 3 cloves garlic |
| ½ cup (60 g) pine kernels |
| Salt and black pepper |
| 1 lb (450 g) fresh tagliatelle |

*To serve:* 2 oz (55 g)
Parmesan cheese

**1** Bring a saucepan of water to the boil for the pasta. Remove and discard the crusts from the bread, break it into pieces, and reduce it to crumbs in a food processor.

**2** Rinse and dry the herbs. Chop enough to give 4 tablespoons of parsley and 1½ tablespoons each of oregano and chives. Add them to the breadcrumbs and process briefly to combine them.

**3** Heat 3 tablespoons of oil in a frying pan over a moderate heat. Peel the garlic and crush it into the oil. Add the pine kernels and stir in the breadcrumb mixture. Season to taste and stir for 5–6 minutes, until the breadcrumbs are lightly browned but still quite soft, then remove the pan from the heat and keep it warm.

**4** Meanwhile, add the pasta and some salt to the boiling water and cook for 3–4 minutes, or until al dente. Grate the Parmesan into a serving dish and set aside.

**5** Drain the pasta thoroughly and place it in a large serving bowl with the remaining oil. Toss well, then add the breadcrumb mixture and toss again. Serve accompanied by the Parmesan.

SERVING SUGGESTION

A tomato salad seasoned with black pepper and scattered with torn basil leaves would make an excellent accompaniment to this satisfying pasta dish.

*NUTRIENTS PER SERVING: calories 977, carbohydrate 106 g (including sugar 4 g), protein 29 g, fat 52 g (saturated fat 9 g), good source of vitamins B group and E, and calcium, selenium and zinc.*

# PASTA WITH FAVA BEANS, ARTICHOKES, AND SPINACH

*Small pasta shapes and a tasty selection of assorted vegetables make this sturdy casserole perfect for a family supper.*

TIME: 30 MINUTES  SERVES: 4

| |
|---|
| 2 tablespoons olive oil |
| 1 medium onion |
| 1 large clove garlic |
| 1 medium red pepper |
| 6 oz (170 g) dried pasta shapes (small shells or rigatoni) |
| Salt and black pepper |
| 1 can (19 oz / 540 ml) chopped tomatoes |
| A pinch of dried oregano |
| ½ teaspoon brown sugar |
| 8 oz (230 g) frozen fava beans |
| 1 pack (350 g) young spinach |
| 1 can (14 oz / 398 ml) artichoke hearts |
| *To serve:* 1 full tablespoon (50 g) Parmesan cheese; 1 Italian loaf |

1  Bring a large saucepan of water to the boil, and preheat the oven to its lowest setting. Heat the olive oil in another large saucepan. Peel and roughly chop the onion, then peel and crush the garlic. Add them both to the oil and fry them gently for 5 minutes, until soft.

2  Rinse, halve, deseed, and slice the pepper. Add it to the onion and fry for a further 2 minutes.

3  Add the pasta and some salt to the boiling water. Return to the boil and cook for 10–12 minutes, until the pasta is al dente.

4  Stir the tomatoes, oregano, sugar, and some black pepper into the onion, garlic, and red pepper. Bring to the boil, then partially cover and simmer for 10 minutes.

5  Put the bread into the oven to heat through. Add the fava beans to the tomato sauce, return to the boil and simmer for 3 minutes.

6  Rinse and drain the spinach, then remove any tough stalks, add the leaves to the sauce, and cook for 3 more minutes.

7  Drain and quarter the artichoke hearts. Drain the pasta. Add both to the sauce and heat through for a minute or two.

8  Turn the pasta and sauce into a warm serving bowl, grate some Parmesan over, and serve with the hot bread.

NUTRIENTS PER SERVING: *calories 741, carbohydrate 92 g (including sugar 16 g), protein 26 g, fat 30 g (saturated fat 6 g), good source of vitamins A, B group, C, E, and folate, and calcium.*

---

### COOK'S SUGGESTION

*You can use canned artichoke bottoms (fonds d'artichaut), the nutty-tasting chunk from the bottom of the artichoke that has no leaves attached, instead of artichoke hearts, if you prefer. Cut them into slices instead of into quarters and add them to the casserole as before.*

# THAI NOODLE SALAD

*This easy salad of crisp fresh vegetables and shrimps, stirred into simple rice noodles, is accompanied by the sharp taste of chilies and lemongrass to make a cold dish full of hot flavors.*

TIME: 30 MINUTES  SERVES: 4

| ½ lb (230 g) snow peas |
| --- |
| 1 yellow pepper |
| 7 oz (200 g) rice noodles |
| 8 green onions |
| ½ lb (230 g) peeled, cooked shrimps |

*For the dressing:*

| 2 stems lemongrass |
| --- |
| 2 fresh red chilies |
| 3 in. (7 cm) piece fresh ginger |
| A large handful of coriander leaves |
| 2 limes |
| 4 tablespoons sunflower or corn oil |
| 2 tablespoons toasted sesame oil |
| 3 tablespoons soy sauce |
| *To serve:* rice crackers |

**1**  Put a kettle of water on to boil. Top, tail, and rinse the snow peas. Put them into a saucepan, cover with boiling water, bring back to the boil, then reduce the heat and simmer for 3 minutes. Rinse and deseed the pepper; slice it thinly.

**2**  Take the snow peas off the heat. Add the pepper and noodles. Leave to stand for 2 minutes, transfer to a colander, rinse, and drain.

**3**  To make the dressing, peel away the outer layers of the lemongrass and slice the stems into chunks. Rinse, deseed, and slice the chilies. Peel and slice the ginger. Rinse, dry, and chop the coriander. Put them all into a food processor or blender.

**4**  Squeeze the limes and add their juice with the vegetable and sesame oils and the soy sauce. Blend just long enough to make a thick, chunky dressing. Alternatively, chop or grind the dressing ingredients with a pestle and mortar.

**5**  Trim, rinse, and dry the green onions. Cut them diagonally into ½ in. (1 cm) pieces and put them into a serving bowl. Add the shrimp and noodle mixture, pour in the dressing, and toss it well together. Serve with the rice crackers.

*NUTRIENTS PER SERVING: calories 654, carbohydrate 71 g (including sugar 7 g), protein 21 g, fat 31 g (saturated fat 4 g), good source of vitamins B group, C, and E.*

### COOK'S SUGGESTION

*The thread-like noodles used for this dish are sold in delicatessens and Oriental grocers, and are sometimes called rice sticks. The salad can be made up in advance and stored for an hour or two in the refrigerator.*

# DUCK CHOW MEIN

*Chow mein, which means fried noodles, makes the perfect base for fresh vegetables and fresh or cooked meat. Stir-fried duck and slightly sweet hoisin sauce give this version a rich flavor.*

TIME: 30 MINUTES    SERVES: 4

| |
|---|
| 1 cup vegetable or chicken stock |
| 9 oz (255 g) medium Chinese noodles |
| 3–4 duck breast fillets, 14 oz (400 g) in total |
| 3 tablespoons soy sauce |
| 1 clove garlic |
| 3 large green onions |
| ⅔ lb (300 g) mixed vegetables, such as cabbage, carrots, broccoli, red pepper, and leeks |
| 2 tablespoons peanut oil |
| 4 oz (110 g) baby corn |
| 2 tablespoons hoisin sauce |
| 1 level teaspoon cornstarch |
| 2 oz (55 g) bean sprouts |

1   Put a kettle of water on to boil. Put the stock on to heat and preheat the oven to a low setting.

2   Put the noodles into a bowl, cover with boiling water, and soak for 6 minutes, or cook according to the package instructions.

3   Remove the skin from the duck breasts and cut the flesh into strips of ½ × 3 in. (1 × 7.5 cm). Put them into a bowl with 1 tablespoon of soy sauce and mix.

4   Peel and chop the garlic, trim, rinse, and slice the green onions, and set them aside. Trim and rinse the mixed vegetables and slice them into matchstick-sized strips. Drain and rinse the noodles.

5   Heat half the oil in a large wok or frying pan. Add the duck and stir-fry for 4–5 minutes. Transfer to a dish and keep warm in the oven.

6   Heat the remaining oil in the wok or frying pan. Add the garlic and green onions, mixed vegetables, and baby corn, and stir-fry them for about 15 seconds in the wok, or for 30 seconds in the frying pan.

7   Return the duck to the pan, add the hoisin sauce and the hot stock, and simmer for a few minutes.

8   Blend the cornstarch with a teaspoon of cold water and stir it into the pan, with the bean sprouts. Cook for 1–2 minutes, then add the noodles and the remaining soy sauce. Toss well, let the noodles reheat for 3–5 minutes, then serve.

*NUTRIENTS PER SERVING: calories 765, carbohydrate 59 g (including sugar 8 g), protein 25 g, fat 50 g (saturated fat 13 g), good source of vitamins A, B group, C, E, and folate, and zinc.*

# SUMMER SQUASH WITH POLENTA

*This colorful and adaptable stew on a base of polenta is an excellent way to deal with a glut of ripe summer vegetables.*

| |
|---|
| 6 oz (170 g) instant polenta |
| 3 tablespoons olive oil |
| 1 small onion |
| 1 clove garlic |
| 1 lb (450 g) mixed yellow and green patty pan squashes and/or young green and yellow zucchinis |
| 4 sprigs of fresh thyme |
| Salt and black pepper |
| 6 oz (170 g) Cheddar cheese |
| 1½ tablespoons (25 g) butter |
| 2 beef tomatoes |
| 1 lemon |
| A few sprigs of parsley |

**1**  Put the polenta into a saucepan with 3 cups of water. Bring to the boil, reduce the heat and simmer for 8 minutes. Stir occasionally to remove any lumps.

**2**  Slowly heat the olive oil in a shallow pan over a moderate heat. Halve, peel, and finely chop the onion, peel and crush the garlic and cook for 5–8 minutes, until soft.

**3**  Meanwhile, rinse, top, and tail the squashes and/or the zucchinis. Cut the squashes into quarters, the zucchinis into rounds, and add them to the onions. Rinse and add the thyme, add salt and pepper, and cook for 10 minutes.

**4**  When the polenta comes away cleanly from the sides of the pan, remove it from the heat. Grate the cheese and beat it into the polenta with the butter, then season to taste, cover, and leave in a warm place.

**5**  Rinse and dice the tomatoes and add them to the squash stew.

**6**  Wash any wax from the lemon, then finely grate the rind. Rinse, dry, and finely chop the parsley. Add both to the vegetables. Remove and discard the thyme, then serve the stew with the polenta.

*VARIATION*

For extra flavor, add eggplants or red and yellow peppers, or enrich the stew with whipping cream.

*NUTRIENTS PER SERVING: calories 485, carbohydrate 39 g (including sugar 15 g), protein 18 g, fat 29 g (saturated fat 14 g), good source of vitamins A, B group, C, E, and folate, and calcium.*

212

# BULGUR PILAF WITH MUSHROOMS

*A bed of healthy grains simmered in stock is mixed with a selection of fresh mushrooms, nuts, and parsley for a gentle and sustaining dish that can also be served as an accompaniment.*

TIME: 30 MINUTES   SERVES: 4

| |
| --- |
| 1 onion |
| ¼ lb (110 g) butter |
| 12 oz (335 g) bulgur |
| 3¼ cups vegetable stock |
| ½ lb (230 g) mixed mushrooms |
| A small bunch of parsley |
| 1 tablespoon olive oil |
| Salt and black pepper |
| 4 tablespoons (50 g) flaked almonds |
| 4 tablespoons (50 g) chopped hazelnuts |

**1** Halve, peel, and finely chop the onion. Heat half the butter in a flameproof casserole, add the onion and fry until it is translucent.

**2** Add the bulgur and cook, stirring frequently, for 3 minutes.

Add the stock, bring it to the boil, then reduce the heat, cover the casserole and simmer it gently for about 10–15 minutes, until all the stock has been absorbed.

**3** Meanwhile, clean and finely slice the mushrooms. Rinse and dry the parsley, chop it finely, and set aside.

**4** Heat the olive oil in a frying pan, add the sliced mushrooms, and fry them until they have softened and are lightly browned. Season with salt and pepper. Pour the mushrooms and any juice on top of the partially cooked bulgur, re-cover the casserole and leave it to continue cooking.

**5** Add the flaked almonds to the frying pan and shake them over a moderate heat for a minute or two,

then add the chopped hazelnuts and cook both until lightly browned.

**6** When the stock is absorbed and the wheat is cooked, stir in the remaining butter, toasted nuts, and parsley. Taste for seasoning and serve straight from the casserole.

*NUTRIENTS PER SERVING: calories 732, carbohydrate 73 g (including sugar 3 g), protein 15 g, fat 44 g (saturated fat 17 g), good source of vitamins A, B group, and E, and iron.*

213

# SALMON TABBOULEH

*Tabbouleh are salads made with nutty bulgur, or cracked wheat. This stylish dish of bulgur and poached salmon has the clean, light taste that comes from fresh herbs and lemon.*

TIME: 30 MINUTES  SERVES: 4

3½ oz (100 g) bulgur
(cracked wheat)

1⅓ lb (600 g) skinned
salmon fillet

6–7 oz (170–200 g)
flat-leaved parsley

2 oz (55 g) fresh mint

8 green onions

1 large lemon

Salt and black pepper

Lettuce leaves
(romaine or iceberg)

6 tablespoons olive oil

*To serve:* lemon wedges
and pita bread

**1**  Put a kettle of water on to boil. Put the bulgur in a saucepan with 1¼ cups of cold water. Bring to the boil, then reduce the heat and simmer for 8–10 minutes, until the bulgur has absorbed all the water.

**2**  Meanwhile, cut the salmon into four equal pieces, put them into a shallow pan, and cover with boiling water. Bring back to the boil, reduce the heat, and simmer for 3 minutes. Transfer to a plate to cool.

**3**  Rinse, dry, and chop the parsley. Rinse, dry, and finely shred the mint leaves. Trim, rinse, dry, and finely chop the green onions. Put all three into a salad bowl.

**4**  Squeeze the lemon and set the juice aside, then rinse and dry the lettuce, and warm the pita bread.

**5**  Rinse the bulgur in cold water, then squeeze it dry in handfuls and add it to the salad bowl with the lemon juice and oil. Season to taste and mix thoroughly.

**6**  Flake the salmon, remove any bones, add to the salad, and toss.

**7**  Line a platter with the lettuce leaves, pile the tabbouleh on top, and serve with lemon wedges and the warm pita bread.

*NUTRIENTS PER SERVING: calories 755, carbohydrate 66 g (including sugar 4 g), protein 33 g, fat 41 g (saturated fat 15 g), good source of vitamins A, B group, C, E, and folate, and calcium and iron.*

# SUMMER TABBOULEH

*Bulgur is perfect with crisp, just-cooked summer vegetables mixed with handfuls of fresh herbs and tossed with a lively honey and mustard dressing to give it an extra bite.*

TIME: 30 MINUTES  SERVES: 4

½ lb (230 g) bulgur (cracked wheat)

½ lb (230 g) fine green beans

½ lb (230 g) frozen peas

Salt

5 large green onions

3 medium tomatoes

1 lemon

A large handful of fresh parsley

A large handful of fresh mint

A large handful of chives or dill

*To serve:* 2 lettuce hearts

*For the dressing:*

3 tablespoons extra virgin olive oil

1 tablespoon red wine vinegar

1 teaspoon honey

1 tablespoon Dijon mustard

Salt and black pepper

**1**  Put a kettle of water on to boil. Put the bulgur in a saucepan with about 3 cups of cold water. Bring to the boil, then reduce the heat and simmer for 8–10 minutes, until the bulgur has absorbed all the water.

**2**  Meanwhile, rinse, top, and tail the green beans and chop them into 1 in. (2.5 cm) pieces. Put them into a saucepan with the frozen peas. Cover with boiling water, add a little salt, return to the boil, cook for 1–2 minutes, then drain.

**3**  Rinse, dry, trim, and thinly slice the green onions. Rinse, dry, and dice the tomatoes. Wash any wax from the lemon, grate the rind, and squeeze the juice. Add them all to the bulgur and fluff the mixture up with a fork.

**4**  Add the beans and peas to the tabbouleh. Rinse, dry, and chop the herbs and add them. Rinse and dry the lettuce leaves and set aside.

**5**  To make the honey and mustard dressing, whisk all the ingredients together in a bowl, then pour it over the tabbouleh and mix well, then serve with lettuce leaves.

*NUTRIENTS PER SERVING: calories 382, carbohydrate 60 g (including sugar 8 g), protein 12 g, fat 11 g (saturated fat 1.5 g), good source of vitamins A, B group, C, E, and folate, and iron.*

---

### COOK'S SUGGESTION

*In the Middle East this salad is eaten by rolling a spoonful of the tabbouleh inside a lettuce leaf and picking it up with the fingers.*

---

**TWO BULGUR SALADS:**
*(top)* SALMON TABBOULEH;
*(bottom)* SUMMER TABBOULEH.

# VEGETABLE COUSCOUS

*Sweet winter vegetables and legumes, mingled with dried apricots and hot spices for a Middle Eastern flavor, make a warm and comforting stew to serve with the mild grains of couscous.*

TIME: 30 MINUTES  SERVES: 2

| |
|---|
| **1 small onion** |
| **1 tablespoon (15 g) butter** |
| **1 tablespoon olive oil** |
| **2 small carrots** |
| **½ small turnip** |
| **1 medium parsnip** |
| **A pinch of cayenne pepper** |
| **A pinch of turmeric** |
| **½ teaspoon ground ginger** |
| **½ teaspoon ground cinnamon** |
| **A pinch of saffron threads, optional** |
| **Salt and black pepper** |
| **12 ready-to-eat dried apricots** |
| **2 oz (55 g) frozen baby peas** |
| **3 tablespoons canned chickpeas** |
| **¾ cup (125 g) couscous** |
| *To garnish:* **2 sprigs of fresh coriander** |

**1** Put a kettle of water on to boil. Peel and chop the onion. Heat the butter and olive oil in a large, heavy, flameproof casserole. Add the onion and fry gently until soft.

**2** Meanwhile, peel the carrots, turnip, and parsnip. Cut them into ½ in. (1 cm) chunks and add them to the onions as you go. Stir in the cayenne pepper, turmeric, ginger, cinnamon, and the saffron threads, if using, and season to taste with salt and black pepper.

**3** Chop the apricots and add them, with the peas. Drain, rinse, and add the chickpeas. Add 1¼ cups of boiling water and bring it back to the boil. Reduce the heat, cover, and simmer for 15 minutes.

**4** Meanwhile, pour 1 cup of boiling water into a saucepan, add the couscous, and stir it, then turn off the heat and leave it to stand,

covered, until the vegetables are ready. Meanwhile, rinse and dry the coriander and set it aside.

**5** Check the couscous and season to taste. Break it up with a fork and transfer it to a serving dish.

**6** Taste and adjust the seasoning of the vegetables, then spoon them and their broth over the couscous. Garnish the dish with a sprig of coriander and serve.

*VARIATION*
Other fresh root vegetables such as celery, fennel, potatoes, or turnips will make an excellent substitute for the carrots, turnip, or parsnip in this adaptable stew.

*NUTRIENTS PER SERVING: calories 600, carbohydrate 95 g (including sugar 37 g), protein 20 g, fat 17 g (saturated fat 5 g), good source of vitamins A, B group, C, E, and folate, and calcium and iron.*

# COUSCOUS WITH SHRIMPS AND MINT

*Couscous is a wonderfully useful basis for any number of quick, light meals, because while it is soaking
you have time to cook some little delicacies, such as these fresh shrimps, to serve with it.*

TIME: 25 MINUTES   SERVES: 4

| |
|---|
| 1⅔ cups fish or chicken stock |
| 2 shallots |
| 1 clove garlic |
| ¾ lb (335 g) small, firm zucchinis |
| 3 tablespoons olive oil |
| Salt and black pepper |
| 1¼ cups (225 g) couscous |
| A handful of fresh mint |
| ½ lb (230 g) peeled, cooked shrimps |
| *To serve:* harissa sauce, optional (see box, below) |

**1** Bring the stock to the boil in a
saucepan. Peel and chop the shallots
and the garlic. Trim and rinse the
zucchinis and slice them thinly.
**2** Heat 2 tablespoons of oil in a
frying pan, add the shallots, garlic,
and zucchinis, stir to coat them
with oil, then fry for 4 minutes until
slightly softened. Season to taste.
**3** Add the boiling stock, return to
the boil, then stir in the couscous.
Remove from the heat, cover, and
leave to stand for 10 minutes, until
the stock is absorbed.
**4** Rinse, dry, and chop the mint
and set aside. Heat the remaining
olive oil in a small frying pan. Stir
in the shrimps and heat through.
**5** Add the shrimps and mint to the
couscous, stir, and season to taste.
Serve, accompanied by a side dish of
harissa sauce, if using.

NUTRIENTS PER SERVING: *calories 279,
carbohydrate 31 g (including sugar 2 g),
protein 18 g, fat 10 g (saturated fat 1 g),
good source of vitamins B group, C, E,
and folate, and iron.*

---

### COOK'S SUGGESTION

*If you like spicy food, you will enjoy
harissa, a fiery sauce made of red
chilies, garlic, and olive oil. Harissa can
be found in Middle Eastern stores
and many supermarkets.*

# SHRIMP PILAF

*Finely spiced rice, turned a tempting golden color with threads of fragrant saffron, needs only a handful of swiftly cooked jumbo shrimps and some fresh herbs to become a memorable dish.*

TIME: 30 MINUTES   SERVES: 4

| |
|---|
| 2½ cups fish stock |
| 1 small onion |
| 1½ tablespoons (25 g) butter |
| 2 tablespoons olive oil |
| 1 clove garlic |
| 2 dried red chilies |
| 1¼ cups (225 g) long-grain rice, such as basmati |
| A pinch of saffron threads |
| 3 bay leaves |
| 1 lb (450 g) peeled, raw jumbo shrimps |
| Salt and black pepper |
| *To garnish:* a few sprigs of fresh flat-leaved parsley, or dill |

**1**   Bring the stock to the boil in a saucepan. Peel and thinly slice the onion. In a large saucepan, heat the butter and oil, then add the onion. Peel and slice the garlic, crumble the chilies, add them, and stir-fry for a few minutes. Then add the rice and stir to coat it in the oil.

**2**   Add the saffron and fish stock to the pan, return to the boil, then add the bay leaves, shrimps, and some salt. Cover, reduce the heat, and simmer for 10 minutes, then remove from the heat and leave to stand, covered, for 4 minutes.

**3**   Rinse, dry, and chop the parsley or dill. Spoon the shrimp pilaf onto a serving dish, season with salt and pepper to taste, and garnish with the chopped herb.

*NUTRIENTS PER SERVING: calories 400, carbohydrate 46 g (including sugar 1 g), protein 27 g, fat 12 g (saturated fat 4 g), good source of vitamin E.*

### COOK'S SUGGESTION

*Saffron threads are expensive, but only a few are needed to infuse a dish with color and aroma.*

# SAFFRON PILAF WITH RAISINS AND NUTS

*This delicately scented Eastern pilaf proves the perfect base for tender fava beans doused in spicy chili oil, and served with a thick sauce of creamy yogurt spiked with fresh coriander.*

TIME: 30 MINUTES  SERVES: 4–6

| |
|---|
| 1½ cups (300 g) long-grain rice, such as basmati |
| 3 tablespoons (50 g) butter |
| 1 medium red onion |
| 2 cloves garlic |
| 1 teaspoon ground coriander |
| 1 cinnamon stick |
| A pinch of saffron threads |
| 4 full tablespoons seedless raisins |
| 4 full tablespoons flaked almonds |
| Salt and black pepper |
| 1 lb (450 g) frozen fava beans |
| 1 small container natural yogurt |
| A few sprigs of coriander |
| 2–3 tablespoons chili-flavored olive oil |

**1** Put a kettle of water on to boil. Put the rice into a bowl, cover it with cold water, and leave to soak, to remove some of the starch.

**2** Melt the butter in a heavy-based saucepan over a very low heat. Peel and chop the onion and garlic and add them to the pan. Increase the heat, and fry for 1–2 minutes or until the onion softens. Stir in the ground coriander and reduce the heat to very low.

**3** Pour the rice into a sieve and rinse it. Add it to the onion and stir in 1½ cups of boiling water. Add the cinnamon stick, saffron, raisins, almonds, and seasoning.

**4** Bring the water to a fast boil, then reduce the heat until it barely simmers. Cover and cook the rice for 15 minutes; do not lift the lid.

**5** Meanwhile, put the fava beans into a saucepan, cover them with boiling water, and bring back to the boil. Then reduce the heat, cover and simmer for 5–6 minutes.

**6** Put the yogurt into a bowl. Rinse, dry, and chop the coriander and stir it into the yogurt.

**7** Drain the fava beans, put them into another bowl, and drizzle with the flavored oil.

**8** Remove the rice from the heat and leave it to stand, still covered, for 3 minutes. Then fluff it up with a fork, discard the cinnamon stick, and serve with the yogurt and spiced fava beans.

*NUTRIENTS PER SERVING, WHEN SERVING 4: calories 646, carbohydrate 84 g (including sugar 16 g), protein 18 g, fat 27 g (saturated fat 9 g), good source of vitamins B group, C, E, and folate.*

# EASY GUMBO

*The flavor of the southern United States has never been more pronounced than in this version of Louisiana's favorite stew.*

TIME: 30 MINUTES  SERVES: 4

| |
|---|
| 1 tablespoon olive oil |
| 1½ tablespoons (25 g) butter |
| 1 medium onion |
| 1 small green pepper |
| 2 sticks celery |
| Salt |
| 1¾ cups (350 g) long-grain white rice |
| 2 tablespoons plain flour |
| 1 can (19 oz / 540 ml) chopped tomatoes |
| 1¼ cups fish or vegetable stock |
| 1 bay leaf |
| ½–1 teaspoon cayenne pepper |
| ½ teaspoon paprika |
| ⅔ lb (300 g) fresh okra |
| ½ lb (230 g) smoked frankfurters |
| 2 cans (4 oz / 113 g) crab meat |
| 9 oz (255 g) canned mussels, smoked or unsmoked |

**1** Put a kettle of water on to boil. Heat the oil and butter slowly in a large saucepan. Peel and slice the onion, add it to the pan, and cook gently until it is translucent.

**2** Meanwhile, rinse, deseed, and roughly chop the pepper and rinse and chop the celery. Add them to the onion and continue cooking for a few minutes.

**3** Pour the boiling water into a large saucepan and add some salt and the rice. Bring back to the boil, cover, and simmer for 15 minutes, or until the rice is tender.

**4** Add the flour to the vegetables, stir it until it has combined with the fat to make a roux, then cook for 2 minutes. Then add the canned tomatoes, fish or vegetable stock, bay leaf, cayenne to taste, and the paprika. Increase the heat and simmer for 15 minutes, until the gumbo is nearly ready and looks thick and soupy.

**5** While the gumbo is cooking, rinse and trim the okra and chop it widthwise into ½ in. (1 cm) pieces, adding it to the saucepan in handfuls as you go.

**6** When the gumbo is almost ready, chop the smoked frankfurters into ½ in. (1 cm) pieces and add them to the pan.

**7** Drain the crab meat and the mussels and add them to the stew. Continue cooking for 2–3 minutes to allow the frankfurters and seafood to heat through thoroughly.

**8** Drain the cooked rice, divide it among four heated serving bowls, then spoon the easy gumbo over the top and serve.

NUTRIENTS PER SERVING: *calories 727, carbohydrate 85 g (including sugar 9 g), protein 30 g, fat 30 g (saturated fat 12 g), good source of vitamins A, B group, C, E, and folate, and iron and zinc.*

### COOK'S SUGGESTION

*The gelatinous juice produced by okra helps to thicken this stew, as does the roux. In traditional gumbo, the roux is often cooked for as long as 45 minutes to give it a rich brown color and smoky flavor. In this recipe, the use of smoked frankfurters and smoked mussels adds the necessary flavor to the quickly made roux.*

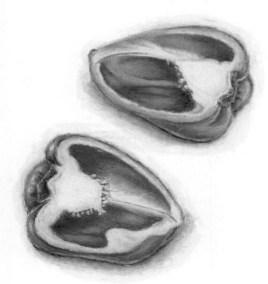

# Egg-topped Kedgeree

*Poached eggs add a melting richness to the rice, smoked fish, and shrimps in this Indian-style brunch.*

**Time: 30 minutes   Serves: 4**

| |
|---|
| 1⅓ cups (280 g) long-grain rice |
| Salt and black pepper |
| 4 tablespoons (60 g) butter |
| 1 small onion |
| 8 oz (230 g) skinned smoked haddock fillet |
| A few sprigs of parsley |
| 1 tablespoon white wine vinegar |
| 4 large eggs |
| 8 anchovy fillets |
| 20 capers |
| ½ lemon |
| ¼ lb (110 g) peeled, cooked shrimps |
| 3 tablespoons light cream |

**1** Put a kettle of water on to boil. Put the rice into a saucepan, add salt and enough boiling water to cover well. Return to the boil, cover, and cook gently for 15 minutes, or until cooked.

**2** Meanwhile, melt the butter in a large saucepan. Peel and chop the onion and fry it in the butter for a few minutes until soft.

**3** Cut the haddock into cubes, removing any bones, then add it to the onion and cook for 5 minutes. Rinse, dry, and chop the parsley and set it aside.

**4** Prepare an egg poacher, or fill a frying pan with 2½ in. (6 cm) of water, add the vinegar, and heat until boiling gently. Poach the eggs for about 3 minutes or until set, but soft in the centers.

**5** While the eggs are poaching, chop the anchovy fillets and capers, and squeeze 1 tablespoon of juice from the lemon.

**6** Drain the rice, stir it into the fish, add the shrimps, and heat through gently. Season to taste with salt and pepper, then transfer to individual serving plates.

**7** Sprinkle the rice with the chopped parsley, anchovies, capers, and lemon juice. Make a hollow in the top of each serving and place a poached egg in it. Pass the cream separately in a jug.

*Nutrients per serving: calories 572, carbohydrate 58 g (including sugar 1 g), protein 33 g, fat 23 g (saturated fat 11 g), good source of vitamins A, B group, and E.*

# EGG FRIED RICE

*The inspiration for this recipe comes from one of the most popular Cantonese dishes, and it is always fresh and different as the vegetables can be varied endlessly, according to the season.*

TIME: 30 MINUTES  SERVES: 4

| |
|---|
| 1⅓ cups (280 g) long-grain rice, such as basmati |
| Salt |
| 3 tablespoons vegetable oil |
| 4 medium eggs |
| ½ lb (230 g) rindless back bacon |
| 3 medium carrots |
| 8 green onions |
| 2 cloves garlic |
| 6 oz (170 g) frozen baby peas |
| 7 oz (200 g) bean sprouts |
| ½ lb (230 g) peeled, cooked shrimps |
| 4 tablespoons soy sauce |
| 4 tablespoons sake, or dry sherry |
| 4 tablespoons mirin, or 1 teaspoon honey |
| 2 tablespoons toasted sesame oil |

**1**  Put a kettle of water on to boil. Put the rice into a pan with a little salt, add 3 cups of boiling water, and 1 teaspoon of vegetable oil. Bring back to the boil, reduce the heat, cover and simmer for 10–15 minutes.

**2**  While the rice is cooking, heat up 1 tablespoon of vegetable oil in a wok or large frying pan. Beat the eggs lightly and pour them into the pan or wok, tipping it to make a thin omelette. Cook over a moderate heat until set, then turn the omelette onto a plate to cool.

**3**  Trim the bacon slices and cut them into strips. Add the remaining oil to the pan and fry the bacon over a moderate heat until crisp.

**4**  Peel and dice the carrots, add them to the bacon, reduce the heat, and leave them to fry. Trim and rinse the green onions, chop them up, and add them to the pan. Peel the garlic and crush it in, and stir in the baby peas.

**5**  Rinse and drain the bean sprouts and add them to the pan. Turn up the heat, stir-fry them for 1 minute, then add the shrimps.

**6**  Transfer half the mixture to another wok or frying pan—using

two pans prevents the mixture steaming instead of frying. Drain the rice, slice the omelette into thin strips, and divide them equally between the two pans.

**7**  Add half the soy sauce, half the sake or sherry, and half the mirin or honey to each pan. Then add half the sesame oil. Mix together thoroughly, stir-fry over a high heat for 5 minutes, or until the mixture is dry. Serve immediately.

**VARIATION**
For a vegetarian version, use water chestnuts and fresh bamboo shoots instead of bacon and shrimps.

**NUTRIENTS PER SERVING:** *calories 736, carbohydrate 68 g (including sugar 7 g), protein 44 g, fat 28 g (saturated fat 5.5 g), good source of vitamins A, B group, and folate, and iron, selenium, and zinc.*

---

**COOK'S SUGGESTION**

*Sake is a wine that is made with fermented rice. It is an important flavoring in Japanese cooking, and can be found in most liquor stores. Mirin is a sweet sake, available from many Asian grocers and some supermarkets.*

---

# SPANISH RICE WITH CHORIZO AND SAGE

*Turmeric gives a warm, golden glow to this hearty, richly flavored Spanish-style dish, where the rice, vegetables, and chunks of spicy sausage are all cooked in one pan.*

TIME: 30 MINUTES  SERVES: 4

| 1¼ cups chicken stock |
| --- |
| 2 tablespoons olive oil |
| 1 medium red onion |
| 1 clove garlic |
| 1 medium red pepper |
| 1 cup (200 g) long-grain rice |
| 1 teaspoon turmeric |
| 1 can (19 oz / 540 ml) chopped tomatoes |
| Salt and black pepper |
| 6 oz (170 g) chorizo sausage |
| A small bunch of fresh sage |
| 6 oz (170 g) frozen peas |

**1** Put the chicken stock on to heat in a small saucepan. Heat the olive oil in a wide frying pan.

**2** Peel and chop the onion and garlic, add them to the frying pan, and cook over a fairly high heat for about 3 minutes, or until the onion is soft, stirring frequently.

**3** While the onion and garlic are frying, rinse, halve, deseed, and roughly chop the pepper. Add it to the pan, with the rice and turmeric, and stir-fry for 3 minutes.

**4** Add the heated stock, the canned tomatoes and their juice, and season to taste. Bring to the boil, reduce the heat, cover, and simmer, stirring occasionally, for about 5 minutes.

**5** Cut the chorizo sausage into fairly thick chunks, then stir them into the rice and continue cooking for 5 minutes.

**6** Rinse and roughly chop the sage and add it to the rice, with the peas. Return to the boil, then reduce the heat, and simmer for 5 minutes until the rice is tender and has absorbed most of the liquid. If the mixture dries out before the rice is cooked, add a little more stock, or some dry white wine. Serve hot.

**VARIATION**

A spicy salami cut into thick slices can be used instead of chorizo if you wish.

*NUTRIENTS PER SERVING: calories 397, carbohydrate 53 g (including sugar 7 g), protein 15 g, fat 14 g (saturated fat 4 g), good source of vitamins A, B group, C, E, and folate.*

# EMERALD RISOTTO

*Young, tender leaves of baby spinach have a vivid color and an extra-fresh flavor that is packed with goodness. Try this risotto for a healthy supper that requires little from the cook except stirring.*

**TIME: 30 MINUTES   SERVES: 4**

---

**5 cups vegetable stock, or 4 tablespoons vegetable bouillon powder**

---

**5 tablespoons white wine**

---

**1 pack baby spinach**

---

**4 tablespoons virgin olive oil**

---

**1 small onion**

---

**2 cloves garlic**

---

**1¾ cups (350 g) risotto rice (arborio, carnaroli, or vialone)**

---

**Salt and black pepper**

---

**Whole nutmeg for grating**

---

**1** Bring the stock to the boil in a saucepan, or stir the bouillon powder into 5 cups of boiling water. Add the wine, reduce the heat, and leave to simmer.

**2** Rinse the spinach leaves, chop them roughly and set them aside.

**3** Heat the oil in a large saucepan or wok. Peel and finely chop the onion and garlic and fry them gently for 2–3 minutes until soft but not brown. Then add the rice and stir-fry until the grains are translucent and coated with oil.

**4** Add a ladleful of stock, adjust the heat to maintain a gentle boil, and stir until most of the liquid has been absorbed. Keep adding stock, a ladleful at a time, and stir constantly for about 15 minutes, until the rice is almost cooked.

**5** Add the spinach and more stock and boil and stir until the rice is cooked—risotto rice should retain a bite, but the mixture should be of a soft, dropping consistency.

**6** Season to taste with salt, pepper, and some freshly grated nutmeg. Serve straight from the pan.

*SERVING SUGGESTION*
Add a mixed-leaf salad and some walnut or olive bread.

*VARIATION*
Emerald Risotto is a vegan meal, but for a nonvegan dish you can add 2–3 tablespoons of grated Parmesan cheese before serving.

*NUTRIENTS PER SERVING: calories 448, carbohydrate 73 g (including sugar 2 g), protein 8 g, fat 14 g (saturated fat 2 g), good source of vitamins A, B group, C, E, and folate.*

---

**COOK'S SUGGESTION**

*Italian risotto rice is a small, fat grain that absorbs the cooking liquid. Never wash the rice before cooking, because it is the starch in the grains that give risotto its lovely creamy texture.*

---

NUTTY SPINACH AND MUSHROOM FRITATTA

# VEGETABLE MAIN DISHES

*The dazzling variety of fresh vegetables, now available year-round at most supermarkets, are the basis for these recipes for omelettes, cheese dishes, fritters, and tarts—all designed to please every palate and each one packed with goodness.*

# VEGETABLE PRIMAVERA

*The secret of this dish lies in the light cooking of a mixture of fine spring vegetables, which gives them a
crisp texture and fresh flavor, and contrasts agreeably with the stuffed pasta.*

TIME: 30 MINUTES   SERVES: 4

½ lb (230 g) baby carrots

5½ oz (155 g) baby corn cobs

½ lb (230 g) young fine green beans

Salt and black pepper

½ lb (230 g) baby or small zucchinis

A small handful of fresh parsley
or chervil

14 oz (400 g) fresh ricotta
and spinach tortellini

1 tablespoon olive oil

½ lemon

1 tablespoon wholegrain mustard

**1**  Put a large saucepan of water
and a kettle on to boil. Preheat the
oven to a low setting.
**2**  Rinse and trim the carrots, corn,
and beans, and cut them into short
lengths. Plunge the vegetables into
the saucepan of boiling water, add
salt, bring back to the boil, then

simmer for 4–5 minutes, keeping
them slightly crisp.
**3**  Meanwhile, rinse and trim the
zucchinis. Cut baby zucchinis in
half lengthwise, small ones into
slices, and set aside. Rinse, dry, and
chop the parsley or chervil.
**4**  Lift the cooked vegetables from
the boiling water with a slotted
spoon, put them into a bowl, and
keep them warm in the oven. Bring
the water back to the boil, topping
up with more from the kettle if
necessary. Add the pasta and boil
gently for 5–6 minutes.
**5**  Meanwhile, heat the olive oil in
a large saucepan, add the zucchinis
and fry them, stirring continuously,
for 2–3 minutes.
**6**  Squeeze the lemon juice into the
zucchinis, then add the drained
vegetables, mustard, and salt and
pepper to taste. Toss gently together.

**7**  Drain the pasta and mix it into
the vegetables. Turn onto a warmed
serving dish, add a sprinkling of
parsley or chervil, and serve hot.
**VARIATION**
Substitute slender asparagus for the
beans, and for a creamy finish, stir
in some sour cream or natural
Greek yogurt just before serving.

*NUTRIENTS PER SERVING: calories 400,
carbohydrate 55 g (including sugar 8 g),
protein 18 g, fat 12 g (saturated fat 5 g), good
source of vitamins A, B group, C, E, and folate.*

---

### COOK'S SUGGESTION

*You can use any of the wide variety of
stuffed pastas to make this dish, such as
agnolotti, cappelletti, ravioli, tortellini,
but it should be fresh rather than dried
to match the fresh vegetables.*

---

# ONION AND FETA CHEESE PIE

*The pie case for this recipe is quickly made using a scone-style dough, and the subtle flavor of fresh thyme makes an ideal accompaniment to the thick, creamy texture of the feta cheese filling.*

TIME: 30 MINUTES  SERVES: 4

| |
|---|
| 1¼ cups (175 g) plain flour |
| 1 teaspoon baking powder |
| 5 tablespoons (85 g) butter, at room temperature |
| ⅔ cup (150 ml) sour cream |
| 1 lb (450 g) onions |
| 2 sprigs of fresh thyme |
| 3–4 tablespoons olive oil |
| ½ lb (230 g) button mushrooms |
| 5 oz (140 g) feta cheese |
| Salt and black pepper |
| *To garnish:* a few chives |

**1**  Preheat the oven to 425°F (220°C). Sift the flour and baking powder into a bowl, then rub in 3 tablespoons of butter. Add 5 tablespoons of the sour cream—just under half—and mix to a soft dough.

**2**  Roll out the dough on a floured surface into a circle about 11 in. (28 cm) in diameter, and use it to line a 10 in. (25 cm) pie plate. Trim the edge, prick the base, line with parchment paper, and fill with baking beans or small balls of cooking foil. Bake blind for 10 minutes.

**3**  Meanwhile, halve, peel, and thinly slice the onions, then rinse and dry the thyme, strip the leaves from the stems, and chop them finely. Heat the oil in a large frying pan, add the onions and thyme, and fry over a moderate heat until the onions are soft and golden.

**4**  Melt the remaining butter in another frying pan. Clean and halve the mushrooms and fry until lightly browned, then stir in the rest of the sour cream and keep warm.

**5**  Remove the paper and baking beans or foil from the pie case, then return it to the oven for a few minutes until the pastry is golden.

**6**  Rinse, dry, and snip the chives. Crumble the feta cheese into the onions. Heat for 1 minute then season to taste. Spoon the mixture

into the pie case and spoon the mushrooms over the top. Sprinkle with chives and pepper and serve.

*NUTRIENTS PER SERVING: calories 674, carbohydrate 46 g (including sugar 10 g), protein 17 g, fat 48 g (saturated fat 26 g), good source of vitamins A, B group, E, and folate, and calcium.*

# NUTTY SPINACH AND MUSHROOM FRITATTA

*This hearty omelette, packed with crunchy nuts, ribbons of spinach, and tender mushrooms, can be served hot for lunch or supper or cut into thick slices for a cold packed lunch or picnic.*

TIME: 25 MINUTES  SERVES: 4

| 1 pack (250 g) young spinach leaves |
| A small bunch of fresh parsley |
| 2 tablespoons olive oil |
| 1 small onion |
| ¾ lb (335 g) small button mushrooms |
| ¾ cup (75 g) roasted cashew nuts |
| 5 medium eggs |
| Salt and black pepper |
| 3 oz (85 g) skim-milk Cheddar or Parmesan cheese |

**1** Preheat the grill to high. Then rinse and dry the spinach and parsley and chop enough parsley to give 2 tablespoons; set aside.

**2** Heat the oil in a large frying pan. Halve, peel, and finely chop the onion. Fry over a moderate heat for 3–4 minutes, stirring, until soft.

**3** Clean the mushrooms, quarter them, add them to the chopped onion, and fry, stirring frequently, for a further 3–4 minutes.

**4** Add the spinach and cook over a fairly high heat, stirring frequently, for 3–4 minutes, until the leaves have wilted and the excess liquid has evaporated. Stir in the cashews and reduce the heat to low.

**5** Break the eggs into a bowl, then add 2 tablespoons of cold water and the chopped parsley. Add seasoning and beat together.

**6** Pour the egg mixture into the spinach and cook for 5 minutes until the egg is just set and golden underneath, lifting the edges to let the uncooked egg run underneath.

**7** Grate the cheese, sprinkle it over the top and grill for 2–3 minutes, until the fritatta is set and golden, making sure that the handle of your frying pan does not burn. Alternatively, place the fritatta on a baking tray underneath the grill.

*SERVING SUGGESTION*
Serve the fritatta, hot or cold, with crusty bread and a tomato salad.

*NUTRIENTS PER SERVING: calories 395, carbohydrate 6 g (including sugar 3 g), protein 22 g, fat 32 g (saturated fat 10 g), good source of vitamins A, B group, C, E, and folate, and calcium, iron, selenium, and zinc.*

# CHEESY CHICKPEA ENCHILADAS

*Spicy chickpeas stuffed into flaky tortilla pancakes and topped with bubbling-hot cheese make a filling dish for an informal meal. Serve with cool yogurt or sour cream for a soothing contrast.*

TIME: 30 MINUTES  SERVES: 4

| |
|---|
| 1 medium red onion |
| 2 tablespoons corn oil |
| 1 clove garlic |
| 1 small, hot, fresh red chili |
| 1 lb (450 g) tomatoes |
| 1 can (19 oz / 540 ml) chickpeas |
| 1 teaspoon ground cumin |
| Salt and black pepper |
| ¼ lb (110 g) old Cheddar cheese |
| 1 small iceberg lettuce |
| 4 store-bought soft flour tortillas, 7–8 in. (18–20 cm) in diameter |
| *To serve:* thick natural yogurt, or sour cream |
| *To garnish:* a few sprigs of coriander |

**1** Preheat the grill to high. Peel and thinly slice the onion. Heat the corn oil in a frying pan and fry the sliced onion over a fairly high heat, stirring, until it is softened and lightly browned.

**2** Peel and crush the garlic, then rinse, deseed, and slice the chili. Rinse and chop the tomatoes. Drain and rinse the chickpeas.

**3** Stir the cumin into the onion, then add the garlic, chili, tomatoes, and chickpeas. Cook them over a moderate heat, stirring occasionally, for 5–8 minutes, until most of the liquid has evaporated, then season.

**4** Coarsely grate the cheese. Rinse and dry the coriander, and rinse, dry, and shred the lettuce.

**5** Lay the tortillas flat and divide the lettuce among them. Spoon chickpea mixture down the center of each, fold the sides over, and lay in an ovenproof dish. Sprinkle with the cheese and grill until it melts.

**6** Serve with yogurt or sour cream, garnished with coriander.

**VARIATION**
You can use ordinary pancakes as a substitute for the tortillas.

*NUTRIENTS PER SERVING: calories 526, carbohydrate 61 g (including sugar 18 g), protein 27 g, fat 21 g (saturated fat 7 g), good source of vitamins B group, C, E, and folate.*

### COOK'S SUGGESTION

*Enchiladas, a Mexican dish of tortilla pancakes stuffed with beans, meat or cheese and topped with a hot sauce, are traditionally baked, but grilling is faster.*

# ORIGINAL OMELETTES

*Whether you introduce an exciting flavor to an omelette with added ingredients or supply a contrasting texture with the crisp crunch of a crouton, stuffing an omelette is an easy way to transform a handful of eggs into a delicious dish in a matter of minutes.*

Omelettes do not have to be stuffed, so, when they are, the mixture should serve some purpose. It can add flavor, such as mushrooms in heavy rich cream, or a generous scattering of fresh herbs (see below). It can build in substance, with cheese melting through diced potato (see below). Or it can offer the chance to use up small quantities of leftovers in a new context—a spoonful or two of warm stew, a cushion of well-seasoned spinach, or smoked haddock with herb cream (see below).

There are no fixed rules for stuffing omelettes, except not to overdo it. The filling should not dominate the omelette, and it should not take long to cook, as the surface of the omelette should still be runny when the filling is added.

### OMELETTE FILLINGS:
*Each of the following fillings will make enough for two 2 or 3 egg omelettes. Make the fillings in a separate pan while you are cooking the omelette, so both are ready at the same time.*

### PEAS IN HERB BUTTER
Melt 2 tablespoons (30 g) of butter in a pan with three torn mint leaves or some chopped tarragon, then add 4 tablespoons of cooked fresh or frozen peas to warm through and season to taste.

### MUSHROOMS IN HEAVY CREAM
Cook 5 oz (140 g) of thinly sliced button mushrooms in 1½ tablespoons (25 g) of butter, then stir in 2 tablespoons of heavy cream or

---

## MAKING A PERFECT OMELETTE

For perfect results, where the egg is light, layered, and slightly runny, always make individual omelettes, using a 6–7 in. (15–18 cm) omelette pan.

1 For two people, break 4–6 eggs into a large measuring jug, season lightly with salt and black pepper, and beat together.

2 Put 2 tablespoons (15 g) of butter into the omelette pan, or a small frying pan, over a high heat. When it is sizzling, pour in half the beaten egg mixture and stir it quickly with a fork.

3 Draw the set mixture into the center and tilt the pan to allow the uncooked egg to run underneath. Cook until the omelette is golden brown underneath but still very moist on top.

4 Remove the pan from the heat, spoon half the chosen filling down the middle of the omelette, but slightly off-center, then fold the rest of the omelette over to enclose the filling as you roll it from the pan onto the plate.

5 Serve it immediately, or cover it with foil and keep it warm in the oven while you make the second omelette.

---

sour cream and 1 teaspoon of flavored oil. Season to taste.

### FINES HERBES
This is the classic French way of flavoring an omelette. Top, tail, and finely shred a green onion and mix it into about 2 teaspoons each of chopped fresh chervil, chives, parsley, and 1 or 2 teaspoons of fresh tarragon.

The chopped herbs can be beaten into the eggs while the omelettes are being made, or they can be stirred into 2 tablespoons of warmed heavy cream, seasoned to taste separately, and used as a filling in the usual way.

---

### POTATO, ONION, AND CHEESE
Peel and slice a medium onion, dice a cooked potato, then grate 1 full tablespoon of hard cheese—Gruyère is gooiest, but Cheddar is a good alternative. Soften the onion in 2 tablespoons of oil over a low heat, add the potato, and cook gently, stirring occasionally, until it is heated through. Season with salt and black pepper, then divide between the omelettes while still very hot and sprinkle the cheese over the top before you fold over the omelette.

### BACON AND CROUTONS
Dice four slices of streaky bacon and fry them in 1 tablespoon of oil until they are crisp; remove with a slotted spoon and set aside. Add more oil, if necessary, and fry 3 tablespoons of finely diced bread over a fairly high heat, until they are crisp all over. Return the bacon to the pan just long enough to heat through, then fold the filling inside the omelettes and serve at once.

### SMOKED HADDOCK IN PARSLEY CREAM
Skin, bone, and flake 3½ oz (100 g) of cooked smoked haddock. Warm the fish through in 3 tablespoons of heavy cream, stir in 1 tablespoon of chopped parsley and plenty of black pepper.

You could also use other smoked or leftover cooked fish for this creamy omelette filling, particularly salmon or trout.

CLASSIC EGG DISH:
OMELETTE FINES HERBES.

232

# SPICY BROCCOLI AND CAULIFLOWER

*Spicy and crisp, this delicious combination of broccoli and cauliflower with capers and pickled green peppercorns is finished off with a tasty double-cheese and breadcrumb topping.*

TIME: 25 MINUTES   SERVES: 4

| |
|---|
| 5 cloves garlic |
| 1 green chili |
| 1 lb (450 g) broccoli florets |
| 1 lb (450 g) cauliflower florets |
| 2 tablespoons olive oil |
| Salt and black pepper |
| 1 tablespoon (50 g) Gruyère cheese |
| 1 tablespoon (50 g) Parmesan cheese |
| 3 tablespoons dried breadcrumbs |
| 2 tablespoons capers |
| 1–2 tablespoons pickled green peppercorns |

**1** Preheat the grill and put a kettle of water on to boil.

**2** Peel and thinly slice the garlic, then rinse, deseed, and chop the chili. Rinse the broccoli and cauliflower florets.

**3** Heat the oil in a frying pan or large wok with a lid. Add the garlic and chili, stir in the broccoli and cauliflower florets, sprinkle with salt and pepper, and add ⅔ cup of boiling water. Cover the pan and cook the vegetables over a high heat for 4–5 minutes, or until they are tender. Stir or toss them halfway through cooking.

**4** Meanwhile, grate the Gruyère and Parmesan cheeses and mix them with the breadcrumbs.

**5** Stir the capers and peppercorns into the vegetables. Transfer them to a shallow, ovenproof dish, sprinkle the cheese and breadcrumb mixture over the top, and place under the grill until the cheese melts and the topping turns golden. Serve hot.

*SERVING SUGGESTION*
For a vegetarian meal, serve with rice, potatoes, or Bulgur Pilaf with Mushrooms (page 213).

*NUTRIENTS PER SERVING: calories 286, carbohydrate 16 g (including sugar 6 g), protein 20 g, fat 16 g (saturated fat 6 g), good source of vitamins A, B group, C, E, and folate, and calcium and zinc.*

# VEGETABLES WITH LIMA BEAN SAUCE

*A simple, creamy sauce made with puréed lima beans, oregano, and lemon juice complements the intense, slightly caramelized flavors of lightly grilled, chunky vegetables.*

TIME: 25 MINUTES  SERVES: 2

| |
|---|
| 1 medium eggplant |
| 1 red onion |
| 2 large zucchinis |
| 1 yellow pepper |
| 3 tablespoons olive oil |
| ½ can (19 oz / 540 ml) lima beans |
| ½ lemon |
| 1 clove garlic |
| 6 sprigs of fresh oregano |
| Salt and black pepper |
| 6 black olives |
| *To serve:* olive bread |

**1** Preheat the grill to high. Rinse and dry the eggplant, trim off the ends, and cut it lengthwise into slices ½ in. (1 cm) thick. Peel the onion and cut it into quarters.

**2** Rinse the zucchinis, trim off the ends, and halve lengthwise. Rinse, deseed, and quarter the pepper.

**3** Pour half the oil into a saucer and oil the vegetables with a pastry brush. Grill them for 6–8 minutes, turning them halfway through and basting again if necessary.

**4** Meanwhile, tip the beans and their liquid into a food processor and squeeze the juice from the half lemon over them. Peel the garlic and crush it into the bowl, then process until smooth.

**5** Rinse the oregano, strip off the leaves, and tear them into the puréed beans. Add the remaining olive oil, season to taste, then process briefly.

**6** Put the grilled vegetables onto individual plates, pour on the sauce, and garnish with the black olives. Serve hot with the olive bread.

*NUTRIENTS PER SERVING: calories 708, carbohydrate 103 g (including sugar 15 g), protein 26 g, fat 22 g (saturated fat 4 g), good source of vitamins B group, C, E, and folate.*

235

# LEEK AND CHEDDAR CHEESE TART

*Ready-made puff pastry lets you turn leeks, cheese, and a dash of mustard into a dish that looks as pretty as a picture.*

TIME: 30 MINUTES SERVES: 4

| |
|---|
| 7–8 slim leeks, about 2 lb (900 g) in total |
| Salt and black pepper |
| ½ lb (230 g) fresh puff pastry |
| 1 tablespoon Dijon mustard |
| 1 medium egg |
| ¾ cup (50 g) Cheddar cheese |

1   Preheat the oven to 450°F (230°C). Put a kettle of water on to boil.
2   Trim the leeks to a length of about 7 in. (18 cm) and rinse them. Arrange them in a single layer in a wide saucepan or frying pan, pour on the boiling water from the kettle, add a pinch of salt, return to the boil, reduce the heat, and simmer, covered, for 6–8 minutes.
3   While they are cooking, roll out the puff pastry on a lightly floured surface to a 10 in. (25 cm) square, then transfer the pastry square onto a baking sheet.
4   Cut a ½ in. (1 cm) strip of pastry from each of the four sides. Dampen the area around the edge of the square with water and trim the pastry strips to fit flat on top of the dampened edges, so that they look like a picture frame; press them lightly into place.
5   Drain the leeks and cool them under cold running water. Drain

again, then wrap them in a folded tea towel and press them gently to remove any remaining moisture.
6   Arrange the leeks inside the pastry case and brush them with the mustard. Break the egg into a small bowl and beat it lightly, then brush the border of the tart with the beaten egg. Grate the Cheddar cheese and spread it evenly over the top of the leeks.
7   Bake on the top rack of the oven for 15 minutes, or until the pastry is risen and golden and the cheese has melted and is bubbling. Then remove it from the oven and cut it into quarters with a serrated-edged knife. Serve hot or warm.
*SERVING SUGGESTION*
Try a leafy salad to accompany this dish, such as Lettuce, Cucumber, and Red Onion Salad (page 98).

*NUTRIENTS PER SERVING: calories 402, carbohydrate 31 g (including sugar 3 g), protein 11 g, fat 26 g (saturated fat 3 g), good source of vitamins A, B group, C, E, and folate.*

---

### COOK'S SUGGESTION

*When you shop for this recipe, buy the well-trimmed, clean leeks which are now available in many supermarkets. This will cut down on your preparation time.*

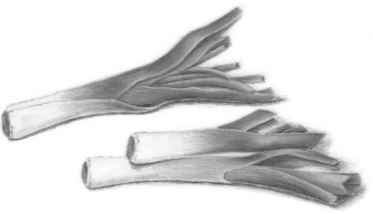

# WARM FLAGEOLET AND CHARRED VEGETABLE SALAD

*Balsamic vinegar enhances the strong flavors of the vegetables in this warm, piquant salad, excellent served as a light lunch.*

**TIME: 20 MINUTES  SERVES: 4**

| |
|---|
| 1 red pepper |
| 1 yellow pepper |
| 1 medium onion |
| 2 medium zucchinis |
| 2 tablespoons olive oil |
| 1 can (15 oz / 425 g) flageolet beans |
| 1 can (15 oz / 425 g) lentils |
| 2 large sprigs of basil |
| 2 medium tomatoes |
| 2 tablespoons crushed sun-dried tomatoes in oil |
| 1 tablespoon balsamic vinegar |
| Salt and black pepper |
| *To garnish:* 12 large black olives |

**1**  Rinse, deseed, and roughly chop the peppers. Peel and slice the onion. Trim, rinse, dry, and thinly slice the zucchinis.

**2**  Heat the oil in a large frying pan and brown the peppers, onion, and zucchinis over a high heat, stirring occasionally.

**3**  Meanwhile, drain and rinse the canned beans and lentils. Rinse, dry, and tear the basil leaves, and rinse, dry, and roughly chop the fresh tomatoes.

**4**  Add the beans and lentils to the pan, stir gently, then add the basil, the fresh tomatoes, the sun-dried tomatoes, and the vinegar.

**5**  Season the mixture, then let it heat through, stirring well. Stone the olives if necessary.

**6**  Turn the salad into a warm dish, garnish with the olives and serve immediately.

### VARIATION

Balsamic vinegar has the best flavor, but you can use a good wine or cider vinegar instead.

*NUTRIENTS PER SERVING: calories 390, carbohydrate 52 g (including sugar 9 g), protein 21 g, fat 11 g (saturated fat 1 g), good source of vitamins A, B group, C, and E.*

---

### COOK'S SUGGESTION

*Use pitted olives if you can: the Greek Kalamata variety have an excellent flavor. To stone olives easily, use a cherry stoner.*

# HOT POTATO SALAD WITH SAUSAGES

*A fine, hot, main-dish salad of tiny new potatoes and spicy vegetarian sausages, garnished with cheddar cheese, gains additional warmth from a dressing made with garlic and French mustard.*

TIME: 30 MINUTES  SERVES: 4

| |
|---|
| 1½ lb (680 g) baby new potatoes |
| Salt and black pepper |
| 1 lb (450 g) spicy vegetarian sausages |
| 2 tablespoons vegetable oil |
| 1 shallot |
| 1 large clove garlic |
| A small bunch of fresh parsley |
| A small bunch of garlic chives |
| 1 teaspoon Dijon mustard |
| 1 tablespoon plain flour |
| ½ lemon |
| 3 tablespoons white wine vinegar |
| 6 tablespoons olive oil |
| 1 tablespoon fine sugar |
| 3 oz (85 g) Cheddar cheese |

**1** Preheat the grill to high. Scrub the new potatoes and boil them in salted water for 15–20 minutes.

**2** Meanwhile, grill the sausages for about 10 minutes, or according to the manufacturer's instructions, turning them often until they are cooked through and browned.

**3** Heat the vegetable oil in a small saucepan. Peel and chop the shallot and the garlic, add them to the pan and cook for 3 minutes, until soft and just turning brown.

**4** Rinse, dry, and chop the parsley and chives. Add them to the pan, with the mustard and flour, and cook for 1 minute.

**5** Remove the pan from the heat. Squeeze 1 tablespoon of juice from the half lemon, and add it to the pan with the white wine vinegar, olive oil and sugar. Return the pan to the heat and bring the mixture slowly to the boil, stirring, until it becomes smooth and thick. Add salt and pepper to taste, then take the pan off the heat.

**6** Drain the potatoes and put them into a serving dish; thickly slice the sausages and mix them with the potatoes; then pour the garlic and mustard dressing on top, and mix it in gently. Crumble the cheese over the top and serve.

*NUTRIENTS PER SERVING: calories 677, carbohydrate 43 g (including sugar 10 g), protein 25 g, fat 46 g (saturated fat 17 g), good source of vitamins B group, C, and E.*

---

### COOK'S SUGGESTION

*Garlic chives add a stronger, much more garlicky flavor to the salad, but if they are difficult to find you can use ordinary chives instead.*

---

# KIDNEY BEAN AND VEGETABLE GRATIN

*Raisins, chilies, and fresh herbs add interesting flavors to a rich, warming casserole of rice, vegetables, and beans, topped with grilled Parmesan cheese and served with cooling Greek yogurt.*

TIME: 30 MINUTES  SERVES: 4

| |
|---|
| 3 tablespoons virgin olive oil |
| 1 medium onion |
| 2 medium sticks celery |
| 2 cloves garlic |
| 1 medium red pepper |
| ⅔ cup (125 g) seedless raisins |
| A pinch of dried oregano |
| A pinch of dried crushed red chilies |
| 1 teaspoon ground cumin |
| Salt and black pepper |

| |
|---|
| 1 can (19 oz / 540 ml) chopped tomatoes |
| ½ lb (230 g) broccoli |
| A handful of fresh coriander |
| 1 can (19 oz / 540 ml) kidney beans |
| 3 cups precooked rice |
| ¼ lb (110 g) frozen corn |
| 2½ oz (70 g) Parmesan cheese |

*To serve:* ⅔ cup (200 g) natural Greek yogurt, or sour cream, fresh crusty bread

**1** Put a kettle of water on to boil. Heat the oil in a large, heavy-based saucepan over a very low heat.

**2** Peel and chop the onion, rinse and thinly slice the celery, and peel and crush the garlic. Add them to the oil; fry gently for 5 minutes.

**3** Rinse, deseed, and chop the pepper and add it to the pan with the raisins, oregano, crushed chilies, and cumin and fry for 2 minutes.

**4** Add salt and pepper, the canned tomatoes, and 5 tablespoons of water. Bring to the boil, reduce the heat, and simmer for 5 minutes.

**5** Rinse the broccoli, cut it into florets, put them into a saucepan, and cover with boiling water. Bring back to the boil, cook for 2 minutes, then drain and set aside.

**6** Preheat the grill to medium. Rinse and chop enough coriander to give 4 tablespoons and set aside.

**7** Drain and rinse the kidney beans and add them to the vegetable mixture, with the precooked rice and corn. Return to the boil, lower the heat, and simmer for 2 minutes. Add the broccoli and heat for a further minute.

**8** Remove the pan from the heat, then stir in the coriander, and grate the Parmesan cheese over the top. Grill for 5–6 minutes to melt the cheese.

**9** Serve accompanied by yogurt or sour cream, and crusty bread.

NUTRIENTS PER SERVING: *calories 625, carbohydrate 85 g (including sugar 36 g), protein 26 g, fat 22 g (saturated fat 8 g), good source of vitamins A, B group, C, E, and folate, and calcium and zinc.*

---

### COOK'S SUGGESTION

*If you do not have a saucepan that will fit under the grill, or if it has a wood or plastic handle, transfer the cooked vegetables to an ovenproof dish before grating the cheese over them.*

# HASTY PIZZA

*You can enjoy a great pizza topping even without the pizza if you take an herb and tomato sauce, add a pepper and artichoke garnish, top with plenty of cheese, and pile it onto toasted crusty bread.*

TIME: 30 MINUTES  SERVES: 4

| |
| --- |
| 2 tablespoons olive oil |
| 1 medium onion |
| 1 medium green pepper |
| 1 medium red pepper |
| 1 can (14 oz / 398 ml) artichoke hearts |
| 2 cups (400 g) canned chopped tomatoes |
| 1 clove garlic |
| 1 teaspoon dried basil |
| 1 teaspoon dried mixed herbs |
| Salt and black pepper |
| ½ teaspoon sugar |
| 1 round loaf multigrain bread |
| ½ lb (230 g) Cheddar or mozzarella cheese, or a mixture of the two |
| 16 black olives |
| *To garnish:* sprigs of fresh basil |

**1**  Heat one tablespoon of the oil in a frying pan over a moderate heat.

Peel and chop the onion and fry it for 3–4 minutes, until soft.
**2**  Rinse, dry, deseed, and finely slice the peppers into rings. Drain the artichoke hearts and cut them in half, then set them aside.
**3**  Pour the canned tomatoes into a bowl. Peel the garlic and crush it into the tomatoes, and add the fried onions, dried herbs, salt and pepper to taste, and sugar. Mix together and set aside.
**4**  Preheat the grill to high. Heat the remaining oil in the pan, then add the pepper rings and stir-fry them for 5 minutes.
**5**  Meanwhile, slice the round top off the loaf and cut the rest across into four ½ in. (1 cm) thick slices and grill on one side. Grate the Cheddar, dice the mozzarella; rinse and dry the basil and set aside.

**6**  Turn the bread over on the grill rack and spread the tomato mixture evenly over the untoasted side of each slice. Arrange the fried pepper and the artichokes on top of the tomato, sprinkle with the cheese, and dot with the olives.
**7**  Grill the slices for 4–5 minutes, or until the cheese has melted and turned golden brown. Garnish with the basil and serve immediately.
*VARIATION*
Sliced mushrooms or avocados could be used in place of artichoke hearts. Meat eaters could add ham or salami, shrimps, or anchovy fillets.

*NUTRIENTS PER SERVING: calories 1011, carbohydrate 104 g (including sugar 14 g), protein 34 g, fat 54 g (saturated fat 15 g), good source of vitamins A, B group, C, E, and folate, and calcium, iron, and zinc.*

# BEAN AND MUSHROOM BURGERS

*Hungry children will love to tuck into these hearty, lightly spiced vegetarian burgers, made with wholesome ingredients and served with pita bread, salad, and a sweet red onion relish.*

TIME: 30 MINUTES  SERVES: 4

| |
|---|
| 1 can (19 oz / 540 ml) red kidney beans |
| 2 medium red onions, about ½ lb (230 g) in total |
| 4 tablespoons olive oil |
| 2 tablespoons red wine vinegar |
| 2 tablespoons light brown sugar |
| ½ lb (200 g) cup mushrooms |
| 1 clove garlic |
| 1 tablespoon garam masala |
| 2 tablespoons whole-wheat flour |
| A small bunch of fresh mint |
| Salt and black pepper |
| *To serve:* 4 pita breads |

**1** Rinse the beans well and spread them out on a kitchen towel to drain. Peel the onions.

**2** To make the red onion relish, heat 1 tablespoon of olive oil in a saucepan. Slice one of the onions thinly and add it to the pan with the vinegar and sugar. Bring to the boil, stirring, then reduce the heat and leave it to simmer, uncovered, for 15–20 minutes, or until the onion is softened and slightly sticky, stirring it from time to time. Then remove the pan from the heat and keep it warm.

**3** Meanwhile, quarter the other onion and put it into a food processor. Clean the mushrooms, add them to the onion, and process until finely chopped. Alternatively, chop them both finely by hand.

**4** Heat another tablespoon of olive oil in a frying pan, add the onion and mushroom mixture, and cook over a fairly high heat, stirring occasionally, for 5–8 minutes, or until golden and dry.

**5** Peel the garlic, crush it into the mushroom mixture, stir in the garam masala and flour, and cook for 1 minute. Rinse, dry, and chop enough mint to give 2 tablespoons. Remove the pan from the heat, add the mint, and season well with salt and pepper.

**6** Put the kidney beans onto a deep plate and mash them firmly with a potato masher, then stir in the cooled mushroom mixture.

**7** Divide the mixture into four and, with lightly floured hands, shape each portion into a burger.

**8** Heat the remaining oil in a large frying pan, add the beanburgers and cook them over a fairly high heat for 6–8 minutes, turning them once, until they are well browned. Warm the pita breads.

**9** Arrange the burgers on a warm dish or individual plates and spoon the onion relish over the top of them. Serve with the warm pitas and a green salad.

*NUTRIENTS PER SERVING: calories 461, carbohydrate 73 g (including sugar 15 g), protein 15 g, fat 13 g (saturated fat 2 g), good source of vitamins B group, E, and folate.*

---

### COOK'S SUGGESTION

*It is important to dry the kidney beans thoroughly before adding them to the mushroom mixture. If the beans retain too much liquid it will make the burgers difficult to handle.*

---

# SPICED CARROT AND CHICKPEA FRITTERS

*These vivid, healthy carrot and chickpea patties are whizzed together in a food processor with fresh herbs and strong spices to produce a really fresh-tasting variation on the veggieburger.*

TIME: 20 MINUTES  SERVES: 4

| |
|---|
| ¾ lb (350 g) carrots |
| 1 clove garlic |
| A large bunch of fresh coriander |
| 1 can (19 oz / 540 ml) chickpeas |
| 1½ teaspoons ground cumin |
| 1½ teaspoons ground coriander |
| 1 large egg |
| 2 tablespoons plain flour |
| Oil for frying |
| *To serve:* hamburger buns and salad |

**1** Peel the carrots, grate them coarsely and set them aside.

**2** Peel and roughly chop the garlic, then rinse, dry, and chop enough coriander to give 6 tablespoons.

**3** Drain and rinse the chickpeas and put them into a food processor with the garlic, coriander, and both ground spices. Process to a rough paste then add the carrot, egg, and flour and process briefly until evenly mixed but slightly rugged.

**4** Heat the oil in a frying pan and divide the mixture into 8 fritters. Fry in batches for 2–3 minutes on each side, until golden, then drain on kitchen paper. Serve in buns with salad.

**VARIATION**
Try making the fritters smaller and serve them as a snack or a side dish accompanied by red onion relish (see recipe above), or with your favorite chutney.

*NUTRIENTS PER SERVING: calories 464, carbohydrate 66 g (including sugar 12 g), protein 21 g, fat 14 g (saturated fat 2 g), good source of vitamins A, B group, and E.*

**HEALTHY VEGGIEBURGERS:** (*top*) BEAN AND MUSHROOM BURGERS; (*bottom*) SPICED CARROT AND CHICKPEA FRITTERS.

# TOFU AND VEGETABLES WITH SESAME SAUCE

*Smoked tofu, or bean curd, adds body and flavor to these grilled vegetables, served with a creamy sesame sauce.*

TIME: 30 MINUTES  SERVES: 2

| 4 tablespoons soy sauce |
| --- |
| 4 tablespoons olive oil |
| ¾ lb (335 g) small firm zucchinis, or a mix of zucchinis and eggplants |
| ¼ lb (110 g) medium cup mushrooms |
| ½ lb (230 g) smoked tofu |

*For the sauce:*

| A small bunch of parsley |
| --- |
| 4 tablespoons light sesame (tahini) paste |
| 1 large clove garlic |
| ½ teaspoon toasted sesame oil |
| 1 teaspoon Dijon mustard |
| Salt and black pepper |

**1** Preheat the grill to a moderate setting. Blend the soy sauce and olive oil thoroughly in a large bowl.
**2** Trim and rinse the zucchinis and slice them into thin rounds. Trim, rinse, and slice the eggplants, if using. Clean and thickly slice the mushrooms, then cut the tofu into bite-sized pieces.
**3** Add the vegetables and tofu to the soy sauce and oil and stir gently until they are well coated.
**4** Spread out in a single layer in the grill pan, or on a baking tray. Grill for about 20 minutes, until cooked and browned, shaking the pan occasionally to prevent the vegetables from sticking.
**5** Meanwhile, make the sauce. Rinse, dry, and chop enough parsley to give 2 tablespoons; set it aside. Pour the sesame paste into a measuring jug, peel the garlic, and crush it into the jug, then briskly stir in just enough water to give the sauce a creamy consistency. Stir in the chopped parsley, toasted sesame oil, and Dijon mustard, and season to taste with salt and pepper.
**6** When the vegetables and tofu are cooked, put them onto a warm serving plate and pour over the sesame sauce. Serve hot or warm.

NUTRIENTS PER SERVING: *calories 586, carbohydrate 8 g (including sugar 4 g), protein 29 g, fat 49 g (saturated fat 9 g), good source of vitamins A, B group, C, E, and folate, and calcium, iron, and zinc.*

# TOFU STIR-FRY WITH CASHEWS

*Soft tofu soaks up the flavor of a tangy, Oriental-style marinade of soy sauce and dry sherry and is then stir-fried with a crisp mixture of vegetables and cashew nuts and served with noodles.*

TIME: 30 MINUTES  SERVES: 4

²/₃ lb (300 g) tofu (fresh or packaged)

½ in. (1 cm) piece fresh root ginger

⅓ lb (150 g) snow peas

3½ oz (100 g) fresh
shiitake mushrooms

1 large red or yellow pepper

1 lb (450 g) Chinese cabbage
or lettuce hearts

1 bunch of green onions

3 tablespoons peanut oil

9 oz (250 g) thread egg noodles

Salt

3 oz (85 g) roasted cashew nuts

*For the marinade:*

2 cloves garlic

1½ tablespoons Japanese soy sauce

2 tablespoons dry sherry

1½ teaspoons toasted sesame oil

1 teaspoon brown sugar

Black pepper

**1** Preheat the oven to a low setting and put a kettle of water on to boil. To make the marinade, peel the garlic and crush it into a bowl. Add the soy sauce, sherry, sesame oil, sugar, and pepper, and stir.

**2** Drain the tofu and cut it into oblongs ½ in. (1 cm) thick, add it to the marinade and leave to soak.

**3** Peel and finely chop the ginger. Rinse, top, and tail the snow peas. Clean the mushrooms and slice them thinly. Rinse, quarter, and deseed the pepper, stack the pieces and slice them into long strips. Set them all aside.

**4** Remove any damaged outer leaves from the cabbage or lettuce, then rinse, dry, and cut it across into ½ in. (1 cm) slices. Trim, rinse, and slice the green onions.

**5** Heat 1 tablespoon of peanut oil in a frying pan over a moderate heat. Drain the tofu, reserving the marinade, stir-fry it for 3 minutes, then remove and keep warm.

**6** Heat the remaining oil in the pan. Add the ginger, snow peas,

and mushrooms and stir-fry them for 2 minutes. Then add the sliced pepper, stir-fry for 2 minutes more, and add the cabbage or lettuce and the spring onions and stir-fry for a further 2 minutes.

**7** Put the noodles into a bowl, add salt and cover with boiling water. Stir gently, cover, and set aside for as long as instructed on the package.

**8** While the noodles are cooking, pour the reserved marinade into the

vegetables, add the roasted cashew nuts and stir for 1–2 minutes until the marinade is hot.

**9** Stir the tofu into the vegetables and keep warm. Drain the noodles. Serve mixed with the vegetables.

*NUTRIENTS PER SERVING: calories 574, carbohydrate 58 g (including sugar 10 g), protein 24 g, fat 30 g (saturated fat 7 g), good source of vitamins A, B group, C, E, and folate, and calcium and zinc.*

# TOMATOES WITH A SPINACH STUFFING

*A generous filling of fresh spinach enriched with pine nuts and Parmesan cheese gives an Italian flavor to the giant tomatoes in this vegetarian dish, and it is equally delicious served hot or cold.*

TIME: 30 MINUTES  SERVES: 2

| |
|---|
| 1½ tablespoons olive oil |
| 1 package fresh spinach |
| 4 large tomatoes, about ½ lb (230 g) each |
| 4½ oz (125 g) pine nuts |
| 1 clove garlic |
| 4½ oz (125 g) Parmesan cheese |
| Salt and black pepper |

**1**  Preheat the oven to 425°F (220°C). Lightly oil a baking sheet. Destalk, rinse, and dry the spinach.
**2**  Heat the rest of the oil in a saucepan and add the spinach, cover and cook for 2 minutes. Uncover, stir, and leave to cook for 1 minute. Drain off the liquid, transfer the spinach to a bowl and set it aside.

**3**  Destalk, rinse, and dry the tomatoes; slice off and reserve the tops. Discard the pith, seeds, and juice from the center of each.
**4**  Lightly toast the pine nuts (see box, right), then add them to the spinach. Peel the garlic and crush it in, then grate over the Parmesan, season to taste with salt and black pepper, and mix.
**5**  Press the spinach mixture into the tomatoes, piling it up, then balance the tops on the stuffing and bake them on the top rack of the oven for 12–15 minutes.

*NUTRIENTS PER SERVING: calories 948, carbohydrate 19 g (including sugar 18 g), protein 40 g, fat 80 g (saturated fat 18 g), good source of vitamins A, B group, C, E, and folate, and calcium, iron, and zinc.*

### EASY DOES IT!

*Pine nuts have a wonderful flavor that is enhanced by toasting. Place them in a dry frying pan over a low heat and cook them, stirring and turning them constantly, until they turn a golden brown color.*

# ASPARAGUS PIPERADE

*In this well-traveled Spanish dish, fresh asparagus, sweet peppers, chunks of chopped tomatoes, and just enough chili to tantalize the palate are temptingly combined with fluffy scrambled eggs.*

TIME: 30 MINUTES  SERVES: 4

| |
|---|
| 1 large onion |
| 1 green chili |
| 1 large red pepper |
| 1 large green pepper |
| 3 tablespoons olive oil |
| 3 cloves garlic |
| Salt and black pepper |
| 1 lb (450 g) asparagus |
| 2 cups (400 g) canned chopped tomatoes |
| 8 slices of bread, or 4 crumpets |
| Butter for spreading |
| 4 large eggs |

**1**  Peel the onion and slice it; rinse, deseed, and dice the chili, then rinse, deseed, and slice the peppers.
**2**  Heat the olive oil in a large frying pan or a wok with a lid. Peel the garlic, crush it into the oil, and add the onion, diced chili and peppers, with salt and pepper to taste. Stir-fry them for 1 minute, then cover and cook over a high heat for 3–4 minutes, shaking the pan occasionally.
**3**  Trim the woody ends from the asparagus and rinse them, then cut each of the spears into four pieces. Add the asparagus to the onions, then cover the pan and leave them to cook for about 7–8 minutes, stirring them occasionally. Preheat the grill to high.
**4**  Stir the canned tomatoes into the vegetables, increase the heat and bring the mixture to simmering

point, then let it cook, uncovered, for 2 minutes.
**5**  Meanwhile, toast the bread or split and toast the crumpets, and butter them.
**6**  Break the eggs into a bowl and beat them lightly, then add them to the vegetables and scramble over a moderate heat, stirring, until the eggs are just set.
**7**  Serve surrounded by buttered toasts or crumpets.

*NUTRIENTS PER SERVING: calories 650, carbohydrate 50 g (including sugar 14 g), protein 20 g, fat 43 g (saturated fat 20 g), good source of vitamins A, B group, C, E, and folate, and selenium and zinc.*

**TEMPTING VEGETARIAN MAIN DISHES:** *(top)* TOMATOES WITH A SPINACH STUFFING; *(bottom)* ASPARAGUS PIPERADE.

POTATO AND GREEN BEAN CURRY

# SIDE
# DISHES

*Delicious and unusual accompaniments, from leek and carrot stir-fry to lemon zucchinis, celery and apple to polenta, provide a perfect partner to the main course.*

# EGGPLANT PARMAGIANA

*In this simple variation on an Italian classic, eggplants are layered with thick tomato passata, aromatic herbs, and creamy mozzarella cheese, and finished with a topping of grated Parmesan.*

TIME: **25 MINUTES**  SERVES: **4**

| |
|---|
| **1 lb (450 g) eggplants** |
| **5–10 tablespoons olive oil** |
| **4½ oz (125 g) mozzarella cheese** |
| **A small bunch of basil or oregano** |
| **¾ cup (200 ml) tomato passata** |
| **Salt and black pepper** |
| **1 oz (30 g) Parmesan cheese** |

**1**  Rinse and trim the eggplants; finely slice them across into rounds.
**2**  Heat a tablespoon of the oil in a large frying pan, or two smaller pans, and fry the eggplant slices in batches over a fairly high heat, turning once, until golden brown. Add more oil as necessary.
**3**  Meanwhile, preheat the grill to high. Thinly slice the mozzarella. Rinse, dry, and chop enough basil or oregano to give 2 tablespoons. Set them aside.
**4**  When the eggplants are ready, arrange them in layers in a wide, shallow, ovenproof dish. Alternate them with layers made up of the mozzarella, tomato passata, basil or oregano, and seasoning.
**5**  Grate the Parmesan over the top layer, then grill for 4–5 minutes or until golden brown and bubbling.
*SERVING SUGGESTION*
Serve with grilled meats, such as lamb cutlets or steak, with simply cooked white fish, or alongside a vegetarian risotto.

*NUTRIENTS PER SERVING: calories 323, carbohydrate 5 g (including sugar 5 g), protein 12 g, fat 28 g (saturated fat 8 g), good source of vitamins B group and E, and calcium.*

---

### COOK'S SUGGESTION

*Passata is a thick, sieved tomato juice that can add a rich tomato flavor to a dish. If you buy a brand with added garlic and herbs, omit the herbs and seasoning when making this dish.*

# EGGPLANTS WITH TAHINI DRESSING

*Lightly steamed eggplants spiked with green onions and sun-dried tomatoes are served in a Middle Eastern dressing of sesame-based tahini, making an unusual alternative to cream or butter sauces.*

TIME: 25 MINUTES  SERVES: 4

**1 lb (450 g) eggplants**

**4 green onions**

**1 oz (30 g) sun-dried tomatoes in oil**

*To garnish:* **a few sprigs of fresh dill**

*For the dressing:*

**1 clove garlic**

**1 lemon**

**1 tablespoon tahini paste**

**3 tablespoons olive oil**

**Salt and black pepper**

**1** Fill a steamer with water and bring it to the boil.

**2** Trim and rinse the eggplants. Halve them lengthwise if they are large, then cut them widthwise into slices about ¼ in. (5 mm) thick. Put them into the steamer, cover, and cook for 6–8 minutes, or until they have softened.

**3** To make the dressing, peel the garlic and crush it into a small bowl, then squeeze 3 tablespoons of juice from the lemon and add it to the garlic. Add the tahini paste and olive oil, season to taste, and mix.

**4** Trim, rinse, and thinly slice the green onions, drain and chop the sun-dried tomatoes, and set aside.

**5** Transfer the cooked eggplants to a colander and press them down firmly with a spoon to remove as much of their juice as possible—do not worry if they break up. Then transfer them to a serving bowl and

stir in the green onions and the sun-dried tomatoes.

**6** Pour over the tahini dressing and toss well. Rinse, dry, and chop enough dill to give 1 tablespoon and scatter it over the eggplants. Leave them to cool for 5 minutes to let the flavor develop before serving.

*SERVING SUGGESTION*

This unusual dish goes particularly well with simple grilled lamb or chicken. It can also be served as an appetizer, accompanied by some hot crusty bread.

*NUTRIENTS PER SERVING: calories 140, carbohydrate 4 g (including sugar 2 g), protein 2 g, fat 13 g (saturated fat 2 g), good source of vitamins B group, C, and E.*

# DAHL

*Indian cookery uses a wide variety of lentils and split peas that are infused with flavor by simmering with spices and served as dahl—a creamy accompaniment to curries.*

**TIME: 25 MINUTES  SERVES: 4**

| |
|---|
| ¾ lb (335 g) split red lentils |
| 1 teaspoon ground turmeric |
| ½ teaspoon chili powder |
| ½ in. (1 cm) piece fresh root ginger |
| 2 cloves garlic |
| ½ teaspoon garam masala |
| Salt |
| 1½ tablespoons (25 g) butter |
| A pinch of ground cumin |
| 1 small onion |

**1**  Put a kettle of water on to boil. Pick over the lentils and remove any small pieces of grit, then put them into a sieve and rinse them under a cold running tap.

**2**  Put the lentils into a saucepan and cover with 5 cups of boiling water from the kettle. Add the turmeric and chili powder, cover, and bring to the boil.

**3**  Meanwhile, peel the ginger, cut it into 4 thin slices, and add them to the lentils. Peel the garlic and crush it into the saucepan. As soon as the lentils reach boiling point, reduce the heat and simmer for 10 minutes, or until they are soft and almost all the liquid has been absorbed.

**4**  Stir in the garam masala, then add some salt to taste and cook the dahl for a further 5 minutes, leaving the pan uncovered if the mixture is still soupy.

**5**  Meanwhile, heat the butter and cumin in a small frying pan. Peel and dice the onion and fry it gently in the spiced butter until soft.

**6**  Transfer the dahl to a heated serving dish, stir in the fried onion and serve hot.

*NUTRIENTS PER SERVING: calories 333, carbohydrate 51 g (including sugar 3 g), protein 21 g, fat 6 g (saturated fat 4 g), good source of vitamins B group and E, and iron and zinc.*

---

### COOK'S SUGGESTION

*Many legumes require soaking in cold water followed by a long period of boiling, but split red lentils do not need soaking, and cook very quickly.*

# POTATO AND GREEN BEAN CURRY

*Tender, sliced new potatoes and fine green beans are cooked in an aromatic mixture of butter and delicate spices, and can be served with rice or nan bread, or as a side dish to another curry.*

TIME: 30 MINUTES  SERVES: 4

| 1 lb (450 g) small new potatoes |
| 1/2 lb (230 g) fine green beans |
| 1 tablespoon (15 g) butter |
| 3 tablespoons sunflower oil |
| 2 small green chilies |
| 1/2 teaspoon cumin seeds |
| 1/2 teaspoon ground turmeric |
| 1/4 teaspoon garam masala |
| 1 clove garlic |
| Salt |

**1** Scrub the new potatoes and cut them into thick slices. Top and tail the green beans, then cut them into 1 in. (2.5 cm) lengths, rinse them, and leave them to drain.

**2** Heat the butter and oil in a wide, shallow saucepan or frying pan, over a high heat. When they begin to sizzle, stir in the whole green chilies and the cumin seeds, turmeric, and garam masala. Peel the garlic and crush it into the pan; stir and fry for 30 seconds.

**3** Add the potatoes to the pan and season with some salt. Stir them until they are coated with the spiced butter and oil.

**4** Stir in the beans, cover the pan, then reduce the heat to moderate and cook for 15 minutes, stirring occasionally. The curry is ready as soon as the potatoes are tender.

NUTRIENTS PER SERVING: *calories 197, carbohydrate 20 g (including sugar 3 g), protein 3 g, fat 12 g (saturated fat 3 g), good source of vitamins B group, C, E, and folate.*

# CHESTNUT AND CELERIAC PURÉE

*This smooth, velvety purée of celeriac and chestnuts, cooked in vegetable stock, is perfect on a cold
winter's night as a wholesome, comforting accompaniment to hot or cold roast meat or game dishes.*

TIME: 30 MINUTES  SERVES: 4

| |
| --- |
| 1¼ cups vegetable stock |
| 1 bouquet garni |
| 1 lb (450 g) celeriac |
| 1 lb (450 g) whole cooked unsweetened chestnuts, canned or vacuum packed |
| A small bunch of chives |
| 1½ tablespoons (25 g) butter |
| 2 tablespoons whipping cream, optional |
| Salt and black pepper |

**1** Pour the vegetable stock into a
large saucepan, add the bouquet
garni, and bring to the boil. Then
reduce the heat, cover the pan, and
leave the stock to simmer while
preparing the celeriac.

**2** Peel the celeriac, cut it into ½ in.
(1 cm) dice, and add them to the
simmering stock. Cover and cook
for 10 minutes or until softened.
**3** Drain the chestnuts, if necessary,
add them to the celeriac, and
simmer for 3–4 minutes more.
**4** Meanwhile, rinse, dry, and chop
or snip the chives.
**5** When the chestnuts and celeriac
are cooked, strain them well and
reserve the stock. Remove the
bouquet garni and purée or blend
the celeriac and chestnuts. Then
return the purée to the saucepan,
add the butter, and place over a low
heat until the butter has melted.
**6** If you are using the whipping
cream, stir it in a tablespoon at a
time so the purée does not become

too thin. If it is still too thick, add a
little of the reserved stock, or one or
two more tablespoons of whipping
cream, to thin it slightly.
**7** Taste, season with salt and black
pepper, then turn it into a serving
dish, and sprinkle with the chives.
*SERVING SUGGESTION*
This purée makes an elegant partner
to a pork roast or to cold turkey on
Boxing Day. It also goes well with
sausages. Or you can serve it as a
vegetarian course, accompanied by a
green salad garnished with apples
and chopped walnuts.

*NUTRIENTS PER SERVING: calories 287,
carbohydrate 48 g (including sugar 1 g),
protein 4 g, fat 9 g (saturated fat 3 g),
good source of vitamins B group, C, and E.*

# SAUTÉED BRUSSELS SPROUTS

*Golden fried Brussels sprouts mingle with crisp morsels of bacon and water chestnuts in this crunchy dish, while wholegrain mustard and a hint of orange add an aromatic touch and bring out the flavor.*

TIME: 25 MINUTES  SERVES: 4

---

1 tablespoon corn oil

---

5 slices (75 g) smoked bacon

---

1 lb (450 g) fresh
Brussels sprouts

---

1 orange

---

3 tablespoons (50 g) butter

---

2 teaspoons wholegrain mustard

---

1 can (4 oz / 115 g) whole
water chestnuts in water

---

Salt and black pepper

**1**  Heat the corn oil in a frying pan, then dice the smoked bacon and fry it for 2–3 minutes until it turns golden brown.

**2**  Rinse the Brussels sprouts, trim them if necessary, and cut in half. Wash any wax off the orange and grate the rind into the frying pan with the bacon and add the butter, mustard, and sprouts. Cook over a moderate heat for 5 minutes, stirring, until the sprouts are crisp.

**3**  Meanwhile, drain and roughly chop the water chestnuts, stir them into the sprouts, and cook them for 3–4 minutes until the sprouts are golden and the chestnuts are heated through. Add salt and black pepper to taste and serve.

*NUTRIENTS PER SERVING: calories 224, carbohydrate 7g (including sugar 5g), protein 8g, fat 19g (saturated fat 9g), good source of vitamins B group, C, E, and folate.*

255

# A HAT-TRICK OF FRESH FLAVORS

### LEEK AND CARROT STIR-FRY

*Two favorite winter vegetables team up with tarragon in this refreshing combination, stir-fried in minutes.*

**TIME: 20 MINUTES  SERVES: 4**

| |
|---|
| 1½ lb (680 g) leeks |
| ½ lb (230 g) carrots |
| 2 tablespoons olive oil |
| 1 large sprig fresh tarragon |
| Salt and black pepper |

**1**  Discard the tough outer leaves and two-thirds of the green tops from the leeks, then slice thinly, widthwise. Place them in a colander and rinse under the cold tap, then drain them well.
**2**  Peel the carrots and grate them.
**3**  Heat the oil in a wok or large frying pan over a moderate heat. Rinse and chop the tarragon.
**4**  Add the leeks to the hot oil and fry for about 2 minutes, or until they just begin to wilt.
**5**  Stir in the grated carrots and add salt, pepper, and the chopped tarragon. Continue to cook for a further 2 minutes, then serve.

*VARIATION*
You can vary the choice of fresh herb to suit your own taste, or use whatever herb is available.

*NUTRIENTS PER SERVING: calories 89, carbohydrate 7g (including sugar 6g), protein 2g, fat 6g (saturated fat 1g), good source of vitamins A, B group, C, E, and folate.*

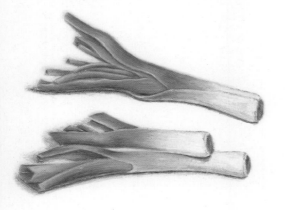

### ORANGE AND SESAME CARROTS

*The natural crunch and sweet taste of young carrots is enhanced by cooking them in orange juice.*

**TIME: 25 MINUTES  SERVES: 4**

| |
|---|
| 1 lb (450 g) small, young carrots |
| 1 medium orange |
| 1 tablespoon (15 g) butter, or 1 tablespoon sunflower oil |
| Salt and black pepper |
| 1 tablespoon sesame seeds |

**1**  Peel the carrots, unless they are organic—if so they will only need scrubbing. If they are very small, leave them whole; otherwise, cut them in half lengthwise.
**2**  Wash any wax off the orange, then remove the rind with a zester and squeeze out the juice. Put the orange rind and juice into a large saucepan, then add the butter or sunflower oil and bring to the boil over a moderate heat.
**3**  Add the carrots to the saucepan, then season them to taste with some salt and black pepper. Bring back to the boil, then reduce the heat to moderate, cover, and simmer for 10–12 minutes, shaking the pan occasionally, until the carrots are tender, but not soft.
**4**  Meanwhile, put the sesame seeds into a frying pan and dry fry them over a fairly high heat for about 2 minutes, shaking the pan, until golden.
**5**  Stir the sesame seeds into the carrots and serve.

*VARIATION*
If small new carrots are not in season, you can use larger, older ones, but these will need to be sliced thinly.

*NUTRIENTS PER SERVING: calories 87, carbohydrate 8g (including sugar 7g), protein 2g, fat 6g (saturated fat 2g), good source of vitamins A, B group, and E.*

### CURRIED PARSNIP PURÉE

*Sweet-tasting parsnips mingle with hot curry and fresh herbs to make a warmly substantial purée.*

**TIME: 20 MINUTES  SERVES: 4**

| |
|---|
| 1½ lb (680 g) parsnips |
| Salt and black pepper |
| 3–4 sprigs of fresh parsley |
| 1½ tablespoons (25 g) butter |
| 1 tablespoon medium or hot curry powder |
| 4 tablespoons sour cream |

**1**  Put a kettle of water on to boil. Peel the parsnips, cut them into small chunks, and put them into a saucepan with a little salt. Cover with boiling water and return to the boil, then reduce the heat and simmer them for 8–10 minutes, or until they are tender.
**2**  While the parsnips are cooking, rinse, dry, and chop the parsley and set it aside.
**3**  Drain the parsnips thoroughly, then return them to the saucepan and mash them coarsely with a potato masher.
**4**  Add the butter, curry powder, and sour cream to the mashed parsnips, season the mixture well with black pepper, and beat it until it becomes a smooth purée.
**5**  Transfer the parsnip purée into a heated serving dish, then fluff it up or swirl over the surface with a fork. As a finishing touch, sprinkle the chopped parsley over the top of the purée.

*NUTRIENTS PER SERVING: calories 162, carbohydrate 16g (including sugar 7g), protein 3g, fat 10g (saturated fat 6g), good source of vitamins B group, C, E, and folate.*

**FRESH AND EASY ACCOMPANYING DISHES:**
(*top*) LEEK AND CARROT STIR-FRY;
(*bottom left*) ORANGE AND SESAME CARROTS;
(*right*) CURRIED PARSNIP PURÉE.

# ITALIAN BAKED ENDIVE

*Plump heads of endive married to the intense Mediterranean flavors of sun-dried tomatoes, lemon, and black olives taste good baked beneath a crunchy crust of Parmesan cheese and breadcrumbs.*

TIME: 30 MINUTES  SERVES: 4

| |
|---|
| 1 medium-thick slice of day-old bread or 2 tablespoons (15 g) fresh white breadcrumbs |
| 1 full tablespoon (40 g) Parmesan cheese |
| 6 sun-dried tomatoes in oil |
| 4 large heads endive |
| ½ lemon |
| 3 tablespoons olive oil |
| Black pepper |
| 16 pitted black olives |

**1**  Preheat the oven to 400°F (200°C). Remove and discard the crusts from the slice of bread, if using, and grind it into breadcrumbs in a food processor. Grate the Parmesan cheese into the breadcrumbs, mix them together and set aside.

**2**  Drain the sun-dried tomatoes on kitchen paper, then chop them and set them aside.

**3**  Remove any blemished outer leaves from the endive heads, neaten the bases, and cut each head into quarters lengthwise.

**4**  Squeeze the lemon half and measure 1 tablespoon of the juice into a large, shallow, ovenproof dish. Then stir in 2 tablespoons of the olive oil.

**5**  Arrange the quartered endive, cut sides up, in the ovenproof dish. Drizzle the remaining olive oil over them, then season them with black pepper.

**6**  Scatter the sun-dried tomatoes over the endive, followed by the black olives, then sprinkle the cheese and breadcrumb mixture over the top. Put the dish into the oven and bake for 15 minutes, until the topping is golden brown.

NUTRIENTS PER SERVING: *calories 189, carbohydrate 7 g (including sugar 1 g), protein 5 g, fat 16 g (saturated fat 4 g), good source of vitamins B group and E.*

# GRILLED ENDIVE AND BEET

*This colorful combination of grilled endive in an orange juice and wholegrain mustard dressing, mixed with sliced beets, can be served either warm or cold with roast or cold cuts of meat.*

TIME: **25 MINUTES** SERVES: **4**

| |
| --- |
| **4 large heads of white endive** |
| **4 tablespoons olive oil** |
| **½ lb (230 g) cooked beet** |
| **1 orange** |
| **3 tablespoons good-quality mayonnaise** |
| **2 teaspoons wholegrain mustard** |

**1** Preheat the grill. Rinse and dry the endive, then trim the heads and remove any damaged outer leaves. Cut the heads of endive in half, lengthwise.

**2** Put the halves on the grill rack, cut sides down, brush with some of the olive oil and grill for 5 minutes, about 4 in. (10 cm) away from the heat. Turn them over, brush with the remaining olive oil and grill for 3 minutes more until the edges begin to char.

**3** Meanwhile, slice the beet into thin discs and set them aside.

**4** To make the orange and mustard dressing, squeeze 1 tablespoon of juice from the orange and stir it into the mayonnaise, then stir in the wholegrain mustard.

**5** Remove the endive from the grill. Arrange it, cut sides up, around a serving dish, like the spokes of a wheel. Spoon the orange and mustard dressing on top and lay the sliced beet in between.

*NUTRIENTS PER SERVING: calories 223, carbohydrate 10 g (including sugar 7 g), protein 2 g, fat 21 g (saturated fat 3 g), good source of vitamins B group, E, and folate.*

# ZUCCHINIS, APPLES, AND PERSILLADE

*Persillade, a wonderfully scented combination of chopped parsley and garlic, contributes a classic French flavoring to this fruity dish of fried zucchini, tomato, onion, and apple.*

TIME: 25 MINUTES  SERVES: 4

| |
|---|
| 1 red or regular onion |
| 4 tablespoons olive oil |
| 1 medium apple |
| 1 medium tomato |
| 1 lb (450 g) small zucchinis |
| Salt and black pepper |
| A medium bunch of parsley |
| 1 clove garlic |

**1**  Peel and thinly slice the onion. Heat 2 tablespoons of the oil in a frying pan, add the onion, and cook over a low heat for 7–8 minutes, until it has softened.

**2**  Rinse and core the apple, chop it into cubes, then rinse and cube the tomato. When the onion is soft, stir in the apple and tomato and cook them over a low heat for 5 minutes, stirring them occasionally.

**3**  Trim and rinse the zucchinis, slice them lengthwise into thin strips, then cut the strips into 2 in. (5 cm) pieces. Sprinkle them with salt and toss with your hands. Heat the remaining oil in another frying pan and fry the zucchinis over a moderate heat until they release their moisture. Increase the heat and continue cooking until all of the liquid has evaporated, shaking the pan to make sure the zucchinis do not burn.

**4**  Reduce the heat, then add the apple, tomato, and onion mixture to the zucchinis and leave to simmer for 5–6 minutes.

**5**  While the mixture is simmering, rinse, dry, and chop enough parsley to give 4 tablespoons, then peel and

crush the garlic and mix it with the parsley to make the persillade. Stir the persillade into the frying pan with the vegetables. Simmer for a few minutes to cook the garlic, then grind in some black pepper and add some more salt if necessary. Serve immediately.

*VARIATION*

This dish can be turned into a main course by stirring ½ lb (230 g) of good-quality chopped, cooked ham into the pan and heating it just until the ham is warmed through, before adding the persillade.

*NUTRIENTS PER SERVING: calories 150, carbohydrate 9 g (including sugar 8 g), protein 3 g, fat 12 g (saturated fat 2 g), good source of vitamins B group, C, E, and folate.*

# LEMON ZUCCHINIS ok

*This is a simple but refreshing dish of thinly sliced, tender zucchinis with a generous sprinkling of finely grated lemon zest, seasoned with flaky sea salt and black pepper.*

TIME: **15** MINUTES  SERVES: **4**

**1 lb (450 g) small zucchinis**
**1½ tablespoons olive oil**
**1 lemon**
**Flaky sea salt and black pepper**

**1**  Trim and rinse the zucchinis and slice them thinly diagonally.
**2**  Heat the olive oil in a large frying pan, then add the zucchinis and fry, stirring them frequently, until they are tender.
**3**  Meanwhile, wash any wax off the lemon and finely grate the rind.

When the zucchinis are cooked, sprinkle the lemon rind over them and season well with flaky sea salt and black pepper.

*SERVING SUGGESTION*
Lemon Zucchinis are a delicious accompaniment to any main dish, especially Chicken Breasts with Apples and Cider (page 180) or plain grilled fish.

*NUTRIENTS PER SERVING: calories 56, carbohydrate 2 g (including sugar 2 g), protein 2 g, fat 4 g (saturated fat 1 g), good source of vitamins B group, C, and E.*

# PARSNIP AND APPLE CREAM

*The tart flavor of cooking apple balances the smooth sweetness of parsnips as they are melted into heavy cream in this luxurious vegetable dish, perfect to offer with plain roasts or grills.*

TIME: 20 MINUTES  SERVES: 4

| 1 lb (450 g) parsnips |
| 2 tablespoons olive oil |
| 1 cooking apple |
| Salt and black pepper |
| ½ lemon |
| 3 sprigs of fresh thyme |
| ¼ cup heavy cream |

**1** Peel and coarsely grate the parsnips. If they are old, cut them into quarters and remove and discard the woody cores before you begin grating.

**2** Heat the olive oil in a large, shallow saucepan, add the grated parsnips, and cook them over a moderate heat.

**3** Meanwhile, peel and coarsely grate the apple, stopping when you reach the core. Stir it into the pan with the parsnips, season, then squeeze in half a tablespoon of juice from the half lemon.

**4** Rinse the thyme, strip the leaves from the stems (see box, right), and add them. Cook for 3–5 minutes more, stirring occasionally, until the parsnips are tender.

**5** Pour the cream into the pan and stir while you heat it through. Transfer to a heated dish and serve.

*NUTRIENTS PER SERVING: calories 212, carbohydrate 17g (including sugar 11g), protein 2g, fat 16g (saturated fat 7g), good source of vitamins B group, C, E, and folate.*

## EASY DOES IT!

*To strip the leaves off the thyme, hold a sprig by the tip and run your thumb and forefinger down the stem, pushing off the leaves as you go.*

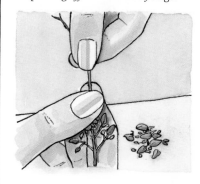

# MIXED BEANS WITH PANCETTA

*Fresh and canned beans mixed with cubes of smoky fried bacon and simmered in a herby sauce go well with any meat or firm fish, especially chicken, rabbit, or salmon.* Nice – Good

### TIME: 30 MINUTES  SERVES: 4

| |
|---|
| 1 cup chicken stock, or white wine |
| 1 bouquet garni |
| ¾ lb (335 g) fine green beans |
| 1 can (19 oz / 540 ml) cannellini beans |
| ½ lb (230 g) pancetta, or rindless, dry-cured smoked bacon |
| 1 medium red or regular onion |
| A few sprigs of fresh tarragon or parsley |
| 1 tablespoon whipping cream |
| Salt and black pepper |

**1** Put the stock or white wine into a small saucepan with the bouquet garni, bring to the boil, and simmer until the liquid has reduced by half.

**2** Top and tail the green beans, cut them into 1 in. (2.5 cm) lengths and set them aside. Drain and rinse the canned beans and set aside.

**3** Cut the pancetta or bacon into small cubes. Fry them in a large, dry frying pan for 1–2 minutes until crisp, then drain on kitchen paper. Discard all but 1 tablespoon of the pancetta or bacon fat.

**4** Peel and chop the onion and fry it in the remaining fat over a medium heat until lightly browned.

**5** Add both lots of beans and the reduced stock or wine to the frying pan. Bring to the boil, cover, then reduce the heat and simmer for about 10 minutes until the green beans are tender. To test them for tenderness, cool a bean under the cold tap, then bite into it. When the beans are ready, there should be almost no liquid left in the pan.

**6** Meanwhile, rinse and chop the herb. Add the whipping cream to the beans, warm it through, then add the pancetta or bacon, the herb, and salt and pepper to taste. Let the meat warm through, then serve.

*NUTRIENTS PER SERVING: calories 322, carbohydrate 19 g (including sugar 4 g), protein 20 g, fat 19 g (saturated fat 2 g), good source of vitamins B group, C, E, and folate.*

# BABY VEGETABLES WITH SOUR CREAM

*This rich, warm trio of crisp steamed vegetables makes an excellent accompaniment to grilled fish or meat dishes, and it can also be served on its own as a vegetable salad.*

TIME: **20** MINUTES  SERVES: **4**

| |
|---|
| ½ lb (230 g) baby carrots |
| ½ lb (230 g) baby zucchinis |
| ½ lb (230 g) fine asparagus spears |
| ¾ cup sour cream |
| 2 teaspoons wholegrain mustard |
| 1 tablespoon (15 g) salted butter, at room temperature |
| Black pepper |

**1**   Prepare a steamer by half filling the bottom pan with water and putting it on to boil.

**2**   Meanwhile, peel and trim the carrots and cut any large ones in half lengthwise. Trim and rinse the baby zucchinis and halve them lengthwise, then trim and rinse the asparagus spears.

**3**   Put the carrots into the steamer, cover them and steam for 5 minutes. Then lay the zucchinis over the carrots, and the asparagus over the zucchinis. Replace the cover and steam for 5 minutes.

**4**   While the vegetables are in the steamer, put the sour cream into a saucepan, then stir in the mustard and heat the mixture very gently until just warmed through.

**5**   Warm a serving bowl, put the vegetables into it, and stir in the

### EASY DOES IT!

*If you do not have a steamer, use a metal sieve resting over a large saucepan. Make sure the sieve sits above the level of the water so that the steam can circulate all around.*

butter and some black pepper. Pour in the warm cream dressing, stir gently to mix it in thoroughly, and serve at once.

***VARIATION***

If asparagus is not in season, replace it with fine french beans.

*NUTRIENTS PER SERVING: calories 170, carbohydrate 7g (including sugar 6g), protein 5g, fat 14g (saturated fat 8g), good source of vitamins A, B group, C, E, and folate.*

# SWEET POTATO RÖSTI

*Grated potato rösti cakes make a crunchy, individual accompaniment to grilled meat or roast game.*
*Here they are given a fresh appeal by using succulent sweet potatoes for their delicious flavor.*

**TIME: 30 MINUTES  SERVES: 4**

1½ lb (680 g) sweet potatoes
Salt and black pepper
3 tablespoons sunflower oil
1½ tablespoons (25 g) butter

**1**  Preheat the oven to its lowest setting. Line a baking sheet with a double thickness of kitchen paper and set aside.
**2**  Peel and coarsely grate the sweet potatoes, then put them into a mixing bowl. Season and mix well.
**3**  Heat half the sunflower oil in a large, nonstick frying pan and add half the butter.
**4**  Take half the potato mixture and divide it into four, then shape each portion into a round patty about ½ in. (1 cm) thick and press

together firmly. As soon as the butter begins to sizzle, carefully place the patties in the pan.
**5**  Cook the rösti cakes over a moderate heat for 5 minutes, or until they become crisp and golden brown underneath, then turn them over carefully with a fish slice and cook for a further 5 minutes (do not worry if the patties break up as you turn them over—simply pat them back into shape). While they are cooking, shape the remaining mixture into 4 more cakes.
**6**  When the first batch is cooked, transfer them to the lined baking sheet and drain for 1–2 minutes. Keep them warm in the oven.
**7**  Add the remaining sunflower oil and butter to the pan, heat until sizzling, and fry the remaining rösti.

**VARIATION**
The rösti can also be cooked in one large cake and divided into eight portions at the table. You can add finely chopped bacon or ham for extra flavor.

**NUTRIENTS PER SERVING:** *calories 233, carbohydrate 28 g (including sugar 7 g), protein 2 g, fat 14 g (saturated fat 5 g), good source of vitamins A, B group, C, and E.*

---

**COOK'S SUGGESTION**

*The skins of sweet potatoes range from white and pink to reddish brown, their flesh from white to orange. The pink-skinned, white-fleshed variety is readily available, but orange flesh has the best flavor.*

# ROAST NEW POTATOES WITH ROSEMARY

*Tiny, tender new potatoes, delicately scented with lemon and flavored with fresh rosemary, are roasted to glowing, golden perfection in this simple, tasty dish that takes very little time to prepare.*

TIME: 30 MINUTES  SERVES: 4

1¼ lb (560 g) even-sized baby new potatoes

2 tablespoons olive oil

1 lemon

2–3 large sprigs of fresh rosemary

Salt and black pepper

**1** Preheat the oven to 450°F (230°C) and put a kettle of water on to boil.

**2** Scrub the potatoes and put them into a large saucepan. Cover with boiling water, bring back to the boil, and boil gently for 5 minutes.

**3** Meanwhile, pour the olive oil into a large, shallow roasting pan and put it into the oven to heat.

**4** Wash any wax off the lemon and finely grate the rind or remove with a zester. Rinse and strip the rosemary leaves from the stems.

**5** Drain the potatoes well. Put them into the hot oil and stir well to coat evenly. Sprinkle the lemon rind, rosemary leaves, and some salt and black pepper over them. Make sure the oil is really hot before you begin roasting—the potatoes should start to sizzle as soon as you put them into the pan.

**6** Roast the potatoes on the top rack of the oven for 20 minutes, until golden.

*NUTRIENTS PER SERVING: calories 158, carbohydrate 25 g (including sugar 2 g), protein 3 g, fat 6 g (saturated fat 1 g), good source of vitamins B group, C, and E.*

### COOK'S SUGGESTION

*Choose tiny new potatoes, about the size of a marble, for this elegant dish. If you can only buy larger potatoes, cut them into halves, or even quarters.*

# CABBAGE WITH BLUE CHEESE AND CREAM

*Savoy, the king of cabbages, with a rich dressing of cream and hot blue cheese, makes a dish that goes well with roast lamb.*

TIME: 20 MINUTES  SERVES: 4

| 1 tablespoon olive oil |
| 1 large onion |
| 1 small savoy cabbage, about 1 lb (450 g) |
| Salt and black pepper |
| 4 oz (110 g) Stilton cheese |
| ¾ cup light cream |

**1**  Heat the olive oil in a saucepan. Peel and finely chop the onion. Add it to the oil and cook gently.
**2**  Meanwhile, trim off and discard any tough or bruised outer leaves from the cabbage. Cut it in half, then remove the core and finely shred the leaves. Rinse the leaves well and drain them.
**3**  Add the cabbage to the saucepan and stir, then cover and cook over a moderate heat for 6–8 minutes, shaking the pan frequently. You may prefer not to add salt as the Stilton will give a salty flavor.
**4**  While the cabbage is cooking, cut the Stilton into small cubes. Remove the pan from the heat, add the cream, Stilton, and some black pepper, then return to the heat and stir until the cheese has melted, but do not allow it to boil. The melted cheese will thicken the cream.

*NUTRIENTS PER SERVING: calories 284, carbohydrate 10 g (including sugar 8 g), protein 10 g, fat 23 g (saturated fat 13 g), good source of vitamins A, B group, C, E, and folate.*

# STIR-FRIED CABBAGE AND SALAD GREENS

*White cabbage contrasts with dark salad greens in this easy stir-fry, while crunchy cashew nuts and celery add flavor.*

TIME: 20 MINUTES  SERVES: 4–6

| ¾ lb (335 g) white cabbage |
| ¾ lb (335 g) salad greens |
| 2 cloves garlic |
| ¾ in. (2 cm) piece fresh root ginger |
| 2 sticks celery |
| 4 green onions |
| 2 tablespoons sesame oil |
| 2 oz (55 g) unsalted cashew nuts |
| *To serve:* light soy sauce |

**1**  Trim, rinse, dry, and shred the white cabbage and salad greens. Peel and chop the garlic, peel and grate the ginger, and rinse, dry, and slice the celery and green onions.
**2**  Heat the sesame oil in a large frying pan and fry the cashew nuts for 30 seconds, until they just begin to turn brown.
**3**  Add the garlic, ginger, celery, and green onions and cook them for 30 seconds, being careful not to let the garlic burn.
**4**  Add the cabbage and salad greens; stir-fry for 3–5 minutes, until softened but not wilted.
**5**  Serve sprinkled with soy sauce.

*NUTRIENTS PER SERVING, WHEN SERVING 4: calories 182, carbohydrate 10 g (including sugar 7 g), protein 7 g, fat 13 g (saturated fat 2 g), good source of vitamins A, B group, C, and folate and calcium.*

**CREATIVE CABBAGE DISHES:**
(*top*) WITH BLUE CHEESE AND CREAM; (*bottom*) STIR-FRIED WITH SALAD GREENS.

269

# MIXED MUSHROOMS WITH BRANDY

*A harmonious mixture of dried and fresh mushrooms, cooked in olive oil and their own juices with onion, garlic, fresh parsley, and a splash of brandy, makes an indulgent side dish.*

TIME: 30 MINUTES  SERVES: 4

| |
|---|
| A small bunch of parsley |
| 1 oz (30 g) dried morels or cèpes |
| 1½ tablespoons (25 g) butter |
| 1 tablespoon olive oil |
| 2 cloves garlic |
| 1 medium onion |
| ½ lb (230 g) white or button mushrooms |
| ½ lb (230 g) shiitake mushrooms |
| ⅓ lb (150 g) oyster mushrooms |
| 1–2 tablespoons brandy |
| Salt and black pepper |

**1** Put a half-filled kettle on to boil. Rinse, dry, and chop enough parsley to give 3 tablespoons. Put the dried mushrooms into a small bowl, cover with 1 cup of boiling water, and leave to soak.

**2** Meanwhile, heat the butter and olive oil in a large frying pan over a moderate heat. Peel and crush the garlic and set aside. Peel and finely chop the onion, add it to the pan, and fry over a moderate heat while preparing the fresh mushrooms.

**3** Clean the mushrooms. Halve the white or button mushrooms, slice the shiitake mushrooms thickly, and cut the oyster mushrooms into strips lengthwise, removing the stalks if they are tough.

**4** Raise the heat under the pan, add the garlic and the mushrooms. Stir-fry for 5 minutes, until the mushrooms are just softened.

**5** Meanwhile, line a sieve with kitchen paper and place it over a bowl. Pour the soaked mushrooms into it so the paper catches any grit

and the soaking water drains into the bowl. Reserve this liquid. Rinse and chop the drained mushrooms.

**6** With a slotted spoon, lift the fried onion and mushrooms from the frying pan and put them into a bowl, leaving their juices in the pan.

**7** Add the drained mushrooms and their soaking water to the pan. Boil rapidly until the liquid has a syrupy consistency.

**8** Stir in the brandy. Return the mushrooms to the pan, season to taste, stir in the parsley, and reheat. Transfer to a warm dish to serve.

*NUTRIENTS PER SERVING: calories 126, carbohydrate 4 g (including sugar 3 g), protein 5 g, fat 9 g (saturated fat 4 g), good source of vitamins B group, E, and folate and selenium.*

# POLENTA WITH SMOKED CHEESE

*In this versatile, colorful, and substantial version of Italian polenta, the thick, creamy, cooked cornmeal is given a mixture of flavors with strong cheese, olives, an aromatic herb, and peppercorns.*

TIME: 20 MINUTES  SERVES: 4

**2 cups instant polenta
(precooked cornmeal)**

**A small bunch of sage,
oregano, basil, or parsley**

**½ lb (230 g) smoked mature cheese
such as smoked Cheddar
or smoked Fontina**

**½–1 tablespoon black
or mixed peppercorns**

**8–10 pitted black olives**

**1** Put the polenta into a saucepan with 3½ cups of water. Place over a high heat, bring it to the boil, then reduce the heat and leave to simmer for 10 minutes, stirring the polenta frequently with a large wooden spoon or paddle to remove any lumps.
**2** Meanwhile, rinse and dry the herb, strip the leaves from the stalks and chop them finely. Grate or dice the smoked cheese and crush the peppercorns. Finely chop the olives.
**3** When the polenta becomes thick and starts to stiffen, stir in the herb, smoked cheese, peppercorns to taste, and the olives. Beat vigorously until the cheese is incorporated and the mixture begins to leave the sides of the saucepan when stirred.
**4** Serve immediately or leave to stand for 5–10 minutes to stiffen further. It will remain hot.

*SERVING SUGGESTION*
While the polenta is standing, steam some green vegetables such as snow peas, or heat up a seasoned stew of eggplant, tomatoes, and green peppers, to serve alongside. For a vegetarian feast, serve with Spinach and Baby Corn Salad (page 103), Italian Baked Endive (page 258), and roasted vegetables.

*NUTRIENTS PER SERVING: calories 238, carbohydrate 46 g (including sugar 10 g), protein 9 g, fat 2 g (saturated fat 1 g), good source of vitamin E.*

---

## EASY DOES IT!

*For a more stylish presentation, when the polenta is stiff, you can mold it into egg shapes, using two large metal spoons.*

# GREAT WINTER VEGETABLES

## CELERY AND APPLE

*Celery is at its best in the crisp, cold days of winter when there is also a good selection of apples available. They are delicious combined with wine, herbs, and capers.*

**TIME: 30 MINUTES  SERVES: 4**

| 1 head celery |
| --- |
| 3 red dessert apples |
| 2–3 tablespoons olive oil |
| 12 fresh sage leaves |
| 1 large clove garlic |
| 1 bay leaf |
| About ½ cup dry white wine |
| 2 tablespoons capers, optional |
| Salt and black pepper |

**1** Trim off the root end of the celery then slice the stalks into thin semicircles, cutting across the entire head. Rinse and set aside.
**2** Rinse and core the apples but do not peel them. Roughly chop them into cubes and set aside.
**3** Generously cover the bottom of a large frying pan with olive oil, and heat it until it shows a haze. Rinse the sage leaves, then snip them into the pan. Peel the garlic and crush it in. Allow the sage and garlic to sizzle for a few seconds, then quickly add the celery, apples, and bay leaf and stir.
**4** After 1 minute, pour in enough white wine to cover the mixture. Continue cooking over a high heat, stirring occasionally, until the celery is cooked but still crunchy. If the mixture dries out before the celery is cooked, add a little more wine.
**5** When the celery is cooked, stir in the capers, if using, and heat them through. Season with salt and pepper to taste, remove the bay leaf from the pan and serve.

*NUTRIENTS PER SERVING: calories 141, carbohydrate 13g (including sugar 12g), protein 1g, fat 7g (saturated fat 1g), good source of vitamins B group and E.*

## TOMATOES À LA PROVENÇALE

*Here is a simple and delicious way to prepare tomatoes. Enhanced by garlic, they are a perfect complement to roast or grilled red meat.*

**TIME: 30 MINUTES  SERVES: 4**

| 4 beef tomatoes |
| --- |
| Salt |
| 1 medium onion |
| 3 tablespoons olive oil |
| 5 oz (140 g) stale bread crumbs |
| A small bunch of fresh parsley |
| 2 cloves garlic |
| Black pepper |
| 1½ tablespoons (25 g) butter |

**1** Preheat the oven to 450°F (230°C). Halve the tomatoes across their middles and remove the seeds. Sprinkle with salt and leave to drain of water.
**2** Peel and finely chop the onion and let it brown in a small frying pan in 1 tablespoon of olive oil. Put the breadcrumbs through the blender. Wash the parsley and chop its leaves. Peel the garlic and press it above the breadcrumbs. Add the parsley and mix well with the onion.
**3** Heat 2 tablespoons of olive oil in a frying pan. Shake the tomatoes, then put them in the hot oil, cut sides up. Cook for one minute, turn the tomatoes, and cook over high heat for one more minute.
**4** Put the tomatoes in an ovenproof dish and season with pepper to taste. Cover evenly with the onion/breadcrumb mixture and top with knobs of butter. Bake in the oven for 10 minutes.

*NUTRIENTS PER SERVING: calories 276, carbohydrate 33g (including sugar 8g), protein 6g, fat 14g (saturated fat 6g), good source of vitamins A, B group, C, E, and folate.*

## GLAZED ONIONS

*Dainty button onions glowing in a golden glaze flavored with soy sauce, mustard, and rosemary make a rich, crunchy accompaniment to roast and grilled meat.*

**TIME: 30 MINUTES  SERVES: 4–6**

| 1 lb (450 g) button or pickling onions |
| --- |
| ½–1 teaspoon dried rosemary |
| 1½ tablespoons (25 g) butter |
| 1 tablespoon dark molasses |
| 2 teaspoons Dijon mustard |
| 1 tablespoon soy sauce |

**1** Put a kettle of water on to boil. Put the onions into a saucepan, cover them with boiling water, and leave them to cook over a moderate heat for 5 minutes. Then pour them into a colander and cool them under a cold running tap. When they are cool enough to handle, drain them and peel off the skins.
**2** Crush the rosemary as finely as possible, using a pestle and mortar or the end of a rolling pin.
**3** Melt the butter gently in a frying pan over a moderate heat. Then add the crushed rosemary, dark molasses, Dijon mustard, and soy sauce and mix them together well to make an emulsion.
**4** Stir in the onions and cook them gently, stirring and basting them with the sauce, for 10–15 minutes, until the glaze has thickened and the onions are tender and golden brown. Watch them continuously as it is important not to allow the glaze to burn.

*NUTRIENTS PER SERVING, WHEN SERVING 4: calories 110, carbohydrate 14g (including sugar 11g), protein 2g, fat 6g (saturated fat 3g), good source of vitamins B group and E.*

**WINTER VEGETABLES:** (*top*) CELERY AND APPLE; (*center*) GLAZED ONIONS; (*bottom*) TOMATOES À LA PROVENÇALE.

Pear Meringue

# DESSERTS, CAKES, & COOKIES

*Nothing rounds off a good meal like ripe, juicy fruit, an extravagant creamy dessert, or a spicy pudding, while coffee break becomes a treat with homemade cakes and cookies.*

# POACHED FRUIT WITH CHOCOLATE SAUCE

*Peaches and figs, poached in brandy and apple juice, are partnered by a lavish white chocolate sauce, enriched with cream to give it smoothness and orange zest for a tangy citrus flavor.*

TIME: 20 MINUTES  SERVES: 4

| |
|---|
| 3 oz (85 g) white chocolate drops or solid white chocolate |
| 1 cup (250 ml) apple juice |
| 1 teaspoon sugar |
| 2 tablespoons brandy |
| 8 small, or 4 large, fresh figs |
| 2 large peaches or nectarines |
| ⅔ cup (150 g) cream |
| 1 orange |

**1** Use a double saucepan or you can put some hot water into a small pan and set a bowl over it, making sure the bottom is clear of the water. Put the chocolate into the bowl (if using a bar, break it into pieces first); bring the water to simmering point. Stir the chocolate as it melts. Do not let the water boil as the chocolate will overheat. When it has melted, remove the bowl and set aside, leaving the pan of hot water for later.

**2** Meanwhile, pour the apple juice into a shallow saucepan or a frying pan with a lid. Add the sugar and brandy, bring the mixture to the boil, then reduce the heat.

**3** Rinse the figs and cut large ones into quarters lengthwise, small ones into halves. Halve and stone the peaches or nectarines, then cut each half into four slices. Add the fruit to the apple juice, cover and poach it gently for 4 minutes. If the skins come off the peaches, remove them.

**4** While the fruit is cooking, stir the cream into the melted chocolate gradually with a balloon whisk, then beat it until smooth. Put the sauce back on the pan of hot water and leave it to sit while you finish off the fruit.

**5** Transfer the poached fruit to a serving dish with a slotted spoon. Boil the juice for 5 minutes, or until it is reduced to a slightly heavy syrup, then pour it over the fruit.

**6** While the syrup reduces, wash any wax from the orange and grate half the rind into the chocolate mixture, then add 2 tablespoons of the juice. Stir the sauce and serve it with the fruit.

NUTRIENTS PER SERVING: *calories 369, carbohydrate 36 g (including sugar 36 g), protein 5 g, fat 22 g (saturated fat 14 g), good source of vitamins B group, C, and E.*

### EASY DOES IT!

*Melt the white chocolate quickly in a microwave oven. In a 650-watt oven, put the chocolate pieces into a bowl, heat on low power for 30 seconds then stir. If lumps remain, cook and stir in further 10-second bursts until smooth.*

# WAFFLES WITH FRUIT AND CARAMEL

*Oranges and bananas soaked in orange juice make a luscious partner to hot, freshly toasted waffles served with a warm, syrupy caramel sauce enriched with heavy cream.*

TIME: 20 MINUTES  SERVES: 4

| |
|---|
| **2 large oranges** |
| **1 large banana** |
| **3 tablespoons (50 g) unsalted butter** |
| **⅓ cup (50 g) dark brown soft sugar** |
| **4 tablespoons heavy cream** |
| **4 regular size waffles** |
| ***To serve:* 4 tablespoons natural Greek yogurt, optional** |

**1** Remove the peel and white pith from the oranges with a sharp knife. Holding each orange over a bowl to catch the juice, remove the segments by cutting between the connecting white tissue, letting each segment fall into the bowl. Squeeze the remaining tissue to extract the rest of the juice.

**2** Peel the banana, slice it into the oranges, and mix gently together. Preheat the grill.

**3** Melt the butter slowly in a small pan over a moderate heat. Add the sugar and stir for about 2 minutes, until it has dissolved. Then add the cream, and simmer the mixture gently for about 3 minutes, stirring frequently, until it turns a caramel color. Remove it from the heat and keep warm.

**4** Toast the waffles according to the instructions on the package and place on four serving plates. Spoon a quarter of the orange and banana mixture onto each, and pour on the caramel sauce. Add a spoonful of yogurt, if using, and serve.

*NUTRIENTS PER SERVING: calories 534, carbohydrate 50 g (including sugar 26 g), protein 7 g, fat 36 g (saturated fat 16 g), good source of vitamins A, B group, C, and E, and calcium.*

---

### COOK'S SUGGESTION

*If you toast the waffles while you are still simmering the cream mixture, make sure that you keep an eye on them, as they burn very easily.*

---

# BAKED APPLE WITH BRIOCHE

*Sweet dessert apples in a spicy orange sauce can be left to bake in the oven while you enjoy your main course, then quickly finished off and served on toasted brioche for a really satisfying dessert.*

TIME: 30 MINUTES  SERVES: 4

---

**4 sweet dessert apples, about 5½ oz (155 g) each**

**1 tablespoon (15 g) butter**

**1 large orange**

**½ teaspoon ground cinnamon**

**2 tablespoons brown sugar**

**4 brioche rolls**

**⅔ cup (150 g) natural Greek yogurt or ⅔ cup (150 ml) whipping cream**

**1** Preheat the oven to 425°F (220°C), and put an ovenproof dish in to heat for baking the apples.

**2** Core the apples, then cut them in half lengthwise and score the skins deeply several times using a sharp knife.

**3** Place the apples, cut sides down, in the heated dish and dot them with the butter.

**4** Wash the wax from the orange, finely grate the rind and squeeze the juice into a bowl. Stir in the cinnamon and half the sugar. Pour the mixture over the apples.

**5** Cover the dish with a lid or foil and bake for 10–15 minutes, or until the apples are tender.

**6** Meanwhile, cut the brioche rolls into two, widthwise; cut off the top and bottom crusts. Preheat the grill to high if you need it for toasting, and whip the cream, if using.

**7** Two minutes before the apples are cooked, toast the brioche slices for about 1 minute on each side, or until lightly browned. Put two slices on each serving plate and place an apple half on each slice.

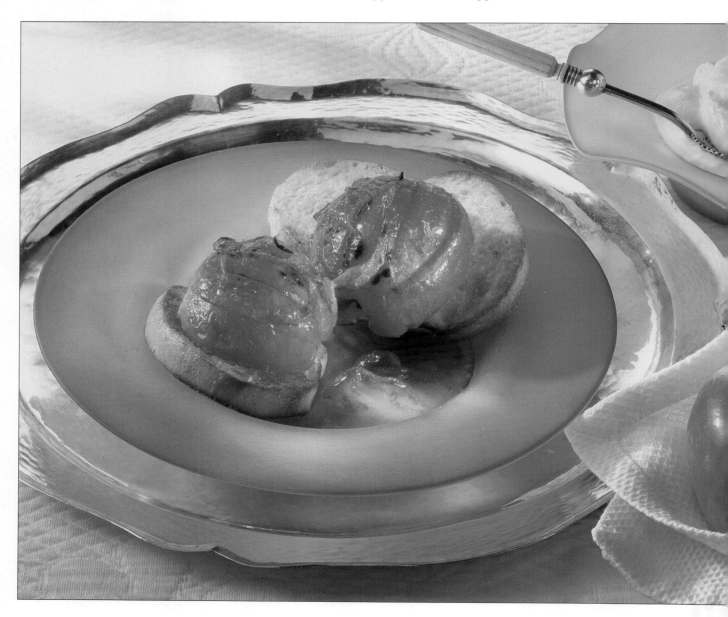

# CINNAMON APPLE FRITTERS

*Served piping hot, these slices of crisp apple in fluffy,
light-as-air batter will fill the house with an irresistible aroma.*

**8** Spoon the cooking juices over the apples, sprinkle them with the remaining brown sugar, and serve hot with the Greek yogurt or whipped cream.

*NUTRIENTS PER SERVING: calories 430, carbohydrate 52 g (including sugar 28g), protein 6g, fat 23g (saturated fat 11g), good source of vitamins A, B group, C, and E.*

TIME: 15 MINUTES  SERVES: 2

| |
| --- |
| **Corn oil for deep-frying** |
| **1 small egg** |
| **Salt** |
| **6 tablespoons sparkling mineral water** |
| **4 tablespoons plain flour** |
| **2 tablespoons sugar** |
| **1 teaspoon ground cinnamon** |
| **2 crisp dessert apples** |

**1** Half-fill a large wok or deep fryer with oil and put it on to heat. Break the egg into a bowl, add a pinch of salt, and whisk until frothy. Whisk in the mineral water, then the flour—you are not aiming for a smooth batter.

**2** Mix the sugar and cinnamon together on a saucer and set aside.

Peel, core, and slice the apples into rings about ¼ in. (5 mm) thick.

**3** Dip each of the apple slices into the batter with a fork. When the oil has reached a temperature of 375°F (190°C), and a few drops of the batter sizzle as soon as they are dropped in, deep-fry the apple fritters in two or three batches for 1–2 minutes each, or until they are puffed and golden, turning them over with a slotted spoon halfway through cooking.

**4** Drain them on kitchen paper and serve very hot, sprinkled with the spiced sugar.

*NUTRIENTS PER SERVING: calories 413, carbohydrate 45 g (including sugar 29g), protein 5g, fat 25g (saturated fat 4g), good source of vitamins B group and E.*

# HOT CHOCOLATE SOUFFLÉS WITH RUM

*Contrary to popular belief, little chocolate soufflés are easy to make. You can start preparing them before you begin your meal and finish them off while the main course is being cleared away.*

TIME: 30 MINUTES  SERVES: 4–6

| |
|---|
| 1 tablespoon (15 g) unsalted butter, at room temperature |
| 6 tablespoons sugar |
| 1 cup (225 ml) milk |
| 3½ oz (100 g) dark chocolate |
| 5 medium eggs |
| 3 tablespoons cornstarch |
| 2 tablespoons heavy cream |
| 3 tablespoons rum |
| 1 tablespoon confectioners' sugar |

**1**   Carefully butter the insides and rims of four 7 fl oz (200 ml) or six 5 fl oz (150 ml) soufflé dishes, then coat them evenly with 2 tablespoons of the sugar.

**2**   Pour the milk into a small saucepan and set it over a moderate heat. Break the chocolate into small pieces and stir it into the milk. As soon as the milk reaches scalding point, remove from the heat, cover, and leave to stand for 2–3 minutes, until the chocolate has melted.

**3**   Meanwhile, separate the eggs, put the whites into a large, dry bowl, and set aside. Put 3 egg yolks into a small bowl—the other two are not needed and can be kept for another purpose.

**4**   Add 3 tablespoons of the sugar to the cornstarch in a large pan, and over a low heat gradually whisk in the chocolate milk to form a smooth paste. Then increase the heat, beating continuously, until the sauce boils and becomes stiff.

**5**   Remove from the heat and beat in the cream, rum, and egg yolks. Scrape the mixture from the sides of the pan with a spatula and cover it with the lid to prevent a skin forming, then set aside.

**6**   Before you begin your meal, preheat the oven to 450°F (230°C). Put a baking tray with a raised edge into the oven to heat.

**7**   When the main course is over, whisk the egg whites until they form soft peaks (an electric beater is quickest). Add the remaining sugar and whisk again until the whites are stiff and shiny.

**8**   Fold a large spoonful of the egg white into the chocolate sauce, then gently fold in all the remaining egg white. Spoon the mixture into the soufflé dishes and put them onto the baking tray in the oven.

**9**   Bake for 8–10 minutes, or until well risen and lightly set, with soft, gooey centers. Remove them from the oven, sift confectioners' sugar over them, and serve immediately.

VARIATION
For a nonalcoholic soufflé, omit the rum and beat some finely grated orange zest into the sauce.

*NUTRIENTS PER SERVING, WHEN SERVING 4: calories 475, carbohydrate 53 g (including sugar 46 g), protein 9 g, fat 24 g (saturated fat 13 g), good source of vitamins A, B group, and E.*

---

### COOK'S SUGGESTION

*For successful soufflés, the oven must be very hot and the egg whites must be whisked in a clean, dry bowl with a clean, dry whisk.*

# HOT RASPBERRY SOUFFLÉS

*Raspberries give these individual desserts a beautiful, soft rose color and a delectable flavor—they must be eaten straight from the oven to capture their deliciously light, melt-in-the-mouth texture.*

TIME: 25 MINUTES  SERVES: 4

| 2 teaspoons (10 g) unsalted butter, at room temperature |
| ⅔ cup (125 g) sugar |
| 9 oz (255 g) fresh raspberries |
| 1 tablespoon kirsch, optional |
| 4 large egg whites |
| 1 tablespoon confectioners' sugar, for sifting |
| *To serve:* heavy cream |

**1** Before you sit down to your main course, preheat the oven to 375°F (190°C). Grease the insides of four 7 fl oz (200 ml) soufflé dishes, or ovenproof cereal bowls, with the butter, then coat them evenly with some of the sugar, tipping out any surplus, and place on a baking tray.

**2** Purée the fresh raspberries by pressing them through a stainless-steel or nylon sieve with the back of a spoon. Stir in the kirsch, if using.

**3** When you have finished the main course, whisk the egg whites with an electric beater until they are stiff but not dry, then gradually whisk in the remaining sugar. Keep whisking until the mixture becomes shiny.

**4** Carefully fold the raspberry purée into the egg whites, then spoon the mixture into the dishes and make a swirl on top of each. Cook in the center of the oven, leaving space above for the soufflés to rise, for 12–14 minutes, or until well risen and lightly set.

**5** Remove the soufflés from the oven, sift confectioners' sugar evenly over them and serve with cream.

*NUTRIENTS PER SERVING: calories 401, carbohydrate 38 g (including sugar 38 g), protein 5 g, fat 26 g (saturated fat 16 g), good source of vitamins A, B group, C, and E.*

# THREE FAST YOGURT DESSERTS

## MANGO BRÛLÉE

*Voluptuous mangoes soaked in rum and cinnamon snuggle beneath a golden, grilled sugar topping.*

**TIME: 20 MINUTES  SERVES: 4**

| |
|---|
| 2 large mangoes, about 14 oz (400 g) each |
| 2 tablespoons rum |
| ½ teaspoon ground cinnamon |
| 1¼ cups (350 g) natural Greek yogurt |
| ½ cup (80 g) brown sugar |

**1**  Preheat the grill to high.
**2**  Peel the mangoes (see box, below), cut off the two fat cheeks and dice them, then cut off and dice the remaining flesh. Half fill four deep, ovenproof ramekin dishes with the fruit.
**3**  Drizzle the rum over the fruit and sprinkle with cinnamon. Spoon in the yogurt, smooth it level, then sprinkle the brown sugar evenly over the top.
**4**  Put the ramekins under the grill, about 4 in. (10 cm) from the heat, and cook for 4–5 minutes, until the sugar melts and turns golden brown. Serve hot or cold.
*VARIATION*
Fresh sliced peaches or bananas, or raspberries or strawberries could be used instead of mangoes.

*NUTRIENTS PER SERVING: calories 315, carbohydrate 52 g (including sugar 52 g), protein 7 g, fat 8 g (saturated fat 5 g), good source of vitamins A, B group, C, and E.*

## RASPBERRIES WITH CEREAL

*Crunchy muesli with raisins and almonds makes a substantial partner for soft, sweet raspberries.*

**TIME: 10 MINUTES  SERVES: 4**

| |
|---|
| 1½ cups (350 g) raspberries |
| 2 tablespoons sugar |
| 1 lb (500 g) natural yogurt |
| 5 oz (150 g) muesli, or crunchy oat breakfast cereal with honey, raisins, and almonds |
| 1 tablespoon runny honey |
| *To decorate:* **a little extra honey or muesli or breakfast cereal** |

**1**  Put the raspberries and sugar into a bowl, mix and set aside.
**2**  In another bowl, mix the natural yogurt with the muesli or breakfast cereal. Add the honey, stirring it in lightly, so the mixture is streaky.
**3**  Divide two-thirds of the mixture among four wide 1 cup (225 ml) glasses. Top with the raspberries, then add the remaining mixture. Drizzle a little honey over the top, or sprinkle with muesli or cereal.
**4**  If it is served immediately, this dessert has a crunchy texture, but if you prefer a softer, creamier texture, chill it for 3–4 hours before serving.

*NUTRIENTS PER SERVING: calories 318, carbohydrate 52 g (including sugar 37 g), protein 14 g, fat 7 g (saturated fat 3 g), good source of vitamins B group, C, and E.*

## STRAWBERRY CLOUDS

*Crushed strawberries mixed into a yogurt and vanilla meringue are transformed into a light-as-air treat.*

**TIME: 20 MINUTES  SERVES: 4**

| |
|---|
| 9 oz (255 g) fresh strawberries |
| ⅓ cup (70 g) sugar |
| 2 large egg whites |
| ⅔ cup (250 g) Greek yogurt, chilled |
| ½ teaspoon natural vanilla extract |

**1**  Rinse and dry the strawberries and hull them, reserving 4 whole ones for decoration. Put the hulled strawberries into a bowl, sprinkle with 1 tablespoon of the sugar and crush them with a fork.
**2**  In a large, dry mixing bowl, whisk the egg whites until they form a soft peak, then gradually add the remaining sugar, whisking well after each addition, to make a stiff meringue.
**3**  Add the yogurt and the vanilla extract to the meringue and gently fold them in with a metal spoon.
**4**  Fold the mashed strawberries and their juice into the yogurt mixture. Be careful not to mix them in too vigorously, as the light, airy texture will be lost.
**5**  Spoon the meringue into four 7 fl oz (200 ml) glasses and decorate with the reserved strawberries. Serve them immediately, or chill for 2–3 hours before serving.
*VARIATION*
Decorate the top of each strawberry cloud with a sprinkling of chopped, toasted nuts.

*NUTRIENTS PER SERVING: calories 165, carbohydrate 23 g (including sugar 23 g), protein 6 g, fat 6 g (saturated fat 3 g), good source of vitamins B group, C, and E.*

---

### EASY DOES IT!

*To peel the mango, score through the skin lengthwise, dividing it into four equal sections, being careful not to cut into the flesh. Then insert a fork into the stalk end to hold the fruit steady, lift up the end corner of each section of skin with a knife and your thumb and gently peel it back.*

**YOGURT DELIGHTS:** (*top*) RASPBERRIES WITH CEREAL; (*center*) STRAWBERRY CLOUDS; (*bottom*) MANGO BRÛLÉE.

# PEAR MERINGUE

*Spicy poached pears are given a featherlight topping of vanilla-flavored meringue and served with a glittering red wine sauce.*

TIME: 30 MINUTES   SERVES: 4

| | |
|---|---|
| Butter for greasing | ½ cinnamon stick or ¼ teaspoon ground cinnamon |
| 4 large, firm, ripe pears | 2 large egg whites |
| 1 lemon | ¼ teaspoon natural vanilla extract |
| 1⅔ cups (400 ml) red wine | 2 tablespoons (25 g) flaked almonds |
| 1¼ cups (250 g) sugar | 2 tablespoons confectioners' sugar |

**1**   Preheat the oven to 425°F (220°C). Lightly butter a shallow baking dish just large enough to hold the pears when they are halved.

**2**   Squeeze the lemon and pour the juice into a saucepan, or a large frying pan with a lid, wide enough to hold the pear halves in a single layer. Add the wine, 6 tablespoons of sugar and the cinnamon. Bring to the boil, then reduce the heat to a simmer.

**3**   Peel, halve, and core the pears. Lower them into the simmering red wine syrup and cook them gently for 10 minutes, until they are just softened, basting them with the syrup from time to time.

**4**   Meanwhile, make the meringue. Put the egg whites into a clean, grease-free bowl and whisk until they are stiff but not dry (this is easiest with an electric beater). Sprinkle in the remaining sugar, one tablespoon at a time, beating well after each addition. Then add the vanilla and beat until the meringue is stiff and shiny.

**5**   Lift out the pear halves with a slotted spoon, draining the juice, and lay them in the baking dish, hollow sides up. Spoon some meringue over each half, sprinkle flaked almonds over the meringue, and sift the confectioners' sugar over the top. Bake on the middle rack of the oven for 5 minutes or until lightly browned.

**6**   Meanwhile, boil the wine sauce until it is reduced to a heavy syrup. Remove the cinnamon stick, if used, and pour the syrup into a jug.

**7**   Lift the dish of pears from the oven very carefully so the meringue does not slip off, and serve them with the wine sauce.

VARIATION

Firm dessert apples, peaches, or fresh pineapple rings can be used in place of the pears, and water may be substituted for the red wine if you prefer.

*NUTRIENTS PER SERVING: calories 451, carbohydrate 90 g (including sugar 89 g), protein 4 g, fat 4 g (saturated fat 0.3 g), good source of vitamins B group and E.*

# APRICOT AND SOUR CREAM FLAN

*Canned apricots are buried beneath an unusual batter made with fruit juice and sour cream and topped with butter and sugar, to make a warming and substantial dessert.*

TIME: 30 MINUTES  SERVES: 4–6

Butter for greasing

2 cans (each 14 oz / 397 ml) apricot halves in natural juice

*To serve:* cream, light or heavy, as preferred

*For the batter:*

⅔ cup (150 ml) sour cream

¾ cup (100 g) plain flour

2 large eggs

½ cup (75 g) soft light brown sugar

A few drops of natural vanilla extract

*For the topping:*

1 tablespoon (15 g) butter

2 tablespoons soft light brown sugar

**1**  Preheat the oven to 400°F (200°C) and grease a shallow, ovenproof dish, 10–12 in. (25–30 cm) in diameter.

**2**  Drain the canned apricots, reserving ½ cup (100 ml) of the juice, and arrange them, cut sides down, in the bottom of the dish.

**3**  To make the batter, stir the sour cream into the reserved apricot juice. Place the flour in a separate bowl and make a well in the center. Add the eggs, sugar, and vanilla extract, quickly whisk into the flour to make a smooth paste, then gradually whisk in the apricot juice and sour cream mixture.

**4**  Pour the batter over the apricots and bake the flan in the oven for 20 minutes.

**5**  Meanwhile, make the topping by blending the butter and sugar together with a fork in a small bowl.

**6**  Remove the flan from the oven after 15 minutes and dot the butter and sugar mixture evenly over the top. Return it to the oven for the remaining 5 minutes, or until the batter is lightly golden on top and puffed up.

**7**  Serve hot, with light or heavy cream.

VARIATION

Instead of the topping, sprinkle the flan with confectioners' sugar before serving. Alternatively, sprinkle it with brandy—an apricot-flavored brandy would be particularly good.

NUTRIENTS PER SERVING, WHEN SERVING 4: *calories 555, carbohydrate 65 g (including sugar 46 g), protein 10 g, fat 31 g (saturated fat 18 g), good source of vitamins A, B group, C, and E.*

# BAKED ALMOND PEARS

*This luscious pear dessert is baked in a glorious fruit syrup and topped with almond-flavored cookies or crisp, browned, roasted almonds, to add a crunchy texture.*

TIME: 30 MINUTES  SERVES: 4

---

3 tablespoons (50 g) butter,
at room temperature

1 tablespoon sugar

4 large, firm, ripe pears

4 tablespoons white wine
or orange juice

3 tablespoons (85 g) apricot jam or
2 tablespoons honey

6 almond cookies or
6 tablespoons (70 g) blanched
almonds

*To serve:* cream or natural
Greek yogurt

---

**1**  Preheat the oven to 400°F (200°C). Grease a shallow, round ovenproof dish with half the butter and sprinkle the sugar evenly over the top to coat the butter.

**2**  Peel the pears and halve them, then cut them lengthwise into slices about ½ in. (1 cm) thick. Arrange the slices in a single, overlapping layer in the bottom of the dish.

**3**  Mix the wine or orange juice with the apricot jam or honey and pour the mixture over the pears.

**4**  Crush the almond cookies with a rolling pin or finely chop the almonds. Sprinkle them over the pears. Dot the remaining butter evenly over the pears. Bake in the oven for 15–20 minutes, until the pears have softened and the cookies or nuts are lightly browned. Serve with cream or Greek yogurt.

**VARIATION**

For a faster dessert, substitute 8 canned pear halves for the fresh pears, sliced or left whole, and mix 2 tablespoons of the juice from the can with 2 tablespoons of orange juice to replace the white wine.

*NUTRIENTS PER SERVING: calories 490, carbohydrate 42 g (including sugar 36 g), protein 2 g, fat 35 g (saturated fat 22 g), good source of vitamins A, B$_6$, and E.*

# GRILLED, HONEYED FRUIT KABOBS

*Tropical and home-grown fruits marinated in scented honey and nut oil make an unusual dessert served as kabobs, sprinkled with toasted hazelnuts, and accompanied by sweetened cream.*

TIME: 30 MINUTES  SERVES: 4

| |
|---|
| 1 firm pear, preferably Williams |
| 1 small, slightly under-ripe banana |
| 2 canned or fresh pineapple rings |
| 8 large, firm strawberries |
| 1 small star fruit |
| 2 full tablespoons (25 g) chopped hazelnuts, optional |
| *To serve:* ⅔ cup (150 ml) thick heavy cream, sweetened to taste |

*For the marinade:*

| |
|---|
| 1 lime |
| 2 tablespoons runny honey, preferably acacia |
| 2 tablespoons hazelnut or walnut oil |

**1** For the marinade, wash any wax from the lime and finely grate the rind into a large, shallow dish. Squeeze the juice and add it to the dish with the honey and the nut oil. Mix and set aside.

**2** Prepare the fruits, adding them to the marinade in turn. Rinse, dry, quarter, and core the pear, then slice each quarter into two. Peel the banana and cut it into four. Drain and halve the pineapple rings. Rinse, hull, and dry the strawberries. Rinse and dry the star fruit, slice off and discard each end, trim along the ridges with a potato peeler, then cut it into four thick slices.

**3** Set the fruit aside for 10 minutes while you heat the grill to medium.
**4** Thread all of the fruit onto 4 metal skewers about 10 in. (25 cm) long, beginning with a piece of pineapple, then a strawberry, some pear, banana, strawberry, then pear, and end with a slice of star fruit, threaded on horizontally so that the star shape lies flat.
**5** Place the skewers on the rack of the grill pan and brush with the marinade. Grill for 3 minutes, baste and grill for 2 minutes. Turn the kabobs over and repeat until the fruit is golden, with some crunchy dark patches.

*This gorgeous dessert features plump fresh figs, scented with rosewater and oozing with beautiful pink juices.*

---

## COOK'S SUGGESTION

*Fruit turns soft when grilled, so make sure you cut it into generous pieces and skewer them centrally so that they do not fall off after cooking.*

---

**6** While the fruit is under the grill, toast the chopped hazelnuts, if using. Transfer the cooked fruit kabobs carefully onto a serving dish, and sprinkle them evenly with the toasted hazelnuts. Serve them with the heavy cream.

**VARIATION**

In summer, these kabobs can be grilled outdoors on a barbecue.

*NUTRIENTS PER SERVING: calories 330, carbohydrate 30g (including sugar 28g), protein 2g, fat 24g (saturated fat 12g), good source of vitamins B group, C, and E.*

---

TIME: 20 MINUTES   SERVES: 4

---

1 tablespoon (15 g) butter at room temperature

8 large fresh figs

1 lemon

A few drops of rosewater, optional

6 tablespoons sugar

6 tablespoons cream

---

**1** Preheat the grill to its highest setting for 10 minutes. Lightly butter a small, ovenproof dish.
**2** Rinse, dry, and remove the stalks from the figs, then cut them in half.
**3** Squeeze the lemon juice into a small bowl and add the rosewater, if using. Toss the figs in the scented juice, then arrange them, cut sides down, in one layer in the buttered dish. Sprinkle the skins liberally with 3 tablespoons of the sugar.
**4** Place under the hot grill and cook for 3–4 minutes. Turn them over, sprinkle the cut sides with the remaining sugar and grill them for a further 2–3 minutes. Serve piping hot, bathed in their pink juices, with the cream.

*NUTRIENTS PER SERVING: calories 311, carbohydrate 36g (including sugar 36g), protein 2g, fat 18g (saturated fat 12g), good source of vitamins B group.*

# PLUM CRUMBLE

*Sweet poached fresh plums are given a buttery, golden topping of crunchy cereal, chopped nuts, mixed spices and brown sugar, then baked in the oven to make a comforting, satisfying dessert.*

TIME: 30 MINUTES  SERVES: 4

| |
| --- |
| 2 lb (900 g) ripe but firm plums |
| ½ cup (115 g) sugar |
| 4 tablespoons (60 g) unsalted butter |
| 1 teaspoon mixed spice |
| 4 oz (110 g) oat cereal |
| ⅓ cup (60 g) brown sugar |
| 6 tablespoons (60 g) mixed chopped nuts |

*To serve:* whipped cream or ice cream

**1**  Preheat the oven to 450°F (230°C). Rinse, dry, and halve the plums and remove the stones. Cut large plums into quarters.

**2**  Put the plums into an ovenproof casserole, about 8 in. (20 cm) in diameter and 2 in. (5 cm) deep. Add 2–3 tablespoons of water and the sugar. Cover, and poach over a moderate heat for 8–10 minutes, until the plums begin to soften, stirring occasionally.

**3**  Meanwhile, melt the butter in a frying pan, then stir in the mixed spice, oat cereal, brown sugar, and chopped nuts.

**4**  Spoon the oat crumble mixture evenly over the top of the plums. Put the casserole into the oven and bake for 12–15 minutes, checking

from time to time, until the cereal is golden brown. Serve with whipped cream or ice cream.

NUTRIENTS PER SERVING: *calories 679, carbohydrate 87g (including sugar 66g), protein 9g, fat 35g (saturated fat 17g), good source of vitamins A, B group, and E.*

---

### COOK'S SUGGESTION

*If you prefer, you can poach the plums in an ordinary saucepan and then transfer them to an ovenproof dish to bake.*

---

# FRUITY BREAD AND BUTTER PUDDING

*Sweet summer fruits make a luxurious, colorful addition to an everyday favorite—an old classic that makes a warming grand finale for a light meal.*

**TIME: 30 MINUTES  SERVES: 4**

| |
|---|
| 1⅓ cups whole milk |
| 10½ oz (290 g) fresh or frozen mixed summer fruits |
| 3 tablespoons (50 g) butter, at room temperature |
| 8 slices whole-wheat bread from a medium-cut loaf |
| 3 tablespoons light brown sugar |
| 2 large eggs |
| ½ teaspoon natural vanilla extract |
| Nutmeg for grating |
| 1 teaspoon confectioners' sugar |
| *To serve:* fresh cream or natural Greek yogurt |

**1**  Preheat the oven to 425°F (220°C). Heat the milk gently in a pan; do not let it boil. If you are using frozen fruit, spread it out on a plate to thaw a little.

**2**  Grease four 1¼-cup (300 ml) ovenproof dishes with a little of the butter.
**3**  Remove the crusts from the bread, butter the slices and cut each one into four triangles or squares.
**4**  Arrange a few pieces of the bread in the bottom of each dish, pointing slightly upward. Add a spoonful of fruit and a sprinkling of the sugar, then repeat until all the bread and fruit are used up, ending with a layer of bread.
**5**  Break the eggs into a bowl, whisk lightly, then stir in the warm milk and the vanilla. Whisk again, then carefully pour the custard mixture evenly over each dish.
**6**  Grate a little nutmeg over the puddings, put them on a baking tray and bake for 15 minutes, or until just set and golden brown.

**7**  When cooked, sift confectioners' sugar over the tops and serve with cream or Greek yogurt.
**VARIATION**
Use two 2-cup (500 ml) baking dishes. Turn puddings out to serve, dusted with confectioners' sugar.

*NUTRIENTS PER SERVING: calories 647, carbohydrate 52 g (including sugar 23 g), protein 15 g, fat 44 g (saturated fat 25 g), good source of vitamins A, B group, C, E, and folate, and calcium, selenium, and zinc.*

### COOK'S SUGGESTION

*You can prepare the puddings some hours ahead of serving and keep them refrigerated. Take them out to return to room temperature 30 minutes before you are ready to bake them.*

# A MOUTHFUL OF HEAVEN

### GINGER AND CHOCOLATE MASCARPONE

*A wickedly rich confection of dark chocolate, rum, and creamy Italian cheese, studded with sweet ginger.*

TIME: **10 MINUTES** SERVES: **4**

**2 pieces preserved stem ginger in syrup**

**2 tablespoons ginger syrup from the jar**

**3 tablespoons dark rum**

**3½ oz (100 g) dark, bitter chocolate**

**4½ oz (125 g) mascarpone cheese**

*To serve:* **4 dessert wafer baskets**

**1** Dice the ginger finely and put it into a bowl with the ginger syrup and the rum. Grate the chocolate into the bowl and stir thoroughly.
**2** Add the mascarpone cheese, mix well, cover, and chill for as long as you can. It will stiffen as it chills.
**3** Scoop the cream mixture into four wafer baskets and serve.
*VARIATION*
Try brandy, sweet sherry, or coffee liqueur as a substitute for the rum.

*NUTRIENTS PER SERVING: calories 385, carbohydrate 34 g (including sugar 32 g), protein 3 g, fat 24 g (saturated fat 15 g), good source of vitamin E.*

### ZABAGLIONE

*A mixture of eggs, sugar, and Marsala fluffed up over a gentle heat that tastes wonderful eaten warm.*

TIME: **15 MINUTES** SERVES: **4**

**4 large egg yolks**

**3 tablespoons sugar**

**½ cup (125 ml) Marsala**

**1** Choose a heatproof mixing bowl and a saucepan on which it will sit firmly. Fill the saucepan with about 3 in. (10 cm) of water and heat until it starts simmering.

**2** Put the egg yolks into the mixing bowl, add the sugar, and whisk until the mixture is light and creamy.

**3** Set the mixing bowl over the pan of simmering water, then add the Marsala and continue to beat with a whisk until the mixture becomes thick and forms soft peaks. Spoon the zabaglione into tall, slim glasses and serve.

VARIATION

For a nonalcoholic zabaglione, use fresh orange juice instead of the Marsala and whisk in 1 teaspoon of orange zest.

NUTRIENTS PER SERVING: *calories 177, carbohydrate 12 g (including sugar 12 g), protein 3 g, fat 6 g (saturated fat 2 g), good source of vitamins B group and E.*

## CHESTNUT BRANDY CREAM

*Chestnut purée fortified with brandy is whipped up into a treat with heavy cream and chocolate.*

TIME: 20 MINUTES  SERVES: 4

| |
|---|
| 1 can (9 oz / 250 g) unsweetened chestnut purée |
| 2 tablespoons brandy |
| 2 tablespoons confectioners' sugar |
| 1 cup (225 ml) heavy cream |
| 1¾ oz (50 g) dark, bitter chocolate |

**1** Empty the can of chestnut purée into a large mixing bowl, pour in the brandy, add the confectioners' sugar, then beat them together thoroughly, until the mixture is smooth, using either an electric beater or a handheld balloon whisk.

**2** Whip the heavy cream until it holds soft peaks, then fold it into the chestnut mixture.

**3** Grate the chocolate and add half to the mixture. Spoon the cream into four glasses, sprinkle the rest of the chocolate over the top, and chill for 15 minutes before serving.

NUTRIENTS PER SERVING: *calories 486, carbohydrate 42 g (including sugar 17 g), protein 4 g, fat 32 g (saturated fat 19 g), good source of vitamins A, B₆, and E.*

## WHIPPED LEMON CURD PUDDING

*A little fresh cream transforms a simple jar of lemon curd into a delicious, mousselike dessert.*

TIME: 12 MINUTES  SERVES: 4

| |
|---|
| 6 oz (170 g) good-quality lemon curd |
| ⅔ cup (150 ml) heavy cream |
| 1 large egg white |
| Salt |
| 1 digestive cookie, or 2 butter cookies |

**1** Spoon the lemon curd into a bowl. Whip the cream until it will hold a soft peak, then fold it into the lemon curd.

**2** Add a pinch of salt to the egg white and whisk until it forms soft peaks, then carefully fold it into the lemon mixture.

**3** Spoon into 4 serving dishes and chill for as long as possible.

**4** Just before serving, crush the cookies and scatter the crumbs over the top of each dessert to give them a sweet crunch.

NUTRIENTS PER SERVING: *calories 313, carbohydrate 31 g (including sugar 19 g), protein 2 g, fat 21 g (saturated fat 12 g), good source of vitamins A, B₆, and E.*

EXQUISITELY RICH DESSERTS: (*left*) GINGER AND CHOCOLATE MASCARPONE; (*center top*) ZABAGLIONE; (*center bottom*) CHESTNUT BRANDY CREAM; (*right*) WHIPPED LEMON CURD PUDDING.

# FLAMBÉED PINEAPPLE AND BANANAS

*The sunny flavor of two of the best-loved tropical fruits is enhanced by the potent sweetness of hot rum for an easy, aromatic dessert, cooled with whipped cream or ice cream.*

TIME: 30 MINUTES  SERVES: 4

| |
|---|
| 1 pineapple, about 2 lb (900 g) |
| 2 tablespoons (25 g) unsalted butter |
| ⅓ cup (60 g) brown sugar |
| 3 large, ripe, firm bananas |
| 4 tablespoons rum |
| *To serve:* whipped cream or ice cream |

1  Peel the pineapple, cut it in half lengthwise and remove and discard the center core. Cut each half across into eight slices, reserving any juice.

2  Melt the butter and sugar in a large, stainless-steel or enamel frying pan, over a moderate heat.

3  Peel the bananas, cut them in half widthwise, then lengthwise.

4  Add the pineapple to the hot butter and sugar and cook over a fairly high heat for 1–2 minutes, then add the bananas and cook for another 2–3 minutes, until heated through.

5  Pour the rum into the frying pan, heat it for a few seconds, then stand well back and set it alight with a match. Allow the rum to burn, shaking the pan very gently, until the flames die down. Pour any reserved pineapple juice into the pan and continue to heat the fruit for 1 minute.

6  Transfer the flambéed fruit onto individual dishes, and serve with whipped cream or ice cream.

NUTRIENTS PER SERVING: *calories 455, carbohydrate 49 g (including sugar 47 g), protein 3 g, fat 25 g (saturated fat 16 g), good source of vitamins A, B group, C, and E.*

# RHUBARB AND STRAWBERRY COMPOTE

*Tart rhubarb and sweet strawberries, simmered in orange juice, make a surprisingly successful combination of flavors and are a refreshing way to use up a glut of fresh summer fruits.*

TIME: 20 MINUTES  SERVES: 4

1½ lb (680 g) rhubarb

4 tablespoons (60 g) sugar

½ cup (100 ml) fresh orange juice

9 oz (255 g) strawberries

*To serve:* ¾ cup (200 ml)
heavy cream

**1**  Trim and rinse the rhubarb, cut it into 1 in. (2.5 cm) lengths, and put it into a large saucepan with the sugar and the orange juice. Cover the pan, bring the mixture to a boil, reduce the heat and simmer gently, uncovered, for 5–6 minutes, stirring occasionally.

**2**  While the rhubarb is cooking, hull and rinse the strawberries, and halve or quarter any large ones. Add the strawberries to the rhubarb and simmer them for 4–5 minutes, or until they are slightly softened but maintain their shape and still have some bite.

**3**  Taste and add a little more sugar if necessary. Transfer the compote to a serving dish and serve warm with the cream.

*NUTRIENTS PER SERVING: calories 317, carbohydrate 24 g (including sugar 24 g), protein 3 g, fat 24 g (saturated fat 15 g), good source of vitamins A, B group, C, and E.*

### COOK'S SUGGESTION

*Use a stainless-steel or enamel pan to cook the rhubarb. If you have no fresh orange juice to hand, squeeze the juice from 2 large oranges.*

# PEACH AND RASPBERRY CROUSTADES

*Golden peaches, nestling among rich red raspberries on a bed of featherlight pastry, bring the sweetness of summer to the table.*

TIME: 30 MINUTES   SERVES: 4

| |
|---|
| **4 firm, ripe peaches** |
| **3 tablespoons good-quality raspberry jam** |
| **4 tablespoons (60 g) unsalted butter** |
| **⅓ lb (150 g) ready-to-use filo pastry** |
| **4 tablespoons (85 g) fresh raspberries** |
| **2 tablespoons confectioners' sugar** |
| *To serve:* cream or whipped cream |

**1**  Preheat the oven to 400°F (200°C). Rinse, dry, halve, stone, and slice the peaches. Melt the jam over a low heat and sieve it into a cup or ramekin. Put some hot water from the tap into a small bowl and stand the container of jam in the water to keep it warm.

**2**  Gently melt the butter, then cut the filo pastry into 12 rectangles about 10 × 4½ in. (25 × 12 cm). The exact size of the rectangles does not matter too much, as the pastry will be crumpled into pleats.

**3**  Lightly brush a baking sheet with some of the melted butter. Place one filo strip on the baking sheet and brush it with butter. Lay another strip on top and brush it with butter, then repeat with the third strip to make the base of one croustade. Repeat the process to make three more bases.

**4**  Place your hands at the short ends of each of the pastry rectangles and gently push the ends together, pleating and scrunching until you have made a "corrugated" croustade about 6 × 4½ in. (15 × 12 cm).

**5**  Arrange the peach slices inside the folds on top of the pastry. Rinse and dry the raspberries and scatter them over the top. Brush with the jam and bake the croustades for 15–20 minutes, or until the pastry has turned crisp and golden. Then transfer them to individual dishes and serve them hot or warm, dredged with confectioners' sugar, with the cream or whipped cream.

NUTRIENTS per serving: calories 550, carbohydrate (including sugar 29 g), protein 5 g, fat (saturated fat 23 g), good source of vitamins group, C, and E.

# WELSH HOT BUTTER CAKE

*Spiced butter soaks through this moist, aromatic cake as soon as it leaves the oven. If you can resist the temptation to eat it all while it is hot, you will find the cake tastes equally delicious served cold.*

**TIME: 30 MINUTES SERVES: 8**

¼ lb (110 g) salted butter, at room temperature

⅓ cup (85 g) sugar

3 large eggs

1 cup plus 1 tablespoon (175 g) self-raising flour

4 tablespoons (50 g) golden raisins

1 tablespoon milk

For the topping

2½ tablespoons salted butter, at room temperature

2 tablespoons brown sugar

½ teaspoon ground cinnamon

**1** Preheat the oven to 375°F (190°C). Grease an 8 in. (20 cm) round sandwich tin with a little of the butter and line the base with baking paper.
**2** Using an electric whisk, cream the rest of the butter and the sugar in a bowl, until light and fluffy. Beat in the eggs, one at a time, then fold in the flour. Add the raisins and milk and mix. Spread the mixture in the tin. Bake the cake in the center of the oven for 15–20 minutes, until it is well risen, firm, and golden.

**3** To make the spiced butter topping, put the butter into a mixing bowl with the brown sugar and cinnamon and mash together.
**4** When the cake is done, remove it from the oven and spread the butter over the top. Leave it to stand until the butter has soaked in, then remove it from the tin, cut it into wedges, and serve.

*NUTRIENTS PER SERVING: calories 300, carbohydrate 36 g (including sugar 20 g), protein 6 g, fat 16 g (saturated fat 9 g), good source of vitamins A, B group, and E.*

# HOME-BAKED TEATIME TREATS

### SIMPLE SCONES

*Homemade scones, oozing with
butter or strawberry jam and cream,
taste best hot from the oven.*

TIME: 30 MINUTES  MAKES: 9

| |
|---|
| 1½ cups (225 g) plain flour |
| 3 level teaspoons baking powder |
| Salt |
| 3 tablespoons (50 g) butter |
| ⅔ cup (150 ml) buttermilk or milk, plus 2 tablespoons milk for brushing |

**1** Preheat the oven to 425°F
(220°C). Sift the flour, baking
powder, and a pinch of salt into a
mixing bowl. Add the butter and
rub it into the flour.
**2** Make a well in the center of the
flour, add the buttermilk or milk,
and mix to a slightly soft, sticky
dough. Knead on a floured surface
for a few seconds until smooth.
**3** Shape the smooth dough into a
ball and roll into a square or round
about 1 in. (2.5 cm) thick. Cut the
square three times each way with a
floured knife to make nine squares,
or cut the round into eight triangles.
**4** Put the scones onto a floured
baking tray and brush with milk.
Bake in the center of the oven for
10–15 minutes until they are well
risen, golden brown, and sound
hollow when tapped on the bottom.
*VARIATIONS*
Add one of the following lists of
extra ingredients after you have
rubbed the butter into the flour:
• 2 tablespoons (50 g) raisins,
2 tablespoons (25 g) sugar and
½ teaspoon of ground cinnamon
or mixed spice.
• 1 tablespoon (50 g) chopped
dates, 2 tablespoons (25 g) chopped
walnuts, 2 tablespoons (25 g) sugar,
and 1 teaspoon grated orange rind.

*NUTRIENTS PER SQUARE SCONE: calories
137, carbohydrate 21 g (including sugar 1 g),
protein 3 g, fat 5 g (saturated fat 3 g),
good source of vitamins B group and E.*

### CHOCOLATE MUFFINS

*These little chocolate muffins
smell so good when they are baking
they will disappear in minutes.*

TIME: 30 MINUTES  MAKES: 18–20

| |
|---|
| 1½ cups (225 g) self-raising flour |
| ½ cup (100 g) light brown sugar |
| 1 teaspoon baking powder |
| 3 tablespoons cocoa |
| Salt |
| 1 medium egg |
| 2 teaspoons natural vanilla extract |
| ½ cup (100 ml) sunflower oil |
| 9 oz (255 g) natural, low-fat yogurt |
| 4½ oz (125 g) plain chocolate chips |

**1** Preheat the oven to 425°F
(220°C). These muffins are smaller
than traditional ones, so use 18–20
paper cake cases, instead of a
muffin pan, and place them on
two baking trays.
**2** Sift the flour, brown sugar,
baking powder, 2 tablespoons of
the cocoa, and a pinch of salt into a
bowl; make a well in the center.
**3** Break the egg into the well; add
the vanilla extract, sunflower oil,
and yogurt. Beat until smooth, then
mix in the chocolate chips.
**4** Spoon the mixture into the
paper cases and bake for
18–20 minutes, until well risen,
firm, and springy.
**5** Remove the muffins from the
oven, sprinkle them with the
remaining cocoa while they are still
hot, and serve.

*NUTRIENTS PER MUFFIN: calories 162,
carbohydrate 20 g (including sugar 10 g),
protein 3 g, fat 8 g (saturated fat 2 g),
good source of vitamins B group and E.*

---

**COOK'S SUGGESTION**

*These scones and cakes are perfect
for visitors because they can be made
in minutes, then left to bake while
you welcome your guests.*

---

### SOFT ROCK CAKES

*When friends drop in for
coffee, tempt them with one of these
softer-than-usual fruit buns.*

TIME: 30 MINUTES  MAKES: 12

| |
|---|
| 1½ cups (225 g) self-raising flour |
| ¼ lb (110 g) soft margarine |
| 1 large egg |
| ¼ lb (110 g) luxury mixed dried fruits |
| 1–2 tablespoons milk |

**1** Preheat the oven to 400°F
(200°C). Line a 12-pan cake pan
with paper cake cases.
**2** Sift the flour into a bowl and
rub in the soft margarine. Beat the
egg, add it to the flour mixture with
all the remaining ingredients, and
mix well. Divide the mixture evenly
among the cake cases.
**3** Bake the cakes for 15–20
minutes until they are well risen,
golden brown, and firm to the
touch, then remove from the oven
and cool on a wire rack.
*VARIATIONS*
For a crunchy topping, sprinkle
with a little brown sugar before
putting the cakes in the oven.
  The mixed dried fruits can be
replaced by one of the following:
• 4 tablespoons (50 g) chopped
walnuts, 1 small, crisp dessert
apple, peeled and grated, and
½ teaspoon ground cinnamon.
• Grated rind of half an orange and
2½ oz (70 g) chopped, mixed peel.
• 2½ oz (70 g) chopped, ready-to-
eat dried apricots and 1½ oz (45 g)
chopped glacé cherries.

*NUTRIENTS PER CAKE: calories 168,
carbohydrate 21 g (including sugar 7 g),
protein 3 g, fat 9 g (saturated fat 3 g),
good source of vitamins B group.*

**QUICK TEATIME TREATS:** (*top left*)
CHOCOLATE MUFFINS; (*top right*) SOFT
ROCK CAKES; (*bottom*) SIMPLE SCONES.

# ALMOND COOKIES

*Using semolina to make the dough and chopped nuts as a topping gives these little cookies a deliciously crunchy crust.*

TIME: 25 MINUTES  MAKES: 16

**1 tablespoon (15 g) blanched almonds**
**1 medium egg**
**½ cup (115 g) sugar**
**½ teaspoon baking powder**
**4 tablespoons (50 g) ground almonds**
**½ cup (115 g) semolina**
**¼ teaspoon natural almond extract**
**Confectioners' sugar, for sifting**

**1**  Heat the oven to 400°F (200°C). Line one large, or two small baking sheets with baking paper. Finely chop the almonds and set them aside.
**2**  Whisk the egg and the sugar together in a bowl until the mixture is thick and creamy. Then sift in the baking powder and stir in the ground almonds, the semolina, and the almond extract.
**3**  With wet hands, roll the almond mixture into 16 balls, each a little larger than a walnut. Dip into the almonds and place on the baking sheet, spaced a little apart, with the chopped nuts uppermost.
**4**  Bake for 8–10 minutes until risen and pale golden. Leave to cool on the baking sheet for 1 minute, then transfer to a wire rack.
**5**  When the cookies have cooled down, sprinkle confectioners' sugar over the top of them.

*NUTRIENTS PER COOKIE: calories 88, carbohydrate 14 g (including sugar 9 g), protein 2 g, fat 3 g (saturated fat 0.3 g), good source of vitamins B group and E.*

# PEANUT BUTTER COOKIES

*These crunchy little peanut butter cookies, lightly flavored with orange and spice, have a soft, cakelike center.*

TIME: 25 MINUTES  MAKES: 12

**1¼ cups (125 g) self-raising flour**
**6 tablespoons (75 g) light brown sugar**
**4 tablespoons (60 g) butter, at room temperature, plus extra for greasing**
**5 tablespoons (75 g) crunchy peanut butter**
**1 medium egg**
**½ teaspoon ground mixed spice**
**1 small orange**

**1**  Preheat the oven to 375°F (190°C). Lightly grease a large baking sheet.
**2**  Put the flour, sugar, butter, peanut butter, egg, and mixed spice into a mixing bowl, and grate the orange rind into the bowl. Beat all ingredients until smooth.
**3**  Spoon 12 tablespoons of the mixture onto the baking sheet, leaving room for each to spread.
**4**  Bake the cookies for 12–15 minutes or until they are golden brown and firm. Leave them to cool for 2–3 minutes on the baking sheet, then lift them off with a palette knife and finish the cooling on a wire rack.

*NUTRIENTS PER COOKIE: calories 137, carbohydrate 14 g (including sugar 6 g), protein 3 g, fat 8 g (saturated fat 3.5 g), good source of vitamins B group and E.*

---

COOK'S SUGGESTION

*These peanut butter cookies freeze really well. If you have time, it is worth making a double batch so that you can freeze half for another time.*

---

**EASY-TO-MAKE, CRUNCHY COOKIES:**
(*left*) PEANUT BUTTER COOKIES
(*right*) ALMOND COOK[...]

# COCONUT MACAROONS

*Simple but richly flavored cinnamon macaroons, with a sweet aroma created by the tropical scents of coconut and vanilla, make a dainty, nut-filled teatime treat.*

**TIME: 30 MINUTES  MAKES: 18**

¾ package (150 g) sweetened shredded coconut

6 tablespoons (85 g) chopped nuts, such as almonds, hazelnuts, or pecans

½ teaspoon ground cinnamon

1 teaspoon natural vanilla extract or ½ teaspoon vanilla essence

2 large egg whites

Salt

⅔ cup (125 g) sugar

**1** Preheat the oven to 350°F (180°C), then line two baking sheets with rice paper or baking paper and set aside.

**2** Combine the coconut, chopped nuts, cinnamon, and vanilla in a mixing bowl and stir together well.

**3** Put the egg whites and a pinch of salt into another bowl and whisk until the mixture forms soft peaks. Sprinkle a tablespoon of the sugar over the egg whites and whisk until the peaks are glossy.

**4** Gently sprinkle the remaining sugar over the egg whites and carefully fold it in using a rubber spatula, then gently fold in the coconut mixture.

**5** Put dessertspoons of the batter onto the prepared baking sheets, about 1 in. (2.5 cm) apart, then bake for 12–15 minutes until golden.

**6** If baked on rice paper, allow the macaroons to cool completely on the baking sheets, then remove and peel away the excess paper from each one. If using baking paper, allow to cool for 2–3 minutes to firm up, then remove them from the paper with a palette knife, place them on a wire rack and leave them to cool completely.

**NUTRIENTS PER MACAROON:** *calories 97, carbohydrate 10g (including sugar 10g), protein 2g, fat 6g (saturated fat 3g), good source of vitamins B group and E.*

---

### COOK'S SUGGESTION

*If you wish to make the macaroons in advance for a special occasion, they will keep for three days if you store them in an airtight tin once they have cooled.*

---

# BROWNIE THINS

*Dark, luscious brownies, flecked with walnuts, are a treat few people can resist, and can be served hot or cold. Their strong chocolate flavor makes them a favorite with adults as well as children.*

TIME: 30 MINUTES  MAKES: 24

| |
| --- |
| ¼ lb (110 g) unsalted butter |
| ⅓ cup (40 g) cocoa |
| Salt |
| 1 cup (200 g) sugar |
| 2 large eggs |
| ⅓ cup (50 g) self-raising flour |
| 1 teaspoon natural vanilla extract |
| 4 tablespoons (50 g) walnut pieces |

1  Preheat the oven to 350°F (180°C), then line a 12 × 8 × 1 in. (30 × 20 × 2.5 cm) baking tin with baking paper.

2  Place the butter in a saucepan, allow it to melt gently, then take it off the heat.

3  Sift the cocoa into the melted butter, add a pinch of salt and the sugar and mix together. Break the eggs into the cocoa mixture and whisk until smoothly blended.

4  Sift the flour into the pan, fold it in, add the vanilla extract and the walnuts and stir gently.

5  Pour the brownie mixture into the baking tin. Bake for 18 minutes, or until just set but still soft (it will firm up as it cools).

6  While it is still warm, turn the cooked mixture out onto a large board and cut into square brownies.

*NUTRIENTS PER BROWNIE: calories 103, carbohydrate 11 g (including sugar 9 g), protein 2 g, fat 6 g (saturated fat 3 g), good source of vitamins B group and E.*

# THE MENU PLANNER

*Delicious meals need not take for ever to cook. These menus mingle wonderful tastes
with clever contrasts of color and texture, yet the preparation and cooking time is cut to the minimum.
There are meals for all sorts of occasions, packed with healthy goodness, and
many with vegetarian options. Meal planning has never been so easy.*

## FAMILY MEALS FOR FOUR

---

**COD BAKED WITH PESTO, WITH
CRUSHED GARLIC POTATOES,** *page 112*
**STEAMED GREEN BEANS**

---◆---

**FLAMBÉED PINEAPPLE AND BANANAS,**
*page 296*

*Firm white fish with a tasty
topping, served with rich mashed
potatoes and simple steamed beans,
is followed by a luscious hot dessert.*

---

### IN ADVANCE
• Peel and slice the pineapple and
whip the cream for the dessert;
cover and chill, separately.
• Peel the potatoes; cover with cold
water. Prepare some green beans.
Skin the cod fillets, if necessary.

### BEFORE DINNER
• Preheat the oven for the cod. Put
the potatoes on to boil. Prepare the
cod and put it in the oven to bake.
Steam the beans over the potatoes.
• While they are cooking, put the
butter and sugar into a large frying
pan ready for cooking the dessert.
Place the pineapple, bananas, rum,
and matches nearby.
• Drain and mash the potatoes
with the garlic, butter, and cream,
then drain the green beans and
serve the main course.

### AFTER THE MAIN COURSE
• Peel and dice the bananas and
flambé them with the pineapple.

---

*The advance planning stages show
how to save time by getting ahead, but
be careful when chilling food to cool it
as fast as possible, and always cover it
before putting it in the refrigerator.
All the recipes in this book can be
easily halved or doubled, so if cooking
for smaller or larger numbers,
just adjust the quantities.*

---

**QUICK CASSEROLE,** *page 164*
**CRUSTY BREAD**
**GREEN SALAD**

---◆---

**MANGO BRÛLÉE,** *page 282*

*This sophisticated version of
sausages and beans is followed by juicy
fruit and soft, creamy yogurt with a
crunchy burned-sugar cap.*

### IN ADVANCE
• Prepare a simple green leaf salad
and a vinaigrette dressing and chill
them separately.
• Make the mango brûlée and chill.

### BEFORE DINNER
• Make the casserole. (If you prefer,
the main course can be made in
advance and then reheated without
losing any of its flavor.)
• Toss the salad in the dressing.

---

**SPICY PORK BURGERS WITH
GUACAMOLE,** *page 157*

---◆---

**BAKED ALMOND PEARS,** *page 286*

*The spicy burgers with their creamy,
piquant sauce are a good contrast to
the buttery fruit dessert.*

### IN ADVANCE
• Make the burger mixture, shape
into burgers and chill.
• Prepare the pears, then place
in a baking dish with the white
wine mixture and chill. Prepare
the almond topping and set aside.
Put the cream or Greek yogurt
into a serving bowl and chill.

### BEFORE DINNER
• Preheat the oven for the pears.
• Cook the pork burgers and
make the guacamole.
• Add the almond topping
to the chilled pears and
syrup and put the pudding
in the oven to bake while
you eat the main course.

---

**CHICKEN WITH MUSHROOM SAUCE,**
*page 170*
**BOILED NEW POTATOES**
**STEAMED BROCCOLI**

---◆---

**PLUM CRUMBLE,** *page 292*

*The main course with its creamy
mushroom sauce is well balanced by a
crunchy, lightly spiced crumble.*

### IN ADVANCE
• Prepare the potatoes and broccoli.
• Prepare and cook the plums,
then prepare the crumble topping
and chill, separately.

### BEFORE DINNER
• Spoon the crumble over the
plums. Whip the cream and chill.
• Boil the potatoes. Fry the chicken;
put in a low oven to keep warm,
then steam the broccoli over the
potatoes. Make the sauce; drain the
vegetables. Remove the chicken
from the oven, increase the heat, and
bake the crumble while you eat the
main course: chilled crumble takes
an extra 5–10 minutes to bake.

BAKED COD WITH GARLIC
POTATOES AND GREEN
BEANS (*right*)
AND FLAMBÉED
FRUIT.

## AN AMERICAN FAMILY MEAL

**CORN CHOWDER**, *page 40*

———•◦•———

**BALTIMORE SEAFOOD CAKES**, *page 107*

———•◦•———

**BLACK CHERRY SPECIAL WITH CHOCOLATE ICE CREAM**, *page 288*

*Crispy seafood cakes are a good follow-up to the sweet creaminess of corn chowder, while dark brownies with ice cream and black cherries are a rich, fun way to end the meal.*

### IN ADVANCE

• Make the chowder up to the end of Step 4, cover and chill.
• Make and shape the seafood cakes, then prepare the salad leaves and chill both, separately.

### BEFORE DINNER

• Put the black cherries and kirsch into a small pan for the dessert.
• Fry the seafood cakes and put them in a low oven to keep warm.
• Finish off the soup, taking care not to let it boil, and serve.

### AFTER THE FIRST COURSE

• Toast the burger buns and add the salad and seafood cakes.

### AFTER THE MAIN COURSE

• Heat the black cherry sauce and assemble the dessert.

## A VEGETARIAN FAMILY MEAL

**CHEESY CHICKPEA ENCHILADAS**, *page 231*

———•◦•———

**CHOCOLATE ICE CREAM WITH PUFFY MARSHMALLOW SAUCE**, *page 288*

*The densely textured main course with its hot spices, and wrapped in pancakes, is well balanced by the smooth texture and sweet creamy flavors of the ice cream dessert.*

### IN ADVANCE

• Make the chickpea and tomato filling for the enchiladas and chill.
• Shred the lettuce and coriander, then grate the cheese and chill, separately. Put the yogurt or sour cream into a serving dish.

### BEFORE DINNER

• Gently reheat the chickpea and tomato filling, then assemble the enchiladas and grill them.
• Put the marshmallows and single cream into a bowl, and put a kettle of water on to boil while you eat the main course.

### AFTER THE MAIN COURSE

• Melt the marshmallows to make the sauce while the main course is being cleared away.

## CHILDREN'S MEAL FOR FOUR–SIX

**PASTA WITH HEARTY SAUCE**, *page 203*

———•◦•———

**RASPBERRIES WITH CEREAL**, *page 282*

*This simple sausage sauce for pasta is always a favorite with children, and they will enjoy discovering the layers of creamy yogurt, juicy fruit, and crunchy cereal that form the dessert.*

### IN ADVANCE

• Make the dessert and chill.
• The sausage sauce can be made in advance (it also freezes well) and reheated, if you prefer.

### BEFORE DINNER

• Cook the pasta, and cook or reheat the hearty sauce.

## A VEGETARIAN CHILDREN'S MEAL

**SPICED CARROT AND CHICKPEA FRITTERS**, *page 242*

———•◦•———

**ROCKY ROAD ICE CREAM**, *page 288*

*These colorful fritters can be served in baps to ring the changes on hamburgers, while the ice cream is packed full of chunky treats that children will enjoy.*

### IN ADVANCE

• Make the rocky road ice cream and return to the freezer to firm up.
• Prepare some salad leaves to accompany the burgers and chill.

### BEFORE DINNER

• Make the fritters and serve in hamburger buns with the salad.

# SPECIAL OCCASIONS

## LUNCHES FOR FOUR

---

SPANISH-STYLE CHICKEN, *page 173*
A CRUSTY LOAF

ZABAGLIONE, *page 294*

*The brightly colored, well-flavored chicken casserole contrasts well with the soft, frothy texture of the zabaglione, intensely flavored with marsala wine.*

---

### BEFORE LUNCH
• Make the chicken casserole.
• While the casserole is cooking, assemble the egg yolks and sugar for the zabaglione and set aside. Put a saucepan of water on to heat while you eat the main course.

### AFTER THE MAIN COURSE
• Make and serve the zabaglione.

---

COOL CUCUMBER SOUP, *page 28*

BAKED COD PLAKI, *page 111*
RICE
GREEN SALAD WITH OLIVES
AND FETA CHEESE

*This summery cucumber and yogurt soup, served cold, makes a sharp and easy appetizer to the hot main course of baked fish with tomatoes and lemon.*

---

### IN ADVANCE
• Make the cool cucumber soup, then cover and leave it to chill for up to 8 hours.
• Prepare some salad leaves and put them into a salad bowl; drain and chop the feta cheese; make a salad dressing, then chill, separately.

### BEFORE LUNCH
• Preheat the oven on a low heat and boil a kettle of water for the rice. Make the cod plaki. While the fish is cooking, put some rice on to boil. When they are both cooked, keep them warm in the oven while you serve the soup.

### AFTER THE FIRST COURSE
• Add the feta cheese, some black olives and the dressing to the green salad leaves and toss.

---

GAZPACHO, *page 29*

LAMB NOISETTES WITH SPINACH, *page 151*

FRUITY BREAD AND BUTTER PUDDING, *page 293*

*Chilled gazpacho provides a chunky contrast to tender lamb noisettes served on a light bed of spinach, and a brilliant fruity pudding rounds off the meal.*

---

### IN ADVANCE
• Make the soup and chill.
• Assemble the puddings (you don't need to heat the milk) but do not bake them, and chill.

### BEFORE LUNCH
• Preheat the oven to low. Make the main course and keep it warm in the oven while you serve the soup.
• Remove the puddings from the refrigerator.

### AFTER THE FIRST COURSE
• Take the lamb noisettes out of the oven, increase the heat and put the puddings in to bake.

---

A NORTH AMERICAN
LUNCH FOR FOUR

WARM CHEESE AND TOMATO
DIP, *page 52*

BLACKENED WHITE FISH, *page 130*
CAJUN POTATO SALAD, *page 102*

*Hot jalapeño peppers give the dip enough power to stand up to the strong flavors of the fish and the Cajun-style salad.*

---

### IN ADVANCE
• Make the dip and chill.
• Make the potato salad and chill.
• Coat the white fish with the crumb coating and leave it to firm up in the refrigerator.

### BEFORE LUNCH
• Gently reheat the dip.
• Preheat the oven; fry the fish and keep it warm in the oven while you serve the first course. Take the potato salad out of the refrigerator to serve at room temperature.

---

SUMMER LUNCH FOR FOUR

WATERMELON AND FETA CHEESE, *page 58*

COUSCOUS WITH SHRIMPS AND MINT, *page 217*

ICE CREAM WITH LEMON CURD SAUCE, *page 288*

*Juicy melon and salty cheese makes a vivid starter to a main course of shellfish and zucchinis followed by a cool dessert.*

---

### IN ADVANCE
• Prepare the watermelon and salad leaves and chill, separately.
• Prepare the zucchinis and chill.
• Add the passion fruit to the vanilla ice cream and refreeze.

### BEFORE LUNCH
• Drain the feta cheese and assemble the first course.
• Make the main course and keep it warm while you eat the appetizer.

### AFTER THE MAIN COURSE
• Make the lemon curd sauce.

---

A VEGETARIAN
LUNCH FOR FOUR

VEGETABLES WITH BUTTER BEAN SAUCE
AND OLIVE BREAD, *page 235*
*(make double quantities for 4)*

APRICOT AND SOUR CREAM
FLAN, *page 285*

*The sweet batter pudding adds weight to the light main course of fresh vegetables with a silky, puréed bean dressing.*

---

### IN ADVANCE
• Prepare the vegetables up to the end of Step 2, make the butter bean sauce and chill, separately.
• Assemble the apricots in their ovenproof dish, make the batter and the butter topping; set aside.

### BEFORE LUNCH
• Preheat the grill and the oven.
• Oil and grill the vegetables and w... the ...
... our ... ... apricots.
Bake ... main course.

## BARBECUES FOR FOUR

SALMON PÂTÉ WITH CRACKERS,
*page 76*

LAMB BROCHETTES WITH PITA
BREAD, *page 154*

GRILLED, HONEYED FRUIT KABOBS,
*page 290*

*The spicy appetizer prepares the tastebuds
for the kabobs, and can be eaten while
they are cooking. The fruit dessert ends
the meal on a clean, refreshing note.*

### IN ADVANCE

• Make the salmon pâté and chill.
• Assemble the lamb kabobs, make
the yogurt dressing, prepare the
salad, and chill, separately.
• Make the marinade for the fruit,
assemble the kabobs, pour the
marinade over, cover, and chill.
Toast the hazelnuts.

### BEFORE DINNER

• Serve the salmon pâté.
• Start cooking the lamb kabobs.
Loosely wrap the cut pita breads
in foil and place on the side of the
barbecue to warm. Toss the salad.

### AFTER THE MAIN COURSE

• Barbecue the fruit kabobs.

---

### A VEGETARIAN BARBECUE

AVOCADO AND WATERCRESS CREAM
WITH MELBA TOAST, *page 76*

BEAN AND MUSHROOM BURGERS WITH
RED ONION RELISH, *page 242*

WELSH HOT BUTTER CAKE, *page 299*

*The luscious spread can be enjoyed
as the intensely flavored burgers are
cooking, while the cake ends the meal
on a warming, starchy note.*

### IN ADVANCE

• Make the avocado cream, cover the
surface closely with plastic wrap to
prevent it turning brown, and chill.
Make the Melba toast and set aside.
• Mix the burger ingredients, shape
them, make the relish, and chill
• ... the r ... w
hot butter ca ... in
the cake tin, ...

---

### BEFORE DINNER

• Preheat the oven for the cake.
Make the spiced butter, cover, and
leave to stand at room temperature.
• Serve the avocado and watercress
cream with the toast while you grill
the burgers, reheat the onion relish,
and warm the pita breads.
• Put the cake in the oven to bake
while you eat the main course.

### AFTER THE MAIN COURSE

• Spread the spiced butter over the
hot cake, allow it a few minutes to
soak in, then serve.

## BRUNCH FOR FOUR

SALMON PIZZAS WITH YOGURT
AND DILL, *page 108*
LOCKET'S SAVORY, *page 58*
MIXED BEANS WITH PANCETTA, *page 263*
RHUBARB AND STRAWBERRY COMPOTE,
*page 297*

*Serve this menu buffet-style for
guests to help themselves. The sturdy
mixed bean dish makes a refreshing
contrast to the two other savory dishes,
and the clean-flavored compote
provides a sweet balance.*

### IN ADVANCE

• Assemble the salmon pizzas.
• Make the compote and chill.

### BEFORE BRUNCH

• Make the mixed beans with
pancetta; this dish can be served
at room temperature.
• Bake the salmon pizzas.
• Make the Locket's savory.

## SUPPER ON A TRAY

SPANISH RICE WITH CHORIZO
AND SAGE, *page 224*

WHIPPED LEMON CURD PUDDING,
*page 295*

*A robust main-course dish of rice, red
pepper, peas, and hot, paprika-flavored
sausage is well balanced by a sweet,
creamily soft citrus dessert.*

### IN ADVANCE

• Make the whipped lemon curd
pudding, cover, and chill.

---

### BEFORE DINNER

• Make the Spanish rice dish for
the main course.

FARFALLE WITH PESTO AND BACON,
*page 202*

FRESH FRUIT SORBET WITH
RASPBERRY COULIS, *page 288*

*The substantial main course, flavored
with bacon and a basil sauce, needs only
a cool and simple dessert to follow.*

### IN ADVANCE

• Make the raspberry coulis sauce,
sieve it and chill.

### BEFORE SUPPER

• Make the pasta dish.
• Transfer the fresh fruit sorbet to
the refrigerator to soften while you
eat the main course.

## SOUP AND A SANDWICH FOR TWO

*(use half quantities of recipes if necessary)*

SPICY CARROT SOUP, *page 35*

TURKEY, AVOCADO, AND PESTO
CROISSANTS, *page 72*

*The rich, assertive flavors of the
buttery croissant will not overwhelm
the carefully spiced carrot soup.*

PEA AND ASPARAGUS SOUP, *page 36*

BRIE AND GRAPE SANDWICHES, *page 72*

*The velvety soup is balanced by the
crunchy texture of the baguette with its
tasty and nutritious filling.*

ZUCCHINI AND WATERCRESS
SOUP, *page 39*

HUMMUS AND NATURAL DATE
PITA BREADS, *page 72*

*Creamy hummus and juicy natural dates
in pita bread make a substantial
sandwich to complement the light soup.*

• Make your chosen soup and leave
it to simmer while you assemble the
accompanying sandwich.

# ENTERTAINING

## DINNER PARTIES FOR FOUR

### TROPICAL SALAD WITH LIME DRESSING, *page 49*

### DUCK BREASTS WITH BLACKBERRY SAUCE, *page 187*
### NEW POTATOES WITH CREAM

### HOT CHOCOLATE SOUFFLÉS WITH RUM, *page 280*

*The peppery appetizer makes a colorful contrast to fanned duck breasts with a berry sauce, and the rich chocolate soufflé is surprisingly filling.*

#### IN ADVANCE
• Prepare the watercress, papayas, and the lime salad dressing and chill them separately.
• Scrub the new potatoes, put in a saucepan, and cover with cold water.
• Prepare the chocolate soufflé mixture up to Step 5.
#### BEFORE DINNER
• Preheat the oven to a low heat.
• Add salt to the potatoes and bring them to the boil. Cook the duck and blackberry sauce. Drain the cooked potatoes and keep the main course warm in the oven.
• Prepare the avocados, arrange the salad on serving plates, and pour over the lime dressing.
#### AFTER THE FIRST COURSE
• When you remove the main course from the oven, raise the heat for the hot chocolate soufflés.
• Stir the cream through the new potatoes.
#### AFTER THE MAIN COURSE
• Finish making the soufflés and bake them while you clear away the main course.

### SMOKED TROUT WITH PEAR AND ARUGULA, *page 56*

### STEAK SKEWERED WITH TWO ONIONS WITH RED WINE SAUCE, *page 143*
### MASHED POTATOES
### ORANGE AND SESAME CARROTS, *page 256*

### STRAWBERRY CLOUDS, *page 282*

*A light salad prepares the way for beef kabobs with a powerful sauce, served with an unusual carrot dish. Then all it needs is a light and airy dessert.*

#### IN ADVANCE
• Make the dessert and chill.
• Prepare the trout and salad, make the salad dressing and horseradish sauce and chill, separately.
• Prepare and assemble the steak kabobs. Prepare the carrots and peel and dice the potatoes, then cover them both with cold water. Dry fry the sesame seeds.
#### BEFORE DINNER
• Preheat the grill to high and the oven to low.
• Prepare the pears, then assemble the smoked trout salad and chill until ready to serve.
• Put the potatoes on to boil. Make the orange sauce for the carrots and cook them. Grill the steak kabobs. Put the kabobs and carrots in the oven while you make the red wine sauce and drain and mash the potatoes, then put them in the oven while you eat the first course.

### GOAT'S CHEESE SOUFFLÉS, *page 50*
### SALAD

### TUNA STEAKS WITH WASABI BUTTER, *page 114*
### STEAMED NEW POTATOES

### SPICED PEACHES WITH MASCARPONE, *page 287*

*The goat's cheese soufflés, served chilled, make a strong prelude to the grilled tuna with its hot butter dressing. The spicy peaches, served chilled, cut through the richness of the first two courses.*

#### IN ADVANCE
• Cook the soufflés, prepare the salad leaves, fry the bacon then make the dressing; chill separately.
• Prepare the wasabi butter for the tuna steaks and freeze.
• Poach the peaches, sweeten the mascarpone and chill, separately.
#### BEFORE DINNER
• Preheat the oven and grill. Steam the potatoes and grill the fish. Take the wasabi butter out of the freezer and slice it. Keep the potatoes and tuna warm in the oven.
• Assemble the salads and carefully turn out the cheese soufflés on top.

HOT CHOCOLATE SOUFFLÉ WITH RUM (*left*); TROPICAL SALAD WITH LIME DRESSING (*center*); DUCK BREASTS WITH BLACKBERRY SAUCE AND NEW POTATOES WITH CREAM (*right*).

## A VEGETARIAN DINNER PARTY

RED PEPPER AND ORANGE VELVET
SOUP, *page 31*

LEEK AND CHEDDAR CHEESE TART,
*page 237*
LETTUCE, CUCUMBER, AND RED
ONION SALAD, *page 98*

GRILLED FIGS WITH CREAM,
*page 291*

*The soup is full-flavored but light
and prepares the palate for the buttery
pastry of the tart, while the salad
provides a crisp texture. Grilled figs with
their sweet juices make a refreshing finale.*

### IN ADVANCE
• Clean and slice the red peppers for
the soup and chill.
• Cook the leeks, drain them well,
and chill. Roll out the puff pastry,
make the tart case, and chill.
• Prepare the salad and walnut oil
dressing and chill, separately.
• Prepare the fresh figs, toss them in
lemon juice and rosewater, and lay
them in a buttered dish.

### BEFORE DINNER
• Make the pepper and orange soup.
• Preheat the oven. Assemble the
leek and cheddar tart and bake it
while you eat the first course.

### AFTER THE FIRST COURSE
• Assemble the lettuce, cucumber,
and red onion salad.
• Preheat the grill for the dessert.

### AFTER THE MAIN COURSE
• Sugar the figs and grill.

## ROMANTIC DINNERS FOR TWO

*(use half quantities of each recipe
where necessary)*

GRILLED OYSTERS, *page 60*

GINGERED PORK ON WILTED
WATERCRESS, *page 159*

TROPICAL FRUIT SORBET WITH RED WINE
AND BUTTER SAUCE, *page 288*

*The salty grilled oysters introduce
an impressive presentation of gingered
pork, while the red wine sauce makes an
adult-only addition to the sorbet.*

### IN ADVANCE
• Prepare 6 oysters, make the
breadcrumb topping and add it to
the oysters, then chill.
• Peel the potatoes and cover with
cold water. Prepare the pork, mix it
with the grated ginger, cover, and
chill. Prepare the watercress; toast
the sesame seeds and make the
omelette, and chill, separately.
• Make the wine sauce; set aside.

### BEFORE DINNER
• Preheat the grill and the oven.
• Put the omelette in the oven to
warm. Cook the pork and its sauce,
then keep it warm in the oven.
Bring the potatoes to the boil and
let them cook on a low heat while
you eat the first course.
• Grill the oysters.

### AFTER THE FIRST COURSE
• Drain the potatoes, slice the
sesame omelette into strips, and
assemble the main course.
• Transfer the fruit sorbet to the
refrigerator to soften a little.

### AFTER THE MAIN COURSE
• Gently reheat the wine sauce and
pour it over the sorbet.

---

FIGS WITH PARMA HAM, *page 58*

STEAK WITH SHALLOTS IN RED
WINE, *page 138*
CURRIED PARSNIP PURÉE, *page 256*

CHEESE AND SHERRY PÂTÉ WITH
WATER BISCUITS, *page 69*

*This menu allows you to spend
plenty of time with your loved one: the
appetizer merely requires good shopping;
the unusual cheese course can be made
well ahead; and the tempting main course
is served with a simple side dish.*

### IN ADVANCE
• Arrange the first course on serving
plates and chill.
• Make the cheese and sherry pâté
and chill.
• Make the parsnip purée and chill.

### BEFORE DINNER
• Put the curried parsnip purée in a
low oven to reheat.

### AFTER THE FIRST COURSE
• Fry the steak, keep it warm, and
make the red wine sauce.

## A FAR EASTERN FEAST FOR EIGHT

*(use double quantities of each recipe)*

---

THAI SALAD WITH COCONUT
DRESSING, *page 88*
THAI NOODLE SALAD, *page 210*
SCALLOPS WITH THAI
FLAVORINGS, *page 129*
THAI-STYLE BEEF SALAD, *page 86*

*A chunky vegetable salad with
satay contrasts with the creamy curried
scallops and spicy beef, while the noodle
dish provides a filling element to
this Thai-style menu.*

---

### IN ADVANCE

• Prepare the vegetables for the Thai
salad, make the coconut dressing,
and chill, separately.
• Make the noodle salad, preparing
extra snow peas and lemongrass for
the scallop dish, and chill.
• Prepare the beef and its salad
ingredients and chill, separately.
• Assemble the other ingredients
together, in separate groups for each
recipe, to help to speed up the final
cooking process.

### BEFORE DINNER

• Preheat the oven to low. Toss the
vegetable salad in its dressing.
• Remove the noodle salad from
the refrigerator.
• Cook the scallops and put them
in the oven to keep warm.
• Stir-fry the beef and lemongrass,
make the hot dressing and add to
its salad ingredients.

## AN INDIAN FEAST FOR EIGHT

*(use double quantities of each recipe)*

---

PUNJABI POTATO PATTIES WITH
CHUTNEY, *page 74*

— · ◆ · —

BEEF BALTI, *page 142*
CHICKEN AND SPINACH CURRY, *page 179*
SHRIMPS MASALA, *page 133*
RICE

*Crisp potato cakes, served
chilled, introduce a main course
where the slightly sweet coconut sauce
of the shrimps masala contrasts with the
strong beefy flavor of the balti dish, and
the light chicken curry. Plain rice is
the only accompaniment needed.*

---

### IN ADVANCE

• Make the potato cakes and chill.
• Prepare the vegetables and beef
for the balti and chill.
• Prepare the vegetables and
chicken for the curry and chill.
• Prepare the onion, garlic,
root ginger, and coriander for
the shrimps masala and chill.
• Measure out the spices for each
dish onto separate saucers.

### BEFORE DINNER

• Put a kettle of water on to boil
for the rice, then preheat the oven
to a low heat.
• Make the one-pot beef balti and
the chicken curry, then keep them
warm on a low heat.
• Meanwhile, put the rice on to cook
with the water from the kettle and
make the shrimps masala.
• Drain the rice and keep it warm
in the oven, with the masala, while
you serve the potato patties.

THAI NOODLE SALAD (*top*); THAI SALAD
WITH COCONUT DRESSING (*center*);
THAI-STYLE BEEF SALAD (*bottom left*);
SCALLOPS WITH THAI FLAVORINGS
(*bottom right*).

TAGLIATELLE WITH BREADCRUMBS

BAKED EGGS WITH CRAB

SMOKED TROUT WITH PEAR AND ARUGULA

# Q, R

**Quail** on a mushroom nest 57
**Rabbit**, mustard-crusted 189
**Radish**, cucumber, and melon salad 101
**Ragouts** *see* **Stews**
**Raspberries**
    hot raspberry soufflés 281
    peach and raspberry croustades 298
    raspberries with cereal 282–83, 307
**Ratatouille**, speedy 137
**Red currants**
    lamb chops with red currants 150
    spiced red wine and [sauce] 138–39
**Rhubarb** and strawberry compote 297, 309
**Rice**
    egg fried rice 223
    egg-topped kedgeree 222
    emerald risotto 225
    Italian rice balls 25
    leftovers 24–25
    pear rice pudding 17
    rice noodles 17, 210
    rice vinegar 20
    shrimp pilaf 218
    Spanish rice, chorizo, and sage 224, 309
    wild rice and fennel salad 85
**Rum**, hot chocolate soufflés with 280

# S

**Saffron** 19
    saffron pilaf with raisins and nuts 219
**Salad greens** stir-fry with cabbage 268–69
**Salads**
    avocado, shrimp, and tomato 53
    bean sprout, feta, and hazelnut 97
    Caesar 100
    Cajun potato 102
    carrot and ginger 98–99
    citrus 58–59
    creamy mixed bean 92
    cucumber, radish, and melon 101
    endive, pear, and Roquefort 94
    fava bean, shrimp, and feta 96
    fruit 23
    goat's cheese and arugula 63
    Greek 87
    hot corn cakes with 78
    hot potato salad with sausages 239
    last-minute 23
    lettuce, cucumber, red onion 98–99, 311
    melon, avocado, and shrimp 93
    mozzarella with tomato dressing 89
    Niçoise 95
    preparation 10
    salmon and asparagus 84
    smoked trout, pear, and arugula 56, 310
    snow peas and pickled ginger 98–99
    spinach and baby corn 103
    strawberry, cucumber, avocado 58–59
    Thai noodle 210
    Thai-style beef 86–87, 312
    Thai with coconut dressing 88
    tomato 75
    tropical with lime dressing 49
    tuna 119
    warm duck breast, wine, apple 90–91
    warm flageolet and charred vegetable 238
    wild rice and fennel 85

**Salmon**
    potato pancakes with smoked salmon 67
    pâté 76–77, 309
    salmon and asparagus salad 84
    salmon filo wraps 118–19
    salmon pizzas, yogurt, and dill 108, 309
    salmon tabbouleh 214–15
    salmon with lime herb butter 114–15
    salmon with tropical fruit salsa 117
    smoked with stir-fried vegetables 120
    "straw and hay" with smoked
      salmon 206
**Salsas** 21
    grapefruit 58–59
    pepper 176
    tomato 154–55, 175
    tropical fruit 117
**Salt** 8
**Sandwich fillings** 72–73, 309
**Sardines**
    sardine and tomato bruschetta 118–19
    sardines in a peppercorn crust 54–55
**Sauces**
    anchovy 118–19
    apples and cider 180–81
    balsamic vinegar 146
    basting 143
    bean 20
    blackberry 187
    black cherry 288
    brandy cream 138–39
    butter bean 235
    caramel 277
    chocolate 17, 276
    chunky tomato 138–39
    Creole 141
    cucumber raita 20
    deglazing 138–39
    garlic 172
    ginger 186
    guacamole 157
    horseradish butter 114–15
    hot pepper 130–31
    hot sherry 167
    ice cream 288–89
    Indian 19
    lime herb butter 114–15
    marmalade 193
    mint-butter and lime 132
    mushroom 170
    mustard 158
    mustard and cream 138–39
    orange 278–79
    port-flavored cranberry 194
    red currant 150
    red wine 143, 284, 310
    red wine and butter 288–89, 311
    sage and apple 138–39
    shallots in red wine 138–39, 311
    soy 20
    spiced red wine and red currant 138–39
    tahini 21, 244
    Thai fish sauce 21
    tomato, chunky 138–39
    wasabi butter 114–15
    wine 192
**Sausage**
    cabbage, potato, and sausage soup 34
    easy gumbo 220–21
    hot potato salad with sausages 239
    Italian spirals with burst tomatoes
      162–63
    mighty burger 156

    pasta with hearty sauce 203, 307
    quick casserole 164, 306
    sausages, spiced wine, and apples 162–63
    Spanish rice, chorizo, and sage 224, 309
    venison sausages with Stilton mash 195
**Scallops**
    scallops grilled with prosciutto 54–55
    scallops with a herb dressing 128
**Scones**, simple 300–301
**Seafood** *see* **Fish**
**Seasoning** 8
**Seeds**: garnishes 22
**Shallots**
    onion and shallot pastries 64–65
    shallots in red wine [sauce] 138–39, 311
**Shellfish**
    avocado, shrimp, and tomato salad 53
    baked eggs with crab 80
    Baltimore seafood cakes 107, 307
    couscous with shrimps and mint 217
    crab and pea tart 118–19
    fava bean, shrimp, and feta salad 96
    grilled oysters 60, 311
    melon, avocado, and shrimp salad 93
    scallops grilled with prosciutto 54–55
    scallops with a herb dressing 128
    scallops with Thai flavorings 129, 312
    shrimp pilaf 218
    shrimps masala 133, 312
    shrimps with chili and mangoes 61
    smoked oyster and potato pan-fry 118–19
    spaghetti alla vongole 204–5
    spicy crab with chili mayonnaise 109
    Thai noodle salad 210, 312
**Sherry**
    cheese and sherry pâté 69, 311
    ham steaks with hot sherry sauce 167
**Shrimps**
    avocado, shrimp, and tomato salad 53
    couscous with shrimps and mint 217
    fava bean, shrimp, and feta salad 96
    melon, avocado, and shrimp salad 93
    shrimp pilaf 218
    shrimps masala 133, 312
    shrimps with chili and mangoes 61
    Thai noodle salad 210, 312
**Skate**, baked 116
**Snacks** *see* **Appetizers and snacks**
**Sole**, grilled with buttery zucchinis 122
**Sorbets**
    instant 14
    red wine and butter sauce 288–89, 311
**Soufflés**
    goat's cheese 50–51
    hot chocolate with rum 280
    hot raspberry 281
**Soups**
    aromatic parsnip 38
    cabbage, potato, and sausage 34
    chunky fish 42–43
    cool cucumber 28, 308
    corn chowder 40, 307
    creamy avocado and coconut 30
    French vegetable 45
    gazpacho 29, 308
    green bean 33
    minestrone 41
    mushroom 32
    oriental chicken broth 44
    pasta 11
    pea and asparagus 36, 309
    red pepper and orange velvet 31, 311
    smoked haddock, bean, and leek 42–43

NUTTY SPINACH AND MUSHROOM FRITATTA

# W

# Y, Z

## ACKNOWLEDGMENTS

*Photographs and illustrations in this book are the copyright of Reader's Digest and the photographer and illustrator for each is listed below.*

### PHOTOGRAPHY

**Martin Brigdale** 28, 29, 38, 39, 66, 67, 77, 78, 84, 85, 90–91, 96, 97, 102, 103, 111, 120, 121, 128, 129, 142, 143, 150, 151, 158, 159, 163, 172, 173, 186, 187, 206, 207, 215, 222, 223, 228, 229, 236–237, 252, 253, 257, 260, 261, 264–265, 268–269, 276, 283, 290, 291, 294–295, 301, 304, 305, 313

**Gus Filgate** 2, 3, 6, 9, 11 (*top right, bottom right*), 12, 16, 18 (*bottom right*), 23 (*bottom*), 26–27, 34, 36, 37, 44, 45, 46–47, 51, 56, 57, 58–59, 62, 63, 68, 69, 72–73, 80, 81, 82–83, 92, 93, 100, 101, 104–105, 110, 112, 113, 119, 122, 123, 132, 133, 134–135, 136, 139, 146, 147, 155, 168–169, 170, 171, 175, 178, 179, 184, 185, 188, 189, 190–191, 192, 193, 194,

195, 198–199, 202, 203, 205, 208–209, 216, 217, 224, 225, 226–227, 231, 233, 238, 243, 245, 248–249, 250, 251, 254, 255, 258, 274–275, 277, 278, 279, 284, 285, 286, 288–289, 293, 298, 306–312, 314, 317

**James Murphy** 7, 30, 31, 35, 43, 52, 53, 60, 61, 71, 79, 88, 89, 99, 106, 107, 115, 124–125, 131, 137, 140, 141, 148, 149, 160, 161, 166, 167, 174, 213, 218, 219, 234, 235, 247, 270, 271

**Peter Myers** 4–5, 32, 33, 40, 41, 48, 49, 55, 64–65, 70, 74, 75, 86, 87, 94, 95, 108, 109, 116, 117, 126, 127, 144, 152, 153, 156, 157, 164, 165, 176, 177, 180–181, 182, 183, 196, 197, 200, 201, 210, 211, 212, 220–221, 230, 239, 240, 241, 244, 259, 262, 263, 266, 267, 273, 280, 281, 287, 292, 296, 297, 299, 302–303, 319

**Jon Stewart** 10, 11 (*top left, bottom left*), 13 (*bottom right*) 14, 15, 17, 18 (*left, top right*), 19, 20, 21, 23 (*top right*), 25

### ILLUSTRATIONS

**Diane Broadley** 1, 6, 8, 10, 12, 16, 19, 22, 24, 39, 42, 49, 63, 71, 91, 92, 101, 107, 111, 112, 124, 130, 137, 143, 145 (*bottom*), 165, 179, 185, 187, 191, 192, 194, 196, 201, 207, 208, 213, 214, 218, 220, 229, 231, 235, 237, 246 (*bottom*), 253, 256, 264 (*top*), 279, 286, 297, 305

**Stan North** 50, 53, 64, 94, 128, 145 (*top*), 173, 180, 182, 204, 246 (*top*), 262, 264 (*bottom*), 271, 276, 282